THE GREAT SOUTH

A RECORD OF JOURNEYS

IN

LOUISIANA, TEXAS, THE INDIAN TERRITORY, MISSOURI, ARKANSAS,
MISSISSIPPI, ALABAMA, GEORGIA, FLORIDA, SOUTH CAROLINA,
NORTH CAROLINA, KENTUCKY, TENNESSEE, VIRGINIA,
WEST VIRGINIA, AND MARYLAND.

Volume II.

BY

EDWARD KING.

PROFUSELY ILLUSTRATED FROM ORIGINAL SKETCHES
BY J WELLS CHAMPNEY.

BURT FRANKLIN: RESEARCH AND SOURCE WORKS SERIES 381
AMERICAN CLASSICS IN HISTORY AND SOCIAL SCIENCE 46

BURT FRANKLIN
NEW YORK

Published by BURT FRANKLIN
235 East 44th St., New York, N.Y. 10017
Originally Published: 1875
Reprinted: 1969
Printed in the U.S.A.
Library of Congress Card Catalog No: 72-80225
Burt Franklin: Research and Source Works Series 381
American Classics in History and Social Science 46

CONTENTS.

XL	The Journey to Florida—The Peninsula's History—Jacksonville	377
XLI	Up the St. John's River—Tocoi—St. Augustine	383
XLII	St. Augustine, Florida—Fort Marion	390
XLIII	The Climate of Florida—A Journey to Palatka	398
XLIV	Orange Culture in Florida—Fertility of the Peninsula	402
XLV	Up the Oclawaha to Silver Spring	408
XLVI	The Upper St. John's—Indian River—Key West—Politics—The New Constitution	416
XLVII	South Carolina—Port Royal—The Sea Islands—The Revolution	422
XLVIII	On a Rice Plantation in South Carolina	429
XLIX	Charleston, South Carolina	438
L	The Venice of America—Charleston's Politics—A Lovely Lowland City—Immigration	444
LI	The Spoliation of South Carolina	454
LII	The Negroes in Absolute Power	460
LIII	The Lowlands of North Carolina	466
LIV	Among the Southern Mountains—Journey from Eastern Tennessee to Western North Carolina	474
LV	Across the "Smoky" to Waynesville—The Master Chain of the Alleghanies	480
LVI	The "Sugar Fork" and Dry Falls—Whiteside Mountain	490
LVII	Asheville—The French Broad Valley—The Ascent of Mount Mitchell	503
LVIII	The South Carolina Mountains—Cascades and Peaks of Northern Georgia	515
LIX	Chattanooga, the Gateway of the South	527
LX	Lookout Mountain—The Battles around Chattanooga—Knoxville—Eastern Tennessee	536

LXI	A Visit to Lynchburg in Virginia	5
LXII	In South-western Virginia—The Peaks of Otter—The Mineral Springs	561
LXIII	Among the Mountains—From Bristol to Lynchburg	569
LXIV	Petersburg—A Negro Revival Meeting	579
LXV	The Dismal Swamp—Norfolk—The Coast	588
LXVI	The Education of Negroes—The American Missionary Association—The Peabody Fund—The Civil Rights Bill	596
LXVII	The Hampton Normal Institute—General Armstrong's Work—Fisk University—Berea and Other Colleges	603
LXVIII	Negro Songs and Singers	609
LXIX	A Peep at the Past of Virginia—Jamestown—Williamsburg—Yorktown	621
LXX	Richmond—Its Trade and Character	626
LXXI	The Partition of Virginia—Reconstruction and Politics in West and East Virginia	639
LXXII	From Richmond to Charlottesville	647
LXXIII	From Charlottesville to Staunton, Virginia—The Shenandoah Valley—Lexington—The Graves of General Lee and "Stonewall" Jackson—From Goshen to "White Sulphur Springs."	656
LXXIV	Greenbrier White Sulphur Springs—From the "White Sulphur" to Kanawha Valley—The Mineral Springs Region	670
LXXV	The Kanawha Valley—Mineral Wealth of Western Virginia	681
LXXVI	Down the Ohio River—Louisville	693
LXXVII	A Visit to the Mammoth Cave	699
LXXVIII	The Trade of Louisville	707
LXXIX	Frankfort—The Blue Grass Region—Alexander's Farm—Lexington	713
LXXX	Politics in Kentucky—Mineral Resources of the State	721
LXXXI	Nashville and Middle Tennessee	726
LXXXII	A Glance at Maryland's History—Her Extent and Resources	733
LXXXIII	The Baltimore and Ohio Railroad	741
LXXXIV	The Trade of Baltimore—Its Rapid and Astonishing Growth	748
LXXXV	Baltimore and its Institutions	757
LXXXVI	Southern Characteristics—State Pride—The Influence of Railroads—Poor Whites—Their Habits	771
LXXXVII	The Carrying of Weapons—Moral Character of the Negroes	777
LXXXVIII	Dialect—Forms of Expression—Diet	784
LXXXIX	Immigration—The Need of Capital—Division of the Negro Vote—The Southern Ladies	792
XC	Rambles in Virginia—Fredericksburg—Alexandria—Mount Vernon—Arlington	795

ILLUSTRATIONS
AND MAPS.

	PAGE.
Moonlight over Jacksonville, Florida	377
Jacksonville, on the St. John's River, Florida	381
Residence of Mrs. Harriet Beecher Stowe, at Mandarin, Florida	383
Green Cove Springs, on the St. John's River, Fla.	384
On the Road to St. Augustine, Florida	386
A Street in St. Augustine, Florida	387
St. Augustine, Florida—"An ancient gateway"	388
The Remains of a Citadel at Matanzas Inlet	391
View of Fort Marion, St. Augustine, Florida	392
Light-house on Anastasia Island, near St. Augustine, Florida	393
View of the Entrance to Fort Marion, St. Augustine, Florida	394
"The old sergeant in charge"	395
The Cathedral, St. Augustine, Florida	396
The Banana—"At Palatka, we first found the banana in profusion"	400
"Just across the river from Palatka lies the beautiful orange grove owned by Colonel Hart"	402
Entrance to Colonel Hart's orange grove, opposite Palatka	404
The Guardian Angel	407
A Peep into a Forest on the Oclawaha	409
"We would brush past the trees and vines"	410
The "Marion" at Silver Spring	412
Shooting at Alligators	414
View on the upper St. John's River, Florida	416
Sunrise at Enterprise, St. John's River, Florida	419
A Country Cart	421
View of a Rice-field in South Carolina	429
Negro Cabins on a Rice Plantation	431
"The women were dressed in gay colors"	432
"With forty or fifty pounds of rice-stalks on their heads"	432
A Pair of Mule-Boots	434
A "Trunk-Minder"	434
Unloading the Rice-Barges	435
"At the winnowing-machine"	436
"Aunt Bransom"—A venerable ex-slave on a South Carolina Rice Plantation	437
View from Fort Sumter, in Charleston Harbor	438
The old Charleston Post-Office	440
Houses on the Battery, Charleston	441
A Charleston Mansion	442
The Spire of St. Philip's Church, Charleston	443
The Orphan House, Charleston	444
The Battery, Charleston	445
The Grave of John C. Calhoun, Charleston	446
The Ruins of St. Finbar Cathedral, Charleston	447
"The highways leading out of the city are all richly embowered in loveliest foliage"	449
Magnolia Cemetery, Charleston	450
Garden in Mount Pleasant, opposite Charleston	452
Peeping Through	453
A Future Politician	459
The State-House at Columbia, South Carolina	460
Sketches of South Carolina State Officers and Legislators under the Moses Administration	462
Iron Palmetto in the State-House Yard at Columbia	465
A Wayside Sketch	473

	PAGE.
"The Small Boy"	474
"The Judge"	476
The Judge shows the Artist's Sketch-Book	479
"The family sang line by line"	481
A Mountain Farmer	482
"We caught a glimpse of the symmetrical Catalouche mountain"	483
The Cañon of the Catalouche as seen from "Bennett's"	484
Mount Pisgah, Western North Carolina	486
The Carpenter—A Study from Waynesville Life	487
View on Pigeon River, near Waynesville	488
The Dry Fall of the Sugar Fork, Blue Ridge, North Carolina	490
View near Webster, North Carolina	492
Lower Sugar Fork Fall, Blue Ridge, North Carolina	495
The Devil's Court-House, Whiteside Mountain	499
Jonas sees the Abyss	501
Asheville, North Carolina, from "Beaucatcher Knob"	504
View near Warm Springs, on the French Broad River	506
Lover's Leap, French Broad River, Western North Carolina	508
View on the Swannanoa River, near Asheville, Western North Carolina	509
First Peep at Patton's	510
The "Mountain House," on the way to Mount Mitchell's Summit	511
View of Mount Mitchell	512
The Judge climbing Mitchell's High Peak	513
Signal-Station and "Mitchell's Grave," Summit of the Black Mountains	514
The Lookers-on at the Greenville Fair	516
Table Mountain, South Carolina	518
"Let us address de Almighty wid pra'r"	520
Mount Yonah, as seen from Clarksville, Georgia	521
The "Grand Chasm," Tugaloo River, Northern Georgia	522
Toccoa Falls, Northern Georgia	524
A Mail-Carrier	526
Mission Ridge, near Chattanooga, Tennessee	527
Lookout Mountain, near Chattanooga, Tennessee	529
The Mineral Region in the vicinity of Chattanooga	531
Map showing Grades of Illiteracy in the United States. (From the U. S. Census Reports.)	532
Map of Middle Atlantic States, southern section, and North Carolina	533
The Rockwood Iron-Furnaces, Eastern Tennessee	533
The "John Ross House," near Chattanooga. Residence of one of the old Cherokee Landholders	534
Catching a "Tarpin"	535
View from Lookout Mountain near Chattanooga	536
Umbrella Rock, on Lookout Mountain	537
Looking from "Lookout Cave"	538
"Rock City," Lookout Mountain	539
View from Wood's Redoubt, Chattanooga	540
On the Tennessee River, near Chattanooga	542
The "Suck," on the Tennessee River	543
A Negro Cabin on the bank of the Tennessee	544

	PAGE.
Knoxville, Tennessee	546
The East Tennessee University, Knoxville	548
At the Ætna Coal Mines	550
"Down in a Coal Mine"	551
The old Market at Lynchburg	552
The James River, at Lynchburg, Virginia	553
A Side Street in Lynchburg, Virginia	555
Scene in a Lynchburg Tobacco Factory	557
"Down the steep hills every day come the country wagons"	558
Summoning Buyers to a Tobacco Sale	560
Evening on the James River—"The soft light which gently rested upon the lovely stream"	561
In the Gap of the Peaks of Otter, Virginia	562
The Summit of the Peak of Otter, Virginia	564
Blue Ridge Springs, South-western Virginia	566
Bristol, South-western Virginia	569
White Top Mountain, seen from Glade Springs	570
Making Salt, at Saltville, Virginia	571
Wayside Types—A Sketch from the Artist's Virginia Sketch-Book	573
Wytheville, Virginia	574
Max Meadows, Virginia	575
The Roanoke Valley, Virginia	576
View near Salem, Virginia	577
View on the James River below Lynchburg	578
Appomattox Court-House—"It lies silently half-hidden in its groves and gardens"	579
"The hackmen who shriek in your ear as you arrive at the depot"	581
"The 'Crater,' the chasm created by the explosion of the mine which the Pennsylvanians sprung underneath Lee's fortifications"	582
"The old cemetery, and ruined, ivy-mantled Blandford Church"	583
"Seen from a distance, Petersburg presents the appearance of a lovely forest pierced here and there by church spires and towers"	585
A Queer Cavalier	587
City Point, Virginia	588
A Peep into the Great Dismal Swamp	589
A Glimpse of Norfolk, Virginia	591
Map of the Virginia Peninsula	593
Hampton Roads	594
The Ruins of the old Church at Jamestown, Virginia	621
Statue of Lord Botetourt at Williamsburg, Virginia	622
The old Colonial Powder Magazine at Williamsburg, Virginia	623
The old Church of Bruton Parish—Williamsburg, Virginia	624
Cornwallis's Cave, near Yorktown, Virginia	624
View of Richmond, Virginia, from the Manchester side of the James River	626
Libby Prison, Richmond, Virginia	627
Capitol Square, with a view of the Washington Monument, Richmond, Virginia	628
St. John's Church, Richmond, Virginia	629
View on the James River, Richmond, Virginia	630
Monument to the Confederate Dead, Richmond, Virginia	631
The Gallego Flouring-Mill, Richmond, Virginia	631

	PAGE.
Scene on a Tobacco Plantation—Burning a Plant Patch	632
Tobacco Culture—Stringing the Primings	633
A Tobacco Barn in Virginia	633
The Old Method of Getting Tobacco to Market	634
Getting a Tobacco Hogshead Ready for Market	635
Scene on a Tobacco Plantation—Finding Tobacco Worms	636
The Tredegar Iron Works, Richmond, Virginia	637
A Water-melon Wagon	646
A Marl-bed on the Line of the Chesapeake and Ohio Railroad	647
Earthworks on the Chickahominy, near Richmond, Virginia	648
Scene at a Virginia "Corn-Shed"	649
Gordonsville, Virginia—"The negroes, who swarm day and night like bees about the trains"	650
The Tomb of Thomas Jefferson, at Monticello, near Charlottesville, Virginia	651
Monticello—The Old Home of Thomas Jefferson, author of the Declaration of American Independence	652
The University of Virginia, at Charlottesville	653
A Water-melon Feast	655
Piedmont, from the Blue Ridge	656
View of Staunton, Virginia	657
Winchester, Virginia	658
Buffalo Gap and the Iron-Furnace	659
Elizabeth Iron-Furnace, Virginia	660
The Alum Spring, Rockbridge Alum Springs, Virginia	661
The Military Institute, Lexington, Virginia	661
Washington and Lee College, Lexington, Va.	662
Portrait of General Thomas J. Jackson, known as "Stonewall Jackson." (From an engraving owned by M. Knoedler & Co., N. Y.)	663
General Robert Edward Lee, born January 19, 1801; died October 11, 1870	664
The Great Natural Arch, Clifton Forge, Jackson's River	665
Beaver Dam Falls	665
Falling Springs Falls, Virginia	666
Griffith's Knob, and Cow Pasture River	667
Clay Cut, Chesapeake and Ohio Railroad	668
"Mac, the Pusher"	668
Jerry's Run	669
Scene on the Greenbrier River in Western Virginia	670
The Hotel and Lawn at Greenbrier White Sulphur Springs, West Virginia	671
The Eastern Portal of Second Creek Tunnel, Chesapeake and Ohio Railroad	672
A Mountain Ride in a Stage-Coach	673
Anvil Rock, Greenbrier River	675
A West Virginia "Countryman"	675
A Freighters' Camp, West Virginia	676
"The rude cabin built beneath the shadow of a huge rock"	677
"The rustic mill built of logs"	678
The Junction of Greenbrier and New Rivers	678
Descending the New River Rapids	679
A hard road for artists to travel	680
The "Hawk's Nest," from Boulder Point	681

	PAGE
Great Kanawha Falls	682
Miller's Ferry, seen from the Hawk's Nest	682
Richmond Falls, New River	683
Big Dowdy Falls, near New River	684
Whitcomb's Bowlder	685
The Inclined Plane at Cannelton	686
Fern Spring Branch, a West Virginia Mountain Stream	687
Charleston, the West Virginia Capital	688
The Hale House, Charleston	688
Rafts of Saw-Logs on a West Virginia River	689
The Snow Hill Salt Works, on the Kanawha River	690
Indian Mound, near St. Albans	690
View of Huntington and the Ohio River	691
The result of climbing a sapling—An Artist in a Fix	692
The Levée at Louisville, Kentucky	693
A familiar scene in a Louisville Street	695
A Waiter at the Galt House, Louisville, Kentucky	696
Scene in the Louisville Exposition	697
Mammoth Cave, Kentucky—The Boat Ride on Echo River	699
The Entrance to Mammoth Cave (Looking Out)	700
Mammoth Cave—In "the Devil's Arm-Chair"	702
The Mammoth Cave—"The Fat Man's Misery"	703
Mammoth Cave—"The Subterranean Album"	704
A Country Blacksmith Shop	706
The Court-House, Louisville	707
The Cathedral, Louisville	708
The Post-Office, Louisville	708
The City Hall, Louisville	709
George D. Prentice. (From a Painting in the Louisville Public Library)	710
The Colored Normal School, Louisville	710
Louisville, Kentucky, on the Ohio River, from the New Albany Heights	711
Chimney Rock, Kentucky	712
Frankfort, on the Kentucky River	713
The Ascent to Frankfort Cemetery, Kentucky	714
The Monument to Daniel Boone in the Cemetery at Frankfort, Kentucky	715
View on the Kentucky River, near Frankfort	719
Asteroid Kicks Up	717
A Souvenir of Kentucky	719
A little Adventure by the Wayside	720
"Steady"	725
The Tennessee State Capitol, at Nashville	726
View from the State Capitol, Nashville, Tennessee	727
Tomb of Ex-President Polk, Nashville, Tennessee	728
The Hermitage—General Andrew Jackson's old homestead, near Nashville, Tennessee	729
Young Tennesseans	730
The old home of Gen. Andrew Jackson, near Nashville	731

	PAGE
Tomb of Andrew Jackson, at the "Hermitage," near Nashville	732
View from Federal Hill, Baltimore, Maryland, looking across the Basin	733
The Oldest House in Baltimore	735
Fort McHenry, Baltimore Harbor	738
Jones's Falls, Baltimore	740
Exchange Place, Baltimore, Maryland	741
The Masonic Temple, Baltimore, Maryland	742
The Shot-Tower, Baltimore, Maryland	742
Scene on the Chesapeake and Ohio Canal	743
The Blind Asylum, Baltimore, Maryland	745
The Eastern High School, Baltimore, Maryland	746
View of a Lake in Druid Hill Park, Baltimore	747
Maryland Institute, Baltimore	748
Woodberry, near Druid Hill Park	749
The new City Hall, Baltimore, Maryland	750
Lafayette Square, Baltimore, Maryland	750
The City Jail, Baltimore, Maryland	752
The Peabody Institute, Baltimore, Maryland	753
First Presbyterian Church, Baltimore	754
A Tunnel through the Alleghanies	756
Mount Vernon Square, with a view of the Washington Monument, Baltimore, Maryland	758
The Battle Monument, seen from Barnum's Hotel, Baltimore	759
The Battle Monument, Baltimore, Maryland	760
The Cathedral, Baltimore, Maryland	760
The Wildey Monument, Baltimore, Maryland	761
Entrance to Druid Hill Park, Baltimore, Maryland	761
Scene on the Canal, near Harper's Ferry	762
The Bridge at Harper's Ferry	763
View of the Railroad and River, from the Mountains at Harper's Ferry	764
Jefferson's Rock, Harper's Ferry	769
Cumberland Narrows and Mountains	767
Cumberland Viaduct, Maryland	768
Harper's Ferry, Maryland	769
Old John Cupid, a Williamsburg Herb Doctor	770
Southern Types—Come to Market	771
Southern Types—A Southern Plough Team	772
Southern Types—Negro Boys Shelling Peas	773
Southern Types—A "likely Girl" with her Baby	775
Southern Types—Catching his Breakfast	776
Southern Types—Negro Shoeblacks	777
Southern Types—A Little Unpleasantness	779
Southern Types—"Going to Church"	780
Southern Types—A Negro Constable	781
Southern Types—The Wolf and the Lamb in Politics	784
Southern Types—Two Veterans discussing the Political Situation	787
The Potomac and Washington, seen from Arlington	800
Homeward Bound	801

XL.

THE JOURNEY TO FLORIDA—THE PENINSULA'S HISTORY. JACKSONVILLE.

I ENTERED Florida on a frosty morning. Thin flakes of ice had formed in the little pools along the railway's sides, and the Northern visitors in the Pullman car shrouded themselves in their traveling-blankets and grumbled bitterly. Here and there, in the forests' gaps, the negroes had kindled huge

Moonlight over Jacksonville, Florida.

fires, and were grouped about them, toasting their heads and freezing their backs. Now and then we caught glimpses of beautiful thickets; we passed long stretches of field carpeted with thick growths of palmetto; with intervening pine-barrens, and freight platforms of logs.

It is 263 miles by the present rail route from Savannah to Jacksonville, the chief city of Florida, and the rendezvous for all travelers who intend to penetrate to the interior of the beautiful peninsula. The train traverses the distance at the comfortable speed of twelve miles an hour; from time to time, half an hour is consumed in wooding up,—an operation performed in the most leisurely manner by the negroes,—and one arrives in Jacksonville after a night's travel. The currents of Northern comers pour in by three great streams—the Atlantic and Gulf rail route from Savannah, the outside steamers from Charleston, which ascend the St. John's river as far as Palatka, and the inland route from Savannah, which conducts the traveler along a series of estuaries and lagoons between the fertile sea islands and the main-land.

By the first of these routes, one passes but few towns of importance. Neither at Live Oak, the junction where one reaches the Jacksonville, Pensacola and Mobile railroad, nor at Wellborn, nor at Lake City, is there anything to answer to one's ideas of the typical Florida town. The rail route passes Olustee, the site of a fierce engagement in February, 1864, between Federals and Confederates, in which the former were defeated. At Baldwin one comes to the Florida railroad, grappled to Fernandina, northward, on the Atlantic, and stretching away through Duval, Bradford, Alachua, and Leroy counties to Cedar Keys, on the Gulf coast.

When we reached Jacksonville the frost had vanished, and two days thereafter the genial December sun bade the thermometer testify to 80 degrees in the shade. Here and there we saw a tall banana, whose leaves had been yellowed by the frost's breath; but the oranges were unscathed, and the Floridians content.

Pause with me at the gateway of the great peninsula, and reflect for a moment upon its history. Fact and fancy wander here hand in hand; the airy chronicles of the ancient fathers hover upon the confines of the impossible. The austere Northerner and the cynical European have been heard to murmur incredulously at the tales of the modern writers who grow enthusiastic upon the charms of our new winter paradise. Yet, what of fiction could exceed in romantic interest the history of this venerable State? What poet's imagination, seven times heated, could paint foliage whose splendors should surpass that of the virgin forests of the Oclawaha and Indian rivers? What "fountain of youth" could be imagined more redolent of enchantment than the "Silver Spring," now annually visited by 50,000 tourists? The subtle moonlight, the perfect glory of the dying sun as he sinks below a horizon fringed with fantastic trees, the perfume faintly borne from the orange grove, the murmurous music of the waves along the inlets, and the mangrove-covered banks, are beyond words.

> "Canst thou copy in verse one chime
> Of the woodbell's peal and cry?
> Write in a book the morning's prime,
> Or match with words that tender sky?"

Our American Italy has not a mountain within its boundaries. Extending from 25 degrees to 31 degrees north latitude, it has an area of 60,000 square miles. Nearly 400 miles in length, it has the latitude of Northern Mexico, the desert of Sahara, Central Arabia, Southern China, and Northern Hindostan; but its heats are tempered by the Gulf of Mexico on the one hand, and the Gulf Stream, which flows along the eastern coast for 300 miles, on the other. Over the level breadth of ninety miles between these two waters constantly blow odorous and health-giving ocean winds, and under their influence and that of the genial sun springs up an almost miraculous sub-tropical vegetation. It is the home of the palmetto and the cabbage palm, the live oak and the cypress, the mistletoe with its bright green leaves and red berries, the Spanish moss, the ambitious mangrove, the stately magnolia, the *smilax china*, the orange, the myrtle, the water-lily, the jessamine, the cork-tree, the sisal-hemp, the grape, and the cocoanut. There the Northerner, wont to boast of the brilliant sunsets of his own clime, finds all his past experiences outdone. In the winter months, soft breezes come caressingly; the whole peninsula is carpeted with blossoms, and the birds sing sweetly in the untrodden thickets. It has the charm of wildness, of mystery; it is untamed; civilization has not stained it. No wonder the Indian fought ferociously ere he suffered himself to be banished from this charming land.

The beautiful peninsula has been the ambition of many nationalities. First came the hardy Venetian, Cabot, to whose father Henry the Seventh accorded the right to navigate all seas under the English flag. In 1497, groping blindly, doubtless, like his father before him, for the passage to Cathay, Cabot touched at Florida. Early in the sixteenth century came Ponce de Leon, the chimerical old Governor of Porto Rico, who vainly sought in the recesses of the peninsula for the fabled "Fountain of Youth," and perished in a broil with the savages. To him our gratitude is due for the name which the fair land has kept through all the changes of domination which have fallen to its lot. During his second search after the treasure, landing on Palm Sunday,* amid groves of towering palm-trees, and noting the profusion of flowers everywhere, the pious knight christened the country "Florida." After him came other Spaniards, bent on proselyting Indians by kidnapping and enslaving them; but speedy vengeance fell on these ignoble fellows; the Indians massacred them by scores. Then Narvaez, and the Spaniards in his train, waded through the dangerous lagoons and dreary swamps, fought the Indians from behind breastworks made of rotten trees, and finally perished in storms along the treacherous coast. Nothing daunted, and fresh from triumphs in other lands, De Soto followed, overrunning with his army the vast extent of territory which the Spaniards claimed under the name of Florida, and which extended from the Chesapeake to the Tortugas.

The definite settlement of Florida by Europeans was consecrated by a massacre, by which the fanatical Spaniard added fresh infamy to his already tarnished name. When Coligny had received from Charles the Ninth of France permission to found a colony upon the peninsula, and Ribault's expedition had erected a monument near the mouth of the St. John's river, ere sailing to found the settlement at Port Royal, the Spaniards were enraged; and as soon as, in 1564, Laudonniere's expedition had founded Fort Caroline on a little eminence a few miles from the mouth of the St. John's (then called the river May), active hostilities were begun by Spain. The counter expedition of Menendez de Avila resulted in the massacre of all the Huguenots at Fort Caroline; and the grim Spaniards placed an inscription on the spot stating that "the murdered ones had

* In Spanish, *Pascua Florida*.

been slain, not as Frenchmen, but as heretics." Two years later came Nemesis, in the person of the brave Protestant Chevalier, Dominique de Gourgues of France, who relentlessly slew the Spaniards settled on the site of the old Fort Caroline, and hanged many of them, averring by an inscription above them that it was not done " as to Spaniards, but to traitors, robbers, and murderers."

The town which Menendez established on the site of the Indian village of Seloo, and which he named St. Augustine, was the first permanent European settlement in North America. In the eighteenth century the British gained possession of Florida. The American colonists had already unsuccessfully tried to gain St. Augustine; but were destined to wait a century longer. In 1781 the English lost their hold, and the territory reverted to Spain, only to be purchased by the United States in 1819, after Fernandina and Pensacola had been taken by American arms. Ceded and re-ceded, sacked and pillaged, languishing undeveloped through a colonial existence of 200 years, shocked to its centre by terrible Indian wars, and plunged into a war of secession at the moment when it was hoping for rest and stability, the lovely land seems indeed to have been the prey of a stern yet capricious fate.

It is not wonderful, in view of the perturbed condition of the peninsula, since its discovery, that to-day it has hardly more than a quarter of a million of inhabitants, and that its rich lands remain untilled. The weight of the slave system kept it down, after the Government of the United States had guaranteed it against the wonted invasions and internal wars; the remoteness from social centres enforced by the plantation life made its populations careless of the enterprise and thrift which characterize a country filled with rich and thriving towns; and the few acres which were tilled were forced to exhaustion by the yearly production of the same staple. Now, with more than 33,000,000 of acres within its limits, it has barely 3,000,000 partially improved, and on its 10,000 farms much is still woodland. Large farms and plantations have, throughout the State, decreased, and small ones have multiplied, but the total yearly value of farm products now rises hardly above $11,000,000 or $12,000,000, while the value of its home manufactures is but a couple of hundred thousand dollars. With 1,100 miles of practicable coast line, studded with excellent bays, and with such noble navigable rivers as the St. John's, the St. Mary's, the Appalachicola, and the Suwanee, it is strange that a larger commerce has not sprung up within the State limits.

We will not be too statistical. Imagine yourself transferred from the trying climate of the North or North-west into the gentle atmosphere of the Floridian peninsula, seated just at sunset in an arm-chair, on some of the verandas which overlook the pretty square in Jacksonville. Your face is fanned by the warm December breeze, and the chippering of the birds mingles with the music which the negro band is playing in yonder portico. The lazy, ne'er-do-well negro boys playing in the sand so abundant in all the roads, have the unconscious pose and careless grace of Neapolitan beggars. Here and there among the dusky race is a face beautiful as was ever that of olive-brown maid in Messina. This is the South, slumbrous, voluptuous, round and graceful. Here beauty peeps

Jacksonville, on the St. John's River, Florida.

from every door-yard. Mere existence is pleasure; exertion is a bore. Through orange-trees and grand oaks thickly bordering the broad avenues gleams the wide current of the St. John's river. Parallel with it runs Bay street, Northern in appearance, with brick blocks on either side, with crowds of smartly dressed tourists hurrying through it, with a huge "National Hotel," with banks, with elegant shops. Fine shell roads run out beyond the town limits, in either direction. Riding toward the river's mouth, which is twenty-five miles below the town, one comes to marshes and broad expanses of luscious green thicket. Passing the long rows of steam saw-mills,—Jacksonville is a flourishing lumber port,—one comes to the point of debarcation for millions of feet of pine lumber, shingles and staves, and great quantities of naval stores. The fleet of sailing vessels used in this trade find at the new city as fine a port as the country can boast.

The St. John's, at Jacksonville, makes a crescent bend, not unlike that of the Mississippi at New Orleans. Nearly two miles broad directly in front of the wharves, it widens to an expanse of six miles a little way above, offering superb opportunities for commerce. The bar at its mouth is nearly always practicable for large ocean steamers, and they run with ease to Palatka, sixty miles above Jacksonville. The journey is charming from the river's mouth, past Baton island, the residence of the hardy river pilots, and the site of two excellent light-houses; past the mounds of oyster-shells, through which tangled shrubbery has pierced a difficult way; past the intensely white dunes, glistening under the sun, and ghastly and weird under the moonlight; past the little eminence known as St. John's Bluff, the location of old Fort Caroline, where Menendez massacred the unfortunate Huguenots; and past Yellow Bluff, with its ancient Spanish ramparts. Along the river-side, on elevated ground beyond the commercial part of the town, many New York and Boston gentlemen have erected elegant residences, and the climate has already seduced them from even a summer allegiance to their Northern birthplaces. The view from "Riverside" is charming.

It is not a score of years since there was a corn-field on the site of Bay street, now the chief avenue of a city of twelve thousand inhabitants. Jacksonville was once known as "Cow Ford." There the "King's Road," in the old days, crossed the river, and connected the northern settlements with St. Augustine. During the war it ran to decay; it was strongly fortified, and was clung to desperately by the Confederates. The Union troops occupied it then several times, and on the third assault a fire sprang out, which did much damage. At the close of the great struggle, the grass stood waist-high in the streets, and the cattle had taken refuge from the sun in the deserted houses. But the North has swept on in such a resistless current that, so far as its artificial features are concerned, the city has grown up according to the New England pattern, though foliage, climate, sun—all these are the antipodes of those of the North!

A good many people fancy that, in going to Florida, they are about to absent themselves from all the accessories of civilization,—that they must undergo considerable privation. Nothing could better correct this impression than a stay of a few days in Jacksonville. Such good hotels as the St. James and the National, such well-ordered streets, such charming suburbs as "Brooklyn" and "Riverside" and "La Villa" and "Wyoming," where the invalid can find the coveted repose and enjoy the delicious climate; such an abundance of newspapers and books, of carriages and saddle-horses, and such convenient access to all other desirable points along the great river, are sufficient to satisfy even the most querulous. Jacksonville is filled with pleasant houses where lodgings are let; and from December until April its population is doubled; society is active; excursions, parties, and receptions occur almost daily; gayety rules the hour. For it is not invalids alone who crowd Florida now-a-days, but the wealthy and the well. One-fourth of the annual visitors are in pursuit of health; the others are crusading to find the phantom Pleasure. Fully one-half of the resident population of Jacksonville is Northern, and has settled there since the war. The town boasts excellent public schools for white and black children; the Catholics have established educational institutions there, and there are several fine churches. The winter evenings are delightful. In the early days of December, on my first visit, the mercury during the day ranged from 79 to 80 degrees, but at nightfall sank to 70 degrees, and the cool breeze from the river produced a most delicious temperature.

XLI.

UP THE ST. JOHN'S RIVER—TOCOI—ST. AUGUSTINE.

THE St. John's river is a capricious stream, and the Indians characterized it for its waywardness as "Il-la-ka,"—meaning that "it had its own way, which was contrary to every other." Its actual source no man knows, though it seems to be formed by a myriad of small streams pouring out of the unexplored region along the Indian river. It is four hundred miles in length, and here and there broadens into lakes from six to twelve miles wide. The banks are low and flat, but bordered with a wealth of exquisite foliage to be seen nowhere else upon this continent. One passes for hundreds of miles through a grand forest of cypresses robed in moss and mistletoe; of palms towering gracefully far above the surrounding trees, of palmettoes whose rich trunks gleam in the sun; of swamp, white and black ash, of magnolia, of water oak, of poplar, and of plane-tree; and, where hummocks rise a few feet above the water-level, the sweet bay, the olive, the cotton-tree, the juniper, the red cedar, the sweet gum, the live oak, shoot up their splendid stems; while among the shrubbery and inferior growths one may note the azalea, the sumach, the sensitive-plant, the agave, the poppy, the mallow and the nettle. The vines run not in these thickets, but over them. The fox grape clambers along the branches, and the woodbine and bignonia escalade the haughtiest forest monarchs. When the steamer nears the shore, one can see far through the tangled thickets the gleaming water out of which rise thousands of "cypress-knees," looking exactly like so many champagne bottles set into the current to cool.

Residence of Mrs. Harriet Beecher Stowe, at Mandarin, Florida. [Page 386.]

The heron and the crane saucily watch the shadow which the approaching boat throws near their retreat. The wary monster-turtle gazes for an instant, with his black head cocked knowingly on one side, then disappears with a gentle slide and a splash. An alligator grins familiarly as a dozen revolvers are pointed at him over the boat's side, suddenly "winks with his tail," and vanishes! as the bullet meant for his tough hide skims harmlessly over the ripples left above him.

The noble stream appears of a dark blue, as one sails along it, but, taken up in a glass, the water is of a light coffee color, a thin scum sometimes rising to its surface. Its slightly brackish taste is accounted for by the fact that the ocean tides are often perceptible as far up as Lake George. Many insist that there must be springs along the channel of the river, as they cannot otherwise account for its great volume. For its whole length of four hundred miles, it affords glimpses of perfect beauty. One ceases to regret hills and mountains, and can hardly

Green Cove Springs, on the St. John's River, Florida. [Page 385.]

imagine ever having thought them necessary, so much do these visions surpass them. It is not grandeur which one finds on the banks of the great stream, it is nature run riot. The very irregularity is delightful, the decay is charming, the solitude is picturesque. The bitter-sweet orange grows in wild profusion along the St. John's and its tributary streams; thousands of orange-trees demand but transplanting and careful culture to become prolific fruit-bearers.

The local steamers which ascend the river from Jacksonville regularly leave the wharves at eleven in the morning, though advertised for nine, as it has been a tradition, time out of mind, that they shall be two hours late. This brace of hours will be well spent by the traveler, however, if he seats himself on the deck and watches the proceedings on the wharf. A multitude of drays, driven by ragged negroes, come and go incessantly, bringing every conceivable kind of merchandise and household goods; the deck hands carry piles of lumber, baskets of eggs, crates of crockery, hoist in kicking and biting mules, toss aboard half-a-hundred chickens tied by the legs; stow away two or three portable houses destined for the far interior, where some lone lumbermen are felling the massive cypresses; and finally fill in the interstices with coal, chains, fertilizers, salt pork, garden seeds, mail-bags, and an unimaginable hodge-podge. Meantime, if the boat you have taken be her favorite, "Aunt Rose," the venerable river stewardess,—one of the characters along the Jacksonville wharves,—has danced up and down the gang-planks a hundred times with various letters and packages. Even though the day be hot, you find that a cool breeze comes from the dense thickets and forests bordering the current, for you go up the stream at a rapid pace when at last the little craft moves off.

It used to be said, a few years since, that the St. John's banks, from its mouth to its source, were strewn with the wrecks of orange groves. After the war, hundreds of Northerners who knew little of Florida rushed in, dug up the wild orange-trees from the swamps, and transplanted them along the river banks; leaving them with the firm belief that they would care for themselves, and that, in a few years, golden fortunes would hang on every tree. But these careless cultivators were doomed to bitter disappointment; hardly any of them succeeded. In their train, however, came Northerners who made a study of the culture, and now there are dozens of noble groves scattered up and down the river, and a score of years hence the perfume of the orange leaf will be encountered at every point along the stream.

When the war closed there was not a wharf left on the river. Federal and Confederate had warred and wasted, and to-day for memento there lies in the stream, some distance above Jacksonville, a sunken gun-boat, its engine gear just showing above the waves. Inquiring of a venerable Floridian how it happened to be there, I was informed that "the durned Yankees' shot was too hot for her."

The journey from Jacksonville to Tocoi is delightful, though one's first experience of the great river has a zest which no subsequent one can rival. Stemming the current, which, under the brilliant noonday sunshine, seems a sheet of molten silver, the steamer passes little tugs, drawing in their train immense rafts of cypress and pine logs; or salutes, with three loud shrieks, the ponderous "City Point" or "Dictator," from Charleston. The cattle, knee-deep in water, are feeding on the fresh herbage springing from the sand-bars; hundreds of little fish are leaping out of the current and falling back again, their shining bodies coquettishly bent as if they were making mock of the sun. Sometimes the boat enters a pleasant inlet, where the pines on the shores have cut across the "hummock" and stand quaintly draped in Spanish moss, as if they had come to be baptized. Fifteen miles from Jacksonville, on the eastern shore, is the pretty town of Mandarin, so called from the culture there of that variety of the orange. Through the trees gleam white cottages. Orange groves, with the golden fruit glistening among the dark leaves, come to the very water's edge. There, in winter, lives

Mrs. Harriet Beecher Stowe, besieged by hundreds of visitors, who do not seem to understand that she is not on exhibition. Mandarin was once the scene of a dreadful Indian massacre; a generation ago, the Seminoles fell upon it and massacred all within its limits.

"Hibernia," on its island, with a lovely promenade under the sheltering branches of live oaks, and "Magnolia," where a large establishment was erected

On the Road to St. Augustine, Florida.

especially for invalids many years ago, and is now very successfully conducted, are on the right, as you ascend, and are much frequented by Northerners. Oak forests border the water, and pines and palmettoes form a striking background. Throughout the winter months these health-resorts have the climate of Indian summer, and at Green Cove Spring, just above Magnolia, where there are sulphur waters of peculiar healing virtues in rheumatism and dyspepsia, a goodly company usually assembles with the first advent of "the season." Crossing the river to Picolata, a wharf with a prospective town, the steamer follows the eastern bank until it arrives at Tocoi, whence an extempore horse-railway conducts the traveler to St. Augustine. The traveler was formerly condemned to journey from Picolata to St. Augustine, over a terrible road, through cypress clumps and masses of briars, and palmettoes, in a species of volante, in which his bones were so racked that he rarely recovered before it was time to make the journey again.

It is expected that a railroad will one day penetrate the country between Jacksonville and St. Augustine, and following the coast as far as Cape Sable, be conducted over trestles to Key West, thus placing Cuba within three or four hours' sail. The road could be built for a comparatively small sum, as it would run through an absolutely level country.

But that road would rob good old St. Augustine of its romance. I object to it on that account; and so, I am sure, will many hundred others. What! mus we lose the pleasure of arriving at nightfall at the Sebastian river, and hearing the cheery horn sounded as we dash through the quaint streets, and alight at the hostelry? *A bas* the railroad! rather let us have the diligence, the mules with tinkling silver bells, the broad-hatted, velvet-jacketed drivers of primitive Spain.

Useless—vain—these protestations; as I stand on the wharf, at Tocoi, I can see that modernism is already here. A horse-car! Ye guardians of the venerable!

Out through a seemingly interminable forest leads a straight road, bordered here by pines, and there by the palmettoes which spring in dense beds from the rolling ground. There is a little group of houses at Tocoi, and along the river bank, under the shade of the beautiful moss-hung oaks, several Northerners have established charming homes. A few miles back from the river, on either side, are good sugar-lands, and the negroes about the station are munching stalks of cane. An old mill near by is half-buried under a wilderness of tropical vegetation. At intervals in the forest, palm-trees shoot up their slender, graceful trunks.

A Street in St. Augustine, Florida. [Page 388.]

It is eighteen miles from Tocoi to St. Augustine. The journey is made partly on iron, partly on wooden rails; but is comfortable, and affords one an excellent chance to see a veritable Florida back-country. There is not a house along the route; hardly a sign of life. Sometimes the roll of the wheels startles an alligator who has been napping on the track; and once, the conductor says, they found two little brown bears asleep in the run directly in their path. It is night ere you approach the suburbs of the old city. The vegetation takes on a ghostly aspect; the black swamp canal over which the vehicle passes sends up a fetid odor of decay; the palm thickets under the moonlight in the distance set one to tropical imaginings. Arrived at the Sebastian river, an arm of the sea flowing in among long stretches of salt-marsh clad in a kind of yellowish grass, and inhabited by innumerable wild fowl that make the air ring with their cries, the horse-car stops, you are transferred to an omnibus, brown-skinned Minorcans and French touters for hotels surround you; the horn sounds ta-ra! ta-ra-ta-ra! and you rattle through the streets to the hotel.

St. Augustine, Florida—"An ancient gateway."

There is no noise in the town; evening has brought with it profound quiet. As for me, alighting at the "Magnolia," in a street as narrow as any in Valencia or Genoa, I stroll, after supper, into the dark and mysterious lanes. This moonless night is kindly; it lends the proper weirdness—the charm which should be thrown about St. Augustine. Walking in the middle of the street, which is overhung by wide projecting balconies, I detect a murmur, as of far-off music—a soft and gentle monotone. Now that I hear it clearly, surely it is the rhythm of the sea, and the warm breeze which blew across my face had a smell of the ocean. There is plainly the sound of water lapping on the shore. Ah! here is a half-ruined cottage built of coquina, with a splendid palmetto overshadowing its remains, and some strange vines which I cannot identify in the darkness, creeping about the decaying windows! A little farther on, an open plain—and here an ancient gateway, with a fragment of a high wall adjoining it; to the right—looming up through the shadows at a little distance—the massive walls and mauresque towers of an antique fortress. Yonder is the beach, and, as I draw near to it, I see two or three stalwart figures pulling in a boat.

I turn again, and wander through other streets, Hypolita, Bay, Treasury Lane. Some of the little alleys are barely eight feet wide. Where is the bravo with his dagger? Not here. St. Augustine is most peaceable of towns. No moss-grown corner of Europe, asleep these two hundred years, shall boast a steadier population than this—our oldest town in the United States.

Here is a sea-wall wide enough to walk upon. Against it the waves are gently beating. The fort yonder seems now but a great blot on the sky. I come to the Plaza, a little park in the city's midst. A few fishermen, a soldier or two, and some visitors are lazily reclining on the benches opposite the venerable Cathedral. A tall white monument stands in the park's centre. I light a match, and climb the pedestal.

Plaza de la Constitucion.

Monument to one of the short-lived forms of government in Spain. Nothing but a plain shaft.

Now every one has left the square. There are no lights, no voices. So I go home to bed.

Morning, in mid-December, brings warmth and sunlight; noon, slumbrous heat. Still roaming in the quiet streets, I see few signs of activity. Hammers are ringing on the walls of the new wooden hotel in which Northern tourists are to be lodged, a splendid coquina wall, which might have stood for another century, having been torn down to make room for this ephemeral box. The old arch, which marked the site of the Treasury, is crumbling, and will soon vanish. The quondam residence of the Spanish Governors, on the west side of the Plaza, has been rebuilt and altered until there is nothing antique in its appearance. It is now a prosaic court-house and post-office, and around its doors daily gather swarms of Northern tourists awaiting their mail. The balconies of the huge St. Augustine Hotel are crowded at evening when the band of the crack artillery regiment plays.

XLII.

ST. AUGUSTINE, FLORIDA—FORT MARION.

ST. AUGUSTINE, which a proud Spanish monarch once called the "Siempre fiel Ciudad," is situated on the eastern coast of Florida. The town is built on a small peninsula between the St. Sebastian river and the harbor. Menendez drew the attention of the Spanish nation to the spot by landing there in 1565; by his joyous return to the little garrison there, and his reception by the priesthood, who glorified him for the zeal he had displayed, after the massacre of the Huguenots at Fort Caroline; and by the subsequent bloody deeds among the dunes of Anastasia Island, at Matanzas Inlet. Menendez, finding that Ribault's Huguenots had been wrecked near this inlet, went to them with seeming protestations of friendship. He heard their pitiable story; how they had lost four galleons in the mighty storm, and that other vessels were missing; how they desired boats with which to traverse the inlet, and to pass through St. Augustine on their way to a fort "which they had twenty leagues from there." Menendez was too thorough a scoundrel and too little of a gentleman to declare open war against them, but he announced boldly that he had massacred the garrison and destroyed the fort. Then they desired that he should enable them to return to France, since "the kings of Spain and of France were brothers and friends." But Menendez told them that, as they were of the new sect, he held them for enemies, and if they would throw themselves upon his mercy he would *do with them what God should of His mercy direct.* Thus, having shifted the responsibility of his crime from himself to his Maker, he enticed the unfortunate Frenchmen into his clutches, and, after tying their hands, his soldiers massacred every one of them. As the two hundred and eight prisoners came, one by one, into a lonely place among the sand-hills, they were poignarded and stricken down by the swords of their treacherous and murderous assailants. It is not strange that the Floridian should to this day speak of the "bloody Matanzas river."

But this was not all. On the very next day after the massacre, the Spaniards, who had returned to St. Augustine, learned that large numbers of Frenchmen had been seen "at the same part of the river as the others had been." This was Ribault himself, with the remains of his shipwrecked company. The Adelantado, Menendez the infamous, at once pushed forward to meet them. A conference was had; the Frenchmen were shown the dead bodies of their comrades, and grimly directed to surrender to the clemency of the noble hidalgos. Terrified and shocked, starving and without any means of escape, Ribault surrendered himself and 150 of the men-at-arms with him, as well as the royal standards, into the hands of Menendez. Two hundred of Ribault's men, well knowing the fate in store for them, had braved the horrors of the wilderness during the night, preferring them to Spanish "clemency." Ribault and the others who surrendered, save sixteen persons, were ruthlessly slaughtered.

In the world's history there is recorded no more infamous massacre than this. The two hundred who fled the night before the final massacre built a fort at some distance from St. Augustine, but were finally attacked by the Spaniards, and great numbers were made prisoners. Menendez did not kill them, perhaps fearing that a fourth slaughter would arouse even the tardy fury of the King of France, but pressed them into his service.

That was three hundred years ago. The remains of a citadel are still visible at Matanzas Inlet, and a Government revenue officer keeps as regular watch there as ever did Menendez, but not exactly with the same intent. The first fort built at St. Augustine is described by the ancient chroniclers as built of logs, and it is said to have been the council-house of the Indian village, on which site the town is founded. The ruins at Matanzas are undoubtedly more ancient than any building in St. Augustine.

The Remains of a Citadel at Matanzas Inlet.

Menendez went to his reward in 1574, and for two centuries thereafter the records of the settlement were eventful. Sir Francis Drake attacked and burned it in 1586; the buccaneers now and then landed and plundered the helpless inhabitants, and Indians massacred the missionaries. At the end of the seventeenth century the Spanish Government saw that the sea threatened to wash away the town, and for half a century thereafter the inhabitants toiled at the erection of a massive sea-wall, the remains of which may now be seen in the middle of Bay street, and which has been superseded by the fine breakwater built by the United States Government between 1837 and 1843.

At the beginning of the eighteenth century, the South Carolinians came in hostile array against St. Augustine by land and sea. The siege by land was successful, the attack by sea was a fiasco, and the invasion failed after having cost South Carolina £6,000, for which she issued promises to pay. A quarter of a century later the Carolinians raided again upon the old town, but went no farther than the gates. In 1740 Governor Oglethorpe, of Georgia, led a movement of Georgians, Carolinians and English against it; but retired, after an unsuccessful siege and bombardment. Shortly thereafter, the garrison of St. Augustine retaliated, and attacked the English settlements in Georgia with a formidable force; it was profitless. Back came Oglethorpe in 1743, carrying fire and death to the very walls of the old fort.

At the time of Oglethorpe's siege, St. Augustine was stoutly walled about and intrenched, with salient angles and redoubts. On the principal fort, fifty pieces of brass cannon were mounted, and growled defiance across a moat two score feet wide to any enemy prowling beneath the walls. There were twenty-

View of Fort Marion, St. Augustine, Florida. [Page 394.]

five hundred inhabitants—of which nearly one-half were Spanish soldiers. Outposts were maintained on the St. John's river, and scouts quickly brought intelligence of any hostile movement.

England obtained the province of Florida by treaty in 1763, and when the red-coats came to St. Augustine, the Spanish inhabitants nearly all left. Many of them or their descendants, however, returned when the English had decided to get rid of the troublesome colony, and recession to Spain occurred in 1783, in exchange for the Bahama islands. In 1821, the standard of Spain, which had been raised by Menendez and his men, 256 years before, over St. Augustine, was hauled down, and the stars and stripes were raised in its place.

Since then, the old town has had its share of vicissitudes. It changed hands three times during our civil war.

A century ago, St. Augustine was, in general plan, very much as it is now. The "Governor's official residence," the present court-house, has lost the beautiful garden which surrounded it; a Franciscan convent stood on the site of the artillery barracks of to-day. An Indian village was still standing upon the little peninsula in those days, and to the town's fortifications had been added a ditch, along whose sides were planted thick rows of the Spanish bayonet, forming an almost impenetrable *chevaux de frise.*" The outer lines of defense can still be traced. The gardens surrounding the solidly built two-story flat-roofed houses were still filled with fruit-trees, as the Spaniards had left them; the fig, pomegranate, lemon, lime, orange, guava and the bergamot, flourished then as now; and over the lattices great vines trailed, bending under loads of luscious grapes.

The romance of the place is now gradually departing. The merry processions of the carnival, with mask, violin and guitar, are no longer kept up with the old taste; the rotund figure of the *padre*, the delicate form of the Spanish lady, clad in mantilla and basquina, and the tall, erect, brilliantly uniformed cavaliers, are gone; the "posy dance," with its arbors and garlands, is forgotten; and the romantic suburbs are undergoing a complete transformation.

The wealth of Northern cities is erecting fine pleasure houses, surrounded with noble orchards and gardens, and in a few years there will be as many villas as at Newport within a half hour's drive from the centre of St. Augustine. A brilliant society already gathers there every winter, and departs reluctantly when the long summer heats begin. Although the majority of those who visit the venerable town are not in search of health so much as of an agreeable climate, and an escape from the annoyances of winter, still, the preservation of health has been found so certain in the genial air of Florida, that hundreds of families have determined to make it henceforth their winter home.

Those invalids who cannot endure a sea-air would do well to avoid St. Augustine, and seek some of the interior towns; but the overworked and careworn, the sufferers from nervous disease, can find speedy relief in the permeating influence of the genial sunshine, which continues almost uninter-

Light-house on Anastasia Island, near St. Augustine, Florida.

ruptedly throughout the winter months. In December, the days are ordinarily bright and sunny, a salt sea-wind blowing across the peninsula; from ten until four o'clock, one can sit out of doors, bathed in floods of delicious light. During my stay at St. Augustine, in December, there were two days in which I gave myself completely up to the mere pleasure of existence. I seemed incapable of any effort; the strange fascination of the antiquated and remote fortress-town was upon me. The sunshine penetrated to every corner of my room. There was no broad and unpleasant glare—no impertinent staring on the sun's part, but a gladsome light which I have never seen elsewhere. I walked out at noonday; the town seemed transfigured: the shadows thereon from the balconies, from the date-trees, from the thickets of roses, were mystical; I sat down on the grass-grown rampart near old Fort Marion, and (forgetting the gnats) let the gentle sea-breeze caress my temples, and memories of by-gone centuries take complete possession of me. At that moment, the rest of the world seemed as remote as Paradise, vague as Ilium, foreign as the Zendavesta.

Falling, at last, to contemplation of the ancient fort, I could not repress my indignation as I remembered that when there was talk of building a railroad to St. Augustine, some enterprising company wished to buy and demolish the quaint

View of the Entrance to Fort Marion, St. Augustine, Florida.

landmark, that they might establish a railway terminus there. Such vandalism would be a disgrace to us. The fort should be tenderly clung to. The more moss-grown it becomes, the more we should love it. It is a grand monument. For more than a century hundreds of men toiled in the quarries on Anastasia Island and along the bay shore, wresting out the material now in the massive walls.

Coquina, of which the fort is built, is a kind of concretion of shell-fragments, often very beautiful. This formation extends along the Floridian coast for more than a hundred miles. It crumbles when exposed for a very long time to the air, but rarely falls to pieces. Coquina resists a bombardment better than ordinary stone, as it is elastic and will bend before the fiery messengers; so that it is quite possible that Fort Marion, decaying and aged though it seem, would stand the broadsides of a foreign man-of-war better than the forts which have been built but a few years.

This fort is built after Vauban's principles, in the form of a trapezium, with walls twenty-one feet high and enormously thick, and with bastions at each corner, originally named after St. Paul, St. Pierre, etc. The Castle of San Marco was its former title. On it the Appalachean Indians labored for sixty years. The garrison was also compelled to contribute to the work, and convicts were brought from far Mexico to labor in the quarries. Thousands of hands must have been employed for half a century in transporting the giant blocks across the bay, and raising them to position in the thick walls. As one traverses the draw-bridge, coming down the town, he sees over the main entrance the arms of Spain, with the globe and cross above them, and an inscription showing that in 1756 Field-Marshal Don Alonzo Fernando Herrera, then "Governor and Captain of the City of San Augustin de la Florida," finished the castle, "Don Fernando Sixth being then King of Spain."

"San Marco," now Fort Marion, has never been taken by a besieging enemy. It is a noble fortification, requiring one hundred cannon and a thousand men as complement and garrison; and it has been so strengthened by the water-battery added to it since the United States came into possession that it is a very formidable defense. The old sergeant in charge exhibits the interior to visitors. You penetrate the cell which was suddenly discovered some years ago by a break in a wall, and which the Spaniards had concealed before ceding the fort to our Government. In this cell were found cages in which men had been confined. Torch in hand, the sergeant leads you through the chapel in the casemate, to the cell whence a Seminole chief once made his escape during the war with his countrymen, and mounts with you to the breezy promenade overlooking the water-battery, flanked at either end by the little Moorish sentry-boxes whence the men-at-arms were wont to watch the forest and the sea for the approach of the enemies who came so frequently. The moss-grown and discolored walls, the worn coquina slits, the gloomy corridors, the mysterious recesses, the grand old moat, with the gigantic walls above it, are too perfect reminders of the past to be allowed to perish. The vandal who shall destroy Fort Marion will deserve banishment.

"The old sergeant in charge."

The cathedral is in real Spanish style, and although it is neither large nor imposing, there is a subtle charm about its gray walls, its time-eaten doorway, its belfry from which bell-notes are always clanging. On Sunday evenings, crowds assemble in the Plaza, and listen to the sweet-voiced choir at vespers, while from the Episcopal Church across the way, one can now and then hear the murmur of Protestant song. I shall not soon forget the startling contrast which I observed one Sabbath evening in the Plaza. The cathedral bells tolled solemnly. I could see, in the open belfry, three bright-faced lads striking the notes on the bells; while out from under the gray portal came a funeral procession,—the young acolytes in their long robes of black and white, then the priests and the mourners, strange, dark-bearded men, and dark-skinned women, facing in sombre fashion toward the little cemetery. It was like a bit out of the seventeenth century. Turning, I saw, on the Plaza's other side, the congregation leaving the Episcopal Church—hosts of richly dressed ladies chatting gayly together; the row of young gentlemen ranged outside to criticise the belles admiringly; an army officer passing, and touching his cap with lofty courtesy; and half-a-dozen Northerners eagerly discussing the latest news from the stock market;—this was the nineteenth century come to St. Augustine.

The Cathedral—St. Augustine, Florida.

The brown maidens, the olive-colored women that you see in the streets, are the descendants of that colony from the Minorcan Islands, which one Dr. Turnbull induced to settle on the coast, at a place called New Smyrna, more than a hundred years ago. Fourteen hundred persons were brought out, and engaged in the culture of indigo, which then commanded an enormous price. Turnbull succeeded in obtaining absolute control over the defenseless colonists, cut them off from all communication with other settlements, and was rapidly reducing them to a condition of actual slavery, when they revolted, but in vain; and it was not until the English attorney-general of the province interfered in their behalf, that they were emancipated from Turnbull's tyranny, and allowed to remove to St. Augustine, where they and their descendants have now been a part of the population for nearly a century. Their old habits and customs, brought from the islands, are rapidly dying out; and the dialect songs which Mr. Bryant heard during his visit, in 1843, have almost entirely disappeared. Many of the women are extremely beautiful in their youth, but they fade early. The men are bold, hardy fishermen, Greek and Italian in type and robustness—while the women have much of the delicacy of form and feature of their American sisters.

Much as one may fear that the influx of Northern fashion may rob the old town of its chief charm, it is easy to see that a delightful watering-place is to be created.

The people of New England, who seem to have taken Florida under their especial tutelage, there meet and mingle freely with those from other sections; even the English and French are beginning to find attractions at St. Augustine, and my lord doffs his shooting suit to spend a few days in the pleasant society gathered in the shade of the orange-trees and the pines. The Florida *Press*, which Mr. Charles Whitney, of New York, has established at St. Augustine, represents Northern sentiment, and in its pleasant editorial parlors gentlemen from all the Northern and Western States gather every morning to exchange opinions. Meantime the ladies are shopping in the tiny box-like shops in the toy streets. They buy rich stores of brilliant wings of flamingoes, or pink curlews (all the hues of the rainbow are found on the feathers of the Floridian birds); or they fill their pockets with alligators' teeth, curiously carved, or send home coquina vases, or box a young alligator a foot long, in Spanish moss, and express him North to a timid friend. Or they visit such superb orange groves as that of Dr. Anderson, where eight hundred noble trees hang loaded with yellow fruit; or visit the cemetery where repose Dade and the brave soldiers who lost their lives in the Seminole war, under the tomahawks of Osceola and his men; or peer into the two convents; or at evening, when the sky near the horizon is filled with Daubigny-tints, wander on the beach, the warm, moist wind blowing across their faces, and the shells and brittle sea-weeds crackling beneath their feet.

The war did not greatly impair St. Augustine. A few fine homes were destroyed, and much suffering and privation were caused by the removal to the Nassau river of such families as refused to take the oath of loyalty. The Federal Government obtained possession in 1862, and kept it. Of course many fortunes were completely broken, and scores of people in the town, as throughout Florida, are living in straitened circumstances doubly painful because they have never before known self-dependence. The town now has good educational facilities for white and black, although before the war it had none. The natives of St. Augustine rejoice as much as do the Northerners at the progress of the free and public schools. But in the back-country, so far as I could learn, there are neither school-houses, schools, nor sentiment in favor of either.

XLIII.

THE CLIMATE OF FLORIDA—A JOURNEY TO PALATKA.

THE climate of Florida is undoubtedly its chief charm. Its beauties and virtues have for a hundred years filled the homes of St. Augustine with people striving to recover from the effects of severer surroundings; and it will always be a refuge. The equable temperature is one of the great excellences of the climate. The thermometer rarely falls below 30 degrees, or rises above 95 degrees. The mean temperature of the winter months at St. Augustine, for 100 years, according to the old Spanish records, averaged a little over 60 degrees. The climate of the State is of course varied, as it extends through six degrees of latitude. The greatest heats in summer are never equal to those experienced in New York and Boston. One writer, who is considered good authority, says that during his eighteen years of residence in Florida, the greatest heat was 96 degrees in the shade. The climate of the whole State from October to June has been characterized as "one continuous spring." Periods of cold or frost never last but a few hours, and rarely come, save in January, once or twice. The nights, whatever the character of the days preceding them, are always cool. Both the winter and summer weather in East Florida is delightful. The winters in that section are so mild that "the most delicate vegetables and plants of the Caribbean Islands," says one writer, "experience there not the least injury from the season;" and the orange, the plantain, the banana, the guava, and the pineapple attain a luxuriant growth. The medical statistics of the army show that the climate of the State as a whole ranks preëminent in point of salubrity. Solon Robinson, formerly the agricultural editor of the *Tribune*, who now resides at Jacksonville, tells me that he considers the climate of East Florida undoubtedly the best in the country. A general impression prevails in the North that on account of the large bodies of swamp land in the State, any one going there to reside, even temporarily, will incur danger of malarial disease. It is, however, established beyond controversy that there is never any danger from malaria in the winter months; and that it is, to quote Mr. Robinson once more, "certainly no worse for immigrants from any of the Northern States than central New York was in its early settlement for those who went into the forests from New England." Despite the fact that there are malarial diseases which attack the careless and unacclimated who remain in the State through all the seasons, it is still true that even with the moribund from half-a-dozen harsh climates sent to her to care for, Florida can show cleaner bills of health than any other State in the Union.

Frost reaches all parts of the State on rare occasions, but has seldom been known to go below latitude 27 degrees. It has sometimes visited Jacksonville and other points along the St. John's river when the mercury stood at 40 degrees. In Eastern Florida it rarely does damage to the sweet oranges, or the banana. In West Florida there is, say the authorities, "a constant struggle between the north-west wind and the trade-wind, and fruit growing incurs dangers." The seasons are the wet and the dry; the rains, which come with astonishing regularity at certain hours during the summer days, fall in heavy showers, and leave a cloudless sky behind them. There is rarely any rain during the winter months. Surgeon-General Lawson in one of his reports announces that while in the middle division of the United States the proportion is one death to thirty-six cases of remittent fever; in the northern division, one to fifty-two; in the southern division, one to fifty-four; in Texas, one to seventy-eight; and in California, one to one hundred and forty-eight,—in Florida it is only one to two hundred and eighty-seven.

If a perfectly equable climate, where a soothing warmth and moisture combined prevail, be desirable for consumptives, it can be found nowhere in the Southern States, save in South-eastern Florida. The number of persons whom I saw during my journey, who had migrated to the eastern or southern sections of the State many years before,—"more than half-dead with consumption," and who are now robust and vigorous,—was sufficient to convince me of the great benefits derived from a residence there. Physicians all agree that the conditions necessary to insure life to the consumptive are admirably provided in the climatic resources of the peninsula. That great numbers of invalids find the localities along the St. John's river, and even on the coast, distressing to them, is said, by some physicians, to be due to the fact that those invalids go there after disease has become too deeply-seated. The European medical men are beginning to send many patients to Florida, cautioning them where to go. It would seem impossible for the most delicate invalid to be injured by a residence anywhere on the eastern or south-eastern coast from St. Augustine down. For those who, from various causes, find that each successive Northern winter,—with its constantly shifting temperature and its trying winds, which even the healthy characterize as "deadly,"—saps their vitality more and more, Florida may be safely recommended as a home, winter and summer. For the healthy, and those seeking pleasure, it will become a winter paradise; for the ailing it is a refuge and strength; for the severely invalided its results depend entirely upon choice of location and the progress which the disease has already made. The perfection of the Floridian winter climate is said to be obtained at Miami, near Key Biscayne bay, on the Miami river. There, among the cocoanuts and the mangroves, invalids may certainly count on laying a new hold upon life.

Returning from St. Augustine to the St. John's river, I continued my journey southward from Tocoi, the terminus of the horse-railroad before mentioned. Over this road, by the way, thousands of Northern people journey yearly; and the wharf, during the winter months, is crowded at the arrival and departure of the boats with fashionably dressed tourists, who seem strangely out of place in the semi-tropical forests. The "Florence," a sprightly steamer, brought me to Palatka early in the afternoon, affording all the way a delightful view of the wide stream, on whose sun-transfigured breast the wild ducks were flushing their eager wings; and over which, now and then, flew the heron and the water-goose uttering strange cries. Dr. Westcott, at Tocoi (a gentleman who spent thirty-three years of his life in the Floridian forests, and who has once been Surveyor-General of the State), told me that the Spaniards called the river at that point Lake Valdes. One finds it wide and narrow alternately until Palatka is reached. There the stream has formed a broad lake, from which there seems no outlet whatever. Palatka is a very pretty town of fifteen hundred inhabitants, on the west bank. It is at the head of navigation for ocean steamers, and is characterized by a richness of vegetation, and a mildness of climate which is not found at Jacksonville. It has become a favorite resort for the Northerners, and I found the Vermonters there in force. Colonel Hart, who went to Florida to die, some years ago, now owns fine properties near and in Palatka, and has drawn around him the sterling New England thrift and management, of which he is such an admirable example. Steamers arrive daily from North and South, and the facilities for travel are quite as numerous and as good as upon the Hudson. The consumptives from the North return yearly to this vivifying and delicious climate, in which they find an arrest of Death's decree against them.

At Palatka we first found the banana and the orange in their richest profusion, and noted what culture would do for them both. The town is backed by an interminable pine forest, through which run but few roads; but the ample space along the river front abounds in grand groves of oak, draped with the cool mosses, hung in most ravishingly artistic forms; and the wild orange grows in the streets. This town has a cheery, neat, New England look; the white painted houses, with their porches nestling in vines and shrubbery, invite to repose. The two old-fashioned, roomy hotels (to one of which an immense wooden addition has been made) are cool and comfortable.

The mornings in December, January, February and March, the four absolutely perfect months of Eastern Florida, are wonderfully soft and balmy; the sun shines generously, but there is no suspicion of annoying heat. The breeze gently rustles the enormous leaves of the banana, or playfully tumbles a golden

The Banana—"At Palatka we first found the banana in profusion."

orange to the ground, that a plump goose or duckling may at once thrust its bill into the tender fruit. The giant cactus in a neighboring garden peers out from among the fruit-trees like some scaly monster. The cart of the "cracker" (the native farmer's appellation), laden with game and vegetables, plies from door to door, and wild turkeys and dappled deer are purchased for dinner. Little parties lazily bestow themselves along the river bank, with books or sketching materials, and alternately work, doze, or gossip, until the whistles of the ascending or descending steamers are heard, when everybody flocks to the wharves. At evening a splendid white moonlight transfigures all the leaves and trees and flowers; the banjo and guitar, accompanying negro melodies, are heard in the streets; a heavy tropical repose falls over the little town, its wharves and rivers.

This was not always so. After the war was over, a few adventurous Yankees betook themselves to Palatka, but were not heartily received by the rude backwoodsmen and dubious "cracker" element which still lingered about there. In war time, 15,000 Union troops had been quartered at Palatka, and previous to that the town had on one occasion been bombarded. The Floridians had suffered a good deal, and there was severe enmity toward the "Yankees." The first attempt to open a hotel by a Northern man was severely resented. Parties of rough horsemen used to ride in and attempt to provoke a fight by sticking their bowie-knives in the hotel door. Shooting affrays were common. I was shown a spot where the sheriff himself tore up the turf during a fight of an hour or two with his own brothers-in-law, who were determined to kill him because he supported the "Yankees," then gradually creeping in. Now and then a negro was massacred.

The river's banks were sometimes the scene of terribly bloody affrays. Of course it was only the rougher classes who had a hand in this — people who rather objected to the march of civilization. It made them uncomfortable. Now the town is as peaceable as the mountain resorts in New Hampshire and Vermont. Property is good there, and has taken on prices which show a real demand for it. Three thousand dollars are asked for a little house and lot which would hardly bring any more in the North. But all the region adjacent to Palatka, and especially on the opposite side of the river, is getting settled up and cultivated.

XLIV.

ORANGE CULTURE IN FLORIDA—FERTILITY OF THE PENINSULA.

JUST across the river from Palatka lies the beautiful orange grove owned by Colonel Hart, in which seven hundred trees, some forty years old, annually bear an enormous crop of the golden fruit, and yield their owner an income of $12,000 or $15,000. The trees bear from twelve to twenty-five hundred oranges each; some have been known to bear four or five thousand. The orchard

"Just across the river from Palatka lies the beautiful orange grove owned by Colonel Hart."

requires the care of only three men, an overseer and two negroes. The myriads of fish to be caught at any time in the river furnish material for compost heaps, with which the land is annually enriched. At the gateway of this superb orchard stand several grand bananas; entering the cool shade—some resplendent December day—one finds the negroes gathering the fruit into bags strapped at their sides, and bearing it away to storehouses where it is carefully packed for the steamers which are to bear it North. On the sand from which the hardy trunks of the orange spring there is a splendid checker-work of light and shade, and one catches through the interstices occasional glimpses of the broad river current. In an adjacent nursery, a hundred thousand young orange-trees await transplanting and "budding."

This culture of oranges will certainly become one of the prime industries of Florida. The natives of the poorer class, who might make fortunes by turning their attention to it, are too idle to develop the country. They prefer to hunt and fish, and, as a rule, cannot be prevailed upon to undertake serious work. The mass of Northern men who undertook orange-raising directly after the war, failed because they did not employ skilled labor. The eastern bank of the river is considered safer than the western for the culture, as frosts rarely reach the former. But for many miles up and down the stream, the culture has proved reasonably successful on both sides. The property is becoming exceedingly good, yearly rising in value. Colonel Hart thinks his grove is worth at least $75,000. In a few years such establishments as those of Mr. Stockwell of Maine, with four hundred bearing-trees; Mr. Burr of Morristown, N. J.; the estate of Masters (two hundred trees); Mr. Brown, a New Yorker (two thousand young trees); Dr. Parsons, the Long Island nurseryman, and others adjacent to Colonel Hart's property, will yield fortunes to their owners. Connected with most of the orchards are many fine lemon and lime-trees. Colonel Dancey, six miles below Palatka, has a lemon grove of two hundred trees. Among the other noticeable groves below Palatka, are those of Dr. Cowgill, the State Comptroller; Colonel Cole of Orange Mills, who has some two thousand trees well started; Doctor Mays, at Orange Mills; a number of New York gentlemen at Federal Point; that of Captain J. W. Stark, nearly opposite Orange Mills, and the fine estate of Captain Rossignol.

Above Palatka, on the eastern banks, where the bluffs are quite high for Florida, and where the magnolia and water oak alternate charmingly with the cypress, the swamp-ash and the palm, there are also many successful orange groves scattered along from Rawlestown (where a hundred years ago an unsuccessful attempt was made to found an industrial retreat for the unfortunate women of London) to San Matteo, Murphy's Island, Buffalo Bluff, Welaka, and Beecher. There are many young groves on the Oclawaha river, and more than a million trees are already budded there. Before the war, acres of land covered with the wild orange were ruthlessly cleared to make room for cotton and cane. It is mainly Northern capital that is invested in orange culture throughout the State at present. In the Indian river region, the woods along the banks are, according to one account, "great gardens of the sour, wild orange, and we often," says the traveler, "had to clear the ground of vast quantities of the fruit before we could pitch our tents." These wild trees can be set out in new lands, and at a proper time budded with the sweet orange. Any time during the winter months is proper for transplanting. The "buds," or grafts, grow enormously the first year; and, in five years at most, if one hundred transplanted trees have been set out on an acre, that acre will yield 10,000 oranges; next year the yield will be doubled, and in ten years from the date of transplanting, with anything like reasonable success, one is sure of an income for life. For the orange is a hardy tree, gives a sure crop, has few insect enemies, and lives for more than a hundred years. A good tree will bear from one thousand to three thousand oranges yearly. Some of the trees in an orchard at Mandarin have produced as many as 5,500, many of the oranges weighing nearly a pound each. One single grove on the Indian river, with 1,350 trees, produced in a season 700,000 oranges. Only a small capital is needed for the starting of a grove, and the rewards of a successful one are very great. Oranges sell at from $25 to $68 per thousand in Jacksonville, and are readily salable in any of the Atlantic seaports. When the necessary dredging and building of canals has been accomplished, so that the Indian river may have an outlet via St. John, the North will be supplied with oranges of more delicate texture than any it has yet seen; and the number of groves along the river will be legion.

Entrance to Colonel Hart's Orange Grove, opposite Palatka.

The fitness of Florida for the growth of tropical and semi-tropical fruits is astonishing. Not only do the orange, the lemon, the lime, and the citron flourish there, but the peach, the grape, the fig, the pomegranate, the plum, all varieties of berries, the olive, the banana, and the pine-apple grow luxuriantly. Black Hamburg and white Muscat grapes fruit finely in the open air; the Concord and the Scuppernong are grown in vast quantities. The guava, the tamarind, the wonderful alligator-pear, the plantain, the cocoanut, and the date, the almond and the pecan luxuriate in Southern Florida. We have within our boundaries a tropic land, rich and strange, which will one day be inhabited by thousands of fruit-growers, and where beautiful towns, and perhaps cities, will yet spring up.

Nothing can be more beautiful than one of the Floridian cottages, surrounded with a flourishing grove of orange-trees. That of Dr. Moragné, at Palatka, is one of the best examples. Down at the river front the good doctor has a long row of flourishing bananas, beyond which the great river is spread out—a gentle lake—before him. From his porch he looks upon several acres of noble trees, with thousands of oranges nestling among the dark green leaves. They come without care; one man picks them and prepares them for market, and they leave a golden, or, at least, a paper harvest annually behind them. Some of the 200 trees within the doctor's inclosure yearly produce 3,000 to 4,000 oranges, and will go on their round of blossom and fruit for half a century.*

* The Union officer in command at Palatka during the war was ordered to destroy all the trees around the town for military purposes. He could not find it in his heart to ruin Dr. Moragné's beautiful grove; so he picketed his cavalry there, and evaded the order.

Palatka was an Indian trading post in 1835. The Government built a road thence to Tampa, and kept a guard upon it, in the days when the Seminoles were still vigorous in their warfare. There are now but few Indians left in the State, and they, though peacefully inclined, remain buried in the Everglades, or among the forests of Indian river. Great numbers of them were ignominiously hunted down at various periods after the wars, and rewards were set upon their heads as if they had been criminals. Soldiers wers employed, or induced, by the hope of money, to follow them into their remotest fastnesses, and to disperse them. Now an occasional warrior, scantily clad, and dejected in appearance, is at rare intervals seen in some of the towns.

At Palatka one may gain a good idea of what culture and the advent of ambitious Northerners can do for Florida. There are so many superior inducements offered by the peninsula to those in search of new abiding-places, that I must content myself with a brief summing up of each. I suppose that the average observer, unfamiliar with the character of a sub-tropical country, would traverse the peninsula constantly remarking that he had never before seen so much good-for-nothing land. The eternal pine woods in many sections would prepossess him unfavorably; he would not even appreciate the exceeding richness of the hummocks until he had been instructed in their qualities. The lands of the State are usually classified into hummocks, pine, and swamp. Through the first-rate pine lands, where forests of pitch and yellow pine grow rankly, runs a dark vegetable mould, under which lies a chocolate-colored sandy loam, mixed with limestone pebbles, and resting on a substratum of marl. Lands of this class are so fertile that they have yielded 400 pounds of long staple cotton to the acre for fourteen successive years without any fertilizing. The second-rate pine lands offer excellent pasturage, and, when re-enforced, will yield 3,000 pounds of sugar to the acre. Upon them also can be grown oranges, lemons, and Cuba tobacco. Even the poorest pine lands have been found admirably adapted to the growth of hemp, and also give a good income from the naval stores which the trees yield.

Throughout these pine lands, at intervals of a few miles, there are hummocks of every size, varying from an acre or two to tracts of 20,000 or 30,000. These are wonderfully rich, and persons wishing to cultivate them can choose their residences on the higher pine lands, where there will be no danger of malarial fevers, and only spend their days among the hummocks. The low hummocks are very fertile, and before the war were the seats of many fine sugar plantations. The high hummocks are considered among the best lands in Florida; their fertility is really extraordinary, and the only preparation which they need for the production of luxuriant crops is clearing and ploughing, while, in addition, the low hummocks require draining.

The swamp lands of the peninsula are still, as it were, in process of formation, and are thought to be of even more durable fertility than the hummocks. They are of alluvial formation, occupying basins into which immense deposits of decaying vegetable matter have been washed from higher lands. Some astonishing results in sugar-planting have been obtained in those swamps. Four hogsheads to the acre were produced near New Smyrna, in East Florida, a production which completely overtops that of Louisiana. While Texas and Louisiana cane-planters are obliged to cut their cane in October, because of early frost, in Florida it may stand unharmed until late in December. Vast bodies of these swamp lands are now lying untilled in Florida, and may be had at two dollars per acre. In Leroy county alone there are said to be 100,000 acres of the best kind of sugar-land.*

While the tracts along the St. John's river are not considered extraordinary in point of fertility, still, within a mile of the banks, there are thousands of acres of fine hummock land which might be tilled with great profit. The counties of Middle Florida offer abundant high hummock lands; so do many counties in the eastern section. As soon as production begins in earnest the producer will learn to appreciate the advantageous situation of Florida. Lying directly across one of the great highways of traffic, and within a day and a-half of New Orleans, three days of New York, and one of Cuba, by steamer; with such harbors as Tampa, Fernandina, Pensacola, Cedar Keys and Charlotte, and with reasonably good means of internal communication by road, and superb ones by river, the State has no reason to complain. Cotton was, of course, the principal staple before the war; but a great variety of production will henceforth be the rule. Indian corn will grow throughout the State, and has been liberally raised, although not yet in sufficient quantities to supply the home demand. Fruit and vegetable culture along the lines of the rivers, with reference to the Northern markets, is becoming one of the principal industries. The culture of cotton at present does not pay in the State; and the production, which in 1860 amounted to 63,000 bales of ginned cotton, is gradually decreasing. Sugar-cane is one of the great hopes of the commonwealth. It is confidently asserted that the yield of this staple in Florida is twice that of Louisiana. Solon Robinson says that "small farmers can grow cane upon any good pine land, and can make sugar as easily as Yankee farmers make cider." He evidently does not believe that the successful culture of the cane is inseparable from the old plantation system. Rice, indigo, silk, coffee, tea, and the ramie plant are likely to be among the other agricultural interests of Florida. The palmetto, scattered so luxuriantly through Florida, is now extensively used in the manufacture of paper, and forms the basis of a great industry. On the entire coast are excellent locations for salt works, and at the commencement of the war, large works had been established on Key West Island for the manufacture of salt by solar evaporation. Along the coast, too, there is such a multitude of oysters, fish, and game, that enterprises for supplying the market from that section should be very successful. The turtle and the fish are celebrated everywhere; and the Indian river oyster deserves a ballad to his charms by some noted gastronomer.

The natural resources for fertilizers are abundant in the State. From the swamp lands may always be had a muck which serves admirably, and the clay itself, which lies next to the sandy soil in a large part of the State, is a fine fertilizer when mixed directly. There are also immense accumulations of shells,

* See Adams on Florida.

of the periwinkle and conch, which are well calculated to strengthen land, and deposits of green marl are easily accessible.

The expense of building is very slight in Florida, for the houses need none of the plastering and weather-tightening so necessary in Northern climates. Simple houses, cellarless, and raised some two feet from the ground on posts, with large, airy rooms, battened instead of plastered, and surrounded by verandas, are best adapted to the climate. In the towns, as a rule, rents are rather high, owing to the lack of building during the past perturbed years.

The Guardian Angel.

XLV.

UP THE OCLAWAHA TO SILVER SPRING.

THE Oclawaha is a small stream running through swamps and still lakes in Putnam and Marion counties. It empties into the St. John's about twenty-five miles south of Palatka, and opposite the settlement called We-la-ka. The river took its name from that of one of the seven clans of Seminoles who once wandered through the swamps which border it, and hunted in the beautiful lakes above it. It is but a few years since the stream was rendered navigable, and to-day its mouth is so embowered in foliage—such great curtains of vines and water plants overhanging it—that the passer-by on the St. John's would hardly notice it. Boats leave Jacksonville and Palatka every Thursday for Lake Griffin, and, traversing the whole forest range through which the Oclawaha runs, furnish the traveler with an admirable opportunity to see some of the most remarkable lowland scenery in the world.

The invalid from the North, anxious to escape not only from the trying climate which has increased his malady, but also the memories of the busy world to which he has been accustomed, could not do better than to drift up and down this remote and secluded stream, whose sylvan peace and perfect beauty will bring him the needed repose. Some years since, an enterprising Yankee, familiar with the charms of the little river, conceived the project of a floating hotel to constantly make trips between Palatka, on the St. John's, and the Silver Spring, one of the most beautiful resorts on the Oclawaha, but until this mammoth project is put into execution the traveler must content himself with the wheezy little steamboats which lazily mount the current, or must come in his own yacht.

Yachting on the Oclawaha and St. John's rivers would certainly be prime amusement in the winter season. There are some curious characters along the little stream,—hunters and trappers, who have spent many years in the woods and swamps, and who could teach the amateur sportsman how to hunt the alligator in his lair, to snare the turtle, and now and then to shoot a noble wild turkey. If neither the floating hotel nor the new line of steamers is placed on this charming water-way, it is to be hoped that large caravansaries for fashionable visitors may be erected at such lovely resorts as Silver Spring and Ocala. The hotel accommodations in the interior of Florida are generally far from excellent, but the tide of travel which is beginning to penetrate even to the remotest corners of the peninsula will soon cause the establishment of hotels which will be thoroughly satisfactory to Northern and foreign visitors. The whole Oclawaha region had not been properly explored until toward

1867, although many travelers who had penetrated as far as the then supposed head of navigation, had told strange and seemingly exaggerated stories of its wonderful beauty. The tales of floating islands, of the grandeur and almost frightful calm of the mighty swamps—of the curious colonies of birds and

A Peep into a Forest on the Oclawaha.

animals—the superb lakes, and the lucent waters, had thrilled many a brain; but only a few had penetrated these watery, sylvan retreats until the prying Northern element demanded to be shown all. Now a journey up the Oclawaha is as fashionable as a promenade on the Rhine, and really more interesting and amusing.

Our party embarked at Palatka on the little steamer "Marion," one cool evening, just after the arrival of the boat from Charleston; and while the officers of her huge sister were still shouting themselves hoarse with commands to the slouching negroes about them, our tiny bark slipped out into the broad current, and set slowly off midstream at the rate of four miles an hour, for a journey to Silver Spring. Although cool, it was not uncomfortable, and one was from time to time startled, as on the Mediterranean, by a warm breath across his face, perfumed with the scent of oranges and the rich forest growth. The lights of cottages along the banks blinked cheerily; occasionally a descending steamer yelled her warning, and we blundered leisurely forward, still in the great stream when midnight came, and sleepily sought the tiny cabins allotted us.

It must have been two o'clock in the morning when I was awakened by a violent brushing and scraping noise, as if the boat were held fast amid the boughs of trees. Lazily gazing out of the cabin I saw, with surprise, the bough of a stout shrub entering the window, then vanishing with a shriek and a whisk, as if it had merely looked in to frighten me.

The whole thicket was lighted up as by some supernatural agency. I saw giant cypresses, their dirty white trunks seeming about to topple down upon me; saw acres of glimmering water, in which the mysterious light cast a thousand fantastic gleams, which shifted uneasily every moment; saw the cypress-knees dotting the thicket in every direction; saw lovely green vines, literally spangled with white and blue flowers, and arrayed in such dense and symmetrical masses that I could not persuade myself they grew wild in the thicket; saw a heron sitting, low-perched, on a shrub; and saw the flash of wings, as from time to time our advancing boat's monotonous refrain of sighs from its two steam-pipes startled the birds reposing in the tree-tops.

The red-bay, the holly, the ash, the maple, the cypress, *toujours* the cypress, floated before my half-closed eyes; then vines again, then more birds,—wondered if I should see an alligator—what they would have for breakfast—another tree coming in at my window—"Look out thar, Bill, for them torches!" and at that point, I think, I fell asleep again.

In the morning it was all explained. I had awakened just after we had entered the Oclawaha, and had seen the glare of the torches by which we groped our way in the narrow channel filled with spring-water. Had we entered in the

"We would brush past the trees and vines." [Page 411.]

day-time, I should have seen immense floating islets of lilies and barnets, gently swayed by the tremulous currents, and hundreds of light-footed birds poising airily upon them; the haughty kingfisher diving for his prey; the wild turkey uttering his startled cry; the crane making himself as invisible as possible, by shrinking until he seemed merely a feather-ball; and the rose-colored curlew rising into the air like a flash of light from a ruby. Then, too, I should have noted the rafts of cypress-trees, girded together with bark and palmetto strings, and as we approached the shores, might have caught sight of the wrinkle-throated alligator wagging his huge tail cheerily in the sunshine.

All day we wound in and out of the recesses of this delicious forest. The banks of the stream were scarcely thirty feet apart, as a rule, although sometimes the current broadened to twice that width. We were perpetually coming to a point in the forest from which there seemed no possible egress, when, rounding a sharp corner, the negro boatmen pushing with their long poles, we would brush past the trees and vines, and once more plod on by cypress, water oak, ash, and orange-tree.

The richly variegated colors of the far-extending thickets were mirrored so completely in the water, that we seemed suspended or floating over an enchanted forest. The clumps of saplings garnished with vines; the stately bosquets of palms, now growing a score together on a little hillock, and now standing apart, like sentinels; the occasional magnolias; the long swamp-ways out of which barges, rowed by negroes, would come to receive the mail, and into which they vanished again, the oarsmen hardly exchanging a word with our captain; the fierce-faced, bearded men, armed with rifles and revolvers, who sometimes hailed us from a point of land, to know if we "wanted any meat," and showed us deer and turkeys, and perhaps the skin of a gray wolf or a black bear,—all these novelties of the tropics and the backwoods kept us in perplexed wonder. When evening came slowly on again, a round moon silvered the water, and enabled us to see even the ducks that floated half submerged, and curiously eyed our little boat. By day, one sees hundreds of turtles, as on the St. John's, sunning themselves. The birds are legion. They chatter in the tree-tops; they offer themselves freely as marks for revolver-bullets; they scold at night as the torchlight awakes them; and they accompany the echo of each unsuccessful shot with loud derisive singing.

The torches of pine-knots placed securely on the boat's roof, and watched there by a habile negro boy, aid the reflection in the water to a new beauty. The cypresses seem more ghostly; the vines more luxuriant; the long-necked white birds more comical; the palms more majestic than by day. Now and then a beacon disclosed some lonely cabin, thatched with palmetto, beside which stood a solitary figure with gun strapped over his back. "Got any terbacker, Cap'n?" or some such question, and we left the figure behind. Penetrating Eureka creek, we wormed our way through a little streamlet only twenty feet wide. At Fort Brooke, large quantities of the rich crops of Alachua county were formerly shipped, but the railroad now transports them.

A little above Fort Brooke one comes to Orange creek, the outlet of a charming lake, in Masson and Alachua counties, with lovely orange groves upon its banks and sulphur springs near by. In conversation with people who came and went at the wayside stations in the swamps, I found that they had all been well-to-do "before" the war, and that they were healthy and happy in their tropic wilderness home. The needs of Florida in the lines of canals and convenient short-cuts were well exemplified in the case of a planter from the St. John's river, who, with some friends, was going on a hunting excursion near Silver Spring. From his home on the St. John's by land across to Silver Spring, it was only at best forty miles; but by the only practicable route he was compelled to travel 175 miles, and spend three entire days on the road.

Silver Spring is certainly one of the wonders of the world. The tradition that it is the "Fountain of Youth," of which the aborigines spoke so enthusiastically to Ponce de Leon, seems firmly founded. The river or spring rises suddenly

The "Marion" at Silver Spring.

from the ground, and after running nine miles through foliage-shrouded banks, more luxuriantly beautiful than poet's wildest dream, empties into the Oclawaha. Transparent to the very bottom, the waters show one, at the depth of thirty or forty feet, the bottom of this wonderful basin, with bubbles here and there denoting one of the sources; and the refraction of the rays of light produces most brilliant effects.

We rowed about on the bosom of this fairy spring, quite overcome with the strangeness of the scene. There is nothing like it elsewhere either in Europe or America; the foliage is even more gorgeously tropical than along the Oclawaha, and its arrangement is more dainty and poetic. We spent hours rocking in little skiffs among the oases of lily pods which extend along the borders of the spring; or in threading the forests which set boldly out into the tranquil stream, not without occasional misgivings as to the quantity and temper of the alligators that might be lurking there.

Nothing befell us, save headaches from the too zealous sun. The thermometer confessed to 90 degrees, and the little boat seemed to bake as she lay at the wharf receiving cotton bales and bags of cotton-seed from Ocala, Marion county's principal town, and from its surroundings. The planters and the negroes from the neighborhood, each superintending the loading of his own cotton, formed a lively group under the wharf-shed at Silver Spring. The tiny steamer was by no means equal to the task demanded of it, and left great quantities of freight awaiting its return. Half concealed among the tall, rustling flags, we sat in our boat watching the grimy negroes as they tussled with the cotton; the young Floridians practicing at the curlews and the herons with their revolvers; and the wonderful dreamy green of the foliage, through which peered hundreds of strange plants and flowers.

Silver Spring was once considered the head of navigation in this direction, but steamers now run far beyond it on the Oclawaha, through lakes Griffin, Eustis, Harris, and Dora, to Okahumkee, a little settlement in the wilderness, where sportsmen delight to spend much of their time while in the peninsula. All the lands near the lakes are specially valuable for cane-growing, and for cotton, corn and fruit. In the vicinity of Lake Harris, frost is seldom known; and sugar-cane matures so as to tassel, which the early frost never permits it to do in Louisiana and Texas.

Colonel Hart, of Palatka, was the explorer of this region, and when his adventurous steamer pushed up through the encumbered channel, the crew had to combat sunken logs, fallen trees, and labyrinths of overhanging limbs. Then "floating islands" were encountered, formed of water-flags securely rooted in a soil under which the current had made its way. These islands are sometimes borne down into the larger streams by the winds and the rising of the waters; and those which had become stationary in the river channel were so tough that a saw was required to cut them in pieces.

This whole lake region seems gradually becoming a marsh, and much labor and expense is required to keep the channel open as far as Okahumkee. A project for cutting a canal through to the Gulf by this route, taking advantage of the lakes and their outlets, has been conceived, and would be of great commercial importance to Florida. The country around Lake Apopka, the source of the Oclawaha river, is considered one of the most remarkable in Florida, and cannot fail when communication is more thoroughly established, to attract large numbers of immigrants. At Okahumkee the waters divide, running into the Gulf by way of Lake Pansoffkee and the Withlacoochee rivers—the route of the contemplated ship canal across the State. The Oclawaha is navigable for about 250 miles, and a semi-weekly line of small steam-packets gives the up-country connection with the outer world. A charter has been obtained for the "Great Southern" railroad to run from Augusta, Georgia, via Millen and Jessup in that State, to Jacksonville in Florida—thence to Palatka, and soon to Key Biscayne Bay and Key West. A large land grant from the State has been accorded the projectors, and the work of laying down the track from Jessup to Jacksonville has been contracted.

Our captain, the cheery and active skipper of the "Marion," had navigated the Oclawaha river for nearly a quarter of the century, and his pilot, formerly his slave, still stands at the helm, a post requiring no small skill in view of the sharp turns which the "Marion" is compelled to make to avoid being ignominiously stuck fast in the swamp thickets. The captain expressed himself better satisfied, on the whole, with free than slave labor; thought that it released

Shooting at Alligators. [Page 415.]

employers like himself from a great many obligations. But he said that the sudden advent of emancipation had greatly hindered the development of hundreds of plantations along the Oclawaha, chiefly because the planters did not wish to encourage more negroes to come into the country, as they were already so formidable a political element. Planters cannot work their broad acres without the very immigration which they dread, and so they suffer them to lie idle. But industrial progress had been very marked in many things since the war. A few manufactories scattered through some of the rich counties traversed by these steamers would, he thought, add greatly to the wealth of those sections. People suffered a great deal from the large prices which they were obliged to pay for manufactured articles brought many hundreds of miles, in a toilsome manner, from the outer world.

Sailing back, we were treated to the sight of an alligator fifteen feet long, sunning himself on a hummock of yellow grass. The wrinkle underneath his lower jaw gave him a good-humored look, and he seemed actually to smile as the bullets hissed around him. The alligator is by no means a trifling enemy; and the Floridian tells strange stories of the creature's strength, fleetness, and strategy. An alligator hunter in Jacksonville gave me an idea of these characteristics, somewhat after the following fashion:

"The 'gaiter, sir, is ez quick as lightning, and ez nasty. He kin outswim a deer, and he *hez* dun it, too; he swims more 'n two-thirds out o' water, and when he ketches you, sir, he jest wabbles you right over 'n over, a hundred times, or mo', sir, ez quick ez the wind; and you 're dead in no time, sir. When a dog sees one he always begins to yelp, sir, for a 'gaiter is mighty fond of a dog and a nigger, sir. Nobody can't tell how old them old fellows is, sir; I reckon nigh on to a hundred years, them biggest ones. Thar 's some old devils in them lagoons you see off the St. John; they lie thar very quiet, but it would be a good tussle if one of you was out thar in a small boat, sir. They won't always fight; sometimes they run away very meek; the best way to kill 'em is to put a ball in the eye, sir; thar 's no use in wasting shot in a 'gaiter's hide. When the boys wants sport, sir, they get a long green pole, and sharpen it; 'n then they find a 'gaiter's hole in the marsh, and put the pole down it; then the 'gaiter he snaps at it, 'n hangs on to it, 'n the boys get together, 'n pull him out, 'n put a rope aroun' his neck and set him to fightin' with another 'gaiter. O Lord! reckon t' would make yo' har curl to see the tails fly."

XLVI.

THE UPPER ST. JOHN'S—INDIAN RIVER—KEY WEST—POLITICS. THE NEW CONSTITUTION.

SOUTHWARD and up the St. John's river from Palatka, the vegetation becomes more tropical, the river narrowing so that one can comfortably inspect the thickets, and widening out only to be merged in grand Lake George, twelve miles wide, Dexter's Lake, and Lake Monroe, at Enterprise. The steamers make the run from Palatka to Enterprise in about twelve hours. In March, when the flowers on the banks are at their perfection, if the moonlight be brilliant, do not

View on the Upper St. John's River, Florida.

neglect the journey by night. The glamour of the Southern moon throws an enchantment over all the splendid foliage which makes it doubly bewitching; the lilies and barnets on the water, and the palms and cypresses on shore, form perfect pictures which none can forget. Welaka, opposite the mouth of the Oclawaha, was well supplied with accommodations for visitors before the war destroyed them. There is a grand hotel there now, near some excellent sulphur springs; and Dunn's Lake, abounding in game, and with many rich plantations on its shores is but eight miles distant. At the southern end of Lake George lies Drayton's Island, where it is said there are some remarkable Indian mounds. A barren rib of land divides the St. John's and the lake from the Oclawaha. The steamers dexterously skim over the dangerous bar at the southern extremity of Lake George, and passing Volusia and Fort Butler, a noted relic of the Indian wars, enter Dexter's Lake, surrounded by its wild and seemingly limitless marshes and hummocks. Beyond this lake, the river flows through a very narrow channel, whose banks are clothed with the omnipresent palm, the maiden cane, and the tall sedge in the meadows. At Lake Monroe, one lands at Enterprise, where a Maine man keeps a hotel, of which, and one or two other houses, the town consists. This is a famous rendezvous for sportsmen who are about to visit the Indian river. On the opposite shore is Mellonville, a promising settlement. All along this lake there is superb hunting and fishing; and the invalid who comes pale and racked with a harrowing cough, is, after a few weeks, seen tramping about in the cool of the morning with gun and fishing rod, a very Nimrod and Walton combined.

The source of the St. John is higher up, in some unknown marsh, and after one has penetrated to Lake Harney and Salt Lake, there is little left to see on the noble stream which, at a distance of nearly three hundred miles from its mouth, flows within seven miles of the ocean into which it empties.

Indian river is difficult of access, but swarms of travelers are now finding their way there. One of the favorite means of reaching it is to row from Enterprise to Lake Harney, and to take a portage across to Sand Point. The entrance from the coast is decidedly less easy than from the St. John's; the deepest of the outlets, Fort Pierce channel, having rarely more than seven feet of water at high tide. The so-called river is really an arm of the sea; its waters are salt; its westward shore was once very highly cultivated by the Spaniards, and it could, with a little renewed attention, be made one of the richest garden spots in America. The westward side presents a sad panorama of ruined sugar plantations and houses, of superb machinery lying idle—and of acres of wild orange-trees, which only need transplanting and budding to produce fruit equal to the best which we receive from Havana. The sportsman who pitches his tent for a few days on the splendid camping ground of this same shore, will see the pelican, the cormorant, the sea-'gull, and gigantic turtles, many of them weighing five hundred pounds; may see the bears exploring the nests for turtles' eggs; may "fire-hunt" the deer in the forests; chase the alligator to his lair; shoot at the "raft-duck," and fish from the salt-ponds all finny monsters that be. Hardly a thousand miles from New York, one may find the most delicate and delightful tropical scenery, and may dwell in a climate which neither Hawaii nor Southern Italy can excel. Settlements throughout this section are few and far between. The mail is carried down the great silent coast by a foot-messenger—for there is a stretch of nearly one hundred miles along which there is not a drop of fresh water for a horse to drink.

The islands extending along the south coast, from Cape Florida to the "Dry Tortugas," lie close to the Gulf Stream, and between the mainland and the dangerous reefs on which so many vessels are annually wrecked. They are only a few feet above tide-water, and are wooded with the mangrove, the bay, the palmetto, the oak, the cocoa and the pine-apple tree, all of which thrive in the rocky soil of these keys. A large trade is here carried on in the gathering of sponges and turtles. The traveler in search of health will find a pleasant recreation in sailing about Biscayne Bay, and penetrating thence into the vast shallow lakes of the "Everglades," where a thousand islands are covered with a wealth of live oaks and cocoas, and with masses of trailing vines, on which, in the season, hang gigantic clusters of grapes. There one may see miles of flower-beds, where every conceivable hue greets the eye; and will find some of the richest lands in the world lying idle, and to be purchased for a trifle. North of Biscayne Bay, on the coast, tobacco, bananas, plantains, oranges, coffee, dates, pine-apples, rice, indigo, sugar and cassava will flourish admirably. The production of sea-island cotton on the Florida coast requires but about one-half the labor necessary in South Carolina, and it is contended that a sugar plantation there can be made for one-fifth of the money required in Louisiana. Biscayne Bay is within four days' easy sail of New York, and there is no reason why vegetables and the great variety of tropical fruits which can be grown there should not find a ready market in the metropolis.

Of course, the labor question in Florida, as elsewhere in the Southern States, is perplexing and startling. The only means by which the State can secure the full development of its extraordinary riches is by inducing immigration on the part of people who live in similar latitudes, and who will find it agreeable and easy to develop the resources of the vast sub-tropical peninsula. While it is evident that Northern and Western people will develop the region bordering on the St. John's, and possibly the northern part of the commonwealth, those who do the work on the vast sugar plantations of the future, and who develop the whole south-eastern coast, must be native to the South. The Floridians have already given some attention to the subject of immigration, and a bureau to take charge of that matter was appointed under the new Constitution. The "Agricultural and Immigration Association of Florida" was organized in 1868, and is composed of the officers of the county associations of the same nature, and of those of the various boards of trade.

Key West, only a short distance from Cuba, is an important Government naval station, and is connected with the world by semi-monthly steamship to Baltimore, Havana, and New Orleans; semi-weekly to Galveston and New York, and by the United States dispatch boats to Fort Jefferson, Tampa, Cedar Keys, St. Mark's, Appalachicola, Pensacola, and Mobile. One may stand on a cracker-box and look over the whole island, which is formed of a species of coralline limestone. Key West town is prettily situated amid "groves of cocoa and of palm;" has five thousand inhabitants; becomes quite lovely in aspect when the fleet rendezvous is fixed there; is famous for the beauty of its ladies, the matchless flavor of its green-turtle, the dexterity of its wreckers, the extent of its salt works and cigar manufactories, its naval hospital and its formidable Fort Taylor, with two hundred heavy guns pointing seaward. All winter long at Key West*

---

* The name Key West is a corruption of the Spanish *Cayo Hueso*, "Bone Key."

the south winds blow; the air is loaded with warmth and perfume; the moonlight is brilliant, and the "northers" considerately come only two or three times a year. From this port steamers run occasionally to the Dry Tortugas, where a thousand prisoners were confined during the war, and where the "conspirators" found a forced seclusion.

Florida accepted reconstruction peacefully, and the new Constitution is, on the whole, a good one. It makes proper provision for schools, and the management of the courts and the provisions with regard to the distribution of lands are wise.

Sunrise at Enterprise, St. John's River, Florida.

The Republican party of the State has suffered a good deal at the hands of some of the men who have been intrusted with its interest, so that many citizens of the State who, on national questions, always vote with Republicans, array themselves so far as regards their local interests with the Conservative faction. The balance of power in the State is at present held by the blacks, led by a few white men; but the Conservative element is rapidly gaining strength, and it is noted as somewhat remarkable that Northerners who settle there gradually find themselves leaning to Conservatism, as they are compelled to do to protect themselves against a torrent of ignorance and vice. Congressman Cox, of New York, was one day at a Republican meeting at Jacksonville, and was invited to address it. He professed great surprise, and inquired how it was "that a Democrat was asked to make an address in a Republican caucus?" He was thereupon informed that it was not a party meeting, but that it was an effort to secure the best men and the best ideas for the service of the State, even if they were found outside party limits. There has been a great deal of fraud and plundering on the part of county officers who, dazzled by the possession of newly acquired power, have not hesitated to put both hands into the public purse. Many have been detected, but some have been so adroit as to completely cloak their iniquities. A firm and thoroughly honest administration of State affairs would bring Florida into front rank among the prosperous States in a short time.

Taxation is about $2.38 on every hundred, but the property owner is allowed to fix his own valuation. This includes a school and county tax amounting to one cent on a dollar. The various railroad enterprises into which the State has been urged have done considerable to embarrass it. The present State debt is nearly $1,350,000, exclusive of a contingent liability of $4,000,000 of bonds, issued by the State to those insincere adventurers who pretended that they desired to complete the Jacksonville, Pensacola and Mobile railroad. This important route is now finished to the town of Chattahoochee, in Florida, the location of the State Penitentiary. The road would be of great advantage to the State, if it were possible to get it freed from the endless litigation surrounding it, and to put even the section which is already completed into decent running order.

It was an enterprise of too much magnitude for the capital or the management of the clever adventurer who got it into his possession, and who obtained everything that he desired from the reconstruction legislature. He having sunk beneath its weight, without having made the tremendous progress anticipated, the project languishes. An act of the last Legislature but one has prohibited the further issuing of bonds for any purpose whatever. The Administration of Governor Stearns has thus far been satisfactory.

At the period of my visit to Florida, the State Superintendent of Education was a negro, and a gentleman of considerable culture and capacity. But neither he nor his predecessors had succeeded in doing much for common schools. The same prejudice which existed against them elsewhere in the South was felt in Florida up to a very recent date; and possibly exists in some degree now, because of the lurking fear of the whites that some day mixed schools may be insisted upon by the black masters of the situation. In such counties as Duval, where the influence of a large and flourishing town has been felt, there are many schools, well supplied and well taught; but as a rule, throughout the back-country, there are no schools, and there is no immediate prospect of any. The scrip which came to Florida, as her share of the national gift for the founding of an agricultural college, was swallowed up by some financial sharks in New York; it amounted to more than $80,000. The establishment of such a college would have been of great value to the State, giving an impetus to effort in exactly the necessary direction.

The educational affairs of each county are managed by a "board of public instruction," consisting of five men recommended by the representatives of the Legislature, and appointed by the State Superintendent. There are about 700,000 acres of "school-lands" in the State, and there are some funds which are used in aiding counties to start schools. There are about 63,000 pupil-children in the State, not more than one-fourth of whom are supplied with good facilities for instruction. The amount annually expended for free education by the State, including donations from the Peabody fund, is $100,000. It was claimed that in 1873, 18,000 children attended the schools. At Gainesville, Key West, Tallahassee, Pensacola, and Madison, there are successful schools for both colored and white children, and at Ocala, Quincy, and Appalachicola, there are colored free schools, liberally aided by the Peabody bequest.

In the backwoods there is an alarming amount of ignorance among the adults; there are hundreds of men and women who have not the simplest rudiments of education, and many amusing stories are told of the simplicity and boorishness of the "crackers." They are a soft-voiced, easy-going, childlike kind of folk, quick to anger, vindictive when their rage is protracted and becomes a feud; and generous and noble in their rough hospitality. But they live the most undesirable of lives, and, surrounded by every facility for a luxurious existence, subsist on "hog and hominy," and drink the meanest whiskey.

The Florida Constitution, adopted under reconstruction, contains some novel features. One clause provides that the Legislature shall enact laws requiring educational qualifications for electors after the year 1880, but that no such law shall be made applicable to any elector who may have registered and voted at any election previous to that time. The Governor is elected for four years. The blacks predominate in the tiny Senate and Assembly, composed of twenty-four and fifty-three members, respectively; and during the sessions, Tallahassee, the capital, situated in a rolling country, in the midst of a beautiful spring region, is the scene of tyro legislation such as at present distinguishes the capitals of Louisiana and South Carolina.

Quincy, St. Mark's, and Monticello, all offer attractions to the traveler; the latter is the site of a sanguinary fight between the forces under General Jackson and the Miccosakie Indians, and there, too, De Soto is said to have encamped on his way to the northward.

A Country Cart.

XLVII.

SOUTH CAROLINA—PORT ROYAL—THE SEA ISLANDS. THE REVOLUTION.

PORT ROYAL, in South Carolina, was once first cousin to Plymouth Rock, in Massachusetts. The rugged New England headland was the refuge and the fortress of the English Puritan; the fertile plain at the mouth of the broad and noble Carolinian river was the resort of the French Huguenot, who preferred exile and danger to the sacrifice of his faith. Jean Ribault and his hardy men-at-arms, sailing northward from the blooming banks of Florida, in 1562, anchored their ships during a great storm at the mouth of a "fair and large harbor," and named it, and the river emptying into it, Port Royal.

The good Frenchmen who had been sent by brave old Admiral Coligny to found an asylum for the oppressed in the New World, wandered delightedly along the shores of the stream, under moss-grown oaks and lofty pines, beneath the cedars and the palmettoes, and shaped visions of future glory. They pictured to themselves the time when the waters of the vast harbor should be covered with noble fleets; when spacious gardens should dot the luxuriant shores; and, after a few days of repose, they raised a stately pillar of stone, with the arms of France graven on it, and in honor of Charles IX., built a fort on an island in the river. A little garrison was placed in charge, and Ribault returned to France, to recount with enthusiasm the wonders of that part of the then province of Florida, destined in future to be named, as the Frenchman called his fort, Carolina.

To-day, more than three centuries after Ribault's adventurous voyage, the site of the old fort and pillar is not even definitely known. Port Royal is an infant town just springing into commercial activity, under the influence of slowly reviving commerce; and the negro slouchingly tills the soil and lounges in the sun on the shores from which the tide of revolution has swept his late master.

In the sixteenth century, the country claimed in America by the Spaniards as Florida, and by the French as "New France," was supposed to extend from the Chesapeake to the "Tortugas," along the coast, and inland as far as the exploring foreigners might choose to penetrate. During many perilous years the States now known as Florida and South Carolina had a common history. The Huguenots continued their explorations until the treachery and murderous fury of the Spaniards had exterminated all of them who ventured into the Florida lands; and had Menendez of Avila, the blackest villain whose life-record blots the annals of American discovery, died in his cradle, South Carolina would, perhaps, at this day have been peopled by Protestant Gauls.

The little settlement at Port Royal suffered many ills. The soldiers left by Ribault, borne down by misfortune and sickness, determined to return home. The Indians aided the soldiers to construct a brigantine, with which the miserable men tried to make their way to France; but they were reduced to starvation on the voyage, and it was only after they had begun to eat each other, that the survivors were rescued by an English vessel.

The settlement founded by Ribault was thus abandoned; and two years elapsed before another Huguenot expedition, led by Laudonniere, founded a settlement near the mouth of the river May, as the St. John's, prince of the streams of Florida, was then called. Had Laudonniere prospered, the Port Royal fort might have been rebuilt; but the Spaniards from St. Augustine, who fell upon both Laudonniere and the re-enforcements which Ribault had brought him, rendered the second of Coligny's attempts disastrous. Even the colossal vengeance which that *preux chevalier*, Dominique de Gourgues, took upon the Spaniards in Florida, two years afterward, did not establish French influence there; and no Huguenot came again to our Southern shores until one hundred and thirty years later, when the revocation of the edict of Nantes in France sent hundreds of the descendants of Coligny's followers to South Carolina. Their illustrious names are still borne by many worthy families in Charleston.

Under the "Palatinate" the development of the province now known as South Carolina was begun. Under a charter from the crown, after the Restoration, all the lands lying between the 31st and the 36th degrees of north latitude were granted to a proprietary government.

The utmost religious liberty prevailed in the newly-organized province. The Constitution, under which the noble dukes and earls who had received the charter proposed that their colonists should live, was framed by the philosopher, John Locke. The eldest of the "lords proprietors" was Palatine, the seven other chief officers were Admiral, Chamberlain, Chancellor, Constable, Chief Justice, High Steward and Treasurer. The province was subdivided into counties, signories, baronies, precincts and colonies. Each signory, barony and colony consisted of 12,000 acres, and it was provided that after a certain term of years the "proprietors" should not have power to alienate or make over their proprietorship, but that "it should descend unto their heirs male." Here was a good foundation for a landed aristocracy. Every freeman of Carolina was authorized to "have absolute power and authority over his negro slaves;" and no person could hold or claim any land in the province except from and under the "lords proprietors."

The first attempt of the English experimenters to settle the country was at Port Royal, in 1670. William Sayle was appointed Governor of the colony, and great inducements were offered to English immigrants. The first site of "Charlestown" was on the western bank of the Ashley river, and the estate where that site was is still known as "Old Town." Subsequently the settlement was removed to the confluence of the Ashley and Cooper rivers.

It was not until 1783 that the town was incorporated. The original expedition of the proprietary government cost £12,000, and in the years between 1670 and 1682, 100 houses were built at "Charlestown," and an ancient chronicler adds that many who went there as servants had become worth several hundreds of pounds, with their estates still increasing.

The Constitution which Locke had framed, after the pattern of Plato's model Republic, was sufficient for the Carolinians only until 1693, and in 1719 Carolina put itself under the protection of King George.

As a colony, a rapid development and a large prosperity were experienced at once, and the people began to turn their attention to their superb material resources with a vigor never before manifested.

One century after the granting of the charter by Charles the Second to the proprietors, Carolina had arisen to considerable commercial eminence. "Charlestown," Beaufort, Purysburg, Jacksonborough, Dorchester, Camden and Georgetown were the principal settlements, but no one, save the first, consisted of more than thirty or forty dwellings. The negroes already outnumbered the whites. In Charleston they were as eight to five; and while the white population of the colony did not exceed 40,000, the negroes numbered 80,000 or 90,000.

At that time it was said of the whites that, "in the progress of society they had not advanced beyond that period in which men were distinguished more by their external than internal accomplishments." They were chiefly known in England "by the number of their slaves, the value of their annual produce, or the extent of their landed estates." They were lively and gay; "all novelties in fashion, ornament and dress were quickly introduced, and even the spirit of luxury and extravagance, too common in England," was beginning to creep among them. It was said that "there were more people possessed of five and ten thousand pounds sterling in the province" than were to be found anywhere else among the same number of persons. "Their rural life and their constant use of arms" kept up a martial spirit among them. The Indians hated the negroes, and there was, consequently, no danger of their conspiring together. The Carolina merchant was an honest, industrious, and generous man.

The province readily obtained all the credit it demanded; the staples which it produced were very valuable, and agriculture and trade were constantly enlarged in their scope by the importations of ship-loads of negroes. A little before the time of the American revolution, the exports from "Carolina" in a single year amounted to £756,000 sterling; but the imports were so extensive that the colony remained indebted to the mother country.

Still the old English critics thought the Carolinians rather slovenly husbandmen, and were astonished at the manner in which they managed their estates. Freeholds of land were easily obtained by patent or purchase, and were also alienable at will; so that the system of husbandry was not carried on according to any established principles or plans. The planter ordinarily cleared a wooded tract, planted it with rice or indigo until it was exhausted, and then neglected it for a fresh location. Nowhere was the soil improved, nowhere were grass seeds sown for enriching the pastures, and the only study was the putting of the largest crop into market. Safe and prosperous, guaranteed royal protection, possessing unlimited credit and indulgence, and owning the labor necessary to produce wealth, the Carolinian of one hundred years ago seemed a most fortunate mortal, and his carelessness was accounted a princely quality.

Port Royal Island and its chief town, Beaufort, are monuments to the disastrous effects of the revolution which has swept over South Carolina within the last generation. Everywhere on the chain of beautiful sea islands along the low coast one finds the marks of the overturn. But Port Royal, situated on the river terminating in what is perhaps the grandest harbor on the American coast, has hopes, and may bring new life to decaying Beaufort.

A railroad has penetrated the low lands, creeping across marshes and estuaries upon formidable trestles, and now drains the rich cotton-fields around Augusta, in Georgia, toward the Broad river. The town is laid out into lots, and the numbers of the avenues run ambitiously high already; an English steamship line has sent its pioneer vessel to the port; and the Home Government talks of establishing a navy-yard upon the stream.

With commercial facilities which neither New Orleans, Savannah, nor Norfolk can boast, Port Royal deserves a great future. The harbor which Ribault 300 years ago enthusiastically described as so large that "all the argosies of Venice might safely ride therein," is certainly ample for the accommodation of the largest fleets known, and is easy and safe of access.

The lowland scenery of South Carolina is as varied as tropical. From the sea the marshes, or savannahs, stretching seventy miles back from the coast, seem perfectly level; but there are in many places bluffs and eminences crowned with delicate foliage. A vast panorama of fat meadows, watered by creeks; of salt and fresh marshes; of swamp lands of inexhaustible fertility, from which spring the sugar-cane and cypress; of the rich, firm soil, where the oak and the hickory stand in solid columns, and of barrens studded with thousands of young pines—salutes the eye.

The innumerable branches which penetrate the low-lying lands from the sea have formed a kind of checker-work of island and estuary. The forests along the banks of the streams, and scattered on the hedges between the marshes, are beautiful. The laurel, the bay, the palmetto, the beech, the dog-wood, the cherry, are overgrown with wanton, luxuriant vines, which straggle across the aisles where the deer and the fox still wander.

In the spring the jessamine and the cherry fill the air with the perfume of their blossoms; in winter the noble oaks, in their garments of moss, and the serried pines, preserve the verdure which the other trees have lost, and give to the landscape an aspect of warmth and life. When the rice plantations are submerged, and the green plants are just showing their heads above the water, and nodding and swaying beneath the slight breeze passing over the hundreds of acres, the effect is indescribably novel and beautiful.

Beaufort, in a soft, delicious climate, where the orange flourishes, is beautifully located, and was once the abode of hundreds of proud and wealthy planters. One reaches it by rail from Yemassee, a little junction in the midst of a pine forest, where the trains from Charleston, Savannah, Augusta, and Port Royal all meet at midday, and indulge in delays which in the North would be thought disastrous, but which seem quite natural in the slumbrous climate of the lowlands.

The journey from Yemassee is through rich woods, and along high ridges; past newly cleared lands, where the freedmen are grubbing for existence; past old and worn-out plantations, now deserted, with no smoke curling upward from the chimneys of the long rows of negro cabins, and no signs of life about the huge, white mansion in the clump of oaks, or in the centre of a once lovely garden. At the little station one sees smartly dressed men mounting fine horses, and galloping down the long, straight avenues in the forests, to the plantations which they own many miles away. One also sees colored people everywhere, of every shade and variety, lounging, riding, talking in high-pitched voices, and with an accent which renders their speech unintelligible to the stranger.

Sometimes a startled doe, followed by her fawns, bounds across the track. There are but few houses to be seen, and they are miles away. You catch a glimpse of some mighty lagoon, lonely and grand; now you are whirled into the lonely forests—along a river bank—across a wide arm of the sea; now through swamps in which innumerable cypress-knees and rotting boughs seem like snakes and monsters in the stagnant water, and now where you note the gleam of the sun on the white walls of some deserted Beaufort mansion.

The long street by the water-side, in Beaufort, was as still when I entered it as if the town were asleep. The only sign of life was a negro policeman, dressed in a shiny blue uniform, pacing languidly up and down. But there was not even a dog to arrest. On the pretty pier in front of the Sea Island Hotel two or three buzzards were ensconced asleep; half way across the stream a dredge-boat was hauling up phosphates from the channel-bed.

I wandered through the town. It was evidently once very beautiful, and even now there are many remains of the ancient beauty. But a silence as of the grave reigned everywhere. Many of the mansions were closed and fallen into decay. The old Episcopal church, surrounded by a high moss-grown wall, seemed indignantly to have shut itself in from the encroachments of the revolution. The whole aspect of the place was that which I afterward found pervading other South Carolinian towns—that of complete prostration, dejection, stagnation.

Here the revolution penetrated to the quick. The planter, when he returned from his enforced exile during the war, found that the negro had installed himself upon his lands, and would not give them up. A practical confiscation had been operated. There was no redress; the government was in the hands of the negroes. It is true that they were the majority, as they had been for many years before they received their civil rights. The victory of the Union armies meant land to these negroes. They had some idea of vengeance; they did not care to respect property, and hundreds of white families were left homeless, moneyless, and driven into cities where they were friendless. The great plantations of sea-island cotton were left untilled; the negro was too busy with politics to work; and the General Government was in no mood for listening to individual complaints. The "acts of forfeiture," passed in 1862, swept all the lands in St. Helena parish and thousands of acres on Port Royal Island into the hands of the United States Government, by whose authority they were in turn sold on long time to the negroes, and liens taken as security. The original owners who dared to return, protested,* but it was of no avail. The lands have been taken from them, and the negro rules over both them and their lands. He and his fellows dispose not only of the revenues of Beaufort, but of the State. The idle and vicious of his race huddle together in gorgeous parlors, once decorated with elegant furniture, purchased by the planters with the proceeds of slave labor.

The City Hall is controlled by the blacks, and the magistrates, the police, and the representatives in the Legislature, are nearly all Africans. In Beaufort township there are ten negroes to one white person; and in all towns in the adjacent country it is a similar story. At Hilton Head there are about 3,000 colored persons and hardly 100 whites. On St. Helena's Island, still in the same county, there are 6,000 negroes and about 70 whites; in Yemassee, nearly 3,000 blacks and barely 200 whites. In the adjoining counties, Colleton and Charleston, the proportions in the towns are about the same, except in Charleston city. On Edisto Island there are nearly 3,000 negroes, and hardly any white persons.

The blacks have formed communities by themselves. They have left the country and gone to town. The result is that in the chief centres of every township they are immensely in the majority. They monopolize everything. Naturally enough, they are in possession of a great deal which they cannot use. They seem, especially on Port Royal Island, contented with a small tract of land on which to raise cotton, and over which their hogs may wander. Some are very industrious; others never do any work; the masses are satisfied with getting a living. They know little about markets, surplus crops, and the accumulation of riches, and care less. They love hunting and fishing; they revel in the idleness which they never knew until after the war. But they are cumberers of the soil; their ignorance impedes, their obstinacy throttles. They are tools in the hands of the corrupt. They lack moral sense, as might have been expected, after a few generations of slavery. They are immoral and irresponsible; emotional and unreliable; not at all unfriendly in spirit toward the whites, their old masters, yet by their attitude in reality doing them deadly harm.

* The act of 1862 provided that if a property owner should fail to pay, within sixty days, the amount assessed by the Land Commissioners for South Carolina, appointed by the General Government, "the title to his land should thereupon become forfeited to the United States;" and that after such forfeiture a sale should follow, by which the title should be vested in the purchaser or in the United States. This act was, of course, based upon the assumption that the States in which it was operative were out of the Union. Inasmuch as the Land Commissioners for South Carolina did not enter upon their duties until one year after the establishment at Beaufort of the military and civil authority of the Federal Government, a large number of those Carolinians who have suffered by confiscation claim that the whole sale of the lands is illegal, and that the titles of the present owners are equivocal and false.

The undoing of the old relations between the two races, and the conferring of political privileges upon him who was formerly the inferior, have been the ruin of certain sections of these fertile lowlands. Neither race seems likely to resume operations on anything like the old scale of grandeur. The sea-island cotton crop, once a source of such wealth, is small now, yet the negroes, with industry, might raise immense crops. In 1870, Beaufort county, with 150,000 acres of improved land, sent to market but a little over 7,000 bales; it has done somewhat better of late. The culture has met with some disasters; caterpillars and foul weather have interfered. The negroes usually plant a little sea-island cotton, no matter how small may be their farms.

The Northern capitalists who have undertaken this difficult but once very profitable culture, have, as a rule, sunk the better portion of their invested capital; and the native planters have gradually taken to planting a less number of acres yearly. During the three years preceding the war, South Carolina sent to market 54,904 bales of sea-island cotton; but in the three years ending September 1st, 1873, only 23,307 bales were sent out. The control of prices abroad has also been lost to the sea-island planter in South Carolina, as in the days of slavery, he carelessly sold the finer seeds to any one from other countries who wished to buy, and now encounters formidable foreign rivalry in Egypt, the Sandwich Islands, and in South America, as well as in our own Gulf States.

If a planter of the days when the royal colony of South Carolina was in the height of its glory could return now, and wander through the streets of moss-grown Beaufort, he would be amazed, but no more so than would the planter of 1850 or 1860, if he too might return.

For it would be found that in a decade and a-half one of the most remarkable revolutions ever recorded in history has occurred. A wealthy and highly prosperous community has been reduced to beggary; its vassals have become its lords, and dispose of the present and pledge the future resources of the State. In ten years the total valuation of the commonwealth has been reduced from nearly $500,000,000 to barely $150,000,000 at the present time; the banking capital of Charleston from $13,000,000 to $3,000,000; the insurance capital is entirely destroyed. The taxes have been increased from $392,000 in 1850, to $2,000,000 in 1870; slaves valued at $174,000,000 have been freed, and set to learn the arts of self-government and civilization. More than 400,000 blacks now inhabit the State, and their number is constantly increasing. Thousands of planters have been so utterly ruined that they can never hope even to attain comfortable circumstances again.

Opposite an elegant mansion, on one of the main streets of Beaufort, is a small, unambitious structure, in which the former occupant of the grand mansion is selling goods at retail. He returned after the capture of the town to find himself stripped of everything, and has been living in view of his former splendor ever since. His fields are held by strangers; his house is converted into offices. In a day, as it were, he and thousands of others were reduced to complete dependence, and compelled to live under the government of the ignorant slaves whose labor they had grown rich upon.

XLVIII.

ON A RICE PLANTATION IN SOUTH CAROLINA.

THE lowlands of South Carolina are the most interesting portion of the State, in a commercial and picturesque point of view, and there the political outlook is also most depressing. The masses of the freedmen and women on the sea islands and in the sea-board counties are very ignorant, and vastly inferior, in natural intelligence and ability, to the negro of the upper and middle sections of the same State, or the type met with throughout Virginia, Maryland, Tennessee, and Kentucky.

The lowland negro of South Carolina has a barbaric dialect, which no external influences have as yet impressed in the slightest degree; the English words seem to tumble all at once from his mouth, and to get sadly mixed whenever he endeavors to speak. The phraseology is usually so odd, too, that even after the

View of a Rice-field in South Carolina. [Page 434.]

stranger has become a little accustomed to the thick tones of the voice and the awkward enunciation, he cannot readily understand. Certainly a Virginian negro from the town could not comprehend these low-country people at all, until his ear had become habituated to the apparent mumbling.

The children of the planters, brought up on the plantations, and allowed to run in the woods with the little negroes, acquired the same dialect; and to-day many a gentleman's son regrets that it is apparent in his speech. These negroes also have their peculiar religious superstitions and ceremonies. I repeatedly asked planters in Beaufort and Colleton counties if the negroes there had changed much in manners and habits since their slave days, and the invariable answer was, "No!" They have learned to understand that the vote gives power; they find work in large bands together on the rice plantations distasteful to them, and they are perfectly happy when they succeed in obtaining an acre or two of land, and in erecting a cabin. To own a mule is the acme of bliss.

The men and women still maintain their old-time servility toward their former masters. When they meet them on the roads the men always touch their hats, and the women, no matter how huge the basket they may happen to be carrying upon their heads, courtesy profoundly. The word "mas'r" is still used, being so intimately associated in the negro's mind with certain individuals, that he has no inclination to drop it.

Friendliest exterior relations are maintained between ex-master and ex-slave, as a rule; and the white Conservatives sometimes bitterly regret that they did not come boldly forward, at the outset of reconstruction, and themselves guide the negro votes. There would, at one time, have been a fair chance for such a fusion; but the races soon drifted into a separate political current, and the negro appeared in his present rôle of corrupt and ignorant legislator. At present, the whites cannot get a fair hearing, and are subject to many tyrannies at the hands of negro justices and constables.

There are honorable exceptions to all the general criticisms which may be made upon the character of the lowland negro; but, as a mass, the race is really very degraded. It is making gradual progress toward a condition of independence; yet ignorance and irresponsibility are still the rule. The marriage relation is almost unknown in many of the lowland counties; men and women live together as long as they can agree, and are called husband and wife.

Passing through a rice-field one morning, in which there were, perhaps, four hundred black men and women at work, I requested the owner of the plantation, whom I accompanied, to ask four men, who were sitting by a rice stack awaiting a barge, some leading question calculated to throw light on their morality. Each of the four had had two "wives," as they termed it; one of the oldest had had four. The causes of separation were various—infidelity, abuse, a hasty word, or laziness. The children who were the fruit of these careless unions were kept by either father or mother, as the couple might agree.

Jealousy is a terrible passion among these people, and sometimes leads to capital crime. All, without exception, are religious; they find a temporary relief and an excitement in the "meetings," and will go to one, no matter how distant it may be. Most of the men are armed; they manage to secure a pistol or a gun, and are as fond of hunting as their white employers. The situation of those gentlemen who had been slave-holders and large planters before the war, was dreadful for a year or two after the fall of the Confederacy. The freedmen were difficult to manage, could not be got to work, and were jealous of anything which seemed like an attempt to get them back to their old places. The intervention of soldiery was constantly necessary to keep the peace.

The low-country planter lived in a luxurious but careless way. Although some few were ignorant, and cherished the belief that there was nothing else in the country so fine as their forests and swamps, most of them were courteous, unaffected, and devoid of pretension. They resided with their families at their country-seats on the plantations, during the winter months, and in the summer removed to pleasant mansions along the Ashley river or on Sullivan's Island, near Charleston. The Heywards, the Manigaults, the Lowndes, the Middletons, the Hugers, the Barnwells, the Elliotts, the Rhetts, went annually to Charleston, where there was choice and polished society.

To-day, the majority of those engaged in planting at the outbreak of the war, are pitiably poor; and just at the close of the war, the spectacle of men who had owned two hundred or five hundred slaves, reduced to driving a cart or tending a grocery, was quite common. The enforced poverty of many is even bitterer

Negro Cabins on a Rice Plantation.

now than it was then, for they are compelled to see, day by day, the poor State, which has already been so impoverished, plundered anew and embarrassed further by the action of the ignorant and vicious legislators.

Many of the lowland negroes were firmly impressed, when first called to use the ballot, that they were to gain property by it, and great numbers of them still have an idea that they have been defrauded of what they were entitled to. They have also been told by so many legislators of their own race, that all the property once their masters' now properly belongs to them, that they literally believe it, in many cases, while, in others, they consider the whole thing a muddle entirely beyond their comprehension.

This assertion that the negroes ought to take the planters' lands has been often made by white politicians who gained control of the negro at the time that the white natives refused to take active part in the elections, or the reörganization of the State. The whole theory of taxation in the commonwealth, as evolved by Nash and the few other colored men of talent in the Legislature, is summed up in these words, from the present Governor's last message: "The taxes fall chiefly where they belong—upon real estate. The owner cannot afford to keep thousands of acres idle and unproductive, merely to gratify his personal vanity, and because he inherited them from his father. Stern necessity, therefore, will compel him to cut up his ancestral possessions into small farms, and sell them to those who can and will make them productive; and thus the masses of the people will become property holders."

Swart Demos in the legislative chair, with artful rogues around him, remembers only that the tax was not raised from land, but upon the slaves, previous to 1860; and when he thinks of it, very likely his blood is hot, and he willingly applies a slashing tax to the land owners. "In the old days," he says, "your cotton acres, worth hundreds of dollars, were only taxed four cents an acre, but on 400,000 wretches, such as I, you placed a tax of sixty cents per head, and made us work it out, thus getting nearly half a million of revenue. Now we will make you work out your tax, and we will wrest your lands away from you." And so bitterness is needlessly provoked on both sides, and oppression flourishes. It is not taxation, nor even an increase of taxation, that the white people of South Carolina object to; but it is *taxation without representation*, and *unjust, tyrannical, arbitrary, overwhelming taxation*, producing revenues which never get any further than the already bursting pockets of knaves and dupes!

Rice culture has been the prominent industry of South Carolina since the time of the Landgrave Thomas Smith, under the proprietary government. With the determination of the planters to make it the chief object of their care, came the necessity for importing great numbers of slaves, and the sacrifice of many hundreds of lives, in the arduous labors of clearing the ground and preparing the soil. The cypress forests gave place to the fields of waving green, and the rivers were diverted from their channels to flood the vast expanse in which the negroes had set the seeds.

"The women were dressed in gay colors." [Page 435.]

"With forty or fifty pounds of rice stalks on their heads." [Page 435.]

In 1724, 439 African slaves were imported to South Carolina, together with a vast amount of other commodities, in exchange for which the citizens gave 18,000 barrels of rice and 52,000 barrels of naval stores. Year by year the importations of negroes increased in numbers; year by year the planter became "more eager in the pursuit of large possessions of land," and "strenuously vied with his neighbor," says a chronicler, "for a superiority of fortune."

The Carolinians were compelled to keep up fortifications on the borders of the Spanish domains, to prevent the negroes from escaping into foreign territory; but they had few other external cares. Their trade grew constantly with New England, New York and Pennsylvania; and in 1738, when there were fully 40,000 negroes in South Carolina, Spanish policy provoked a formidable insurrection on the part of the blacks. This brought on open hostilities between Spaniards and Carolinians, and the latter made an unsuccessful expedition against St. Augustine.

It should be borne in mind that the following statistics, showing how rapidly the exportation of rice increased in quantity, also shows how swiftly the slave population of the province grew. From 1720 to 1729, the export was 44,081 tons; from 1730 to 1740, it was 99,905 tons; and in the single year of 1740, 90,000 barrels were sent away, the gain upon which was estimated at £220,000. In 1771, the exports of the State amounted to £756,000 sterling. Shipping crowded the harbors; money was plenty; the planters commanded the best of everything from Great Britain and the West India Islands. There were at that period no taxes whatever upon real or personal estate; but the revenues were raised by duties on "spirituous liquors, sugar, molasses, flour, biscuit, negro slaves," etc., and amounted to several thousand pounds per annum.

And so, for many generations, the rice culture and the slave system went hand in hand upon the fertile Carolina lowlands. Good authorities have assured me that they believe there were 1,000,000 acres of rice-lands in cultivation in South Carolina at the outbreak of the civil war. At the present time there is hardly one-fourth of that area cultivated, but there is a steady increase.

The blows struck by immediate emancipation upon this once gigantic industry were crushing. Under the slave *régime*, the planters successfully competed with other producers in all the markets of the world. From 1850 to 1860, they exported 705,317,600 pounds of rice, valued at $24,619,009. The total production of rice in the United States in 1850 was 215,313,497 pounds; even in 1860, it was 187,162,032. Such figures are eloquent. The rice-producing States suffered severely at an early period of the war; the fields were abandoned; and in South Carolina the production has decreased from 119,100,524 pounds, in 1860, to 32,304,825, in 1870. The annual product in Georgia, Louisiana and the Carolinas, from 1865 to 1871, will show that the industry is gradually struggling to its feet once more:

Year.	Pounds.	Year.	Pounds.
1866	12,002,080	1869	48,837,920
1867	19,368,060	1870	54,117,320
1868	27,566,740	1871	59,000,000

Some of the rice plantations cover thousands of acres even now; and the employment of from five to eight hundred men, women and children by a single person, is not at all uncommon. I visited the celebrated plantation at Green Pond, in Colleton county, the property of Mr. Bissell, who has 3,500 acres under his control. He, in common with others, was broken by the war, and is struggling with the hundred ills which beset the planter in the changed condition of affairs.

Mr. Bissell's broad fields lie seven miles from the Charleston and Savannah railroad, at the rear of extensive pine forests, in which, now that the white man is so poorly represented in the Legislature, the poacher wanders unreproved. The plantation extends across the Combahee river into Beaufort county, and at various points rice-pounding mills and little villages, in which the workers live, are established. A morning ride in the soft, Italian-like autumn across this or similar plantations, is a delicious experience. Mounted on a stout mule or on a Kentucky horse, you gallop through the perfumed avenues of the forests until you reach the wide expanse of fields, cut into squares by long trenches, through which water from the river in the background is admitted to every part of the land.

The breeze rustles musically in the tall cane along the banks, in whose sedgy recesses the alligator and the serpent hide. In the distance an antlered deer may break from his cover, and after one defiant glance, stamp his foot, and be gone! A white sail glides on the horizon's rim, as the little schooner from Charleston works her way around to the mill, where long processions of black boys and girls, with baskets on their heads, and their mouths filled with horrible jargon, are waiting to load the rice.

The injury done to all the plantations in these lowland counties, by the neglect consequent on the war, is incalculable. Most of these plantations have been reclaimed from the waters; have been diked, ditched, furnished with "trunks," by means of which the planter can inundate or drain his land at will.* A rice plantation is, in fact, a huge hydraulic machine, maintained by constant warring against the rivers. The utmost attention and vigilance is necessary, and the labor must be ready at a moment's notice for the most exhaustive efforts. Alternate flooding and draining must take place several times during the season, and one part of the crop must be flooded, while the other adjacent to it is dry.

Fields are divided into sections, and trunks or canals convey water from the river to each separately. "The whole apparatus of levels, flood-gates, trunks, canals, banks, ditches," says a prominent planter, "is of the most extensive kind, requiring skill and unity of purpose." The slightest leak in the banks or dikes may end in the ruin of the whole plantation. Freshets, too, commit frightful havoc from time to time. At one fell swoop the produce of a

A Pair of Mule-Boots. [Page 435.]

A "Trunk-Minder." [Page 435.]

* Speech of Hon. F. A. Sawyer, of South Carolina, in the U. S. Senate, in 1872.

thousand acres on Mr. Bissell's plantation was swept away in 1872. The cost of reclaiming rice-lands, and fitting them for culture, was about $100 per acre before the war, and so greatly had they been damaged by long neglect that more than half that sum has been expended in their rehabilitation. Once well prepared, the annual cost of cultivation is now about thirty dollars as compared with ten dollars in former days; but it is steadily decreasing.

We wandered over perhaps 700 acres, in Colleton and Beaufort counties. The men and women at work in the different sections were under the control of field-masters. The spectacle was lively. The women were dressed in gay colors, with handkerchiefs uniting all the colors of the rainbow, around their temples. Their feet were bare, and their stout limbs encased in uncouth flannel wrappings. Most of them, while staggering out through the marshes with forty or fifty pounds of rice stalks on their heads, kept up an incessant jargon with one another, and indulged in a running fire of invective against the field-master.

Unloading the Rice-Barges.

The "trunk-minders," the watchmen on whose vigilance the plantation's safety depends, promenaded briskly; the flat-boats, on which the field hands deposited their huge bundles of rice stalks, were poled up to the mill, where the grain was threshed and separated from the straw, winnowed, and carried in baskets to the schooners which transported it to Charleston, and the "pounding-mills." During harvest-time 800 hands are employed on this plantation.

Harvest is hardly completed by March, when the sowing begins again. The trunks are opened in each section the day it is planted, and the fields are flooded. The mules, that annually drag the ploughs through the marshes, are booted with leather contrivances, to prevent them from sinking into the treacherous ooze. To the negroes is given the rice that grows along the margins, and considerable profit is obtained from its sale. The fields in autumn are yellowish in hue, tinged here and there lightly with green, where young rice is upspringing from the shoots recently cut down. The rice lies in ricks, but is ill protected, swarms of birds carrying away great quantities.

While we were strolling afield, one stout negro came up and asked "Mas'r Ben" to buy him a mule with $100 which he had saved. "Mas'r Ben" agreed to do it, and informed me that such a purchase was a sign of a negro's assured prosperity. The wages paid the rice-field hands ranged from twenty-five cents to one dollar and seventy-five cents daily, but the manager on this, as on many other plantations, found great difficulty in keeping the labor organized and available. The men found that by two or three days' work they could procure money enough to support them in idleness the next week, and sometimes the overseers were at a loss what to do for help.

Beautiful were the broad and carefully cultivated acres, stretching miles away on either side of the placid, deep, and noble Combahee; picturesque were the granaries, almost bursting with the accumulated stores of the precious grain; and novel and inspiring the vistas of the long sedge-bordered canals, through which the morning breezes lightly whistled. The sea-myrtle was neighbor to the cane, and the tall grasses twined lovingly around them both.

At the "store," about whose entrance were grouped packs of hounds, leaping and fawning about their masters, who were mounting their horses, we saw crowds of negresses, barefooted and barelimbed, bringing poultry or eggs to exchange for corn, or chattering frantically, or bursting into boisterous laughter which echoed over many a broad acre.

One could not help thinking that in due time a vast amount of labor-saving machinery must come to take the place of this rude and careless negro element upon the rice plantation. At present, the planters admit, there is an enormous waste, and the climate's character renders it impossible to introduce white labor and intelligence into the section. The negro men and women whom I saw were certainly of a low and degraded type, distinctively,—as a Frenchman, with his quick instincts, said on seeing a group of these same lowland people,—"a broken down race!"

"At the winnowing-machine."

At the threshing-mill, at the winnowing-machine, among the great rice stacks where they were packing and sorting and unloading from barges, the women were coarse, brutish, and densely ignorant; the men, in the main, the same. There were types of face in which the savage still stood out in splendor. Many women of sixty or seventy years of age were at work in various places about the field. They had evidently been untouched by the spirit of the war. I doubt if they realized the change in their condition. Their conversation with me was confined to inquiries as to how much tobacco I would give them, and an appeal to me to tell Mas'r Ben that they "bin want" a new handkerchief, and hoped he would not forget them. The men as a rule were civil, but a little suspicious in demeanor, as if they did not intend to allow any advantage to be taken of them. If looked at sharply, they would wince, and finally, wreathing their lips with broad grins, would bow and shuffle away.

The planters throughout this section, where the Middletons and the Heywards once tilled so many acres, and whence they drew great incomes, admit that the labor question is the most serious one with them. The profits of rice-planting are enormous, but the system of large plantations will, perhaps, have to be adhered to, and African or Chinese labor can alone sustain the trials of the summer climate. The production of the State, and the adjacent lowlands in other States, will doubtless again reach the figure attained before the war, although the present condition of South Carolina would not seem to justify prophecies of any prosperity within her limits, save in Charleston.

"Aunt Bransom."— A venerable ex-slave on a South Carolina Rice Plantation.

XLIX.

CHARLESTON, SOUTH CAROLINA.

AND why prosperity in Charleston? Mainly because the venerable city has established in addition to her important cotton trade, a large number of manufacturing enterprises, for which her location is particularly advantageous; and because her business men have an elastic spirit and a remarkable courage, which reflect the highest credit upon them. A veritable phœnix, always springing triumphantly from the ashes of terrible conflagrations, as well as from the ruins caused by hurricanes and bombardments, the South Carolinian metropolis is, in itself, a standing reproof to the too oft-repeated assertion that the ancient commonwealth lacks enterprise.

When the war closed there was not a completed railroad ending in Charleston. Those now known as the North-eastern, giving connection with the

View from Fort Sumter, in Charleston Harbor. [Page 440.]

route to Wilmington; the South Carolina, running north-westward to Columbia, Aiken, and Augusta; and the Savannah and Charleston, penetrating the lowlands and reaching to the Georgian seaport, were worn down and almost completely wrecked. Costly bridges and trestles had been destroyed, depots burned, tracks torn up, and the amount of rolling-stock was absurdly inadequate to immediate wants. The rebuilding and equipment were begun in 1866. All the old rail connections are now resuscitated, and Charleston is reaching out for a wider range of commerce than, before the war, she would have deemed possible. The South Carolina railroad and its feeders, the Greenville and Columbia, and the Macon and Augusta, in Georgia, send vast quantities of freight, which heretofore went northward, to the Carolinian metropolis. The North-eastern, and the Savannah and Charleston, are important links in the shortest route from New York to Florida, and with the sea-board line, from New York to New Orleans. Many steamship companies were compelled to suspend communication with the city during the war; now there are two steamer lines between New York and Charleston, comprising eight fine steamers, capable of carrying away 30,000 bales of cotton monthly. On the Baltimore line there are three steamers, on the Philadelphia two, on the Boston two, with a carrying capacity altogether of about 14,000 bales monthly. The splendid line to Florida has been reopened, and the connections with Savannah, Beaufort, Georgetown, Edisto, and the Peedee river are also resumed, and are very prosperous.

The increase in steamship freights from Charleston since 1860 has been 300 per cent., but the sail tonnage is not larger than it was in 1862, as much of its trade has been transferred to steamers. The following receipts of cotton at Charleston for eight years since the war also indicate a marked prosperity:

Years.*	Bales of Cotton.	Years.	Bales of Cotton.
1865–66	111,714	1869–70	250,761
1866–67	165,316	1870–71	356,544
1867–68	246,018	1871–72	282,686
1868–69	200,764	1872–73	385,000

A large proportion of this cotton was sent to Charleston for sale, not merely to pass through. The exports of rice from Charleston, from September, 1865, to September, 1873, amount to about 250,000 tierces. The increase in the number of naval stores reported has also been remarkable, as shown by the following table

Years.	Barrels.	Years.	Barrels.
1865–66	32,136	1869–70	79,156
1866–67	54,026	1870–71	90,297
1867–68	62,852	1871–72	151,553
1868–69	72,279	1872–73	225,683

The lumber exports since the war have also been large, footing up at least 140,000,000 of feet. The rich pine forests of the State are annually of increasing importance. Charleston, Beaufort and Georgetown are all daily receiving great stores of lumber from the forests, which still stretch over thousands of acres. The swamps furnish the best of material for ship-building, and Charleston has built many fine lumber-mills in which to prepare the pine and other useful trees for shipping. The city sadly needs the addition of several millions to its banking capital to enable it to carry out its schemes. The three National and four State banks now have hardly $3,000,000 of paid up capital. There are four savings banks, with a little more than $1,000,000, much of which represents the savings of the freedmen, on deposit. Private bankers are also doing a good deal for the city's interests.

Very lovely is the old city, lying confidingly on the waters, at the confluence of the broad Ashley and Cooper rivers, and fronting on the spacious harbor, over whose entrance the scarred and ever memorable Sumter keeps watch and ward.

* The commercial year begins September 1.

Nature has lavished a wealth of delicious foliage upon all the surroundings of the city, and the palmetto, the live and water oaks, the royal magnolias, the tall pines, the flourishing hedges, and the gardens filled with rich, tropical blooms, profoundly impress the stranger. The winter climate is superb, and the sunshine seems omnipresent, creeping into even the narrowest lanes and by-ways.

In 1680, the people who had been encouraged to remove from the badly chosen site of a settlement which they had selected on the banks of the Ashley river in 1671, laid the foundations at Charleston, and the town at once sprang into activity. It began its commerce in dangerous times, for pirates hovered about the mouth of the Ashley, and many a good ship, laden with the produce of the plantations, and bound for Great Britain, was plundered, and its crew set on shore, or murdered, if resistance was offered. A hurricane also swept over the infant town, half ruining it; and then began a series of destructive fires, which, from 1680 to 1862, have, at fearfully short intervals carried havoc and destruction into the homes of the wealthiest.

In later years, too, the fleets of hostile Spaniards or Frenchmen sometimes brought panic even to Charleston bar; and the beacon fires on Sullivan's Island, in the harbor, warned the citizens to be on their guard. In 1728, a hurricane created an inundation, which overflowed the town and lowlands, forced the inhabitants to take refuge on the roofs of their dwellings, drove twenty-three fine ships ashore, and leveled many thousands of trees. In the same year came the yellow fever, sweeping off multitudes of whites and blacks. After the surrender, by the proprietary government, of its control of the province, into the hands of the sovereign of Great Britain, on the payment of a round sum of purchase money, Charleston became more prosperous than ever before. In 1765 it was described as "one of the first cities in British America, yearly advancing in size, riches and population."

The approaches to Charleston from the sea are unique, and the stranger yields readily to the illusion that the city springs directly from the bosom of the waves. The bar at the harbor's mouth will allow ships drawing seventeen feet of water to pass over it. The entrance from the sea is commanded on either side by Morris and Sullivan's Islands, the former the scene of terrific slaughter during the dreadful days of 1863, and subsequently one of the points from which the Union forces bombarded Charleston; and the latter at present a fashionable summer resort, crowded with fine mansions. On the harbor side of Sullivan's Island, Fort Moultrie, a solid and well-constructed fortification, frowns over the hurrying waters. Passing Sumter, which lies isolated and in semi-ruin, looking, at a dis-

The old Charleston Post-office. [Page 441.]

tance, like some coral island pushed up from the depths, one sails by pleasant shores lined with palmettoes and grand moss-hung oaks, and by Castle Pinckney, and anchors at the substantial wharves of the proud little city.

Many ships from many climes are anchored at these wharves, and the town seems the seaport of some thriving commercial State, so little does it represent the actual condition of South Carolina. The graceful Corinthian portico and columns of the new Custom-House, built of pure white marble, rise up near the water-side. There is a jolly refrain of the clinking of hammers, the rattling of drays, and the clanking of chains, which indicates much activity. Here some foreign vessel, which has come for phosphates, is unloading her ballast; here a rice-schooner is unloading near a pounding-mill. On one hand are lumber-yards; on another, cotton-sheds, filled with bales. Hundreds of negroes, scream-

Houses on the Battery—Charleston.

ing and pounding their mules, clatter along the piers and roadways; a great Florida steamer is swinging round, and starting on her ocean trip to the Peninsula, with her decks crowded with Northern visitors. Along "East Bay" the houses are, in many places, solid and antique. The whole aspect of the harbor quarter is unlike that of any of our new and smartly painted Northern towns. In Charleston the houses and streets have an air of dignified repose and solidity. At the foot of Broad street, a spacious avenue lined with banks and offices of professional men, stands the old "Post-office," a building of the colonial type, much injured during the late war, but since renovated at considerable expense. Most of the original material for the construction of the edifice was brought from England in 1761. Within its walls the voices of Rutledge, Pinckney, Gadsden, Lowndes and Laurens were raised to vehemently denounce the Government against whose tyranny the "Thirteen original States" rebelled; from the old steps Washington addressed the Charlestonians in 1791; and for many years during this century it was an Exchange for the merchants of Charleston and vicinity. When the British occupied Charleston, the building was the scene of many exciting episodes. The basement was taken for a prison, and all who were devoted to the cause of American liberty were confined therein. From that prison the martyr, Isaac Hayne, was led to execution; and in the cellar one hundred thousand pounds of powder lay safely hidden from the British during the whole time of their occupation. On the site of this building stood the old council-chamber and watch-house used in the days of the "proprietary government."

A Charleston Mansion.

The original plan of Charleston comprised a great number of streets running at right angles, north and south, east and west, between the two rivers. But many of these streets were very narrow, being, in fact, nothing more than lanes; and they have remained unchanged until the present day. The darkness and narrowness of the old lanes, the elder colonists thought, would keep away the glare of the bright sun; but the modern Charlestonians do not seem of their opinion, for they open wide avenues, and court the sun freely in their spacious and elegant mansions on the "Battery." Some of the Charleston avenues present a novel appearance, bordered as they are on either side by tall, weather-stained mansions, whose gable-ends front upon the sidewalks, and which boast verandas attached to each story, screened from the sun and from observation by ample wooden lattices, and by trellised vines and creepers. The high walls, which one sees so often in France and England, surround the majority of the gardens, and it is only through the gate, as in New Orleans, that one can catch a glimpse of the loveliness within. In some of the streets remote from the harbor front, the stillness of death or desertion reigns; many of the better class of mansions are vacant, and here and there the residence of some former aristocrat is now serving as an abode for a dozen negro families.

On King street one sees the most activity in the lighter branches of trade; there the ladies indulge in shopping, evening, morning, and afternoon; there is located the principal theatre, the tasty, little "Academy of Music," and there also, are some elegant homes. Along that section of King street, near the crossing of Broad, however, are numerous little shops frequented by negroes, in which one sees the most extravagant array of gaudy but inexpensive articles of apparel; and of eatables which the negro palate cannot resist. The residence streets of the "Palmetto City," on the side next the Ashley river, are picturesque and lovely. They are usually bordered by many beautiful gardens. A labyrinth of long wooden piers and wharves runs out on the lagoons and inlets near the Ashley, and the boasted resemblance of Charleston to Venice is doubtless founded on the perfect illusion produced by a view of that section from a distance. The magnificent and the mean jostle each other very closely in all quarters.

The Spire of St. Philip's Church—Charleston.

The stranger visiting Charleston is surprised to find that little has been done toward rebuilding that portion of the city swept away by fire in 1861. There are still gaps left in the heart of the populous sections; one suddenly comes upon the scarred and scorched walls of a huge church, or the foundations of some immense block, in a location which it seems folly to leave unimproved. But the Charlestonians explain that they do not need to rebuild as yet, for though the population is gradually increasing (it is now more than fifty thousand) the altered circumstances of some classes in society have compelled them to retire and make room for others.

L.

THE VENICE OF AMERICA—CHARLESTON'S POLITICS. A LOVELY LOWLAND CITY—IMMIGRATION.

IF we climb into the tower of the stately building known as the "Orphan House," some pleasant evening, when the sunset is beginning to throw the dark walls and picturesque groupings of the sea-girdled city into strong relief, we can get a panoramic glimpse of all the chief features of Charleston's

The Orphan House — Charleston.

exterior. We shall, perhaps, be too far from the Battery and its adjacent parks to note fully the effect of the gay group promenading the stone parapet against which the tides break gently, or to catch the perfect beauty of the palm-girt shores so distinctly visible beyond the Ashley's current, now that the sunset has given them a blood-red background. The Battery is not crowded with carriages, as in those merry days when the State was still prosperous, or on that famous day when yonder black mass in the harbor was aflame, and when the flag of the nation which floated over it was hauled down. But it is one of the airiest and most elegant promenades possessed by any Southern city, and the streets leading to it are quaint and beautiful. The church spires here and there are noticeable, and that one glistening in the distance was a white mark for many a day for the Federal batteries; yet few shells struck the stately steeple of St. Michael's, the old-fashioned, staid Episcopal house of prayer.

Beyond this church one sees a mass of buildings, whose queer roofs and strangely shapen chimneys remind him of Antwerp or of Amsterdam. These date from colonial times; it is the Charleston of pre-revolutionary days which one sees clustered around St. Michael's. The bells were removed during the siege of Charleston to Columbia; were captured and accidentally cracked; were recovered, sent to England, and recast in the foundry in Whitechapel, from whence they were originally obtained. After the war they were put back in their place in the steeple with great rejoicing amongst the old Charlestonians. Yonder, nearer the harbor, out of Church street, arises another spire, the counterpart of St. Martin's in the Fields in London. It is the tower of St. Philip's, also an Episcopal church, and in the old graveyard opposite is a simple tomb in which repose the bones of John C. Calhoun. The statesman rests in an antiquated, yet beautiful corner of the town. The venerable cemetery is embowered in trees, and hemmed round about by old buildings with tiled roofs. The remains were removed when the Union forces seemed likely to capture Charleston, but were replaced in 1871. The formidable ruin, which the sunset-glow throws so sharply upon your vision, is the old cathedral of St. John and St. Finbar, destroyed in the last great fire. On its site, when the Charlestonians were compelled to surrender to the British, occurred a tremendous explosion, occasioned by the rage of the conquered.

The Battery—Charleston.

They were compelled to deposit their arms at the arsenal, which was also a powder magazine, and all coming at once, and hurling down upon the ground hundreds of fire-arms, an explosion took place, igniting twenty thousand pounds of powder and blowing to atoms the adjacent Lunatic Asylum, Poor-House, Guard-

House, and Barracks, as well as conquerors and conquered. The city has many other interesting churches, among them the Huguenot, which has on its walls numerous interesting ancient inscriptions. Grace Church (Episcopal) is the resort of the fashionable worshipers.

There is nothing remarkable in the secular architecture of Charleston; yet this old Orphan House, from whose tower we survey the others, with its lovely

The Grave of John C. Calhoun—Charleston. [Page 445.]

garden hedged in from the street, with its statue of William Pitt, which the grateful citizens erected when the "stamp act" was repealed, is imposing. It was founded in 1790, is bountifully endowed, and thousands of orphan boys and girls have been well cared for within its walls. John C. Fremont and the Carolinian Memminger were educated there. There is an institution of the same class for the colored people. Neither the hotels nor the banks are distinguished for architectural excellence. The Charleston Hotel has an immense stone-pillared piazza fronting on Meeting street, but the Mills House and the Pavilion are simply solid blocks.

The Charleston Club-House is an elegant structure, and the building of the South Carolina Hall is fine in interior arrangement. The Club-House has become the seat of the Federal courts, and white and black men sit together in juries there. The Court-House and the City Hall are substantial edifices, fronting each other on corners of Broad and Meeting streets. Around them are always lounging crowds of negro men and women, as if they delighted to linger in the atmosphere of government and law, to the powers and responsibilities of which they have lately been introduced. At the Guard-House one may note white and black policemen on terms of amity.

Charleston prospers despite the anomalous condition of politics and society in the State. What might she not become if the commonwealth were developed to its utmost? The citizens suffer many trying ills, the most aggravated of which is the small rôle that the present leaders of the majority permit them to play in State politics. The Legislature has out-Napoleoned Napoleon III. in measures for the corruption of suffrage, and has enacted an infamous law, which allows Governors of the State to control the ballot-box completely through commissioners appointed virtually by himself. Its vote is swallowed up in the vote of Charleston county, and consequently it is represented only at second-hand in the State Assembly, getting but a meagre and partial hearing through a score of ignorant negroes, sent from the plantations and small towns in the vicinity.

The first election in Charleston after reconstruction was held in 1868, and the Republican candidate for Mayor, Pillsbury, was elected by a majority of twenty-three in a poll of 10,000. He remained in office until the summer of 1871, when the Conservatives attempted a fusion, and ran a ticket composed of white and black candidates, against the Republicans, with John A. Wagener, a German, for Mayor, and elected him by 777 majority. This administration had continued to the date of my visit, in 1873, when a new election took place, and exhibited in the most glaring light some of the atrocities of the present system. The Conservatives alleged, and it was, indeed, clearly proven, that four hundred negroes were imported from Edisto Island at one time, to create a majority in Charleston for the so-called "Republicans." None but Radical supervisors of the elections were appointed, and the right of challenge at every poll-precinct was denied. The law required every person voting to swear that he was a citizen of Charleston, but the imported voters were provided with the printed forms of the oath, from which the clause concerning the place of residence was omitted.

With no power of interference, and no chance to dispute at the polls or in the counting of the votes, this city of 50,000 inhabitants, possessing $30,000,000 worth of taxable property, was delivered over, bound hand and foot, to the tender

The Ruins of St. Finbar Cathedral—Charleston. [Page 445.]

mercies of the ignorant and the vicious. The party then in power admitted the abnormal condition of affairs. Governor Moses told an editor in Charleston that every citizen of South Carolina could vote in that city, if he chose, without hindrance; the Charlestonians could not help themselves.

The result of this latter election, in which the negro party was, of course, victorious, was a ferment, culminating in mass-meetings, investigations, and finally in a series of arguments. It was charged and shown that the commissioners for the elections did not designate all the polling-places so that the general public would know where they were, but that they stealthily opened them during the election, and there "rushed through" the illegal voters. It was also affirmed by the supporters of the corrupt State Government that a "residence in the city without limit as to time," in the county, sixty days, and in the State, one year, were qualifications sufficient for a voter under the act of 1873. The board of managers consisted, at the city election in 1873, almost entirely of negroes. Several hundred special deputy sheriffs were appointed to "maintain order" if the Conservatives made any attempt to challenge voters at the polls; and the managers refused to give the reporters of the city press any information concerning the changes made in the polling-places the night before the election. The Republican or Radical ticket was elected, and the protest of the citizens of Charleston having been entered, the "board of commissioners," appointed by the Legislature, then published a formal announcement that the election was "legal and valid," and that the "protest was overruled."

The Conservatives were bitterly grieved at this, as they had made a very firm stand, and it showed them how completely they were at the mercy of their present masters. They were not especially dissatisfied with the choice for Mayor, as the successful candidate, Mr. Cunningham, is an honest man; but the other municipal officers elected they regarded quite differently. The present police force of the city is about equally divided into black and white, and there are nine colored aldermen in the new board. It is not because of the presence of the negro in these offices of trust and honor that the Charlestonians are angry and grieved, but because he refuses them their proper share in the government. As they are now situated, the intelligence and property of the city are as completely shut out from political representation as if they were imprisoned within walls of adamant.

Charleston's city tax, in 1872, amounted to two per cent., but in 1873 was somewhat reduced. The combined city, county, and State tax, however, now amounts to three and a-half per cent. The assessments are always fully up to, and usually over, the actual value of property. The property holder, in the first instance, makes his returns. If the county auditor is not satisfied with the estimates, he changes them to suit himself; and the citizen then has the refuge of appeal to a "board of equalization." The Constitution requires that all property be taxed at its value.

The present city debt is nearly $5,000,000, some of which was incurred by subscriptions to railroads before the war. The city, before the war, invested $1,000,000 in the Blue Ridge railroad, and the State about $1,300,000. In 1868 or '69, the State stock, a majority, was sold for $13,000, to a ring. Shortly before this the State had guaranteed $4,000,000 of bonds of the road; these were hypothecated by the company. The ring secured the passage of a law authorizing the State Treasurer to issue $1,800,000 of revenue bond scrip upon the surrender to him of the $4,000,000 guaranteed bonds, said scrip receivable for taxes. Exchange was made, and bonds have been canceled, but the State Supreme Court has decided that the act authorizing the issue of the scrip is unconstitutional and void. The "licenses" which business and professions are already compelled to submit to are grievous burdens, and the people consider them such an odious form of municipal taxation that when the Legislature passed a law for collecting State licenses also, it was resisted, and finally its repeal was deemed expedient. The astute legislators even imposed a license-tax upon the railroads, which were, of course, already licensed by charter.

Thus cut off, politically, Charleston, with grim patience, awaits a turn in the tide of affairs, and catches a little inspiration from the development of the scheme for a new railway route from Chicago to Charleston. This superb air line, when built, will pass by Columbia and Spartanburg, in South Carolina, northward to Asheville, in the North Carolina mountains—thence through Cumberland Gap into Lexington, in Kentucky, and so onward to Chicago, giving an outlet on the sea 100 miles nearer the North-west than New York now is by any existing line. The towns mentioned above are situated directly on the route originally projected for the connection between the North-west and the Atlantic, and pronounced by all who have surveyed it as one of the most economical and practical ways across the Blue Ridge and the Alleghanies "to be found from the head-waters of the Susquehanna to the southern termination of those ranges."

"The highways leading out of the city are all richly embowered in loveliest foliage." [Page 451.]

The extensive marl-beds of the South Carolina lowlands, all comparatively near Charleston, have long been known; but they were first especially noticed by Edmund Ruffin, of Virginia, a noted agriculturist, who had been very successful in renovating worn-out lands in his own State with marl. He examined the South Carolina marls, and found them much richer in carbonate of lime than those of Virginia, but the carbonate was so combined with and mineralized by silex, oxide of iron, phosphate of lime, and other substances, as to necessitate a chemical change by burning before it could be applied to agricultural purposes.

Among these marl deposits, which abound in the immediate vicinity of Charleston, are found hard nodular bodies of all sizes, varying from that of a pin's head to masses weighing hundreds of pounds. These nodules are now known as phosphate rock, and have been described as "incalculable heaps of animal remains thrown or washed together." Beautiful specimens of ribs, vertebræ, and teeth of land and sea monsters of the early tertiary period are found in profusion at a little distance below the surface, and are readily dug up with pick and shovel. The negroes are said even to dive for them to the river-beds, and to bring up large quantities.

The people have at last awakened to the immense value of these deposits, and a number of establishments devoted to their conversion into phosphate-manures have sprung up since the war. In these manufactories the nodules are baked thoroughly dry, then ground to a powder, which is finally mixed with sulphuric acid and charged with ammonia. The Wando Company, which first

Magnolia Cemetery — Charleston. [Page 451.]

undertook the production of these fertilizers, made thirty per cent. profit, and there are now two dozen companies in the State organized for the purposes either of mining or manufacturing these phosphates. One company is organized with a capital of $2,000,000 to mine in all the navigable rivers in the State; and there are several manufacturing corporations which have each a million dollars capital. The Etiwan Company claims to have the largest acid-chamber in the United States; and in the Wando, Etiwan, Pacific, Guano, Atlantic, Stono and Wappoo mills, four or five millions of dollars have been invested since 1868.

Important as is this industry, there are a variety of others already developed in Charleston which promise great future success. In the manufacture of doors, blinds, sashes, and machinery, and in ship-building, a large capital is invested. The enterprising citizens are even constructing ready-made houses and churches, which can be shipped in sections to new States and territories. A cotton-mill and several tanneries are projected. The "truck farms" vie with those of Norfolk, and are supplying the Northern markets with early vegetables. The city's jobbing trade amounted to about $6,000,000 in 1872, and steadily increases at the rate of twenty-five per cent.

The highways leading out of the city are all richly embowered in loveliest foliage; the oak, the magnolia, the myrtle, the jessamine, vie with each other in tropical splendor. Splendid shell roads have been projected, but are not yet completed. The visitor hardly knows which most to admire—the cultivated bloom and glory of the gardens, the tangled thickets where the luxuriant cane rises thirty and forty feet, the shimmering sheets of water on the marshes, or the long sandy pathways, over which stretch the long arms of moss-hung oaks. A palmetto, standing lonely under the rich glow of the splendid Southern moon, will fill even the prosaic with poetic enthusiasm; a cabin, overgrown with vines and tendrils, and half concealed in a green and odorous thicket, behind which one catches the gleam of the river current, will make one enamored of the sweet silence and restful perfection of the lowland capital's suburbs. The mansion with closed doors, and decaying verandas, from which

"Life and thought have gone away,"

will recall the late revolution's worst phase to him who had almost forgotten it in the city's commercial bustle.

Along the Ashley, the old manorial houses and estates, like Drayton Hall and the Middleton homestead, stand like sorrowful ghosts lamenting the past; on James's Island one may wander among rich cotton plantations, now overspreading the maze of fortifications which sprang up during the war; there is no more silence and absolute calm, as there is no more of beauty and luxuriance, in Magnolia cemetery, than in the vast parks surrounding these ruined and desolate homes. The monuments in the cemetery to Simons, and Legare, and Colonel Washington, and Vanderhorst, are beautiful and tasteful; so are the battered and broken monuments to a dead civilization and a broken-down system which one finds upon the old plantations.

There is a wide belt of forsaken plantations near the Cooper river, along the famous Goose creek, upon whose banks stands the venerable St. James's Church, built in 1711. Around this ancient building the ambitious forest is fast weaving a network difficult to penetrate; and the very graves are hidden under festoons of wild vines and flowers. Along the harbor there are also deserted and bankrupt towns, like pretty Mount Pleasant, filled with moss-grown and rotting houses, whose owners have fled, unless too poor to get away.

The climate of South Carolina being as mild and genial as that of the most favored portion of southern Europe, it is not strange that the lower classes of Italy and other countries should feel inclined to emigrate to the Palmetto State. But the people have been slow to show a proper intelligence on the subject of immigration. The legislators have taken care to encourage certain Northern classes to come—since they are sure that they will not; and have discouraged foreigners from attempting to settle in the State, since they fear that might lead to a new deal in politics. The Italians who went into the commonwealth some time since were offered $100 per year, and a little meal and bacon weekly; but they haughtily rejected any such terms. The white laborer who enters South Carolina must be offered good wages and given land at cheap rates; and the sooner the natives learn that he is not to be expected to work and live as the negroes do, the better it will be for their interest.

Recently the whites have become thoroughly aroused to the importance of this subject, and there is a great change in the temper with which immigrants are now received. The determination seems to be to make much of them as

Garden in Mount Pleasant, opposite Charleston. [Page 451.]

a sure, if slow, means of working out the political regeneration of the State, and securing its material prosperity. A State Commissioner of Immigration was appointed by the late Taxpayers' Convention, and the counties are appointing local Commissioners. An effort is now making at Charleston to establish a direct steamship line to Liverpool, which, it is hoped, will not only give a stimulus to immigration, but to inward freights as well.

The negro is not especially anxious to see immigration come in. The spirit of race is strong within him. He is desirous of seeing the lands in the commonwealth in the hands of his own people before the rest of the world's poor are invited to partake. He is impressed with the idea that South Carolina should be in some measure a black man's government, and is jealous of white intervention. This is not the sentiment, certainly, of the intelligent and refined colored people, but the mass are ignorant, and think that they are right in taking that stand. The black man lets the African in him run riot for the time being. He even dislikes to see the mulatto progress; and when he criticises him, it is as he were necessarily an inferior.

So, too, the negro secretly dislikes the white adventurer, or " carpet-bagger," as our Southern friends call him. Black rogue has quickly learned from white rogue all he wishes to know, and now proposes to go alone. The idea of Nemesis, added to the negro's lack of moral consciousness, which has become so pronounced in the two centuries of servitude, makes the negro believe that he is right in stealing and oppressing. He has found, now that he has obtained power, a strange fascination in the use of political machinery for purposes of oppression and spoliation. He thinks too, grimly, in the words of the Carolinian black's savage song:

"De bottom rail 's on de top,
An' we 's gwine to keep it dar."

Peeping Through.

LI.

THE SPOLIATION OF SOUTH CAROLINA.

THE political troubles between the white and the black natives in South Carolina began directly after the close of the war. The mass of undisfranchised whites, embittered by and disgusted with the revolution, refused to have anything whatever to do with the new edifice which the negroes were trying to upbuild. Had they frankly accepted the situation, they might have had a share in the framing of the new Constitution. The negroes, left alone, were soon interested in the advent of white strangers, who agreed to teach them the political rôle they were called upon to play. Some of these newcomers were honest men; others were thieves. The convention for the making of a new Constitution was at once a ludicrous and an impressive gathering. The Constitution was ratified at a general election, held on the 14th, 15th, and 16th days of April, 1868. South Carolina then entered upon her first experience of negro government.

Governor Orr left the State executive chair on July 6, 1868. The commonwealth then had a bonded debt of about $5,500,000, and a floating indebtedness amounting to perhaps $1,500,000 more. While the condition of the finances was not hopeful, it was still far from desperate. People hoped that a new railroad development would open up fresh trade, that money would flow in. The abominable and atrocious outrages of the Ku-Klux, however, were an effective obstacle to Northern immigration.

The Klan was imported into South Carolina in 1868, before the present State Government was organized; and the white population of the ruder and remote counties tried to inaugurate a reign of terror among the negroes. The chairman of the Republican State Central Committee was brutally murdered in the fall of 1868. Hundreds of men were taken from their homes at night and whipped; some were murdered. The result was the interference of the Federal Government, the arrest and imprisonment of members of the organization, and the breaking up of its secret operations.

But while society was completely unsettled, while the whites were smarting under the humiliation of being crowded out of the representation to which they were entitled, while the negro was master, and was beginning to be insolent and aggressive, the Legislature met. The first session after reconstruction was held in August of 1868. At a later session, Governor Scott, formerly an agent of the Freedmen's Bureau, sent in his first message, in which he reviewed the financial condition of the State, and the Ku-Klux outrages, then at their height, and counseled moderation and firmness.

The negroes nearly filled both Senate and House; there were but few white members during the first session, when the ignorant blacks were learning parliamentary forms, for which, by the way, they have an extraordinary aptitude. Jobs began to appear, and the first drawing of blood may be said to have been in connection with the job for the redemption of the bills of the bank of the State. The strong influenced the weak; the negro, dazzled and enlivened by the prospect of the reception of sums which seemed to him colossal fortunes, soon became an apt scholar, and needed but little prompting from his white teachers. Measures for authorizing the Governor to borrow on the credit of the State were at once inaugurated; and then began a series of acts whose results are without a parallel in the history of revolutions.

During the four years from 1868 to 1872 inclusive, the bonded debt was increased from five and a-half to sixteen millions, and the floating debt, which could be only vaguely ascertained, amounted to several millions more. The following tabular statement of the debt is compiled from the books of the State Treasurer:

Legal bonded debt	$9,886,627.35
Illegal bonded debt	5,965,000.00
Legal floating debt	2,429,272.95
Illegal floating debt	2,692,102.94
Contingent liabilities	4,797,608.20
Total	$25,770,611.44

If the actual and contingent liabilities, bonded and floating debt, legal and illegal, are to be taken into account, then the actual debt is the whole amount stated above; and less in proportion as any of the constituent items are excluded.

Honest Republicans had raised their voices loudly against the infamies which were the cause of this terrible increase; had endeavored to oust the thieves, and failing, had left the party in disgust. The negroes were intoxicated with power, and would hear of nothing which seemed likely to better the condition of their old masters.

In 1870, the Conservatives, as the white natives style themselves, alarmed at the riot of corruption and the total disregard of decency manifested by the governing powers, rallied and made a decided effort to get the State into their own hands. They nominated R. B. Carpenter, a Republican Circuit Judge, for Governor, on the simple yet broad platform of retrenchment and reform. On their tickets a few negroes were represented, and for the first time in the history of the State, negroes and Conservative whites spoke upon the same political stump. But the leaders of the negroes refused to believe in the sincerity of the ex-Confederates, and Governor Scott was re-elected over Carpenter. The Ring which was soiling its guilty fingers with plunder was jubilant; honest Republicans hung their heads with shame and gave up all hope of the State; the native white Carolinians, angered and distressed, and fearing that the negroes might undertake some measures to which resistance would be necessary, formed themselves into a "council of safety." This is said really to have been simply an organization to enable planters to protect themselves against strikes, at most a purely defensive organization, and not an attempt at a revival of Ku-Kluxism, as it has sometimes been called. It had no hold in the lower part of the State, but in the upper counties seems to have been perverted into Ku-Kluxism.

The offer of amity which it had cost the pride of the Conservatives such an abasement to make is not likely to be repeated at once. The struggle was great, the result unsatisfactory. People now grimly submit to be robbed without attempting resistance save at election-time. But the hostility which they naturally feel toward the acts of the present State Administration is constantly increased; and in the biting criticisms evoked from the press of Charleston so much truth has been told that the outside world has begun to believe in the statement that the revolution has been made an instrument of fraud and oppression.

Although it would seem an infamy simply to deliberately increase the debt of a State which had been so terribly impoverished as had South Carolina by the war (her total valuation having decreased in ten years from $489,319,128 to $164,409,941), this was but the beginning of the outrage. Not only was the debt increased, but the revenues of the State were diverted from their proper channels into the pockets of the thieves; and it has been incontrovertibly proven that millions have been added to the State debt without the authority of the Legislature. By the official statement of the Treasurer of the Commonwealth, the public debt at the close of the fiscal year ending October 31, 1871, amounted to $15,851,327.35. This showed an actual increase since the advent of the reconstruction legislature of $10,500,000, of which amount only $4,389,400 had ever been in any manner authorized by the legal representatives of the State. And it is considered certain that in 1872 there were already afloat upon the market, very possibly in the hands of innocent holders, without any authority in their original issue, some $6,000,000 in conversion bonds; and it was found necessary to introduce an act, in 1872, to ratify and confirm this illegal issue, for which the "Financial Board," composed of the Governor, the State Treasurer, and the Attorney-General, were responsible.*

Immense sums of money were collected during the four years from 1868 to the beginning of 1872. The people of the State contributed $3,780,000 in taxes, and the financial agents at New York sold bonds to the amount of $2,282,000. Add to this $1,000,000 of taxes collected up to the close of 1872, and it will be seen that more than $7,000,000 went into the Treasury during two administrations.

This revenue, which, in view of the impoverishment caused by the war, was very encouraging, has been stolen from the State in a variety of ways. The officers have never been governed by the Appropriation acts; have never been limited by them. The money appropriated for one purpose has been unblushingly expended for another. No honest debts were paid with all the money collected from the white people who are denied the right of representation in this

---

*At the last session, 1873-'74, an act was passed declaring that these bonds, known as Conversion Bonds, amounting to $5,965,000 were put upon the market "without any authority of law," and were "absolutely null and void." A joint resolution was passed for the prosecution of the ex-State Treasurer, but this joint resolution is "lost" from the records.

black Legislature,—not a debt during the year 1873. The bondholders have not received the interest upon their bonds.

The frauds to which the Legislature lent itself and which private individuals perpetrated, were contemptible. A land commission was established. It was ostensibly beneficent. Its apparent purpose was to buy up lands, and distribute them among the freedmen. An appropriation of $700,000 was granted for that purpose. The State was at once robbed. Worthless land was purchased and sold at fabulous sums to the Government. The commissioners were generally accused of extensive corruption. When at last an honest commissioner came in it was found that a quarter of a million dollars had been stolen. The "Sinking Fund Commission," is another "oubliette" into which money raised from the State sinks mysteriously. The commissioners of this fraud were authorized to take and sell real and personal property belonging to the State, and to report annually to the Legislature the sums received. Public property has rapidly disappeared, but no report has ever been made.* The pockets of an unknown few contain the proceeds of much valuable State property.

This is mighty theft; colossal impudence like this was never surpassed. Never was a revolution, originally intended as humane, turned to such base uses. Never were thieves permitted to go unpunished after such bold and reckless wickedness. Never before were a people, crushed to earth, kept down and throttled so long. The manliness which we received as a precious legacy with our Anglo-Saxon blood demands that we should cry out, "Hold off your hands! Fair play!"

The complete centralization which has been the result of the long continuance in power of an ignorant Legislature, controlled by designing men, is shown in the history of the elections since reconstruction. The Governor has the power to appoint commissioners, who in their turn appoint managers of elections in the several counties. In this manner the Governor has absolute control of the elections, for the managers are allowed to keep and count the votes, and are not compelled to report for some days.

The chances thus given for fraud are limitless. For the last four years men who have been elected by overwhelming majorities have been coolly counted out, because they were distasteful to the powers that be. The negroes intimidate their fellows who desire to vote reform tickets, very much as the Ku-Klux once intimidated them. "The villainy you teach me I will execute."

People will say that this is a black picture. It is; there is no light upon it. There seems small hope for a change. The election this year will oust some plunderers, but will not be likely to check corruption. The white people of the State are powerless to resist; they are trampled completely down.

It is impossible to here review in detail all the transactions of the Legislature since 1868. Besides the schemes for corruption above mentioned, there

*An investigating committee of the State Senate on the sinking fund reported, in February 1874, that the proceedings of the Sinking Fund Commission have resulted in nothing but loss to the State; that a large amount of property had been sold, and not a dollar of the public debt had been extinguished.

have been very many others. Nothing has been safe from the taint. Bribery has been necessary to secure the passage of almost every bill. Railroad legislation has been a stench in honest men's nostrils. The pay certificates of the Legislature have even been abused. The Speaker of the House has issued these certificates to the amount of *more than a million dollars*, while the legitimate demand for them has not amounted to $150,000. They have been spread broadcast. The refurnishing of the new State-House cost hardly $50,000, but a bill for $95,000 was presented. Members of the Legislature, both black and white, publicly threatened that unless they received sums which they named they would vote against certain bills. A Governor stands charged by men of his own party with spending nearly $400,000 of the public money to get himself re-chosen. A bill to establish a militia became a gigantic "job." The whole course of legislation in the State tended to absolute tyranny, which is all the more dreadful because the deluded ignoramuses who make up the body of the assemblies are not aware that they are doing anything especially blameworthy. They look upon it as the result of a normal condition of things, and intend to keep it up as long as there is any vestige of State credit left.

Columbia has been the capital of South Carolina since 1790. It occupies a high and commanding position in the centre of the State, and is but 130 miles from Charleston. It borders upon the Congaree river, near the mouth of the Saluda, in the heart of a rich cotton region. The water power which might be made available in its immediate vicinity is much superior to that of most of the New England manufacturing towns. The canal near by was purchased from the State several years ago by Governor Sprague, of Rhode Island; but no cotton factories have as yet arisen along the banks. The town is one of the most beautiful in the South; its climate rivals that of Italy; and the broad, richly shaded avenues; the gardens filled with jessamines and japonicas, laurels and hawthorns and hollys, and the perfect groves in which the live oaks, the pines, the magnolias, and the wild oranges vie with each other in charm, give it an especial fascination. Columbia arose with sorrowful but reliant air out of the ashes in which it was laid by the war; and if its people had not been weighted down by the incubus of an ignorant and dishonest government, they would have done more even than they already have toward rebuilding. The little city, which now has about 12,000 inhabitants, is on the through route from Charlotte in North Carolina, to Augusta in Georgia, and also sends its commercial influence into the north-western counties, along the line of the Greenville and Columbia railroad, on which Newberry and other thriving towns are located. It has also an excellent connection with Wilmington on the North Carolina coast via Sumter, a busy town, a short distance to the westward of Columbia.

The counties of Richland, Sumter, Orangeburg, Lexington, and Clarendon, in the neighborhood of the capital, are exempt from the malaria of the lowlands, and cotton, corn, and other cereals, grow superbly. The great conflagration at the time of the evacuation of the city by the Confederates, swept away the Government armory, the old State-House, some manufactories, all the railway stations, a fine legislative library, St. Mary's College, with many valuable collections of paintings; the retreating Confederates destroyed the bridges over the river, and ruin reigned everywhere.

The exterior aspects of Columbia are to-day fair indeed. The venerable University (from which all the white professors and scholars retreated when the first black student was received) nestles charmingly in the midst of a grand tree-dotted park; the State Lunatic Asylum, a noble building, is likewise embowered in a splendid shade; the city buildings and hotels are large, and in excellent taste; a fine United States court-house is springing out of blocks of native granite; and the numerous private institutions of learning give the casual visitor the impression that he is visiting a "grove of Academe," rather than a perturbed and harassed capital. Many Northern families have purchased fine estates in the neighborhood; at evening the avenues are crowded with splendid teams, whose owners drive to the parade ground, and loiter, while six companies of United States troops go stiffly through the prescribed drill, and the band thunders the hackneyed music.

A Future Politician.

LII.

THE NEGROES IN ABSOLUTE POWER.

BUT it is at the State-House in Columbia that one arrives at the truth. The mammoth building, which yet lacks the stately cupola to be given it in a few years, is furnished with a richness and elegance which not even the legislative halls of States a hundred times as rich can equal. In the poorly constructed and badly lighted corridors below are the offices of the State Government—that of the Governor, the Treasurer, the Secretary of State, and the Superintendent of State Schools—each and all of them usually filled with colored people, discussing the issues of the hour. The Secretary of State is a mulatto, who has entered the law school at the University, and carries on his double duties very creditably.

In the House and Senate the negro element stands out conspicuous. On the occasion of my first visit I was shown into the room of the House Committee on the Judiciary for a few moments. While awaiting the assembling of the honorable members a colored gentleman, in a gray slouch hat, and a pair of spectacles, engaged me in conversation, and, as I inquired what was the present question which was exciting the patriotism and sacrifice of the virtuous members, he rolled up his eyes, and with a tragic air, said:

"Dar 's a heap o' bizness behin' de carpet heah, sah."

It was true, in more senses than one.

The House, when I visited it, was composed of eighty-three colored members, all of whom were Republicans, and forty-one whites; the Senate consisted of fifteen colored men, ten white Republicans, and eight white Democrats. The President of the Senate and the Speaker of the House, both colored, were elegant and accomplished men, highly educated, who would have creditably presided over any commonwealth's legislative assembly. In the House the negroes were

The State-House at Columbia, South Carolina.

of a much lower grade, and more obviously ignorant, than in the Senate. They were perpetually preventing the transaction of necessary business by "questions of privilege," and "points of order," of which, sometimes, as many as a hundred are raised in a single day. It being an extra session, they were endeavoring to make it last until the time for the assembling of the regular one; and their efforts were extremely ludicrous. The little knot of white Democrats, massed together in one section of the hall, sat glum and scornful amid the mass of black speakers, a member only rising now and then to correct an error of "his friend" the colored man, who had the floor.

But some of the sable brethren were trying to the visitor's patience, even, and after I had heard one young man talk for a half hour upon the important subject of what his constituents would say if he allowed himself to be brow-beaten into an immediate adjournment, it was with difficulty that I could suppress a yawn. This youth persisted in repetitions; his voice occasionally would be heard rising above the general hum, precisely reiterating the words he had uttered five minutes before.

The negro does not allow himself to be abashed by hostile criticism. When he gets a sentence tangled, or cannot follow the thread of his own thought in words, he will gravely open a book—the statutes, or some other ponderous volume lying before him—and, after seeming to consult it for some minutes, will resume. He has been gaining time for a new start.

There are men of real force and eloquence among the negroes chosen to the House, but they are the exception. In the Senate I noticed decorum and ability among the members. Several of the colored Senators spoke exceedingly well, and with great ease and grace of manner; others were awkward and coarse. The white members, native and imported, appeared men of talent at least. The black pages ran to and fro, carrying letters and documents to the honorable Senators; and a fine-looking quadroon, or possibly octoroon woman, and the ebony gentleman escorting her, were admitted to the floor of the Senate, and sat for some time listening to the debates.

To the careless observer it seems encouraging to see the negroes, so lately freed from a semi-barbaric condition, doing so well, because their conduct is really better than one would suppose them capable of, after having seen the constituency from which they were elevated. One cannot, of course, prevent reflections upon vengeance and retribution drifting into his mind,—it was, doubtless, to be expected that some day the negro would lord it over his master, as the law of compensation is immutable,—but there is danger in the protraction of this vengeance. We must really see fair play. Ignorance must not be allowed to run riot. If we saw it consummating, as a Commune assembled in Paris, one thousandth part of the infamy which it effects as a Legislature in South Carolina, we should cry out angrily for interference.

But this is an epoch of transition. When the negro is a little older as a politician, he will be less clannish. The masses of the blacks will divide more fully into parties. Then there will be some chance for the setting aside of the dreadful question of race against race. At present the blacks in the State move solidly together. Their eyes are fixed on the spoils which the white men have taught them to gather. They have not yet begun to understand that in stripping the State, compromising her credit and blackening her reputation, they injure themselves much more than they harm their old masters. They will learn in time that they have committed a grave error in allowing the whites to be virtually excluded from representation, and that both races will be forced to labor together, honestly and faithfully, to save the State, and to insure their own future prosperity.

I visited the University a day or two after the revolution caused there by the entrance of the first colored student, the Secretary of State himself. In the library, where the busts of Calhoun and Hayne seemed to look down from their

Sketches of South Carolina State Officers and Legislators, under the Moses Administration.

niches with astonishment upon the changed order of things, I saw the book from whose lists the white students had indignantly erased their names when they saw the Secretary's round, fair script beneath their own. The departure of the old professors and scholars was the signal for a grand onward movement by the blacks, and a great number entered the preparatory and the law schools. They have summoned good teachers from the North, and are studying earnestly. The University attained its present title in 1866. It was founded as a college at the beginning of the century, but now consists of ten distinct schools, and is rich in libraries and apparatus for scientific studies. While I was in the library, a coal black senator arrived, with two members of the House, whom he presented to the head of the faculty as desirous of entering the law class. I was informed that dozens of members were occupied every spare moment outside of the sessions in faithful study; but this has been the case for a short time only.

Except in the large towns, however, the educational prospects throughout the State are not very good. In 1873, the schools were much cramped for resources. Not a cent of an appropriation of these $300,000 for educational purposes, made in that year, reached the schools, and great numbers of them were closed. The difficulty of obtaining good teachers has also been very great. Charleston has had a fine school system for many years. Another High School there, an excellent institution, has been established since 1839. The local school tax for 1873 was nearly $45,000. There are about 2,500 white children in the public schools, and about the same number of colored pupils, for whom separate accommodations are provided. One single edifice for the black has room for 1,000 scholars.

Four colored schools are supported in Charleston by Northern funds: The Shaw Memorial, a large and efficient institution, assisted by the New England Freedmen's Aid Society; the Wallingford Academy, by the Presbyterian Church North; the Avery Institute, by the American Missionary School Association; and the Franklin Street High School, by the Episcopal Church North. All the city free schools are considered exceedingly good. The Normal School in Charleston has a fine edifice, and is sending out some excellent teachers. The Peabody fund has given aid here and there throughout the State to great advantage.

There are, at least, two hundred thousand children in the commonwealth; and it is safe to assert that not more than seventy-five thousand have been afforded school facilities. Charleston county shows an attendance of nearly 8,000; in the other coast counties there has latterly been a large decrease in attendance. On the sea-islands there are still some schools. An educational effort was first made there in 1862, and the school originally established in St. Helena is yet in existence, supported by Philadelphia societies. At one time there were twenty schools on St. Helena Island alone, supported by Northern funds. But now that this aid has been generally withdrawn, education there languishes. The school tax of three mills on the dollar would serve very well, if the State's affairs were not so wretchedly confused, and the pay of the teachers so uncertain. The corruption in the legislative halls demoralizes even the free school system, which the negro once so longed for, as the lever which was to lift him up to happiness. Columbia, Beaufort, the mountain towns of consequence, and the shire towns of upland counties, take much interest in the free school system, and encourage it as their means will permit.

The private institutions of learning in Charleston and the State are remarkably excellent. Few cities can boast of better medical colleges than that in

Charleston. It was first incorporated half a century ago, and had a brilliant career until the late war, during which it was nearly ruined. The Roper Hospital, which adjoins it, is a fine institution. Charleston is divided into health districts, over each of which a physician is appointed, with orders to give daily attendance upon the poor. This was a much needed charity, since the mortality among the negroes who came flocking into the city after the war was fearful, and the blacks neglect themselves, unless looked after, until it is too late to heal them.

The burden of charity is by no means small. The alms-house has more than sixteen hundred regular "outdoor pensioners," that is, poor residents who receive "rations or half-rations," regularly. The city and main hospitals are filled with colored patients, who are cheerfully cared for at the city's expense. Charleston is jealous of her sanitary reputation, and each successive year that passes without bringing the yellow fever only makes her more vigilant in the matters of her tidal drainage, her well-ordered markets, her cleanly docks, and her careful supervision of the personal health of her citizens.

Two of the noted institutions of Charleston are a little fallen into decay, but are still interesting. The Military Academy, a quaint, mauresque building, has become the head-quarters for the United States troops quartered in the city; and its splendid school is broken up. The Charleston College is still in operation. It was chartered in 1795, and has graduated many distinguished men. The establishment of the museum of natural history at the college was first suggested by Agassiz in 1850, and it is to-day, although a portion of the collection was burned in war-time, one of the finest in the country. The libraries of the private institutions are good, but Charleston greatly needs a public one, such as all the Eastern cities possess.

The development of South Carolina presents an interesting problem for solution. It seems, now, as if the system of large plantations were the only one under which rice culture can be successfully pursued. Yet the freedmen yearly manifest stronger disinclination for work in gangs on other people's land, and desire to acquire small farms, and to live independently, however rudely. It is singular that some of them have not developed the business capacity requisite to establish large plantations of their own, and to influence their fellows to work well with them on a coöperative basis.* The wealth in the great pine forests cannot be made available until some one besides the negro goes to work in them. The sea-island cotton-lands are certainly very unlikely to get the needed recuperation by much effort on the part of the negro. A new element of immigration must be had; but it will not go to the State in its present political condition.

Will, then, the State extricate herself from that position? There seems but little hope of any thorough immediate change, perhaps not for four years. Cumulative voting has been advocated in the State for some time, and in 1870 the Attorney-General and Governor Scott professed to be strongly in favor of the adoption of that principle. If this plan, as suggested by Mr. Pike in his

---

* There is, I am told, one highly prosperous colored settlement on the communal plan in Marlborough county.

excellent book on the subject, or some other method of gaining protection for the rights of the minority, could be successfully adopted; and if Charleston could receive her just dues politically, the course of events would, in due time, be changed. Her phosphates, her railway connections, her cotton receipts, her manufactories cannot fail to make her rich; but that will not benefit the State, as she is at present situated. Very little reliance is to be placed on any hopes of immigration, save of families who are well-to-do, toward centres like Aiken and Columbia.

The farmers in the upland regions are forcing their lands too harshly in their desperate effort to make a great deal of cotton, and are neglecting the needed diversity of crops, so that they will, perhaps, be in distress by and by. There are hundreds of superb chances for investment in the State which will never for a moment be considered by capitalists so long as a State Government so unjust, tyrannical and centralized as the present one maintains itself in office. It is a frightful incubus which drags down every earnest man who desires to make an effort at a rebound after the collapse caused by the war; it is a disgrace to our system; it is a stumbling-block to the negro; an embodied corruption which public opinion ought to sweep out of existence; a usurpation for which there is no excuse save the complete ignorance of one race, and the utter helplessness of the other.

Iron Palmetto in the State-House Yard at Columbia.

LIII.

THE LOWLANDS OF NORTH CAROLINA.

NORTH CAROLINA comprises an area of a little more than 50,000 square miles, or 34,000,000 of acres. From the Atlantic ocean it stretches 500 miles, back to the Tennessee line, and is from 100 to 150 miles wide, between Virginia and Georgia. It embraces within its limits almost every variety of soil and climate. It is very plainly separated into three natural divisions. The first is the "flat country of swamps and marshes and sluggish streams, supposed by geologists to have been upheaved by the sea."* This extends 100 miles inland from the coast. This is the country of the long-leaved pine, the sandy bottoms, and the turpentine forests, inhabited by a low and almost worthless population. There, too, however, are flourishing towns and prosperous people.

The second region is that of wheat, corn, tobacco, and cotton. The soil is undulating, fertile, and the rivers afford fine facilities for transportation. The third division is that of the mountains.

There is a marked difference between the upland and lowland people of North Carolina. The mountaineers seem, in some measure, a race by themselves, and have sometimes made strong efforts to secure a division of the State. To-day there are a few enthusiastic advocates of the creation of a new commonwealth out of the mountain regions of North Carolina and Tennessee. The mountains have certainly supplied North Carolina with many of her famous politicians, with fine instances of prosperity, and with the example of loyalty when she sadly needed it. But the residents of the two sections know little of each other. The railroads through the mountains will open to the lowlanders a Paradise which has been at their very doors, yet little known by them.

The North Carolina coast, as seen from the ocean, is flat and uninteresting. There is an aspect of wild desolation about the swamps and marshes which one may at first find picturesque, but which finally wearies and annoys the eye. But the coast is cut up into a network of navigable sounds, rivers and creeks, where the best of fish abound, and where trade may some day flow in. The shad and herring fisheries in these inlets are already sources of much profit. The future export of pine and cypress timber, taken from the mighty forests, will yield an immense revenue. The swampy or dry tracts along the coast are all capable of producing a bale of cotton to the acre. They give the most astonishing returns for the culture of the sweet potato, the classic peanut, or

---

*From a published letter from Rev. Dr. Mason, rector of Christ's Church, Raleigh, North Carolina.

"guber," the grape, and many kinds of vegetables. Malarial fevers will, of course, seize on the inhabitant of this region who does not pay proper attention to the drainage all about him. It is believed that along this coast great numbers of vineyards will in time be established, for there are unrivaled advantages for wine-growing.

The extreme eastern limit of the State is a narrow strip of land, separating the ocean from the interior waters. It is called the Banks, and is here and there broken by inlets, the most important of which are Hatteras, Ocracoke, Beaufort, and the mouth of the Cape Fear river. On this narrow strip, which the ocean has with great unwillingness conceded the State, lives a singular race, "half-horse, half-alligator," subsisting by fishing and pilotage. The central point of this projecting and protecting arm of land is the far and ill-famed Hatteras, the terror of the voyager along the stormy coast.

"Currituck Sound," one of the notable features of the lowlands of North Carolina, separates the "Banks" from the main land just south of the Virginia line. It is a fresh-water strait, varying in width from three to fifteen miles, and in winter is a sportsman's heaven. Myriads of wild ducks, geese and swans resort there during the cold months, and amateurs from every climate under heaven visit the marshes and slaughter the fowls for months together. Albemarle and Croatan sounds are also notable fishing resorts; through Croatan one enters into Pamlico, and thence penetrates to Beaufort Inlet, on which the town of Beaufort stands.

Beaufort possesses one of the best harbors on the Atlantic coast. Vessels can come directly from the deep sea to the wharves of the Atlantic and North Carolina Railway Company at Morehead City, opposite Beaufort. The town has relapsed into comparative obscurity since its brilliant war history, when it was the rendezvous of many navies, and the point of departure for many hostile expeditions. Fort Macon, at the entrance of its harbor, and its surroundings, are interesting, and there are throngs of summer visitors along the ample beach. The railroad, connecting Beaufort with the interior of the State, runs northwestward through Newbern to Goldsboro. The former is an old and pleasant town of five or six thousand inhabitants, at the confluence of the Neuse and Trent rivers, and the latter is a newer and smarter place, owing its growth mainly to the increase of railroad facilities. Newbern boasts a line of steamers to New York, and once had many elegant mansions and gardens, most of which have latterly fallen into decay.

North Carolina is very well supplied with railways in her lowland and middle districts. The North Carolina road extends from Goldsboro to Charlotte; the Raleigh and Gaston road, from Raleigh to Weldon, thence giving an outlet through Virginia; the Western road from Fayetteville, on the Cape Fear river mountainward (probably before many years to be completed); the Wilmington and Weldon road runs directly north and south through the State; and the Chatham railroad penetrates from Raleigh to the coal and iron-beds in Chatham county. The Air Line road from Atlanta gives a direct route from Charlotte in North Carolina, to Danville in Virginia, and thence north and east.

The lower regions of the State abound in beautiful though quiet rural scenery. There are no towns of considerable size. Raleigh is a sleepy, delightful, shaded old place. Wilmington, although busy, is not large; Charlotte is small but lively. Salisbury and Greensboro are in the centre of a rich mining region, where copper, iron, coal, and gold are to be found; the former is the centre of a lively tobacco trade, and the latter is the point whence one takes the railroad to Statesville and Morganton, the charming towns at the outer line of the mountain region. Salisbury was the seat of a famous Confederate prison in which many a Union soldier languished and died, or starved through weary months.

The North Carolinians are accustomed now-a-days to wonder why immigrants do not rush into their State, and settle upon the lands which can be had so cheaply; and finding that but few come, and that the State is in a general condition of discouragement and decay, financially, they have relapsed into an indolent attitude, and let progress drift by them. In some of the small towns I found the people more inclined to bitterness and less reconciled to the results of the war than anywhere else in the South. Many towns, too, had a deserted and neglected look which was painful.

The State, of course, suffered greatly by the war. It was one of the foremost of pro-slavery communities; held nearly 350,000 slaves when the war broke out; and had a firmly-seated and exclusive aristocracy, which has naturally been very much broken up by recent events. The present population is 1,071,361, of whom 678,470 are blacks, of by no means the highest type. The revolution decreased the value of real and personal estate in North Carolina from $292,297,602, in 1860 to $132,046,391 in 1870, and the decrease within the last four years has been very rapid.

The evils of universal suffrage have been very great in this State. The great mass of densely ignorant and ambitious blacks suddenly hurled upon the field created the wildest confusion, and crushed the commonwealth under irredeemable debt. The villainy and robbery to which the white population of the State was compelled to submit, at the hands of the plunderers maintained in power by the negro, did much to destroy all possibility of a speedy reconciliation between the two races. Still, the citizens are loyal to the Union, and are anxious to be on friendly terms with the North; yet continue to regard Northerners as in some way the authors of the evils which have befallen them. They do not, however, reproach the North with having sent them a carpet-bagger; as the man who did them most harm, and whose conduct has been most sharply criticised, was a citizen of their own State.

The reconstruction convention in 1868 was a singular gathering. Its proceedings bordered on the ridiculous. It finally secured a Constitution which has since been much amended. The judges and other officers placed in power were notoriously incompetent; and Mr. Holden, who was appointed first provisional Governor of the State under reconstruction, was the author of so much questionable work that he was successfully impeached and removed. There was, at one time, imminent danger of civil war in the State; several counties were in insurrection; the Ku-Klux flourished and committed all kinds of infamous outrages. Holden was an original secessionist, and his newspaper, the *Standard*, printed at Raleigh, was the mouth-piece of the Democracy until 1860, when this unblushing "scallawag," as the Southerners call political renegades, threw his Democratic sentiments out at window, and went in for the Union cause. Of course he did this with an eye to future plunder. Mr. Holden was, in 1873, Postmaster at the State Capitol, and seemed but little affected by his forcible removal from the executive chair.

At the close of the wild carnival of robbery and maladministration which marked the career of the first reconstruction government, North Carolina found that her debts were between $36,000,000 and $40,000,000. This was an appalling exhibit, for the mere payment of the interest was enough to stagger the impoverished and struggling agriculturists. The money had gone, alas! none save the thieves knew where. The plundered people only knew that out of $16,000,000 voted by the Legislatures for "public works of improvements," but $500,000 had ever been devoted to that purpose; and the ignorant negro himself was puzzled to discover what had become of the resources which, at the outset of his political career, he had imagined to be unfailing.

The main villainies had been consummated at a time when the mass of the white natives who took part in the war were excluded from office, and when the negro vote was overwhelming. As soon as Governor Holden was impeached, the white population succeeded in gaining a fair share of influence again, and when he was removed they came into power, Governor Caldwell, Holden's successor, working pretty harmoniously with them. The political troubles may now be considered as nearly over, and if the industrial opportunities of the State are improved, there will be a return to some degree of prosperity. Many of the most influential citizens believe that an attitude of perfect frankness on the part of North Carolina toward its creditors will be the only thing that can save the State. They are anxious to see a compromise effected as speedily as possible, that both white and black may know just how they are situated, and may set their shoulders to the wheel in earnest.*

The State-House at Raleigh is delightfully situated in the midst of lovely foliage, and its massive granite columns and superb dome, modeled after the Parthenon, are very imposing. Raleigh once boasted an exquisite statue of Washington, from the master hand of Canova; but it was destroyed with the first State-House in the disastrous fire in 1831. The town, which was named for Sir Walter Raleigh, and was established as the seat of government in 1788, is built around a ten-acre lot called Union square, in the centre of which the State-House stands. It would not be an excess of generous remembrance on the part of the North Carolinians to erect in their capital a statue of the illustrious Essex, who did so much three hundred years ago to further the colonization of the region now within the State's limits. At Raleigh there is a large and well-filled Penitentiary, and the Deaf and Dumb and Lunatic Asylums are situated in the outskirts. The town has only 8,000 inhabitants, half of whom are negroes.

* This chapter was written in the summer of 1874.

Northward from Raleigh, toward Charlotte, lie many fertile counties, filled with the remnants of once famous plantations, and with small farms, even now prosperous. At Chapel Hill the State University, now much fallen into decay, is located; and at Hillsborough, one of the oldest towns in the State, the visitor is still shown the house once occupied by Lord Cornwallis, and is reminded that Governor Tryon had his home there; that there the provincial Congress and the Legislature of North Carolina first assembled, and there, too, many unhappy "Regulators" were executed.

The State certainly needs to make progress in education, for the illiteracy at present within its borders is shocking. One of the United States Senators gave it me his belief that there were as many as 350,000 persons in North Carolina who could neither read nor write. The State Superintendent of Instruction said that, late in 1873, there were only 150,000 out of the 350,000 pupil-children actually at school. The free school system, he thought, up to that date, could by no means be called a thorough success; coming, as it did, directly after the war, when people were striving to save money with which to replace their lost stock and farming implements, the dollar tax demanded for the schools was odious to the masses. Still, from $250,000 to $400,000 is annually collected for school purposes; while before the war there was no system worthy the name. The same provision is made for whites and blacks; there is not much desire on the part of ex-Confederates there to deprive the negro of the advantages of an education, as they now realize that it helps him to become a better laborer. There are 40,000 colored children now in the free schools of the State; 530 black teachers passed the Board of Examiners in 1873, and these teachers were paid $46,000 per year. There are several small colleges, each having five or six score students. Prominent among them are Trinity, at Hyde Point (Methodist), Davidson, at old Mecklenburg, where the State first publicly renounced her allegiance to the British crown (Presbyterian), and the Wake Forest (Baptist) College, near Raleigh.

The school law of the State requires that public free schools shall be maintained "four months every year in every school district in each county of the State in which the qualified voters shall vote to levy the additional school-tax for that purpose." This, of course, gives people an opportunity to reject the system entirely, but there are few counties so rude as to refuse all educational facilities, although nearly all the people in the back-country have a most unaccountable aversion to paying "school-taxes." If the Legislature would inaugurate a system which would bring the people up to its level, as was done in Virginia, a reform might be readily effected. Wilmington has at last made the free schools which have long existed in its midst city institutions, and it is hoped that this good example will be followed by a like movement in all the large towns. Raleigh, strange to say, is hindered from taxing itself to support a system of graded schools by the State law, which is very crotchety, and needs amendment. The Peabody fund distributes $12,000 to $13,000 annually in the State, supporting some two score thriving schools. At Newbern and Washington the citizens have shown considerable spirit in establishing free schools.

The capital receives 35,000 or 40,000 bales of cotton yearly, but the great bulk of the State's crop goes by rail to Wilmington. Edgecombe, Caswell, Rockingham, Stokes, and Warner are the great cotton counties, the former growing 18,361 bales in 1872. The cotton production of the State varies from 100,000 to 150,000 bales annually.

The range of climate covered by the State may be taught by the statement that buckwheat can be grown on the mountains in Ashe county, and oranges flourish in the soft, sweet air of Wilmington. There is a tropical luxuriance of flowers and trees in Wilmington, which is almost astonishing, for one sees all plants possible at Charleston or Savannah flourishing in the gardens of this more northern town. Wilmington lies on the banks of the Cape Fear river, and on the hills which extend backward from those banks. It is but twenty-eight miles from the mouth of the river, and was one of the havens most sought after by blockade-runners during our civil war. At the mouth of the river stand Forts Fisher and Caswell, the former one of the strongest forts on the Atlantic coast, as it proved itself in the terrible days of 1865, when Porter and Terry knocked at its doors and finally burst them open.

Wilmington has important railway connections, notably the Wilmington, Rutherford, and Charlotte road, which will give the port direct communication with Tennessee, Kentucky, Ohio, and Illinois, and will immensely increase her trade. All the counties through which the road, when completed, will pass, are rich in mineral and agricultural resources. The other routes leading to Charleston and Richmond also command a considerable trade.

The Cape Fear river, at Wilmington, is a wide and noble stream, and the scene along its banks, in the brilliant sunshine of the autumn morning when I saw it, was inspiring. Cheerful gangs of negroes were rowing huge scows from side to side of the stream, standing upright and steering by means of long poles or sweeps; one might have fancied them a species of African gondoliers. Swedish ships were loading with naval stores; huge piles of lumber, and heaps and long rows of barrels of turpentine, and pitch and rosin, were ranged on the wharves. There were great numbers of negroes who looked idle, although many were employed. Some were fishing, others slept in corners; one or two groups seemed discussing politics, and in the centre of a crowd of jet black men I heard the following question and answer, isolated fragments of a deep religious discussion:

"Wha's de reason dar's so many degrees (sects) o' Baptis' now, when dar wa'n't on'y one John de Baptis', hey?"

"Lor, nigger, we ain't 'sponsible fur dat; dat a'nt got nuffin to do wid godliness!"

Front street is a fine avenue, lined with many elegant blocks devoted to business. Market street is a broad, central promenade, crowded with the omnipresent negroes, who chatter and "discuss" all day long. The blacks seem to fancy that labor is incompatible with the enjoyment of a city life.

In that portion of the town devoted to the residences, churches, and public buildings, perfect tranquillity prevails. Nowhere is there hum of wheels, clatter of teams, or braying of whistles. On Third and Fifth streets there are many elegant mansions, and gardens filled with rarest tropical and costly plants. The City and Thalian halls, the jail, and one or two of the churches are quite imposing, but the city is not rich in architecture. The cemeteries are pretty sylvan retreats, and the sleepy moss-grown suburb of "Hilton" is a favorite resort for excursions.

Commercially, Wilmington has every reason to hope for great development. The principal articles of export are spirits of turpentine in barrels, crude turpentine, rosin, tar, pitch, cotton, peanuts, and lumber in all shapes.* The foreign trade is mainly with Liverpool, Queenstown, Antwerp, Belfast, London, Cardenas, Rotterdam, Havana, Bristol, Hamburg, Cape Haytien, Demerara, Jamaica, Nassau and Hayti. The steamship lines running to Philadelphia, Baltimore and New York, have an aggregate tonnage of 40,000 tons monthly. In 1872, 22,000,000 feet of lumber were shipped from the port. After the war, the exports of spirits of turpentine and rosin were encouraging until 1870; since then their development has not been so great, but the constant growth of the cotton trade makes amends for their failure. The fine regions extending along the road to Weldon, and on both sides of the Wilmington, Columbia and Augusta railroad, as well as on the new Rutherford route, are very rich in turpentine and timber. The section traversed by the two Cape Fears and the

* Comparative statement of exports, coastwise and foreign, from Wilmington, North Carolina, from January 1, 1860, to December 31, 1870:

Articles.	Coastwise. 1860.	Coastwise. 1870.	Foreign. 1860.	Foreign. 1870.
Spirits Turpentine, bbls..	127,562	68,966	20,400	32,889
Crude Turpentine, bbls..	52,175	12,929	23,548	3,258
Rosin, bbls............	440,132	483,546	57,425	26,127
Tar, bbls..............	43,056	54,090	6,120	6,107
Pitch, bbls............	5,489	4,624	784	190
Cotton, bales.........	22,851	51,617	....	20
Cotton Yarn, bales....	1,561	72	....	....
Cotton Sheeting, bales..	1,750	547	....	....
Peanuts, bushels.......	99,743	124,296	....	....
Lumber, P. P., feet....	9,126,176	11,515,123	9,882,078	8,378,861
Timber, P. P., feet....	22,600	290,789	20,000	85,400
Shingles.............	730,880	4,804,890	2,887,870	2,339,334
Staves, Cypress.......	....	482,253	....	....
Staves, Oak..........	94,723	....	10,000	....

It will be seen by the above that the export of naval stores, both coastwise and foreign, except in one instance, has fallen off greatly during the past decade, while, on the contrary, there has been a heavy increase, say about 120 per cent., in the shipments of cotton. This is due, mainly, to the fact that latterly, and in the country supplying the city, every interest was made subservient to the culture of cotton. Even the production of turpentine was of secondary importance compared with the zeal with which cotton was planted, so that Wilmington, the greatest naval store depot in the world, only exported coastwise one and one-third barrels of spirits turpentine to the bale of cotton; that is to say, the number of bales of cotton exported was seventy-five per cent. of the number of barrels of spirits turpentine.

South and Black rivers are, perhaps, richer in turpentine stores than any other in the world. A new railway line on the lowlands of the coast, and terminating at Wilmington, is contemplated.

The little city has a valuation of only $7,000,000, a debt of $600,000, an excellent city government, and many enterprising merchants. There is still some bitterness among those of the aristocrats who were ruined by the war, but it is rapidly mellowing into a regret which has but little of unkindly feeling toward the North mingled in it. A determination on their part to make Wilmington all that it has opportunities to be, would soon increase its population from 14,000 to many times that number.

Fayetteville and Charlotte are the sites of prosperous cotton factories. The water power of the former place has never been utilized; and it is astonishing that it is not taken advantage of. Fayetteville is connected by rail with the mining region in Chatham and Moore counties, and is on the line of one of the important routes to the South, *via* Columbia and Augusta. Charlotte bids fair to become a prominent centre for manufacturing interests, on account of its railroad facilities and fine water power. Its historic importance, as the place where the first American Declaration of Independence was made in 1775, by the patriots of Mecklenburg county, assembled in convention, cannot be denied. The British troops occupied Charlotte in 1780; and there it was that General Greene took command of the Southern army, after the departure of Cornwallis. The United States Government has an assay office at Charlotte, and gold mining is from time to time carried on in the adjacent counties. The town also boasts a military institute, and a prosperous seminary for young ladies.

A Wayside Sketch.

LIV.

AMONG THE SOUTHERN MOUNTAINS—JOURNEY FROM EASTERN TENNESSEE TO WESTERN NORTH CAROLINA.

"YOU ain't a show, be ye?" said the small boy.

The question was pardonable; the travelers alighting, that rainy June evening, from their weary and mud-bespattered horses at the door of a little tavern in a Tennessee mountain town, and proceeding to unload their baggage-wagon, certainly presented a singular spectacle. Such mysterious array of traps the small boy's round, wondering eyes had never seen before. He controlled his curiosity until a tin case containing artists' materials was produced, when he gave a prolonged whistle, and forthwith proceeded to inquire our qualities. Visions of magic lanterns and traveling mountebanks danced before his eyes; his heated imagination hinted at even the possibility of play-actors.

Two days of swift railway travel had brought me from St. Louis to join a merry party of excursionists through the noblest mountain ranges of the South. We had come from Morristown, in Eastern Tennessee, and at the end of our first day's journey on horseback, crawled, drenched and fatigued, into a hamlet for shelter. Let me show you the party as it then appeared.

First alighted the Colonel, coming down with a solid thump in the sticky mud, and unbuckling from his saddle capacious bags and rolls of blankets;

"The Small Boy."

then taking from the wagon certain mysterious packages, he propounded the inquiry which is of such thrilling interest to mountain travelers after nightfall:

"Can we get to stay here to-night?"

"Reckon we can accommodate ye."

Next descended the Judge, his long, gray beard and Arabian mustache streaming with rain, his garments bedraggled, and his eyes dim with the sky-spray. He, likewise going to the wagon, took from it seductive valises, boxes which gave forth a cheering rattle of apparatus, and cans of various patterns, and hastened to shelter. A new accession of small boys silently viewed these proceedings with awe.

But ah! the next figure which galloped lustily to the door, mounted on a prancing, delicate Kentucky mare! How did the juvenile by-standers gape at that short, alert youth, with spectacles on nose, and riding-whip swung cavalierly in hand; with white Marseilles trowsers mottled and drenched with mud and water; with jaunty gray hat, flabby and drooping; with overcoat tied about his neck, and a collection of minerals knotted in his handkerchief at his saddle-bow. He was no common traveler. It must—it must be a show!

Or he with camp stool and dripping umbrella slung on his shoulders, with broad slouch hat crushed down over his eyes, and a variegated panorama of the road along which he had passed painted by the weather upon his back—the artist, whose hands were filled with the mystic tin box; behold him! the envied cynosure of boyish eyes.

Then the writer,—clambering down from his horse's smoking sides, and hastening to join the others before the crackling and leaping flame in an old-fashioned fire-place, overhearing as he entered, however, a new come boy's wild guess:

"If 't ain't a show, it 's 'rock-hunters,' *I* reckon."

What mattered rain and mud, the ferrying of swollen streams, the breaking down of wagons, and the weary climbing of hills? The prospect before us was none the less inspiring. We were about to enter upon that vast elevated region which forms the southern division of the Appalachian mountain system, and constitutes the culminating point in the Atlantic barrier of the American continent. We stood at the gate of the lands through which runs the chain of the Iron, Smoky, and Unaka mountains, separating North Carolina from Eastern Tennessee.

Beyond the blue line of hills faintly discerned in the rainy twilight from the windows of our little room lay the grand table-land, 2,000 feet above the heated air of cities and the contagion of civilization; and there a score of mountain peaks reached up 6,000 feet into the crystal atmosphere; torrents ran impetuously down their steep sides into noble valleys; there was the solitude of the cañon, the charm of the dizzy climb along the precipice-brink, the shade of the forests where no woodman's axe had yet profaned the thickets. It was a region compared to which the White mountains seemed dwarfed and insignificant, for through an extent of more than 150 miles, height after height towered in solemn magnificence, and the very valleys were higher up than the gaps in the White mountain range! Through the thick rain-veil, during our first day's wandering, we had seen the noble outlines of English mountain, and the distant and rugged sides of the Smoky; had passed over hill-sides covered with corn, where the white tree-trunks in the "deadenings" stood like spectres protesting against sacrilege; along banks of streams overhung with dense and richly-colored foliage, and past log farm-houses, where tall, gaunt farmers, clad in homespun, were patiently waiting for the rain to cease—until we came to the "Mouth of

Chucky," as the ford just above the junction of the Nolichucky and French Broad rivers is called.

Time was when all the country bordering the rivers at their junction was romantic ground. The "great Indian war trail," upon which so many scenes of violence and murder were enacted, ran not far from the banks of the Nolichucky, and the war-ford "upon the French Broad" was but a short distance from Clifton, where we had halted for the night. From the time of the settlement along the banks of the two rivers, one hundred years ago, until early in the present century, the settler took his life in his hands daily, and the war-cry of the Indian was a familiar sound to his ears.

The Nolichucky, at the ford, ran rapidly between great mountain banks, whose sides were so steep as to be inaccessible on foot, and just below gave itself to the racing and roaring rapids of the "French Broad," which seemed angry at being pent up among the cliffs. A long halloo brought the ferryman with his flat-boat from the opposite bank; the clumsy ark drifting us safely over to the stretch of winding road which finally led us through a still old town, hidden and moldering at the base of a hill, whence we followed along picturesque paths until we reached the placid Pigeon river, with the mountains near it mirrored in its bosom, and, crossing it, dismounted at Clifton, to be confronted by the small boy with the abnormal appetite for "shows."

The rain ceased when we were safely housed; and having placed our drenched garments by the fire to dry, we waited for the supper of bacon and biscuits, flanked by molasses-syrup and the blackest of coffee, meanwhile catching a glimpse of the prosperous little town set down in a nook in the mountains, with a single railroad line, running directly through the main street, giving it a hold on the outer world. The river was fringed with trees and overhanging vines and creepers; in every direction was the blue stretch of far-away hills, or the shadow of luxuriant woods. Our lullaby that night was the murmur of the river and the cry of the whip-poor-will. Before dawn we were astir, and while the dwellers in cities were still asleep our little cavalcade was vigorously *en route* for the North Carolina line.

"The Judge." [Page 473.]

Ahead, caracoling merrily from side to side of the highway on his coquettishly-pacing mare "Cricket," whose very motions were poetry, rode Jonas of the blond locks, our German companion, in his saddle graceful as a Centaur, in his motions alert as a cat, for he had ridden to many a battle in the cavalry of Prussian William's victorious army. There was a dash of the trooper in him still—the erect military port, the joyous outburst into song, now roystering, now tender; the enviable familiarity with all the secrets of road and woodland life, and a calm, æsthetic sense, never disturbed by weather or the rude inconvenience of travel.

Our route that morning lay through the forest, along unused road-ways; and, constantly ascending, we caught from time to time exquisite views of the summits of English, the Smoky, and other mountains. Great mists were moving lightly away; now and then some monarch of the ranges had his lofty brow wrapped in the delicate embrace of white clouds, which spread into fantastic shapes of smoke-wreaths and castles and towers, sometimes even seeming to take the contour of the mountains themselves.

Now we came to a log-house, with sloping roof, set on some shelf of a hill-side, whence one could look down into deep valleys, and around whose doors sheep and goats were huddled, lying in the shelter of the fences until the sun came out. A shepherd dog would bark at us; a tall maiden, clad in the blue or greenish homespun of the region, would tell us which road to take, and how to turn and "foller the creek," and so we wandered on. Sometimes the hill-sides were so steep that we preferred to dismount and lead our horses rather than take the risk of being pitched over their heads. Rapid little streams here and there foamed across the roadways, and hid themselves in the forests.

Beneath a great oak, or wide-spreading willow, we found a cool spring with a gourd upon a board above it, and travelers halting for shade and rest, with whom our party would exchange courtesies and interrogatories. Still we went on climbing up and up—nearer to some of the peaks, and within view of the clearings upon their sides, and the bald patches where the rocks stood out in the light.

By and by, at a lonely log-house, on a beautiful mountain side, whence one could see the hills craning their long necks in every direction, we halted for dinner; but before we had hitched our horses there came a sudden blinding storm of wind and rain, in the midst of which we hurriedly gave the animals over to our impervious mulatto wagon-driver, and with the lunch baskets beat a retreat for the cabin porch.

The typical Tennessee woman of the mountains, tall and thin, but kind and graceful, the mother of ten children, who stood ranged around her in inquiring attitude, welcomed us, and a loaf of hot corn-bread soon smoked upon the table. Very humble and simple were the appointments of this cabin home. The bare floor, however, was extremely clean; the spinning-wheel, with the flax hanging to it, stood in a corner of the porch; in the great kitchen in the rear of the cabin was a fire-place, in the ashes of which another corn-cake was baking, and the good woman offered us wild honey, buttermilk, and the berries of the mountains.

"No man-folks nigh home now," she said. "Air you rock-huntin'?"

Assuring her that we were not looking for minerals, she questioned us no farther, and seemed to be puzzled when the Colonel hinted that we were in "search of information."

Once more the rain-cloud lifted and the skies were clear. Andy hitched up, singing a cheerful melody, and we rode on; now through gaps in the chain of hills where level fields were in cultivation, and where the women were at work side by side with the men hoeing corn; now by the banks of some creek which rippled merrily over a pebbly bottom, and was overhung by short, densely-set willows; until, at last, we came into a valley where there were a few scattered frame houses and a little mill, around which were gathered some twenty mountaineers. Here our over-loaded wagon suddenly broke down directly opposite a cabin, in which, through the interstices, we could see anvil, bellows, and other appurtenances of the blacksmith's trade.

The afternoon was waning, and the punctual Judge had planned that we should spend that night in North Carolina. But before us lay a tremendous height, whose rugged sides seemed interminable. Riding on in haste to find the blacksmith, we were suddenly surrounded by a threatening mob of half-drunken mountain men clad in rude garb, some mounted, some on foot, but not one of them with a friendly look. Our inquiry for help, as Jonas and the writer backed their horses rapidly, was met with an oath, and a peremptory demand why we were "racketing about the country."

This not being answered in the most satisfactory manner, demonstrations of violence were made, and it dawned upon the advance guard of the wagon that perhaps a retreat would be prudent. There were bad and drunken faces among the rough men; two or three hands were clutching stones plucked from the wet roads, while the circle gradually narrowed in toward us. So galloping back, we reported "breakers ahead." Patching up the wagon we all moved forward together; but upon our approach to the mill the threatening attitude of the mountaineers was resumed, the motley crowd falling in behind when we had passed, and seeming to await some signal. Presently the Colonel and the Judge were assailed with questions like this from the pursuing group: "Reckon ye don't want to steal nothin', do ye?" This being succeeded by more pointed remarks.

At last hostilities became so imminent that we were forced to stop and explain. Gathering around the wagon, we answered the inquiries, "Whar be ye from?" "What do ye want yer?" "What mout your name be?" etc., and by much parleying demonstrated that we meant no harm. Finally man by man dropped off, but, much to our discomfort, two or three of the more drunk and uproarious followed us toward the ford at the base of the mountain in a manner which plainly indicated attack.

We were now entering upon a wild and lonely by-road, and even the heretofore incredulous of our party had suspicions of mischief afoot. The ascent, wooded and sombre, was before us.

At this juncture another man approached, and said he would walk with us to the mountain top. He was sober, and, producing from his pocket a flask of "moonshine" whiskey, invited us to drink. The secret was out. We had evidently been mistaken for a party of revenue officers, on a mission to seize some of the concealed stills in the gorges and caves of this wild region.

We drank of the blistering fluid, and presently, to our great relief, the drunken horsemen behind reluctantly retired. After consulting vaguely together for a little time in the road, they disappeared, our companion assuring us that they would do us no harm. "But ye can't always tell," he added. "A man wants to keep his eye out in these regions when the boys 've ben drinkin'."

The ascent of the Chestnut mountain now became tedious and painful. The road ran zigzag along the edges of banks and rocks, and over our heads hung mammoth embankments, which might have crushed a caravan. But how delicious the sunlight on the tree-stems, through the forest glades; how delicate the green mosses clothing the trunks of fallen monarchs; how crystal and sweet the water which we drank from the foamy brooks!

For miles we clambered along this lofty road until night was at hand. Our companion, who paused from time to time to treat himself from the bottle, and to importune us to drink, finally left us at a cross-road, advising us to stay at Parson Caton's. We could get to stay with the parson—he kept folks; would we have some more "moonshine?" No? Good luck to us. So we hurried on to Parson Caton's.

A by-road, leading into a thicket where wild vines grew luxuriantly; steep descents and lofty knolls, crowned with strong tree-stems; a woodland path; then a clearing, and we were at the humble cabin of the parson.

The Judge shows the Artist's Sketch-Book.

LV.

ACROSS THE "SMOKY" TO WAYNESVILLE—THE MASTER CHAIN OF THE ALLEGHANIES.

ON our way up the mountain we had passed "the church." It was a rude structure of boards and logs, which we should have mistaken for some deserted shanty, had not our friend of the "moonshine" whiskey pointed it out.

The parson's cabin stood in an enclosure, guarded by a rough fence, and, as we approached, a stalwart young fellow opened the little gate, and some hounds followed him out, making the woods ring with their yelping. A tall matron and two of "the girls"—young women, at least five and a-half feet high, dressed in straight, homespun gowns—peered out at us, and we were presently invited to remain at the cabin all night, as "the parson never refuses nobody."

The pigs and the geese had just come home together from their day's ramble in the woods, and were quarreling over the trough which ran along the fence. The cows wandered about the clearing, watched by the hounds; and the "boys" busied themselves in hewing logs of wood into sticks for the fire. Behind the cabin rose a rib of the mountain, on which was a corn-field, and near this ran a brook.

The whole cabin did not seem large enough to house a family of four; yet Parson Caton's stalwart brood of ten children lived there happily with himself and wife, and found the shelter ample. There were but two rooms on the lower floor, each lighted by the doors only; above was a loft, in which were laid truckle-beds. Supper was speedily cooking on the coals in the fire-place; the scent of bacon was omnipresent. In the smaller of the two rooms there were four large beds, covered with gay quilts, and shoved closely together. Around the room hung collections of herbs and several rifles; for furniture there were a few rude chairs, and a small table, on which were some antiquated books.

As we returned from a wash at the brook the parson came home, and was greeted with a cheery welcome from the hounds. Every inch of his face was filled with rugged lines, which told of strong character. He stood leaning on his staff and looking us over intently for some moments before he said, "Good evening, men." Then he greeted us heartily, and our invalid wagon was forthwith dispatched to the rustic forge near the cabin for repairs. There Andy held a pine knot, while the parson's son, a stout smith, worked.

This old man, in his mountain home, was as simple and courteous in his demeanor as any citizen. After the frugal supper was over, he asked us many questions of the outer world, which he had never visited; New York and Louisville seemed to him like dreams. By and by the family came crowding in to evening prayers. It was quite dark, and the forest around us was still.

The parson took down a well-worn Bible, and opening it at the Psalms, read, in a loud voice, and with occasional quaint expoundings, one or two selections; after which, taking up a hymn-book, he read a hymn, and the family sang line by line as he gave them out. They sung in quavering, high-pitched voices, to the same tunes which were heard in the Tennessee mountains when Nolichucky was an infant settlement, and the banks of the French Broad were crimsoned with the blood of white settlers, shed by the Indians.

The echoes of the hymn died away into the depths of the forest, and were succeeded by a prayer of earnestness and fervor, marked here and there by strong phrases of dialect, but one which made our little company bow their heads, for the parson prayed for us and for our journey, and brought the prayer home

"The family sang line by line."

to us. Another hymn was lined, during which the hounds now and then joined in with their musical howls, and at last the family withdrew, leaving us in the spare-room. Presently, however, the parson reappeared, and announced that he and his wife would share the room with us, which they did; and we were wakened to the six o'clock breakfast by the good woman, who joined with her husband in reproving us for continuing our journey on the Sabbath day.

As we started once more, the wagon, carefully mended overnight, broke down again! So then the parson stripped a hickory bough with his own hands, and bound together the pieces. A mile farther on, coming to another forge, we halted until a second smith tried his hand at a permanent mending, although he said he "mout get fined by the authorities for working on a Sunday." The

Judge amused the smith's children with the artist's sketch-book, while the hammer rang on the anvil.

The country here and henceforward was of the wildest and most romantic character. The mountaineers, scattered sparsely along the ridges, cultivated the land in corn, of which there were huge fields visible in the clearings, but sent nothing to market in winter, and, while the crops were growing, were idle. The houses were almost invariably of logs. Often, as in Switzerland, looking down a high bank, we could see the tree-tops in a long valley below us, and the cabin of some farmer, with his cob-house granary and little cattle-pen nestling by a creek. Here, by the hard, firm roadways, the mountain laurel, the ginseng and the gentian abounded, and pines and spruces, poplars, hickories, walnuts, oaks, and ash grew in the valleys and along the banks.

A Mountain Farmer.

We were now climbing over the hills of the Great Smoky range, making our way toward the elevated gap, through which we were to enter North Carolina. Every turn in the angular highway brought a new vista of mountains, blue and infinite, behind us; now in serrated ranks, receding into distance; now seeming to close up near at hand, and shut out the world from us. The rare atmosphere of these high regions gave new zest to the journey, and we hardly knew that evening was at hand when we reached the State line and began to descend into the valley to "Hopkins's," the first station in North Carolina.

In this remote and mountain-guarded dell,—this cup hollowed out of the Great Smoky range, visited only by the post-rider once a week, and the few farmers who go to the far towns of Eastern Tennessee to market,—we found the mountaineer in his native purity. No contact with even the people of the lowlands of his own State had given him familiarity with the world.

The people whom we passed as we rode on to Hopkins's, traveling along the roads out of Tennessee into North Carolina, were tall and robust; their language was peculiar, and their manners, although courteous, were awkward and rough. The gaunt, yellow-haired women were smoking, and trudged along contentedly beside the men, saying but little. They were neatly dressed in home-made clothes, and their hair was combed straight down over their cheeks and knotted into "pugs" behind. There were none of the modern conventionalities of dress visible about them. The men were cavalier enough; their jean trowsers were thrust into their boots, and their slouch hats cocked on their heads with bravado air. The hills rose high up around the humble log-dwelling of Hopkins, and a little road ran beside a roaring torrent which came down from the mountain through a delicious valley, making charming nooks and niches among the round polished stones.

Once a prosperous farmer, the war had left the venerable mountaineer only the wrecks of his home. Both parties had guerrillaed through the gorges and gaps; one "army" burned Hopkins's cabin, and the other stole his produce. High on the hill-sides grew the native grape; a little cultivation would have turned the whole valley-cup into a fruitful vineyard; but Hopkins said it was too late for him to try. It was, too, an excellent sheep-grazing country; the wolves sometimes made cruel havoc, but shepherd-dogs could easily keep them off. Along the slopes of the Smoky beyond his home grew the finest of building timber, and water power was abundant; yet there were no frame houses for miles around.

"Wal, you uns don't understand, I reckon," said Hopkins. "I hain't had a mighty sight o' git up since the war."

Supper was served in the kitchen by one of the tall females we had observed upon the road, who was Hopkins's housekeeper, and who laid aside her pipe to come to the table and wait upon the strangers, whom, she said, she did not understand, "for you uns don't talk like we uns;" adding that she "reckoned we found this a mighty fine country."

Half a day's journey from this nook in the mountains brought us to the gap near Mount Starling, where we crossed through the Smoky range, and began to descend on the other side into Haywood county, a division of North Carolina, extending over 750 square miles, and annually producing more than 200,000 bushels of corn. The chain of the Smoky mountain which we had traversed extends for about sixty-five miles, from the deep gorge through which the French Broad river flows at "Paint Rock" to the outlet of the Little Tennessee; and Professor Guyot, who is authority upon the Appalachian system, calls it the master chain of the whole Alleghany region.

The dominant peaks in this line of mountains north of Road Gap are Mount Guyot, 6,636 feet high; Mounts Alexander, Henry, South, and Laurel Peaks, the True Brother, Thunder, Thermometer, Raven's, and Tricolor Knobs, and the Pillar Head of the straight fork of the Oconaluftee river. South of Road Gap rise the peaks known as "Clingman's Dome," 6,660 feet high; Mounts Buckley, Love, Collins, and a dozen others, more than 5,000 feet high.

Each of these rises to 6,000 feet elevation above mean-tide water, and many of them overtop Mount Washington, the monarch of the East, by several hundred feet. Seen from a distance, these mount-

"We caught a glimpse of the symmetrical Catalouche mountain." [Page 484.]

ains seem always bathed in a mellow haze, like that distinguishing the atmosphere of Indian summer. The gap through which we passed was at an elevation of at least 5,000 feet; beneath us were vast cañons, from which came up the roar of the creeks.

We looked down upon the tops of mighty forests, and now and then, descending, caught a glimpse of the symmetrical Catalouche mountain, fading away into distant blue. There are no gaps in the Smoky range which fall below the level of 5,000 feet, until Forney Ridge is passed; and there is a surprising number of peaks and domes rising higher than 6,000 feet.

The Cañon of the Catalouche as seen from "Bennett's." [Page 485.]

Once having traversed the barriers created by this vast upheaval, one enters the mountainous region comprised between the Blue Ridge and the chain of the Iron, Smoky, and Unaka peaks. This region properly begins at the bifurcation of the two chains in Virginia, and extends across North Carolina and into Georgia for 108 miles. The chain of the Blue Ridge to the eastward is fragmentary, and the gaps are only from 2,000 to 3,000 feet high. All the interior region between the Blue Ridge and the Smoky is filled with spurs and chains, of which, perhaps, the most noticeable is the great Balsam, whose highest point, called the Richland Balsam, or Caney Creek Balsam Divide, reaches the height of 6,425 feet. Into this cluster of highlands, extending to the extreme western boundary of North Carolina, we now daily made our way.

This day's journey was but a succession of grand panoramic views of gorge and height. Descending, we rode for several miles along a path cut out of the mountain's steep side; and hundreds of feet below us saw the tops of tall pines and spruces. Not a human habitation was to be seen; there was no sign of life save when a ruffled grouse or a rabbit sprang across the track.

Now we came into a valley, through which a wide creek flowed rapidly, finding its outlet between two hills towering thousands of feet above us, and there, at a rude cabin, stopped to feed our weary horses, and to partake of the milk, the honey, and the corn-bread set before us; to lie on the turf beside the cool stream, and to drink in at every pore the delicious inspiration of the pure mountain air. Remounting, we climbed along the side of shaggy "Catalouche," until, late in the afternoon, we came to "Bennett's."

Imagine a little frame house set on a shelf on the road, so that its inmates can look for miles down a deep straight valley, through which flows a river between banks fringed with dense foliage, and by rocks over which pines lean and straggle in wildest confusion. At the far end of this river valley looms up a tall mountain peak, so beautiful that one's soul is lifted at very sight of it. As our little company drew rein at the edge of the steep bank leading to the cañon, there was a universal cry of delight. Bennett's folks called to us at that moment, "Won't you 'light,' strangers, 'n come in?" We sat long in the little porch, gazing at Oconoluftee's height, and the Balsam mountains, dimly shadowed beyond the point where the valley was lost in the breast of the hills. The grandeur of the sentinel mountain, standing alone at the end of the chasm; the reflections of high rocks and mighty tree-trunks in the far-away stream; the dizzy precipices which overhung the rarely frequented valley, lent a charm which carried its terror with it.

The road grew narrower and rockier as we clambered along Catalouche; but the air was cooler, purer, the laurels more abundant, the vistas more charming; until just at sunset we came to the "Cove Creek Gap." In front lay a narrow valley, over which the mountain known as Jonathan's Bald threw his shadow; but beyond!—

High on the horizon lay a wavy line of hills, sharply outlined in the strong glare of the sunset, their delicate blue colors springing so suddenly upon our vision against the purple and crimson of the evening tints that we were surprised and delighted. As far as eye could reach, to right, to left, in front, stood the long line of uplifted crags, from which there seemed no outlet! Turning our horses on the crest of the mountain, and looking Tennesseeward, we saw our old friends of the Great Smoky, scattered for miles in friendly groups among the dark forests; westward and eastward deep ravines, and, beyond them, uncounted peaks, which the very sky seemed tenderly to bend over and kiss.

It was fast growing dark as we rode on to the winding road in the valley of Jonathan's creek. As we were rattling by a log farm-house in a deadening, a loud voice cried:

"Strangers, wait a minnit till I ketch my ole mule, or he'll foller you uns clean down to Boyd's, I reckon."

The owner of the voice, carrying a log on his shoulder, came up through the fields as he said this, and, throwing down his burden, secured the restive mule, who was looking over the low fence; after which he turned to each one of the party, and asked:

"What mout be your name?"

Having satisfied his curiosity thus, he gave us good evening civilly enough, and struggled with his log again.

Farther on a young farmer crossing the creek came to us as we inquired the distance, and, before giving us the desired information, said, "What mout be your names?" "Whar are ye from?" After which he added carelessly, "Mile 'n half; good evenin'."

Mount Pisgah, Western North Carolina. [Page 487.]

Troops of children played about the doors of all the cabins along these roads. Families of ten and twelve are by no means uncommon. Girls and boys work afield with their parents in the summer, and pass the winter with but limited chances for culture.

Passing around the base of "Jonathan's Creek Bald," we came into a more open and fertile country, where the farm-houses were neatly built and painted, and the wheat-fields were wide and well stocked. The creeks were numerous, and everywhere bordered by fascinating foliage; at each turn in the road there was a picture; one was constantly reminded of the rich views in the Loire country in France, or of the fat fields of Alsatia.

On the plain of Waynesville, 2,756 feet above the level of tide-water, and in the shadow of the great Balsam range, stands Waynesville town. The approaches to it are lovely, but the view from the town itself is lovelier still. On all sides rise the mountains; the village nestles between the forks of the Pigeon river, nowhere more beautiful than within a few miles of this nook.

To the westward lie the Balsam peaks, seven of which, Amos Plott's, the "Great Divide," Brother Plott, Rocky Face, Rockstand Knob, and the two Junaleskas, tower more than 6,000 feet high. They are clad, upon their summits, in the sombre garb of the balsam, the sad and haughty monarch of the heights, whose odorous boughs brush against the clouds, and whose deep thickets, into which the sun himself can hardly penetrate, afford a refuge for the wolf and the bear. The balsam is emphatically an aristocratic tree; it is never found in the humble valleys, and rarely lower than an elevation of 4,000 feet; it consorts with the proud rhododendron, whose scarlet bloom was the object of the Indian's most passionate adoration, and its grand stem springs from among the decaying and moss-grown rocks.

On these Balsams, as on the great Black mountains, the moss offers an elastic carpet sometimes a foot thick, and is tough and hard as the hides of the bears who delight to disport upon it. Here and there on the sides of the Plott peaks there is a long furrow which marks the path cut by some adventurous woodsman. The peaks are not romantically named; the unimaginative early settlers called them after the men who owned or lived near them; and many of the most imposing heights are still nameless.

The Bald mountains,—so called because their summits are destitute of forest, and because the sun makes the rocks on their tops glisten like a bald man's shining poll,—are numerous in the vicinity of Waynesville. North and north-east of the town lie the "Crab Tree" and "Sandy Mush" Balds, and beyond them in the same direction rises "Bear Wallow" mountain. On the south and south-east are "Mount Pisgah," the "High Tower," and Cold mountain, which rises 6,063 feet out of the "Big Pigeon" valley; and away to the south and south-east stretches the chain of the "Richland Balsam."

The dry and pure air of Waynesville gives new value to life; the healthy man feels a strange glow and inspiration while in the shadow of these giant peaks. The town is composed of one long street of wooden houses, wandering from mountain base to mountain base. It has a trio of country stores; a cozy and delightful little hotel, nestling under the shade of a huge tree; an old wooden church perched on a hill, with a cemetery filled with ancient tombs, where the early settlers lie at rest, and an academy.

There is no whir of wheels. The only manufacturing establishments are flour-mills located on the various creeks and rivers, or a stray saw-mill; while here and there a wealthy land owner is building an elegant home with all the modern improvements. By nine o'clock at night there is hardly a light in the village; a few belated horsemen steal noiselessly through the street, or the faint tinkle of a banjo

The Carpenter—A Study from Waynesville Life.

and the patter of a negro's feet testify to an innocent merry-making. The Court-House of Haywood county, and the Jail, both modest two-story brick structures, are the public buildings, the Jail having only now and then an inmate, for the county is as orderly as a community of Quakers. The Marshal, as in most of these small Western North Carolina towns, is the power which maintains and enforces the law. No liquor is sold within a mile of the town's boundary; some lonely and disreputable shanty, with the words "BAR-ROOM" inscribed upon it, on a clearing along the highway, being the only resort for those who drink "spirits." The sheriff, the local clergyman, the county surveyor, and the village doctor, ride about the country on their nags, gossiping and dreamily enjoying the glorious air; nowhere is there bustle or noise of trade. The county court's session is the event of the year; the mail, brought forty-five miles over the mountain roads from the nearest railroad, is light, and the stage-coaches bring few passengers from the outer world.

But what a perfect summer retreat; what chances for complete rest; what grandeur of mountains; what quiet rippling of gentle rivers; what noble sunsets; what wealth of color and dreaminess of twilight; what breezy morn-

View on Pigeon River, near Waynesville.

ings, when the mists fly away from the deep ravines in the mountain chains, and shadow and sun play hide and seek on the dense masses of the Balsam tops!

The great counties of Haywood, Jackson, Macon, Cherokee, Buncombe, Henderson, Madison and Yancey, contain the principal portion of the mountain scenery of western North Carolina. The mighty transverse chains of the Nantahela, Cowee, Balsam and Black mountains, run across these counties from the Smoky range to the Blue Ridge, and the traveler wandering from county seat to county seat must constantly climb lofty heights, pass through rugged gaps, and descend into deep valleys.

Western North Carolina is not only exceedingly fertile, but abounds in the richer minerals, and needs but the magic wand of the capitalist waved over it to become one of the richest sections of this Union. Occupying one-third of the entire area of the State, and possessing more than a quarter of a million of inhabitants, its present prospects are by no means disagreeable; but its prominent citizens, of all walks in life, are anxious for immigration and development of the rich stores of gold, iron, copper, mica, and other minerals now buried in the hills.

Let no one fancy that this mountain region is undesirable as an agricultural country; there are few richer, or better adapted to European immigration. The staple productions of Haywood county are corn, wheat, rye, oats and hay; all vegetables grow abundantly, and the whole county is admirably fitted for grazing. The level bottom-lands on Pigeon river and its numerous tributaries are under fine cultivation; the uplands and the slopes produce rich wheat; the ash, the sugar maple, the hickory, and the oak, are abundant; and white pine is rafted down the Pigeon river in large quantities yearly.

But the exceptional fertility of most of the ranges throughout all the counties mentioned is the great pride of the section. The sides and tops of the mountains are, in many cases, covered with a thick, vegetable mould,* in which grow flourishing trees and rank grasses. Five thousand feet above the sea-level one finds grasses and weeds that remind him of the lower region swamps. Cattle are kept in excellent condition all winter on the "evergreen" growing along the sides of the higher chains. Winter and summer, before the ravages of the war thinned out their stocks, the farmers kept hundreds of cattle on the mountains, feeding entirely on the grasses. In the spring the herds instinctively seek the young grasses springing up on the slopes, but with the coming of winter they return to the tops to find the evergreen. The balsam-tree can easily be banished, for, after being felled for a few months, it will burn easily, and in its stead will spring up thick coats of evergreen. On some of the mountain farms corn yields one hundred bushels to the acre, and wheat, oats, rye and barley, flourish proportionately. In the "deadenings," where the large timber has been girdled and left to die, and the undergrowth has been carefully cleared, timothy and orchard grass will grow as high as wheat.

The native grape, too, flourishes on all the hill-sides, within certain thermal lines established by observation of the elder mountaineers; and varieties of grapes can be selected, and so planted as to ripen at different periods of the autumn. The negro population is not numerous in Western North Carolina. Wherever the black man is found, however, he is industrious, faithful, and usually quite prosperous. In some of the small tows, as at Waynesville, we found a gentleman's valet of other days officiating as village tailor, barber, errand boy, coachman and "factotum."

* Testimony of Professor Richard Owen, of the Indiana State University.

LVI.

THE "SUGAR FORK" AND DRY FALLS—WHITESIDE MOUNTAIN.

IT is sometimes said that Western North Carolina is shaped like a bow, of which the Blue Ridge would form the arc, and the Smoky mountains the string. Within this semicircle our little party, now and then increased by the advent of citizens of the various counties, who came to journey with us from point to point, traveled about 600 miles on horseback, now sleeping at night in the lowly cabins, and sharing the rough fare of the mountaineers, now entering the towns and finding the mansions of the wealthier classes freely opened to us. Up at dawn, and away over hill and dale; now clambering miles among the forests to look at some new mine; now spurring our horses to reach shelter long after night had shrouded the roadways, we met with unvarying courtesy and unbounded welcome.

As a rule, the younger men with whom we talked were hopeful, very much in earnest; generally free from the mountain rustic dialect; took in one or two newspapers, and were interested in the outer world and general legislation; but their fathers, the farmers of the "befo' the waw" epoch, were discouraged and somewhat discontented at the new order of things; looked upon mineral hunters

The Dry Fall of the Sugar Fork, Blue Ridge, North Carolina. [Page 497.]

and railroad route surveyors with coldness or contempt; and were wont to complain of their own lot and of all the results of the war. The young and prominent men in most of the counties were good companions and enthusiastic friends; they had none of the artificial manners of the town, none of its guile.

Wherever we went we found the "rock-hunters" had been ahead of us, and a halt by the wayside at noon would generally bring to us some denizen of the neighborhood, who would say, "Good mornin', gentlemen. After rocks?"— and would then produce from his pockets some specimens which he was "mighty certain he did n't know the name of." Many a farmer had caught the then prevalent mica fever, and some had really found deposits of the valuable mineral which were worth thousands of dollars.

There is little danger of overestimating the mineral wealth of this mountain country; it is really very great. There are stores of gold, silver, iron, copper, zinc, corundum, coal, alum, copperas, barytes, and marl, which seem limitless. There are fine marble and limestone quarries whose value was unsuspected until the railroad pioneer disclosed it. The limestone belt of Cherokee county, a wild and romantic region still largely inhabited by Cherokee Indians, contains stores of marble, iron and gold; Jackson county possesses a vast copper belt; and the iron-beds of the Yellow mountains are attracting much notice. The two most remarkable gold regions are in Cherokee and Jackson counties.

The Valley river sands have been made, in former times, to yield handsomely, and now and then good washings have been found along its tributaries. The gold is found in veins and superficial deposits in the same body of slates which carries limestone and iron. Before the war liberal arrangements had been made for mining in Cherokee, but since the struggle the works remain incomplete. It is supposed that the gold belt continues south-westward across the country, as other mines are found in the edge of Georgia.

The gold of Jackson county is obtained from washings along the southern slopes of the Blue Ridge, near the mountains known as "Hogback" and "Chimney Top;" and Georgetown creek, one of the head streams of the Toxaway, yielded several hundred thousand dollars a few years ago. In this wild country, where the passes of the Blue Ridge rise precipitously 800 and 1,000 feet, there lie great stores of gold.

Overman, the metallurgist, unhesitatingly declares that he believes a second California is hidden in these rocky walls. The monarch mountain "Whiteside" is said to be rich in gold.

It is possible that the iron ore of these mountains will not be speedily developed, as capital is now so powerfully attracted to Missouri, and other States, where remarkable deposits exist; but there is no denying the richness of Cherokee, Mitchell, Buncombe, Haywood, Jackson, and Macon counties in that mineral. In Cherokee the hematite ores outcrop in immense quantities along the Hiawassee and Valley rivers, and, when wrought in the commonest county bloomeries, have yielded an astonishing per cent. Rivers flow directly through the iron regions in this section, furnishing every needed facility for transportation; and limestone and forest fuel abound. Magnetic ores are found in Madison, Haywood and Macon counties; and there are large outcroppings of hematite in Buncombe.

Our expedition grew rapidly after we left Waynesville, and our group of horsemen, followed by "the baggage train," toiling along the mountain roads, caused a genuine excitement at the farms by the way. One of our most memorable trips was that from Waynesville to Whiteside and the return.

Upon the beautiful country through which we were now wandering the Indian lavished that wealth of affection which he always feels for nature, but never for man. He gave to the hills and streams the soft poetic names of his expansive language— names which the white man has in many cases cast away, substituting the barbarous commonplaces of the rude days of early settlement.

The Cherokee names of Cowee and Cullowhee, of Watauga, of Tuckaseege, and Nantahela, have been retained; and some of the elder settlers still pronounce them with the charming Indian accent and inflection. The Cowee mountain

View near Webster, North Carolina.

range runs between Jackson and Macon counties, and the valley of Tuckaseege, walled in four crooked, immense stretches, includes all of Jackson county which lies north of the Blue Ridge.

The river itself, one of the most picturesque in the South, "heads" in the Blue Ridge, and swelling into volume from a hundred springs of coldest, purest, most transparent water, which send little torrents down all the deep ravines, it goes foaming and dashing over myriads of rocks, sometimes leaping from dizzy heights into narrow cañons, until it comes to, and is lost in, the Tennessee. Where the Tuckaseege forces its way through the Cullowhee mountains there is a stupendous cataract.

The little inn at Webster, the seat of justice of Jackson county, was none too large to accommodate our merry cavalcade. We came to it through the Balsam mountains from Waynesville, along a pretty road bordered with farms and giant mulberry-trees. In the valleys we saw the laurel and the dwarf rosebay, the passion flower and the Turk's-cap lily, and on the mountain sides the poplar or tulip-tree, the hickory, ash, black and white walnut, the holly, the chincapin, the alder, and the chestnut, each in profusion.

Webster is a little street of wooden houses, which seem mutely protesting against being pushed off into a ravine. For miles around the country is grand and imposing. A short time before our arrival the residents of the county had been edified by the execution of the only highwayman who has appeared in Western North Carolina for many years. The hanging occurred in front of the jail in the village street, and thousands flocked to see it from all the section round about.

Sunset came with a great seal of glory. Before the dawn we were once more in the saddle, *en route* for the Cowee range. Just below Webster we crossed the Tuckaseege river at a point where once there was a famous Indian battle, and wound up the zigzag paths to the very top of Cowee, now and then getting a glimpse of the noble Balsam left behind. Now we could look up at one of the "old balds," as the bare peaks' tops are called. (The Indian thought the bare spots were where the feet of the Evil One had pressed as he strode from mountain to mountain.) Now we stopped under a sycamore, while a barefooted girl brought a pitcher of buttermilk from the neighboring house; now a group of negro children, seeing a band of eight horsemen approaching, made all speed for the house, evidently thinking us Ku-Klux or "Red Strings" resuscitated; and now a smart shower would beat about our heads, and die away in tearful whisperings among the broad leaves. The mile-stones by the roadside were notched to indicate the distance; and from hour to hour, in the mountain passes, stops were made to whoop up the laggards.

In the rich coves in Jackson county the black mould is more than two feet in depth, and the most precipitous mountain sides are grazing pastures, from which thousands of fat cattle are annually driven down to the seaboard markets. In the ranges, too, where the winter grass grows luxuriantly from November until May, great numbers of horses and mules are raised. Fruit grows with Eden-like luxuriance; the apple is superb, and on the thermal belt in all this section the fruit crop never fails.

Near Franklin, close to the site of an old Indian fortification, we crossed the "Little Tennessee," a stately river, along whose banks are noble quarries of marble, never yet worked. The chief town of Macon county was fair to look upon, seated amidst well-cultivated fields, and in the immediate vicinity of a grand grazing country; but we pushed on into the mountains once more, anxious to pass the Blue Ridge and climb the ribs of "Whiteside." Three hundred thousand acres still remain unimproved in Macon, and at least one-third of these are rich in minerals.

We were now approaching the extreme western border of the State. A little beyond lay Cherokee and Clay counties, a territory taken from the Indians by treaty no later than 1835-36. They lie in the valley of the Hiawassee, which is famous as the place where the first successful treaty was made. We pushed on until dark, and our little party was dispersed at the various farm-houses on the road, with instructions to gallop up and meet in the morning before reaching the foot of the Blue Ridge.

The stream along whose banks we were now ascending the mountain is known as the "Sugartown" or "Sugar Fork" of the Tennessee river, and comes foaming down the wild slopes of the Blue Ridge through some of the most romantic scenery in America. Beautiful as the Rhone in the Alps, majestic in its tremendous waterfalls, and the wild grandeur of the passes through which it flows, it is strange that few travelers from other States have ever penetrated to its upper waters.

It was not without difficulty that our party reassembled the next morning. The Colonel and the sprightly Jonas came galloping from a town ten miles away, where they had been compelled to remain overnight, and the others came straggling to the rendezvous. The village physician from Webster, who knew every foot of the way for forty miles around, the cheery landlord from Waynesville, and the writer climbed the steep hill-side slowly under a broiling sun; the artist, hungry for sketches, browsed lightly on the delicate vistas afforded by every turn in the road; and the Judge, who had enlisted in our service that genial and venerable mountaineer, Silas McDowell, was actively hunting for the obscure pathway leading to the lower falls; while the colored servant guided an overloaded buggy along the rocky road.

As we reached the crest of the hill a sound like the sweep of the wind through the forest in autumn, or the distant echo of the rush of a railway train, drifted to our ears. Now it was swept away, now came back again powerfully. It was the voice of the fall in the cañon below, and old Mr. McDowell, reining in his horse and placing his hand to his ear, listened intently a minute, then announced that the pathway to the falls was not far, between Lamb and Skittles mountains, from that spot. So we began to search for it, some one meantime volunteering the information that the ravines abounded with rattlesnakes, and that one must tread carefully.

"What do you think of that?" said one, turning to the gray-haired guide. "Had we better go down this way?"

"Sir," said he, fiercely, "I have a contempt for snakes, sir. I kick them out of my way, sir. I kill them before they have a chance to bite me, sir."

Cold comfort, but no alternative; and, Indian-file, we moved toward the descent. After a walk of 200 yards through a pleasant grass-grown space, we came to the hill's abrupt sides, broken by ledges and clothed with tangled vines and underbrush. A slight and scarcely perceptible trail led along the dizzy height, but was now and then lost entirely as one came to a rock, over which he was compelled to crawl and drop cautiously into black-looking caves and dens, out of which the only sortie was another still more difficult scramble.

Bears are often seen in these mountains now-a-days, and "hard times" will bring them into the vicinity of the farmers' cabins. The bear of this region is black, grows somewhat larger than in the swamps of the eastern part of the State, and has a glossy fur-like coat of hair. One sometimes comes upon the wallows in the moss where Bruin has been taking his siesta.

Half-way down the mountain we could hear the roar of the fall, and sometimes, through an opening in the trees, catch a glimpse of the white foam as it poured over the rocks. Guided by the Judge's cheery halloo, and the occasional crack of a revolver, we reached the valley, swinging down by branches of trees, and tearing our hands against the rough rocks. The Colonel suddenly disappeared.

Many a halloo failed to bring him, and I waded through the cold pool at the foot of a great ledge, staggered out of the knee-deep, chilly water on to a

Lower Sugar Fork Fall, Blue Ridge, North Carolina.

shelving platform, clambered over a half-rotten tree-trunk, and reached a pinnacle midstream, from whose jagged summit I could see the top of the falls and the twin pine-trees leaning over the huge chasm as if it awed at the spectacle. Around this pinnacle ran a whirlpool, which made a fierce eddy at the very base of the projection on which I stood. Forcing myself up among the extending boughs of another pine-tree, with my boots in one hand and my staff in my mouth, I was just reaching the top when a limb gave way, and I slid rapidly down twenty feet directly toward the pool. A desperate wrench at a knot on the tree stopped me, however, and I finally reached my perch in safety.

To the right was a ledge, a hundred feet high, down which trailed moss and vines, and along which grew tiny white blossoms in dense masses. Far below this ledge on a rock, which he had reached by a dexterous drop, sat the artist, sketching. In the distance was Jonas, clambering on all fours up a wet stone directly under the shadow of the fall, and now and then turning to whoop at the others. No Judge, no Colonel visible! but now and then a faint halloo showed them still struggling in the glens.

A gap in the mountains, high up, was pierced by a rapidly flowing stream, which boiled into whitest foam as it sprang down the sides of a great rock from a shelf jutting out of the mass. At the right grew tall trees and infinite small foliage, clothing the walls, which descended hundreds of feet, with living green, and with blue, white, and red blossoms; on the left the ledge ran up into a peak in front, then receded toward the crest of the hill which we had left. Eighty or ninety feet below the shelf from which the foam leaped it met some obstacle, and, springing to the right in blinding clouds of spray, which at times filled the cañon for some distance, it formed a second fall extending thirty feet down to the lower channel.

On the left, across the face of the lower part of the cliff, ran minor torrents, bubbling and seething, and everywhere the current was swift, strong, and musical. Landing as I did midstream, and facing the fall, there seemed no exit from the valley save by balloon. On every side the walls appeared to rise perpendicularly, and, indeed, the trail was found only after vexatious scrambling among the rocks. When I reached the top, the others had departed, and I overtook them at a log-cabin, where they had halted for dinner. The Colonel smilingly presented himself.

"I got a fall from a high rock," said he, in apology, "and lost the antidote for rattlesnake bites, which I carried for you others, out of my pocket. It took me a good hour to find it again. Besides, I have seen the falls once before."

The cabin where we rested stood on a very steep hill-side, and was composed of two solidly-constructed square log buildings, connected by a porch. The furniture was of the simplest character. There was a fire-place, a rough board-table, with benches around it, a spinning-wheel, and a quilting-frame, at which three tall girls were busily working. The rude walls and the plank floor were bare.

In the other room stood one or two high bedsteads, of simple pattern; a mirror, a few inches square, hung near them; a little stand with a Bible on it, and a rustic bureau pushed against the wall. The venerable matron of the household, with her gray hair combed smoothly back under her sun-bonnet, which she kept on, stood guard over the table with a fly-brush, and while she gossiped with the Doctor, served buttermilk from an earthen jar.

"Jeems—Jeems is my youngest son's name, Doctor. He'll be eighteen this year; 'n he's a right smart boy."

Although sixty, at least, the matron was strong and hearty; had reared a large family, and never felt the need of anything more than she possessed. "Reckoned them folks that was huntin' for rocks better tend to ther corn, *she* did."

A little higher up the mountain, in the mica-lands, our artist was confronted by the belle of that region. She was pretty. She had evidently been informed as to our coming by the cunning mischief of the urbane Colonel, and approaching the man of pencils remarked, with a delightful bashfulness:

"I want you to take my picture."

Imagine him trying to explain.

"Well, they said anyway that you 'd take all our pictures, 'n my sister 's waitin' up t' our house's, 'n law! how fur'd you uns come this mornin'? Jim Lawson! ef you don't keep thet horse's heels away from me!" to a North Carolina cavalier, anxious to show us his horsemanship by plunging down a steep bank.

Straightway she led the gentle artist captive,—the pretty mountain girl with her hair combed smoothly down over her cheeks, and with her comely form robed in green.

By and by, in the afternoon, the reunited party, as it crept skyward, plunged, Indian-file, into the forest, and took its way to the "Dry Falls." A silence, not of gloom but of reverence, seemed to fall upon all as we entered the aisles of the grand wood, and climbed the knolls which rose like whales' backs every few hundred yards. We were already well upon the Blue Ridge, and crossing toward its southern side, in which the monarch rocks "Whiteside," "Black Rock," "Stooly," and "Fodder Stack," are rooted. Here and there the "Surveyor," who had joined us, stopped to look for his mark on a tree, and his sturdy little horse seemed by instinct to find his way athwart the furze.

After two miles of climbing, sometimes where the hills were so steep that in descending a misstep of the horse would have cost one a broken limb, we came to a long line of laurel thicket. Here, taking our oil capes, we scrambled into the bushes, and, stooping, worked our way to a cliff, down which rugged steps were cut, and stood where we could overlook the cañon into which the upper fall of the Sugar Fork sent its leaping water.

The Hibernianism by which this glorious cascade gets its designation of the "Dry Falls," was suggested by the possibility of passing beneath the giant shelf, over which it pours, without severe wetting, although the spray is at times blinding. The river, coming to a dizzy height, leaps out with such force, that the water is projected far from the rock, and the beholder seems to see a lace veil, at least sixty feet long, dependent from the hoary walls of the cañon. Passing under it, along the slippery rocks, one comes out upon another stone under beetling precipices, from which little streams run down, and around which the mist and spray rise, and can note the changing gleams of the sunshine as they play on the immense mass of foam suspended between earth and sky.

Below, the stream passionately clutches at the rocks, and now and then throws them down into the chasm; there are hollows in the stones, which have been worn to a considerable depth by the pattering of the spray upon them for hundreds of years. Here a mass of wall rises dozens of feet from the chaos of rocks which is huddled at the fall's bottom. Many of the rude figures seem to have human resemblances, and one might imagine them giants rising from the cañon's depths to tear away the veil which has been drawn across the entrance to their cavern.

A hundred and fifty feet below the summit of the falls, the stream runs on in whirlpools and eddies, now forming into inlets in which reeds, ferns and blossoms flourish, and now making a deep, steady current, cold and crystal clear. The pines and spruces seventy feet high seem but toys by the sides of these immense walls; the light, too, in the gap through the mountain, is strange and fantastic, and seems to cast a glamour over every minute object. Even the pebbles, and the ferns and tiny grass-sprouts in the soil beneath the shelf over which the fall pours, are purple.

Then the voice—the voice of the fall! Heard from the laurel thicket, it seems to come from the very ground under your feet; heard from the cavern into which you pass, it is sombre and complaining, like the winter wind about the house chimneys; and its echoes from the foot of the rapids, to which you may descend if you have firm nerves and a quick step, are like those from some unseen choir in a cathedral gallery,—some chant of priests at High Mass, monotonous, grand, inspiring; "the height, the glow, the gloom, the glory," all blended, shock and awe the soul.

Here is a fall upon whose virgin rocks no quack has painted his shameless sign; whose precipices have not been invaded by the mob of the grand tour; whose solitary magnificence thrills and impresses you as if in some barren land you came upon the dazzling lustre of a priceless diamond. But to this, and its brother a few miles below, the feet of thousands of the curious will hereafter wander.

The shadows were creeping over the mighty hills as we hastened back across the wooded slopes, and leaving the main road a little farther on, entered a narrow trail, obstructed by swampy holes and gnarled tree-roots. Three miles brought us to "Wright's"—the little farm-house in a deadening from which we obtained a view of "Short-Off,"—and the forest which hid the approaches to "Whiteside." For some time we had felt the exhilarating effects of the keen, rarefied air, and had noticed the exquisite atmospheric effects peculiar to these regions. The figure of the distant mountain stood out with startling clearness against the heavens; it seemed near at hand, whereas it was in reality miles away. The land is of wonderful fertility; even the imperfect cultivation which it has received in the clearings gives surprising results; and the timber is magnificent. All the land is suitable for small grains and roots, gives fine pasturage, and there are numerous quartz veins running through the hills, indicating the presence of gold in large quantities. The Indians once mined successfully for silver along the slopes of the Blue Ridge, near "Whiteside;" but, although they left the region only thirty years ago, and search has often been made for their riches, no traces of them have yet been found.

The Spaniards once prospected for minerals, and with evident success, in all these regions; and in Cherokee county immense excavations, supposed to be the work of De Soto and his army, have been discovered. Some years ago copper crucibles, with traces of white metal still remaining in them, were unearthed at a place where a vein of lead, silver and gold may be noted.

The summit of Whiteside is perhaps 5,000 feet high, but its peculiar location enables one to gain from it the most striking prospect in North Carolina. It overlooks a country of peaks and projections, of frightful precipices, often of naked rock, but generally fringed with delicate foliage; a country dotted with fertile clearings set down in the midst of forests; of valleys inaccessible save by

The Devil's Court-House, Whiteside Mountain.

narrow passes; of curious caves and tangled trails; of buttes and knobs, reached only by dangerous passes, where one finds the bluff's base thousands of feet down in some nook, and as he looks up sees the wall towering far above him.

At dawn of next day we plunged into the woods beyond "Wright's," and wound through a trail whose trace we of the cities should soon have lost, but in which our companions of the neighborhood easily kept until we reached a wooded hill-side, whence we could see the "Devil's Court-House," and catch a glimpse of "Whiteside's" top.

The former is a grand, rocky bluff, with its foot planted among the thickets, and its brow crowned with a rugged castle-like formation. The ragged sides are here and there stained like the walls of an old building, and it is not difficult to imagine that one is beholding the ruined walls of some giant castle. The "Surveyor" urged us forward, and our stout horses soon brought us to the clearing, where we were compelled to leave them, and climb the remaining distance on foot.

Here, more than 4,000 feet above the ocean-level, the sun beat down with extreme fierceness, and was reflected back from the hard white of the rocks with painful intensity. The horses tethered, the Judge sprang up the narrow pathway, and regardless of rattlesnakes, we clambered on all fours, clinging sometimes to roots, sometimes to frail and yielding bunches of grass and ferns; now trod breathlessly a path in the black dirt on the edge of a rock sixty feet high; now hung, poised by our hands, from one ledge while we swung to another; and now dug out footholds in the stone when we ascended an almost perpendicular wall.

Finally we came to a plateau covered with a kind of gorse, and with laurel bushes scattered here and there; pushing through this, we wound, by a gradual ascent, to the summit of Whiteside, and the edge of the precipice. There we were face to face with the demon of the abyss.

Let me tell you how the Surveyor saw him.

"One day," said the Surveyor, seating himself with admirable carelessness on the dreadful slope of a rock overhanging the awful depths, "I was taking some levels below, and at last thought I would climb Whiteside. While I was coming up a storm passed over the mountains, and when I reached the top everything was hidden in such a dense mist, fog, or cloud, that one could hardly see his hand before his face. I strolled on until I reached a spot which I thought I recognized, and sat down, stretching my feet carelessly.

"Luckily enough, I did n't move; I was mighty still, for I was tired, and the fog was solemn-like; but pretty soon it blew away right smart, and dog my skin if I was n't perched on the very outer edge of this line of rock, and about two inches between me and twelve hundred feet of sheer fall.

"I saw the trees in Casher's valley, and the clearings, and then the sky, for I did n't look twice at the fall below me; but I flattened myself against the rock, and turned over; and I never want to come up here in a fog again."

Imagine a waterfall 2,000 feet high suddenly turned to stone, and you have the general effect of the Whiteside precipice as seen in the single, terrified, reluctant glance which you give from the top. There is the curve and the grand, dizzy bend downward; were it not for occasional clumps of foliage down the sides, the resemblance would be absolute.

The mountain itself lies rooted in the western slope of the Blue Ridge. The veteran McDowell has compared it to the carcass of some great monster, upon whose head you climb, and along whose mammoth spine you wander, giddy with terror each time you gaze over the skeleton sides.

The main rock stands on a hill 1,600 feet high, and its upper crest is 2,400 feet above the branch of the Chattooga river, which runs near the hill's base.

From top to tail of the mammoth skeleton the distance is 800 feet. Viewed at a proper distance, in the valley below, from its south-east front, it is one of the sublimest natural monuments in the United States. The sunshine plays upon walls which are at times of dazzling whiteness, and the sheer fall seems to continue to the very level of the valley, although it is here and there broken by landings.

But the outlook! It was the culmination—the finishing stroke of all our rich and varied mountain surprises! When we were seated on the white crag, over which a fresh breeze perpetually blew, the "wrinkled" world beneath us literally "crawled." Everything seemed dwarfed and insignificant below. Even the brother crags—to the south-west, Fodderstack and Black Rock, and Stooly, to the north-west—although in reality rising nearly to the elevation of Whiteside, seemed like small hills.

To the north-east, as far as the eye could reach, rose a multitude of sharply defined blue and purple peaks, the valleys between them, vast and filled with frightful ravines, seeming the merest gullies on the earth's surface. Farther off than this line of peaks rose the dim outlines of the Balsam and Smoky ranges. In the distant south-west, looking across into Georgia, we could descry "Mount Yonah," lonely and superb, with a cloud-wreath about his brow; sixty miles away, in South Carolina, a flash of sunlight revealed the roofs of the little German settlement of "Walhalla;" and on the south-east, beyond the precipices and ragged projections, towered up "Chimney Top" mountain, while the "Hog Back" bent its ugly form against the sky, and "Cold" mountain rose on the left. Turning to the north, we beheld "Yellow" mountain, with its square sides, and "Short-Off." Beyond and beyond, peaks and peaks, and ravines and ravines! It was like looking down on the world from a balloon.

Jonas sees the Abyss.

The wealthy citizens of South Carolina have long known of the charms of this section, and many of them annually visit it. In a few years its wildness will be tamed; a summer hotel will doubtless stand on the site of "Wright's" farm-house, and the lovely forests will be penetrated by carriage roads; steps will be cut along the ribs of Whiteside; and a shelter will be erected on the very summit. A storm on the vast rock, with the lightning playing hide and seek in the crevices of the precipice, is an experience which gives one an enlarged idea of the powers of Heaven.

There is one pass on Whiteside which, though eminently dangerous, is now and then essayed, and Jonas and one of the woodmen of our party resolved to try it. While we commoner mortals drank in the wonderful view, and hobnobbed with the clouds, these adventurers climbed down the precipice's sides, and coming to a point not far from the Devil's Court-House, where the pass begins, launched themselves boldly forward. To gain a cave which is supposed in former times to have been the abode of an Indian sorcerer or medicine man, they were compelled to step out upon a narrow ledge running along the very side of the cliff, turning a corner with no support above or below. The ledge or path is, at its beginning, two feet wide, and as it nears the cavern, not more than eighteen inches in width. A single misstep or a failing of the nerves would have precipitated them a thousand feet into the valley, and above them the comfortless rock rose 300 feet. Hugging the wall, and fairly flattening themselves against it, they calmly went forward and reached the cavern in safety. Returning, with their eyes blinded by the shadows of the rocky crevice, the demon of the abyss seized upon Jonas, and prompted him to look down. One glance, and the awful depths seemed to claim him. He shrank toward the wall, dug his finger-nails into the crevices, uttered a faint cry, looked up, and was saved. His companion, following imperturbably behind, did not trouble himself about the depths, and striding coolly forward, with his hand filled with mineral specimens, came out upon the plateau unmoved, while Jonas seemed to have seen spectres.

From time to time "Indian ladders,"—huge trunks of trees with the boughs so chopped off as to form steps,—have been found on Whiteside, indicating that the savages frequently visited the mountain, and the tradition that it was the scene of some of their superstitious rites seems well authenticated. Now-a-days a few young men wander about its hills and ravines, inspecting their bear-traps, and sometimes are fortunate enough to encounter a shaggy bruin, wallowing in moss or ensconced near a tree.

At evening, as we reposed at Wright's, the thunder broke along the sky, and the lightning struck among the rocks on the adjacent hills. The storm was mighty and beautiful; a strange, rushing wind came with it, bending the forest growths like willows, and then the clouds covered the mountain top, and a fine mist fell. The sky was luminous, the lightning seeming to rend it in twain, and we were mute and frightened before the terrific grandeur of the battling elements.

"Whiteside" stands near the extreme south-eastern border of Macon county. We descended from it down the Tuckaseege valley into Jackson. Through both these counties runs an extensive copper belt; the ore in Jackson county being mainly bisulphuret or green carbonate of copper. In this region the advantages for the location of grazing-farms are superb, because the high mountains arrest the passing clouds, and condense them into rain so often that the lands are never parched or dry. Snow rarely lingers long there, and even in a hard winter the mountain herbage and ferns are readily made into hay.

LVII.

ASHEVILLE—THE FRENCH BROAD VALLEY—THE ASCENT OF MOUNT MITCHELL.

ON a bright Sunday we descended toward the course of the Tuckaseege and a violent storm delayed us at a lowly cabin, near the path by which a visitor now and then penetrates to Tuckaseege cataract. According to the custom of the country, we carried our saddles into the porch and sat down on them to talk with the residents. The tall, lean, sickly farmer, clad in a homespun pair of trowsers and a flax shirt, with the omnipresent gray slouched hat, minus rim, drawn down over his forehead, courteously greeted us, and volunteered to direct us to the falls, though he "was powerful afeard of snakes."

Buttermilk and biscuit were served; we conversed with the farmer on his condition. He cultivated a small farm, like most of the neighbors in moderate circumstances; only grew corn enough for his own support; "did n't reckon he should stay thar long; war n't no schools, and he reckoned his children needed larnin'; schools never was handy; too many miles away." There was very little money in all the region round about; farmers rarely saw fifty dollars in cash from year to year; the few things which they needed from the outside world they got by barter. The children were, as a rule, mainly occupied in minding the innumerous pigs about the cabin, and caring for the stock. The farmer thought sheep-raising would be "powerful peart," if folks had a little more capital to begin on; thought a man might get well-to-do in a year or two by such investment.

He welcomed the mineral movement gladly; reckoned may be we could send him some one to buy his farm, and let him get to a more thickly settled region; but seemed more cheerful when we suggested that emigrants might come in and settle up the country, bringing a demand for schools with them. "He reckoned there war n't no Ku-Klux these days; never knew nothin' on 'em. Heerd nothin' furder from 'em sence the break-up."

The housewife was smoking her corn-cob pipe, and sitting rather disconsolately before the fire-place, warming her thin hands by the few coals remaining in the ashes. The rain dripped in through the roof, and the children were huddled mutely together where it could not reach them. The furnishings were, as everywhere among the poorer classes in the mountains, of the plainest character. But the log barns were amply provisioned; stock looked well, and a few sheep and goats were amicably grouped under the shed.

The rain had so submerged the country that we gave up a visit to the cataract, said to be superior to the two other falls we had seen; and, as we rode on, there came a pause in the shower. Presently we overtook a party of mountaineers going to church. The women, perched on the horses behind the men, peered curiously at us from beneath their large sun-bonnets, and the men talked cheerily. The church, which we passed, was ruder than Parson Caton's in Tennessee. It was merely a log-cabin, inside which benches were placed. The congregation was singing a quaint hymn as we rode by, and a few men, for whom there was no room inside, lounged near the saplings where their horses were hitched, listening intently.

The copper region of Jackson county is fascinatingly beautiful. While there is the same tropical richness of foliage which distinguishes the other counties, there is a greater wealth of stream-side loveliness; there are dozens of foamy creeks and by-ways, overhung with vines.

The hills are admirably fertile in the vicinity of the Way-ye-hutta and Cullowhee copper mines, and many of the vineyards are exquisitely cultivated. The Cullowhee mountain is charming; no region in the South can furnish stronger attractions for emigrants. "Look at that valley," said an English resident to me, "a few farmers from England, with their system of small farms and careful cultivation, would make this an Eden." And he did not exaggerate.

Asheville, North Carolina, from "Beaucatcher Knob."

Give all that section immigration, and railroads cannot be kept out of it, even by the rascality of such gigantic swindles as have been forced upon North Carolina. The copper mines in Jackson were worked extensively before the war, and Northern capital and shrewd English mining experience are once more developing them.

The ore is "hauled," as the North Carolinians say, more than forty miles over a wagon road. The Blue Ridge tracts and the lands in Jackson county demand the attention of such men as Joseph Arch and other English agitators of the agricultural revolution in Great Britain. Vast tracts of the lands in Western North Carolina can be sold to colonists or capitalists at from one to two dollars per acre.

Some days later, the Judge enthusiastically pointed out to us the beauties of Asheville, the Mecca of the North Carolina mountaineer. We had journeyed thither down the valley of the Pigeon river,—a tranquil stream, with flour-mills here and there perched in cozy nooks along its banks. A thirty mile wagon ride from Waynesville landed us at the great white "Eagle Hotel," from whose doors the Asheville stages ply over all the roads west of the Blue Ridge. In the valley where Asheville lies the capricious "French Broad" receives into its noble channel the beautiful Swannanoa, pearl of North Carolinian rivers.

Around the little city, which now boasts a population of 2,500 people, are grouped many noticeable hills; out of the valley of "Hommony" creek sombre Mount Pisgah rises like a frowning giant, and from the town the distant summits of the Balsam range may be faintly discerned. From "Beaucatcher Knob," the site of a Confederate fort, overhanging Asheville, the looker toward the southwest will see half-a-hundred peaks shooting skyward; while in the foreground lies the oddly-shaped town, with the rich green fields along the French Broad beyond it. Asheville Court-House stands nearly 2,250 feet above the level of the sea; and the climate of all the adjacent region is mild, dry, and full of salvation for consumptives. The hotels, and many of the cheery and comfortable farm-houses are in summer crowded with visitors from the East and West; and the local society is charmingly cordial and agreeable.

Buncombe county, of which Asheville is the central and chief town, was named after Colonel Edward Buncombe, a good revolutionary soldier and patriot; and its name has become familiar to us in the quaint saying so often used in the political world, "He's only talking for Buncombe," when a legislator is especially fervent in aid of some local project. At Asheville, we were once more in a region of wooden and brick houses, banks, hotels and streets; and although still some distance from any railroad, felt as if we had a hold upon the outer world.

Asheville has heretofore been comparatively unknown. Enthusiastic invalids, who there regained their health, have from time to time sung its charms, but the little town, situated 250 miles from the State capital, has only a fleeting fame. The war brought it now and then into notice; General Stoneman, with his command, fought his way through the passes to Waynesville, and at a short distance from Asheville the last Confederate battle east of the Mississippi occurred.

The town has grown steadily and remarkably since the war, and now has banks, good churches, well-furnished stores, three newspapers, and ample hotels; while in the vicinity the tobacco which grows so abundantly in Buncombe is prepared for the market, and great quantities of cheese are annually manufactured. Beautiful natural parks surround it; superb oaks cast their shadows on greenest of lawns, and noble maples, ash and walnuts border the romantic roadway. A few miles from the town's centre are excellent white sulphur springs, from which a variety of exquisite views are to be had, and only nine miles north of the town are the so-called "Million Springs," beautifully situated in a cave between two ranges of mountains, where sulphur and chalybeate waters may be had in profusion.

The town of Asheville will in future be the railroad centre of Western North Carolina, and must grow to be a large and flourishing city. The present poverty of the section as to railroad communication is largely due to the discouragement consequent on the manner in which the confidence of those subscribing to the principal enterprise has been betrayed. The unfinished embankments, the half-built culverts and arches of the Western North Carolina railroad, which are to be seen in many of the western counties, are monuments to the rapacity and meanness of a few men in whom those counties placed confidence.

The plan of this railroad is a fine one, and would soon develop the noble mountain country into a very wealthy section. It proposed to supply a route from Salisbury, North Carolina, to Asheville, and thence by two lines to give advantageous outlets. One of these was to run down the valley of the French Broad river to "Paint Rock," on the Tennessee line, connecting with the Cincinnati, Cumberland Gap, and Charleston railroad, leading to Morristown, Tennessee, which would have connections with the through route from New York to New Orleans, at Morristown, and would complete the great air line from Charleston, in South Carolina, to Cincinnati in Ohio, by connecting at Lexington

View near Warm Springs, on the French Broad River. [Page 507.]

or Paris, in Kentucky, with the Kentucky Central road. The other outlet was to be by the main line passing due west from Asheville through the western counties to Ducktown, in Cherokee county, and thence on to Cleveland in Tennessee, whence it is but a short distance to Chattanooga. Thus the gates of this now almost unknown region would be unlocked, and the best sections penetrated by rail routes. But the work lies incomplete under the very eyes of the hard-working mountaineers who have been swindled. The money which they subscribed has been spirited away, and still the eastern division of the road has only reached Old Fort, twenty-five miles from Asheville.

The other routes are few and insufficient. The "Central North Carolina," formerly the Wilmington, Charlotte, and Rutherford railroad, is to run from Wilmington on the coast via Wadesboro', Charlotte, and Lincolnton to Cherryville, and is intended to reach Asheville, but has eighty-five miles yet to build from Cherryville.

The Union and Spartanburg railroad, leading from Alston, in South Carolina, to the Greenville and Columbia route, twenty-five miles north of Columbia, is to be extended to Asheville, a distance of seventy-four miles, crossing the Blue Ridge at Butt Mountain Gap; and the Laurens and Asheville Railroad Company intends to build a road from Laurensville via Greenville, in South Carolina, to Asheville, which will furnish a means of connection with the Atlanta and Richmond Air Line.

The importance of the extension, which would give a through direct line from Cincinnati to Charleston, can hardly be overestimated. The links still to be built would develop not only a rich, but a wildly romantic and picturesque country. The valley of the French Broad river conforms with perfect accuracy to the general direction of an air line between the two cities.

And what a valley it is! The forty-four miles from Asheville to Wolf creek form one of the most delightful of mountain journeys. The rugged wagon road runs close to the river's banks all the way to Warm Springs, a charming watering-place a short distance from the Tennessee line. As you penetrate the valley the river grows more and more turbulent; its broad current now dashes into breakers and foam-flakes, as it beats against the myriads of rocks set in the channel-bed; now twirls and eddies around the masses of drift-wood washed down from the sides of the gigantic mountains which rise almost perpendicularly from the tiny stretches of sand at the water's edge; now, deep and black, or in stormy weather yellow and muddy, it flows in a strong, steady current beside banks where the trees are grouped in beautiful forms, creating foregrounds over which the artist's eye lovingly lingers.

The Indians named the French Broad "the racing river;" and, as it hurls its wavelets around the corner of some islet or promontory, one sees how faithfully the name describes the stream. Each separate drop of water seems to be racing with every other. A party of American hunters named the stream after their captain, French, during the days of early settlement, and from "French's Broad" the name finally assumed its present form.

One can hear the voice of the river always crying among the cliffs, and moaning and sighing as it laps the low banks in the narrow gorge. It was the rare good fortune of our party to journey beside the stream during a terrific storm. As we reached the little town of Marshall,—a few white buildings grouped beneath immense cliffs,—a wild tempest of wind and rain, which snapped the locusts like paper twine, blew down oaks, made "land slides," and prostrated the crops, came through the valley; and then the roar of the river was sublime.

Straggling along in the storm, we gave ourselves completely up to the grandeur of the occasion. The creeks which came down from the rocks were so swollen that they would have carried the stoutest horse out into the wild chaos of the dashing and leaping stream, and drowned him in the mysterious eddies.

Night came, and we slept in a little farm-house, with the river singing its delicious songs of unrest and impatience at its mountain bounds in our ears. Skillful fording in the morning enabled us to pursue our journey along the washed-out road, where beetling crags almost shut the light; where there was not room for two carriages abreast, and some stone monarch of the glen leaned toward the stream's edge as if just about to topple downward. For miles the rocks towered up loftily, and miniature torrents ran down their sides, rippling across the road into the river, upon whose farther bank there was no refuge whatever; only the sheer rock with its coating of foliage; the tangled thickets on the height; the gleam of the streamlet piercing its way athwart the stones 1,500 feet in air!

The traveler who is not strongly moved by his first gaze upon this valley must be indeed *blasé*. The approaches to Warm Springs exceed in grandeur any other portion of the gorge. Pyramidal hills rise on either hand; the soft breeze of the south brings perfume from the borders of little river lakes, where the current has set backward, and is held in place by banks covered with delicate flowers.

Mountain Island," two miles from the Springs, is a hilly islet in the impetuous stream; its shores and its slopes are rich in beauty, carpeted with evergreens, and all the colors of the rich North Carolinian flora. Below it the river becomes smooth, and moves majestically, only to break up anew into sparkling and fantastic cascades Suddenly leaving the looming mountains, with the famous rock "Lover's Leap" on the right, one finds that the south-west bank of the river recedes, and gives place to a level plain, in whose centre is a beautiful grove. From this clump of trees peer out the white pillars of the Warm Springs Hotel. It is not far from the banks of the French Broad, which there is more than 400 feet wide, and traversed by a high bridge.

Lover's Leap, French Broad River, Western North Carolina.

The Warm Springs were discovered late in the last century by some adventurous scouts, who had penetrated farther than was prudent into the then Indian country. The springs boil up from the margins of the river, and of "Spring Creek," and have a temperature of 105 degrees. Thither the rheumatic, and those afflicted with kindred diseases, repair yearly in large numbers, and find speedy relief. From a spacious lawn one can look up-river at massive cliffs and mountains clad in rich foliage; and for miles and miles around there is a succession of quaint and oddly shaped rocks. Nine miles beyond the Springs the railroad from Wolf creek gives prompt connection with the through line to New York.

Five miles below, on the Tennessee line, is the "Paint Rock," 200 feet high, a titanic mass of stone whose face is marked as with red paint, and which seems to have been pounded by some terrible Thor-hammer into multitudinous fragments, some of which overhang the highway. Not far from this point one comes also to the "Chimneys,"—the unpoetic name given to jagged stone monuments rising 400 feet into the air, serene, awful, gigantic, while the "racing river" cries and caracoles at their bases. Hundreds, nay, thousands of fragments, shaped like diamonds, or squares, of round flint and sandstone, and almost every other kind of stone, lie scattered below, as though hurled down by a thunderbolt; and swarms of turkey-buzzards hover in and out among the crags.

Buncombe county is very fertile; the tobacco raised there has frequently taken the first and second premiums at the Virginia State fair. Fruit culture prospers; iron ores crop out here and there. Stock-raising is one of the chief occupations of the wealthier residents. Beaufort harbor will be Asheville's nearest port, and a very convenient one, if ever the Western North Carolina railroad is completed. Manufacturing is needed, and would find superior advan-

View on the Swannanoa River, near Asheville, Western North Carolina.

tages, in all the region round about Asheville. In the valley of the French Broad there are many admirable mill sites, the river at Asheville being quite as large as the Merrimac at Lowell, in Massachusetts. The water power is generally superb, because most of the mountain streams, before they flow out into Tennessee, have a fall of 1,000 feet. Timber is abundant, and when the railroad comes, it will run through finely-timbered regions.

Our journey along the Swannanoa was a revelation. We missed the noisy grandeur of the French Broad valley, but we found ample compensation in the quiet loveliness of the stream which the reverent Indian named "beautiful." Four miles from Asheville, going north-eastward, toward the Black mountains, we reached the river, and followed its placid current through a beautifully-cultivated valley. A rich carpet of green covered its banks, and there was the same charming effect produced by the trailing of the vines over the trees which we had noticed in the mountains.

The river was sometimes deeply dark in color; now and then faintly blue or purple, as the sunshine played upon it through the thickets; here and there we came to a place where it had formed a little lake, across which a rustic bridge was thrown, and where one of the long, slender canoes of the country was moored to a sapling; now, where some rich farmer's mansion stood on a lawn, dotted with oaks and hickories; now, where we caught a glimpse of the distant Potato Top mountain; now, where an old mill was half hidden under clusters of azaleas and the low-laurels.

The summit of the Black mountains is the highest point in the United States east of the Mississippi river, and the rugged range, clad in its garments of balsam and moss, glorious with its vistas of apparently endless hills and fancifully-shaped valleys, is the chief pride of the North Carolinian mountaineer. Our party left Asheville late one bright morning, sped along the Swannanoa to "Alexander's," a good halting-point, seven or eight miles from the mountain's foot, and then pushed on to Patton's, the collection of humble cabins nestled at the very base of the chain of peaks. Our German companion sang his merriest songs that afternoon, and the Judge's cheery halloo was heard at every mile, for the loveliest phases of nature gave us their inspiration.

As we approached Patton's, the long ridges of "Craggy" loomed up like ramparts to the eastward, and the sun tinged the sky above them crimson and purple. The music from the ripples of the fork of the Swannanoa, which we were now ascending, drifted on the evening air; the kalmias, the azaleas, and the honeysuckles, sent forth their perfumes; the wood-choppers, their feet well protected against the snakes by stout boots, were strolling supperward, and gave us hearty good evenings; the cow-bells tinkled musically, and in a corner of Patton's yard a mountain smith was clanging his hammer against his anvil, seemingly keeping time with the refrain to which all nature was moved. The evening was still and warm, even in that elevated region. While some of us remained in the cabin below and listened to tales of Black Mountain adventure, the aspiring Jonas, with a companion, pushed on a few miles beyond, that he might see sunrise from the heights, even though he had to sleep in a crazy and decaying house on the edge of a dizzy cliff, with the floor for his bed and his saddle for a pillow.

It is twelve miles from Patton's to the summit of Mitchell's Peak, and the ascent, which is very arduous, is usually broken by stop at the "Mountain House," four miles from the foot, and another at the point where the Government once maintained an observatory, on a rock 6,578 feet high, and three miles

First Peep at Patton's.

from the topmost height, which rises suddenly from the range, a mass of ragged projections, covered with deadened tree-trunks.

At early dawn we were on our road to the Mountain House, at first through thickets, then along a creek-bed, where the cautious mountain-horses walked with the greatest difficulty; now fording a creek twenty times in half an hour, now bending as we came to tree-trunks half-fallen across the trail. A slip upon a smooth stone frightened one of the horses so that he stood still and trembled for a moment, so well did he realize the result of a fall or roll backward; sometimes the animals would stand and listen, with their ears ominously cocked as if watching for snakes; often they paused as if in mute despair at the task before them.

But after an hour and a-half of this laborious climbing, during which we had ascended at least 1,500 feet, we heard the halloo of Jonas and his companions, and scrambling up the track of a little water-course, came out upon the plateau on whose edge stands the Mountain House.

The "house" is a small Swiss cottage, once solidly built of stout beams, but now fast decaying. It was built by William Patton, a wealthy citizen of Charleston, and before the war was often the resort of gay parties, who dined merrily on the cliff's verge, and saluted the sunset with champagne. It stands but a few yards from the edge of the Balsam growth, where the vegetation changes and the atmosphere is rarer than below. It is 5,460 feet above the sea-level at the point in front of the Mountain House, where one looks down into the valley, and sees the forest-clad ridges creeping below him for miles; notes the twin peaks of Craggy and their naked tops; then turns in wonder to the wood above him, and searches in vain for the peaks beyond. While at the windows of the Mountain House we seemed to be gazing from mid-air down upon the Blue Ridge. The illusion was perfect. Below us the mists were rising solemnly and slowly; peak after peak was unveiled; vast horizons dawned upon us; we seemed to have risen above the world.

The "Mountain House," on the way to Mount Mitchell's Summit.

We turned from this view of the valleys and entered the balsam thickets, pushing eagerly forward to Mount Mitchell.

And now we came into the region of the pink and scarlet rhododendrons. Whenever there was an opening in the trees the hill-side was aflame with them. Masses of their stout bushes hung along our path, and showered the fragile red blossoms upon us. The white mountain laurel, too, was omnipresent, but the scarlet banner usurped the greatest space.

When we came to a narrow trail, where slippery rocks confronted us, and ragged balsam-trunks compelled us to clamber over dangerous crags, we found the way strewn with a crimson carpet after our horses had struggled through. Here, too, were masses of evergreen, and red-pointed mosses, and the azaleas again along the border of streamlets, and purple rosebay and the tall grasses in the clearings, in whose midst nestled timorously tiny white blossoms and ground berries.

To climb Vesuvius is no more difficult than to scale the Black mountain, for although one can reach the very top of the latter on horseback, he is in constant danger of breaking his limbs and those of his horse on the rough pathway. By the time we had reached "Mount Mitchell" and seated ourselves upon its rocks, our horses were as thoroughly enthusiastic as we were, and peered out over the crags with genuine curiosity.

View of Mount Mitchell.

From Mount Mitchell we saw that we were upon a centre from whence radiated several mountain chains. To the south we could see even as far as the Cumberland line, and could readily discern the "Bald" mountain and our old friend the Smoky; while nearer in the same direction, we noted the Balsam range. Sweeping inward from the north-east coast were the long ridges of the Alleghanies; on the north the chain of the Black culminated in a fantastic rock pile; while on the south the ridges of Craggy once more stood revealed.

To the east we could overlook the plains of North and South Carolina; on the north-east we saw Table Rock and the "Hawk Bill," twin mountains, piercing the clouds; while beyond them rose the abrupt "Grandfather" mountain, and the bluff of the Roan. On the south were the high peaks of the Alleghanies, the Pinnacles, Rocky Knob, Gray Beard, Bear Wallow, and Sugar Loaf.

Another hour and a-half of climbing; then, dashing through a clearing, we suddenly saw above us a crag 200 feet high, with a stone-strewn path leading up it. Our horses sprang to their risky task; they rushed up the ascent,—slipped, caught against the edges of the stones, snorted with fear, then laid back their ears and gave a final leap, and we were on Mitchell's high peak, utterly above Alleghanies, Blue Ridge, or Mount Washington. Our horses' ears brushed the clouds. In a few moments we were at Mitchell's grave.

Here we were above the rhododendrons, and only a gnarled and stunted growth sprang up. The trees were nearly all dead; those still alive seemed lonely and miserable. The rude grave of the explorer, with the four rough slabs placed around it, recalled the history of the man, and the origin of the peak's name.

The Rev. Dr. Elisha Mitchell, a native of Connecticut, graduate of Yale and an eminent professor in the University of North Carolina, established the

The Judge climbing Mitchell's High Peak.

fact by measurements, made from 1835 to 1844, that the Black was the highest range east of the Rocky mountains in the United States. He grew very much to love the work of studying these heights, and spent weeks in wandering alone among them. The rough mountaineers learned to revere him, and he became as skillful a woodsman as any of them.

In June of 1857, after accomplishing some difficult surveys, and, as it is supposed, having ascended the pinnacle which now bears his name, he was descending into Yancey county, when, overtaken by night and a blinding storm, he strayed over a precipice on "Sugar Camp" creek, and was discovered some days afterward, dead, at the bottom of a waterfall, his body perfectly preserved in the limpid pool. His friends the mountaineers, who mourned his loss bitterly, buried him in Asheville; but a year later his remains were carried to the mountain top and there placed in a grave among the rocks he had loved so well.

Near the grave the Government has established a signal-house, where two brave fellows dare the storms which occur almost daily. The anger of the heavens, as witnessed from this stony perch in mid-air, is frightful to contemplate, and many a day the lonely men have expected to see their only shelter hurled down into the ravines below.

The view from the topmost peak is similar, in most respects, to that from lower Mount Mitchell; but the effect is more grand and imposing, and the mountains to the south and east seem to stand out in bolder relief. A tremu-

Signal-Station and "Mitchell's Grave," Summit of the Black Mountains.

lous mist from time to time hung about us; the clouds now and then shut the lower world from our vision, and we seemed standing on a narrow precipice, toward whose edges we dared not venture.

As we descended, that afternoon, the pheasant strutted across our path; the cross-bill turned his head archly to look at us; the mountain boomer nervously skipped from tree to tree; the rocks seemed ablaze as we approached the rhododendron thickets; the brooks rippled never so musically, and the azalea's perfume was sweeter than ever before.

Each member of the party, dropping bridle-rein on his weary horse's neck, as we came once more into the open space where stands the "Mountain House," and looked down thousands of feet into the yawning valley; as the peace and silence, and eternal grandeur of the scene ripened in his soul, involuntarily bared his head in reverence. Goethe was right:

"On every height there lies repose."

LVIII.

THE SOUTH CAROLINA MOUNTAINS—THE CASCADES AND PEAKS OF NORTHERN GEORGIA.

THE new link in the New York and New Orleans Air Line, connecting Charlotte in North Carolina with Augusta in Georgia, had been finished but a few days when I passed over it. This road, which gives the most direct route from Atlanta to Richmond, opens up a large portion of North-eastern Georgia, and traverses a rich mineral region for 600 miles.

The country between Charlotte and Greenville in South Carolina is interesting, though still in the rough. The better class of people all through this section, and especially in North Carolina, possess and manifest that boldness and independence of spirit which made the colony the first of the original thirteen to claim independence, and prompted the settlers on the Cape Fear river to refuse a landing to the stamps brought from England in one of King George's sloops-of-war. There is a good deal of ignorance and prejudice among the low class of whites; they are hardly the stuff out of which the old heroes were made.

The mountain region of South Carolina, lying between North Carolina and Georgia, contains some of the most exquisite scenery in the United States. Entering it from Charlotte, one passes Spartanburg and near the site of the famous battle of King's Mountain, and following the Air Line may pause at the busy town of Greenville.

I found there more activity and less embarrassment on account of the distressing political situation than anywhere else in South Carolina south of Columbia, the State capital. The negroes were far less ignorant than their fellows of the coast and the central counties, and were disposed to be more reasonable in their political views. It is true that, after the war the Ku-Klux organization committed abominable outrages throughout York, Union, Spartanburg, Laurens and Chester counties. It was shown, at the time of the exposure consequent on the military arrests, that 2,000 male citizens of a single county belonged to the Ku-Klux, and actively participated in the coercive measures which it had foolishly adopted.

But the mountaineers have learned the folly of such attempts, and there are no longer any reports of whippings and midnight massacres. The railroad and the advent of Northern men here and there, as well as the impetus which the universal use of the new fertilizers has given to the production of cotton upon lands where, before the war, it would not have been deemed wise to plant it—all have aided in building up new feeling, and in banishing most of the old bitterness. Had it not been for the supreme rascality of the hybrid State Government, the citizens of this upland region might have possessed even more railroad facilities than they at present enjoy. The "Blue Ridge" route was intended as a railroad into Kentucky and Tennessee, running across the southern end of the Blue Ridge, in South Carolina, which latter State and the city of Charleston owned nearly all the stock in the road up to 1871.

After about $3,000,000 had been expended in the construction of a portion of the road, and the State had guaranteed $4,000,000 of bonds, in support of fur-

The Lookers-on at the Greenville Fair. [Page 517.]

ther construction, upon certain conditions intended to protect its own interests, a gigantic fraud was consummated. The "sinking fund commission," composed of the State officers, self-appointed, passed the railroad into the hands of a corporation, robbing the State of its interest in the work, and then secured a legislative enactment annulling the conditions on which depended the issue of the four millions in bonds.

In addition to this, the Legislature authorized a further issue of "Blue Ridge" scrip to the amount of $1,800,000, and made it available by declaring it receivable for taxes. This afforded "operators" the chance they desired for plundering the State treasury; and meantime the Blue Ridge railroad remains unfinished.

It was late in the autumn when I reached Greenville, but the weather was warm and delightful. The small planters from all the country round were crowding the roads with their mule-carts, laden with one, two, or three bales of cotton. The agents for the sale of fertilizers were busy in the town looking after their interests, for many a planter had given them a lien upon his crop, and they wished to claim their money when the crop was brought to market.

There was a variety of testimony as to the profit made by the cotton-raisers who only planted two or three acres each; some insisted that they made handsome profits, others that, after they had paid for their fertilizers, and their own support during the year, they usually had nothing left. The "lien" which the seller of phosphate takes, when he delivers a ton of the coveted stimulating substance to the farmer, is a formidable document. It engages not only the growing crop, but in many cases the household goods, if the crop fails, and sometimes the unlucky wight who has a poor crop on his few acres finds himself in danger of a practical eviction.

But a good crop puts money and prosperity into this section, where the people are altogether better off than in the lowlands. They have every facility for enriching themselves, as soon as they can and will diversify the culture of their farms; and I noticed with pleasure the introduction of the "Agricultural fair" as a means of creating ambition in the direction of thorough farm culture. Greenville held its first fair of the kind during my stay there.

All along the highways leading into Greenville cotton whitened the fields; although it was late in November, there were immense fields yet to pick; and I was told that the whole crop is often not all picked before the advent of the spring months. The bareheaded negroes were lazily pulling at the white fleeces, wherever we passed, but seemed animated by no desire for results; it was easy to see why the crop was not all gathered before spring. Emigrants from other States would find every chance for enriching themselves in these charming uplands, where the climate is so delicious; where the streams and the hills are so beautiful, and where the soil is so fertile.

Greenville lies at the base of the Saluda, near the Paris mountain, and is delightfully situated on a range of breezy hills. Summer visitors from the lowlands crowd its hotels and private mansions; it has, like its neighbor, Spartanburg, a number of excellent schools and colleges, and a university. It is near the source of the Reedy river, and the approaches to it from Columbia are along the banks of that lovely stream, the Saluda. To the eastward, daintily enshrined in a nook in the Blue Ridge, near the North Carolina frontier, lies Walhalla, a German settlement, where the vine is cultivated with rare success; the county of Pickens is rich in mountain outlooks and noble waterfalls; and not more than twenty miles from Greenville, that superb monarch of the glens, Table mountain, with its ledges, each a thousand feet high, rises in rocky grandeur to the height of 4,300 feet above sea-level.

From the Greenville post-office, the stage-coach will speedily convey one into the heart of the Swannanoa and French Broad valleys in North Carolina. The road to Asheville leads through Saluda Gap, and past the beautiful summer resort, once the refuge of so many wealthy lowlanders, " Flat Rock." This was a species of Saratoga for the South Carolinians, and in the sweet valley there are still some noble mansions, like those of the Draytons and Memmingers, surrounded by gardens filled with rarest and costliest of shrubbery and flowers. Another route from Greenville leads to " Cæsar's Head," a lofty mountain like the "Whiteside," and a trysting place for hundreds of merry pilgrims during summer months.

Along the road, between Greenville and Asheville, and the rugged yet delightful routes which lead from Asheville to Charlotte, lies one of the great pleasure regions of the future. The falls of Slicking, at the base of the Table mountain, the banks of that prince among mountain streams, the wonderful Keowee, the sweet vale of Jocasse, and the adjacent Whitewater cataracts, vie with Mount Yonah, Tallulah, Toccoa, and Nacoochee, their Georgian neighbors, in variety and surprising beauty.

Table Mountain—South Carolina.

From Charlotte to Centreville the scenery is sublimely beautiful. By this route one passes through the Hickory Nut Gap, a grand gorge in the Blue Ridge, through which a creek flows until its waters are merged in those of the rocky Broad river. Where the latter stream forces its passage through a spur of the Blue Ridge, its bed is encumbered with myriads of rocks, rooted deeply in the almost unyielding soil; mountain bluffs hem it in; the scene is one of fearful solitude and grandeur. The Gap is hardly anywhere more than half a mile wide, and, seen from a little distance, it seems but a narrow path cut between gigantic buttresses of stone, which rise 2,500 feet.

Midway up the front of the highest bluff, on the south side of the Gap, stands an isolated rock resembling some antique and weather-beaten castle turret. The rains of thousands of years have washed the granite cliffs smooth, and one may fancy them the walls of some huge fortification. Shooting out over the cliff, and falling into some as yet undiscovered pool, a spray-stream comes pouring; and near the base of the awful precipice are three violent and capricious cascades, which, by centuries of persistence, have worn wells from forty to fifty feet deep in the hard stone beneath them. When one approaches the Gap, he sees before him nothing but the limitless ocean of peaks, pointed sharply, like the apexes of waves, against the crystal vault of the sky. Everywhere Nature seems to have thrown out barriers, and to have determined to prevent one from entering her favorite retreat.

Then suddenly one comes upon the narrow defile of the "Hickory Nut Gap."

Beyond it, penetrating to Rutherfordton, one sees the sublime sentinels of the Blue Ridge range jealously guarding the approaches, and at last reaches a point whence the panorama of the Pinnacle, and Sugar Loaf, and Chimney Rock, and Tryon mountains all burst at once upon the vision. The road thither winds along a ravine-side; steep rocks overhang it, and beneath it a rushing torrent screams its warning. An opening in the forest shows anew the vast expanse of peaks, and in their midst the Monarch, the Cloud-piercer, the sombre controller of the whole magic realm, Mitchell's high peak!

Miles away, to the westward, one can dimly discern a silver line on a faintly defined mountain: it is a torrent leaping down the almost perpendicular sides of its parent height.

Southward from Greenville toward Atlanta, the Air Line road runs through the forests of Northern Georgia. I found many small towns, built of rough planks, growing briskly in the forest clearings. The railway station and a long platform, a store, a few plain houses, with fat hogs rooting among the stumps in their immediate neighborhood, a carpenter's shop, and, possibly, some small and primitive manufactory, made up each of these "towns." The hotels were two-story wooden buildings, through whose thin walls came the keen autumn winds, and whose slender partitions allowed one to hear every movement and tone of voice of all his adjacent fellow-sleepers.

The fifteen counties of North-eastern Georgia cover a territory of 7,000 square miles, traversed here and there by the Appalachian chain, which, leaving North Carolina on its western boundary, pushes into hundreds of spurs and outliers which shape the romantic scenery of Rabun, Habersham, Towne, Union, White, Fannin, Gilmer, and Lumpkin counties. There, in valleys elevated nearly 2,000 feet above the sea-level, are rivers and rivulets upon whose courses some of the most majestic cascades on the continent are found. Attracted by the fame of those noble waterfalls, Toccoa and Tallulah, I left the line of rail, and with a friendly company, wandered in and out among the peaks and ravines for several days.

Rabun Gap is the passage from Western North Carolina, through the Blue Ridge, into the Georgia gold and iron field. Rabun county itself is one succession of dark blue giant ridges, over which, descending gradually, one reaches the little town of Clayton. The populations in the mountains along the border devote some attention to illicit distilling, and are, consequently, a little suspicious of strangers who penetrate to their fastnesses. A worthy clergyman from the lower counties was journeying peacefully on a religious errand to the neighboring

State, through the passes of Rabun, shortly before our visit, when he suddenly, one day, saw thirteen guns pointed at him by as many men, and had to dismount and prove, at the rifles' muzzles, that he was not a revenue officer.

From "Whiteside," in North Carolina, to Rabun Gap, it is only forty-five or fifty miles on an air line, but the detours through the ravines make it farther to the traveler. When one arrives at Clayton he feels much as if he had left the world behind him. The quaint hamlet lies in a valley encircled with mountains. As you enter, you have that feeling of being imprisoned and of desire to escape, so common to the wanderer among the Alleghanies and on the Blue Ridge. There seems no possible outlet; the town appears to have been conveyed there by enchantment; yet a little careful observation will show you the

"Let us address de Almighty wid pra'r." [Page 521.]

roads piercing the passes in the valleys. Not far from Clayton are the falls of the Estatoia, or, as the mountaineers call them, "Rabun Falls," where a succession of brilliant cascades plunge down the chasm in a mountain-side. Clambering to the top of this natural stairway in the rocks, one may obtain an outlook over the valley of the Tennessee, miles beyond Clayton, and may note the mountain billows rolling away, apparently innumerable, until the eye tires of the immensity!

I have had occasion to describe the mountain "hack" to you—a red wagon mounted on super-fragile springs, and graced with seats, which, at every start made by the horses, bid fair to leave the vehicle. In such a conveyance, behind two splendid horses, did we depart from one of the forest towns on the Air Line railway one morning in mid-October, and climb the red hills of Northern Georgia. Mile after mile we journeyed through lands which might be made very valuable by a year or two of careful culture, by plantations or farms whose owners had deserted them, or tracts which the old settlers, having adopted the

Mount Yonah, as seen from Clarksville, Georgia. [Page 522.]

new labor system, were putting into most wonderful order; now dashed over firm roads, through stretches of dreary forest, where battalions of black-jacks guarded the solemn way; and now along mountain-sides, where paths were narrow and ravines were on either hand.

A few miles from the little hill-town of Clarksville, whither we were journeying, we came upon a large assembly of negroes in a high, open field, backed by a noble uplift of mountains in the distance. It was Sunday afternoon, and the dusky citizens were returning to their devotions, the scene of which was a log-cabin, inhabited by a negro, whom we judged to be the neighborhood blacksmith, as a shop near by was encumbered with wheels and old iron.

As we approached the "bars" leading into the meadow, the mass of the negroes had gathered inside and outside the cabin, and were singing a wild hymn, marked with that peculiar monotonous refrain which distinguishes all their music. Nothing could have been more picturesque than this grouping of swart and gayly-costumed peasantry, disposed around the humble cabin, with the afternoon sun glistening on their upturned faces. The noble peaks in the far background, mysterious in their garments of subtle blue, and inspiring in their majesty, added deliciously to the effect of the whole.

As the singers became excited, their bodies moved rhythmically, and clinging to each other's hands, they seemed about breaking into the passionate warmth of some barbaric ceremony. But our momentary fears of barbarism were checked when we heard the cracked voice of the venerable pastor, and saw the assembly kneel, and bow their heads at the words—

"Let us address de Almighty wid pra'r."

While the minister was praying, the young negroes who, during the singing, had been disporting near a neighboring brook, left off their pranks, and hastened to join the kneeling throng about the cabin. As we drove away we could hear the solemn pleading of the ebony Jacob as he wrestled with the angel of prayer, and the nervous responses of the brethren and sisters when their souls took fire from the inspiration of the moment.

From Clarksville, pleasant summer resort of the citizens of Savannah and other land towns, we caught a new glimpse of Mount Yonah, that lonely monarch of the northern counties. The village is small and quiet; there are few farm-houses in the immediate vicinity; there is no bustle of trade, no railroad, and no prospect of one. Seven miles away the new Air Line gives communication with the outer world. Habersham county, of which Clarksville is the county seat, was laid out by the famous "lottery act" of 1818, and has in it many valuable lands adapted to the raising of wheat and corn.

A ride from Clarksville to the valley of Nacoochee, which comprises within its limits a series of the most exquisite landscapes in the world, is one of the charming specimens of this mountain journey. There a gentleman who has forsaken the lowlands has built a grand mansion with conservatories, lawns, and parterres; there he and his visitors strike terror into the hearts of the mountain trout, and wander over the peaks and down the valleys at their will. Mount Yonah's summit affords beautiful glimpses of a wide expanse, covered with rich farms—for the Nacoochee valley is fertile, and its vicinity is thickly settled.

The other visitors at Clarksville considered us aristocrats because we maintained the dignity of a red wagon on our journey to Tallulah Falls. They had usually accomplished the route in the somewhat fatiguing but cautious ox-cart. The famous falls, unquestionably among the grandest objects of natural

The "Grand Chasm," Tugaloo River, Northern Georgia. [Page 524.]

scenery in America, are thirteen miles from Clarksville, and a portion of the journey lies over a new road through the forest, which I may safely condemn as execrable.

On the border of a vast rent in the hills stands a little hotel built of pine boards. From its verandas you look up at ravine-sides of solid brown stone; down into leaping and foaming rapids, which seem singing war songs; over the tops of swaying pines, which, in the rich moonlight of a delicious autumn evening, stand out, black and frightful, like spectres; and along paths cut in the steep descents, leading to rocky projections and treacherous knolls.

These falls were named by the Cherokees, who called them Tarrurah or Tallulah—"the terrible." The stream in which they are formed is the western branch of the Tugaloo river, and the rapids are, perhaps, ten miles from its junction with the Chattooga. For more than a mile the impetuous stream passes through a ridge of mountains, with awful parapets of stone piled upon either side, and finally rattles away through the "Grand Chasm."

The rocky banks are in some places five hundred, in others not more than two hundred feet high; their bases are worn into fantastic and grotesque forms by the action of the dashing waters; and the stream, at no point very wide, breaks into four cataracts, which vary from fifty to eighty feet in height, and into many others from twenty to thirty. From the highest points on the cliffs to the bottom of the river-bed, at one or two localities, the depth is nearly 1,000 feet; and the spectator, dizzy and awe-struck, can but do as we did—look once, and turn his frightened and bewildered eyes away!

The "Lodore," the "Tempestia," the "Oceana," and the "Serpentine," are the names given to the four principal falls. The third fall, sometimes called the "Hurricane," is the most remarkable and interesting. Climbing to a rock directly overhanging it, and beneath which the waters are breaking across irregular shelving masses of stone, and foaming and dancing in passion in a whirlpool eighty feet below, one may gaze down stream to the sortie from the cañon.

There the whole valley seems to pitch violently forward, as if it were the entrance to Avernus; its rocky sides are mottled with lichens and the beautiful colt's-foot; and on the crests of the cliffs flourish pines, hemlocks, masses of ferns, and a profusion of grays and browns which no painter's brush can reproduce. Many trees lean as if looking shudderingly, and drawn involuntarily, toward the abyss. Beyond is a sheer precipice draped in hemlocks only, and still beyond, a projection which, when I saw it, was ablaze with the strong autumn colors of the leaves, red, and scarlet, and yellow, above which runs up a hundred and fifty feet of naked, glittering rock, towering tremendously above the tallest trees, and standing in giant relief against the sky.

Coming back to the banks near the "Hurricane" fall, we noticed that the ledges bent downward in three or four immense layers of dark flint, and that grasses grew over them, like strange beards upon monsters' faces. Here and there an old white tree-trunk hung tottering on the ravine's edges. The descent to this fall is down a gully almost perpendicular in steepness: one is also compelled to pass through the "Needle's Eye," a low passage beneath rocks, and the "Post-office," where it was once the custom for the hundreds of visitors to write their names upon the smooth walls of a cave.

The cascades themselves are not so remarkable as the scenery around them. The rocks and the precipices are so gigantic that the stream seems but a silvery thread among them. Seen from the dizzy height known as "The Devil's Pulpit," or "The Lover's Leap," the cascades are like tiny lace veils, spread in the valley, or like frostbeds, such as one sees on meadows in the morning.

The effect of a sojourn among the rocks at Lover's Leap at night, when the moonlight is brilliant, is magical. Far below you the valley seems sheathed in molten silver; the song of the cascades is borne, now fiercely, now gently, to your ears by the varying breezes; while you grovel among the slippery pine and hemlock sprays and twigs, clinging to a rock, which is your only protection against a fall of a thousand feet down to the jagged peaks below.

At the "Grand Chasm," which is properly the end of the ravine, where the stream, free from its barriers, becomes tranquil,—after it has fought its way around the base of a mountain of dark granite,—the formation of rock changes. There are no more of the slanting shelves, of the Avernus

Toccoa Falls, Northern Georgia. [Page 525.]

gates; but instead, there are rounded battlements, which, sloping and yielding, end in a ragged hill-side, strewn with bowlders, with blackened hemlocks, and with tree-trunks prone, as if waiting for some landslide to hurl them into the stream.

On the right looms up another cliff, with a slope like that of walls rising from a castle-moat; this is thatched with foliage; hemlocks straggle along its summit; and in the recesses of the thickets which stretch in all directions from it, the holly spreads its thorny leaves, and the laurel its pendants.

Finally the stream is lost to view and flows under rocks, through a symmetrical gap half a mile away,—beyond which one can see a succession of peaks, whose heads are wrapped in cloud.

After "Tallulah," the falls of Toccoa, a single spray jet, falling one hundred and eighty-five feet, over a shelving rock, is a relief. Seated in a quiet and forest-enshrouded valley, through which Toccoa creek runs, one can look up to the pouring waters with a sense of admiration, but without the awe inspired by the chasms and cascades of "The Terrible." Toccoa is situated near Toccoa City, an ambitious fledgling town on the Air Line railroad, and thousands of visitors yearly watch its tremendous leap from the crag, around which a steep road winds along the ascents that conduct to "Tallulah."

The copper region of Northern Georgia is a continuation of the remarkable one in Eastern Tennessee. A vein of copper seventeen feet thick has been found in one of the counties. In Fannin county there are large bodies of marble, and there is an iron-field on the southern slopes of the Iron mountain range. A great deal has been said about the gold mines in the northern counties. There are, no doubt, extensive deposits there. The mines in the Nacoochee valley, when first worked, on a very small scale, and with rude machinery, yielded from $2,000 to $3,000 to each workman yearly; and several millions of dollars have been obtained from the deposits since 1828. The Loud, Sprague, and Lewis mines, in the vicinity of Nacoochee, are believed to be exceptionally rich. In Rabun, Habersham, Carroll, and White counties there are known to be extensive deposits. In the Nacoochee valley immense works for carrying out the California hydraulic process were erected before the war; but have since that time been only feebly worked.

In the section between the Tray and Yonah mountains some few diamonds have from time to time been found. Not far from this point are the head-waters of the Tennessee, which, passing through Rabun Gap, plunge downward through the Appalachian, the Smoky, the Chilhowee, and Cumberland ranges, until, merged in a broad and noble stream, they enter the fertile fields of Tennessee and Alabama. There, too, the Savannah rises; there the waters of the rain-storm divide, and flow in separate directions in the channels of the two mighty rivers. It is said that several good gold mines in Hall county have been opened, and worked as low as the water-level, and that they pay a small but steady profit. In Hall county is also situated the "Harris Lode," a notable silver mine; and in the neighboring divisions of Lumpkin, Forsyth and Clarke, topaz,

amethysts, beryl, gold, plumbago, iron, granite, and gneiss have been found.*
In Clarke county, where the Georgia University is located, there is remarkable water power, and some cotton and woolen factories have been erected.

This mountain region, so rich in resource, has been as yet but little developed. With the completion of the railroad system, which is very comprehensive, and puts almost every county within easy reach of markets, the more enterprising of the present residents think that new population and new methods of agriculture will come in.

The valley lands now readily yield twenty to thirty bushels of corn and fifteen of wheat to the acre, without manures, and with no culture of consequence; deep ploughing and rotation of crops would treble these amounts. The local farmers need the example of Northern agriculture before their eyes. With lands which will produce infinitely finer and larger crops of clover and timothy than those of Massachusetts, they still send to the Bay State for their hay. But living is cheaper than in the Western States, game is plentiful, and good land, "improved" in the Georgia sense, is to be had at reasonable prices.

*At Dahlonega, in Lumpkin county, a pretty town commanding fine mountain views, the United States has a branch mint, and gold mines are quite extensively worked in the vicinity.

A Mail-Carrier.

LIX.

CHATTANOOGA, THE GATEWAY OF THE SOUTH.

AT a little distance from the locality known as Bird's Mill, not far from the boundary line between Tennessee and Georgia, and within the limits of the former State, there stands, among tangled underbrush, a massive yet simple monument. Around it the envious brier has crept, and the humbler headstones which here and there dot the thicket are also hedged about with

Mission Ridge, near Chattanooga, Tennessee. [Page 528.]

weeds and creepers. Neglect and oblivion seem, to the hasty observer, to have so effectually covered the spot with their wings, that even the dwellers in the neighborhood hardly know whom or what the marble and the stone represent.

Yet these obscure memorials call to mind some of the most touching and remarkable episodes in our history as a nation. They point backward, through the miraculous years of the last half century, to the time when the Cherokees held all the country about them; to the time of the mission-schools, and the heroic efforts of the "American Board" to establish them. A weather-beaten inscription on the marble monument discloses the fact that beneath it is the resting-place of the good Dr. Worcester, first Secretary of the Board, and an enthusiastic laborer among the Cherokees. A hundred rods away stands one of the old mission-houses, now a decaying ruin, inhabited by a horde of negroes. Cherokee and missionary have gone their ways together; there is not one to be encountered in any nook of the forest; the current of Fate has swept the Indian to the West, and the priests who labored for him into almost forgotten graves.

At the beginning of the present century the Indian still held the territory of North-western Georgia secure against the intrusion of the white man's laws, and also roamed over extensive tracts in Alabama, Tennessee and North Carolina. In the deep coves between the parallel ranges of the Cumberland, along the vast palisades by the winding Tennessee, and through the furrowed and ridgy lands extending toward Virginia and Kentucky, he wandered unrestrained. But the pale-race was on his track, anxious first to gain his good-will, and then to reason him into a cession of his beautiful lands. It was with the bitterness of despair in his heart that one of the chieftains said he had "learned to fear the white man's friendship more than his anger."

But the Cherokees did not seem to dread or detest the missionaries of the American Board. They knew them for men without guile or desire for personal gain, and they learned to love them. When good Cyrus Kingsbury founded the mission of Brainard, in 1817, on the banks of that Chickamauga whose waters, a few years since, ran red with the blood of civil war, it was with the cordial consent of all the principal chiefs. Schools and churches were founded; log mission-houses erected; even the President of the United States allowed the use of the public funds for the building of a school-house for girls. Kingsbury, Cornelius, Evarts and Worcester became eloquent champions of the Indians when their rights were assailed, and each missionary successively risked his liberty and life for the much wronged aborigines. At last a crisis arrived. The State of Georgia began to extend her criminal jurisdiction over the lands claimed by the Cherokees, and with scorn disregarded all efforts of the Indians to protect themselves by an appeal to the Supreme Court of the United States. Angered because the missionaries sided with the Cherokees in the exciting question, the officers of the Georgia Government imprisoned the noble Worcester and one of his fellow-laborers in the penitentiary, for "illegal residence among the Indians," and "because they gave advice on political matters." This last charge the missionaries solemnly denied, but refused of their own will to quit their posts, and the pardon which had been offered them was withdrawn. While they spent weary months in prison, the Cherokees were occupied with internal dissension, and with ineffectual resistance to the encroaching Georgians. At last the treaties which virtually banished the Indians from their homes were signed, and in 1838 the troops gathered up into one long and sorrowful procession thousands of men, women and children, and hurried them from the State. Depleted and worn down by every imaginable privation, more than 4,000 of the unfortunates died on their long march of 600 miles to their new homes west of the Mississippi,— forming a ghastly sacrifice to commemorate the white man's greed.

Leaving the brier-invaded grave-yard and the tumbling mission-houses, and climbing to the summit of Mission Ridge, a vision of perfect beauty is before one. To the east is Chickamauga valley, following the course of the historic creek, and dotted with pleasant farms and noble groves; westward one looks down upon a rich and broad interval, bounded by high bluffs with rocky faces, along whose bases the noble stream of the Tennessee flows with many an eccentric turn, until, as if amazed and startled at the grandeur of Lookout mountain, which rises just within the vale to 2,400 feet above the sea-level, it turns inland once more in a western course, becoming rapid and turbulent as it descends through gorges and forests, to Northern Alabama. "Lookout" is an outlier of the Cumberland table-land, and extends across the Tennessee line into Georgia. One may travel for more than forty miles along its breezy height without finding anywhere a really advantageous point at which to descend. Between Mission Ridge and Lookout mountain lies Chattanooga valley, the "Crow's Nest," as the Indians called it, and as its name signifies. It is, indeed, not unlike a nest or cup securely set down among huge mountain barriers, through which one can discern no pass,

Lookout Mountain, near Chattanooga, Tennessee.

and which only the birds can afford to despise. Everywhere ridges, sharply-projecting spurs from the Cumberland, caves, forests, rocks, bluffs! How can traffic find its way through such a country?

Far below, as you stand on Mission Ridge, with "Lookout's" shadow thrown across the brilliant sunlight, falling on the slopes up which Grant sent his men on that day of blood in 1863, you may see the city of Chattanooga, "the gateway of the South." On the present site of the town, the south bank of the Tennessee river, there stood, in 1835, a Cherokee trading post. In 1837 a good many white families from Virginia and the Carolinas had moved there, and a post-office called Ross's Landing was established. The original lots into which the town was partitioned were disposed of by lottery, after the expulsion of the Indians, and the vast commerce that to-day uses the Tennessee's current as the chief transporting medium soon created quite a trading post. From upper Eastern Tennessee came iron and ironware, corn, wheat and whiskey, and Virginia sent down great quantities of salt. In 1838 a new town was started and christened Chattanooga.* Ten years later, railroad communication, via Atlanta, with Charleston and Savannah, gave the little town 40,000 bales of cotton as its annual shipment; and when Robert Cravens began to manufacture charcoal iron there, at a cost of $10 to $14 per ton, shipping it to New Orleans, St. Louis and Cincinnati, for from $30 to $40 per ton, the settlers multiplied very rapidly. The cotton trade was lost to Chattanooga by the building of the Memphis and Charleston railroad, which did away with the painful navigation of the Tennessee up from Alabama, and the portage around "Muscle Shoals;" but the grain and stock trade steadily increased, and in 1861 the town boasted 3,500 population. Then the war came to it.

Planted at the very mouth of the narrow passes, through which trade and travel pick their difficult way, Chattanooga has sprung, since the war's close, from a village into a prosperous city of 12,000 inhabitants. Its aspect to-day is that of a North-western settlement, Northern and Western men having flocked to it in large numbers. The men who campaigned among the mountains around it, and who fought so desperately to get to it, year after year, noted its wonderful advantages as a railway centre in one of the richest mineral regions in the world, and when they were mustered out settled there. The march of progress began. It was a revelation to the people of the surrounding country—that steady and rapid improvement at Chattanooga. They had always known that there were coal, iron and oil in the vicinity in such quantities that, in the words of a public speaker who once upbraided them for their lack of enterprise, "within sight of the city might be found Pittsburg ploughs that had been worn out upon the iron ore lying loosely on the hill-sides;" yet they had not dreamed that with cheap iron and cheap coal at their doors they had the elements of empire in their hands. To-day Chattanooga is connected with the outer world by five trunk lines of rail, and the surveys for the sixth, and in some respects the most remarkable, have been completed. The Western and Atlantic connects the city with Atlanta and the South; the Nashville and Chattanooga line pierces the Cumberland, and gives a route to Louisville and the Ohio; the East Tennessee, Virginia, and Georgia road reaches to Bristol, giving direct connection with Lynchburg, Washington and New York; the Alabama and Chattanooga runs through marvelous coal and iron fields to Meridian, in Mississippi, whence there is a direct line to the "Father of Waters," and the Memphis and Charleston opens up a vast fertile section in Northern Alabama and a corner of Mississippi, a section unhappily strewn at present with wrecks of once prosperous plantations. The track of the war is visible through all the beautiful Tennessee valley, and for miles one sees nothing but ruins and neglected lands. The "Cincinnati Southern" railroad is intended to run from the Ohio metropolis to Chattanooga, and

---

* This was done at the suggestion of Mr. John P. Long, one of the prominent citizens of Chattanooga, who is very familiar with the Indian language and legends.

will operate as an outlet from the Ohio valley to the south-eastern seaboard, while it will also furnish a desirable connection with the Gulf system of roads. It will penetrate some of the richest regions of Kentucky, will cross the Cumberland river at Point Burnside, and run through the Sequatchie valley, along an almost unbroken coal-field.

With so many important and really finely-built lines of travel stretching from it in all directions, one would naturally suspect Chattanooga of an inclination to

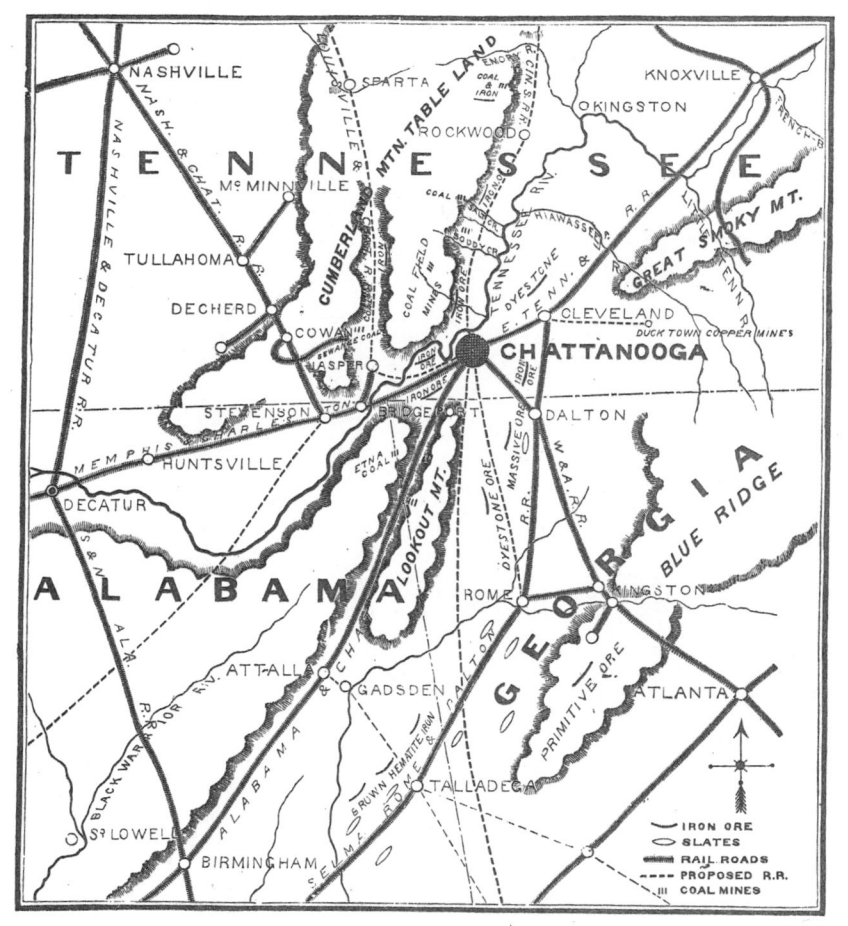

The Mineral Region in the vicinity of Chattanooga.

disregard her river traffic, yet she is by no means unmindful of it. Operating as the distributing point for the whole river-valley, and indeed for the far South, the city crowds her storehouses yearly with corn, wheat, and bacon, brought hundreds of miles in flat-boats and small steamers along the winding river from Kentucky, Virginia and North Carolina. At high water season the stream is crowded with rustic crafts of all kinds, and the jolly raftsmen who have been for months in the forests, and have drifted down stream on broad platforms of pine logs, make merry in highways and by-ways. Transportation of coal

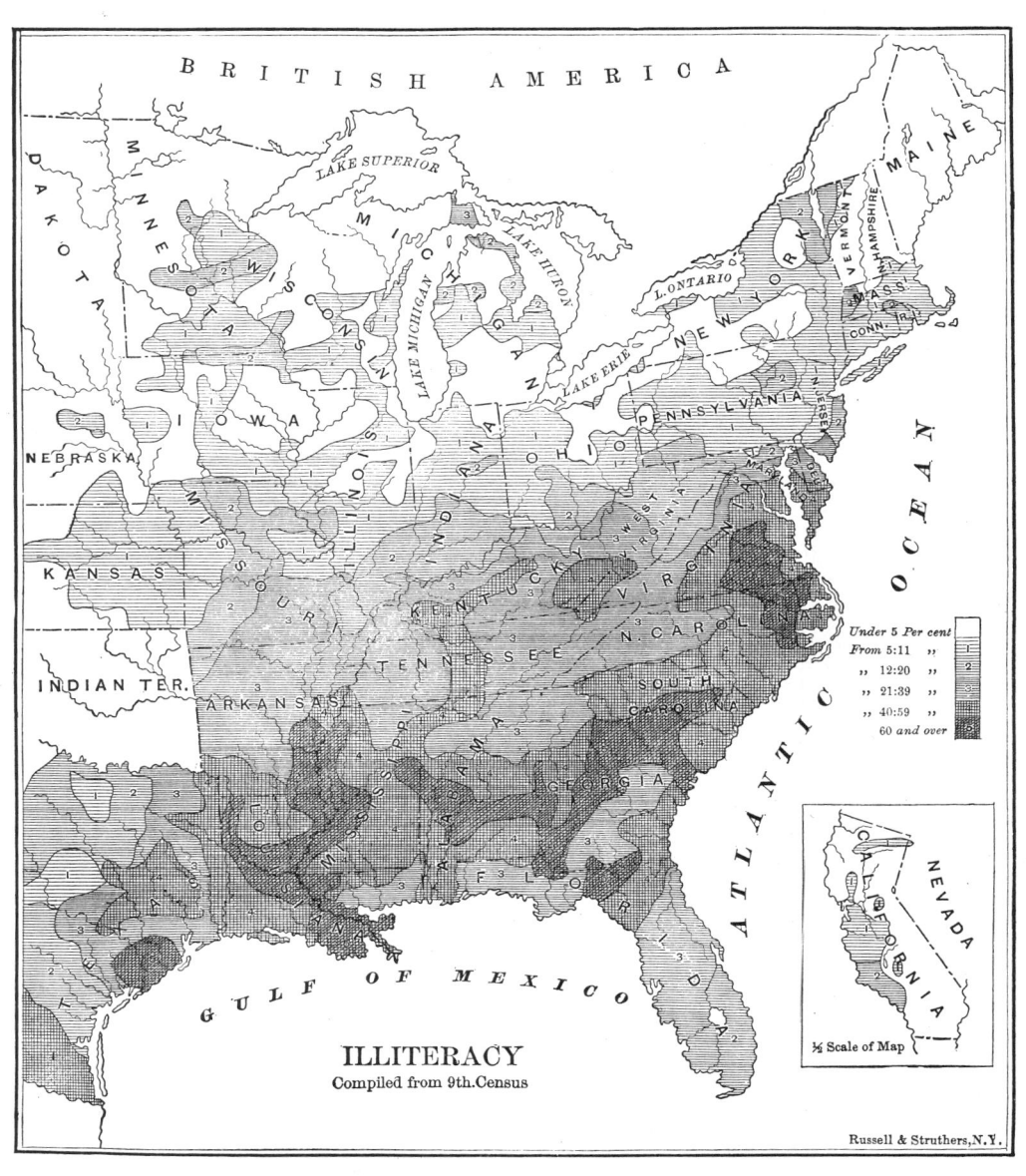

MAP SHOWING GRADES OF ILLITERACY IN THE UNITED STATES.

MIDDLE ATLANTIC STATES, SOUTHERN SECTION, AND NORTH CAROLINA.

Physical and Political

By A. Guyot

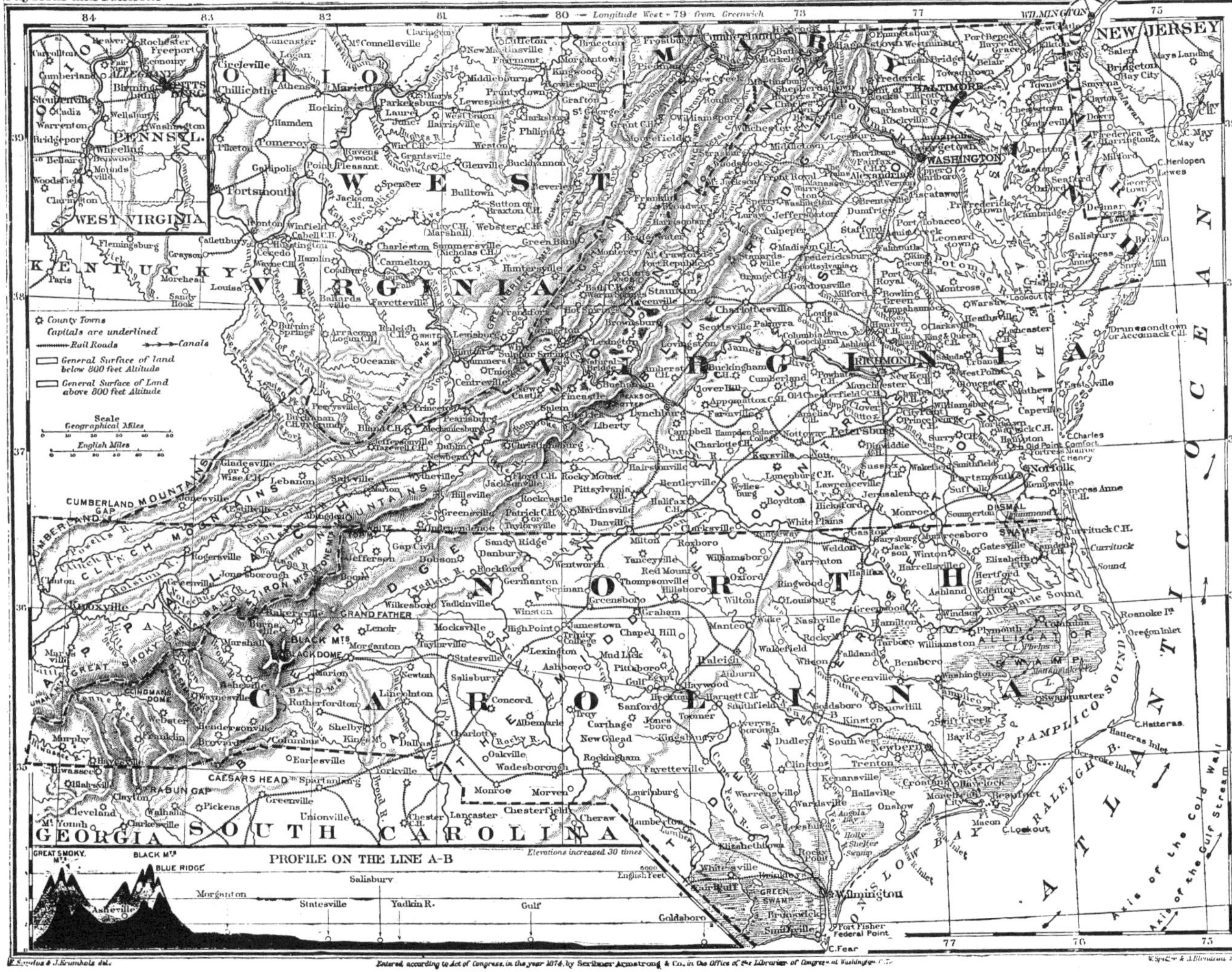

E. Sandoz & J. Krumholz del.

Entered according to Act of Congress, in the year 1874, by Scribner Armstrong & Co., in the Office of the Librarian of Congress at Washington D.C.

W. Spelle & A. Bierstadt Sculpt.

and iron by river would not cost more than one-fourth the sum demanded by the railways.

The surroundings of Chattanooga are of the wildest and most romantic beauty, and in gazing down from "Lookout," or from the humbler Mission Ridge, upon the lovely valley, with its majestic river and lordly ledges, one cannot repress a fear that some day all these natural beauties will be hidden by the smoke from the five hundred chimneys which will be erected in honor of the god Iron. For it is to be a town of rolling-mills and furnaces, giant in its traffic, like Pittsburg and St. Louis, and inhabited by thousands of hard-handed, brawny-armed artisans. There is hardly a county in Eastern Tennessee where the resources destined to make Chattanooga one of the commercial centres of the country do not abound. Along the Great Unaka chain, in those counties bordering upon the Smoky, over which we passed on our way to the North Carolina mountains, lie some of the richest sections of the "eastern iron belt"—which extends northward into Virginia and southward into Georgia. In the "Valley," that rich and populous quarter of Tennessee, on whose ridges and in whose nooks are raised some of the noblest physical specimens of the American man, the mineral development seems incredible. In what is known as the "Dyestone Belt" the immense layers of red hematite run without a break for 150 miles, swelling sometimes to eight or ten feet in thickness, but never sinking below five. One hundred pounds of this stratified red-iron rock, soft and easily crushed, will yield seventy pounds of pure iron. It is the same ore which, outcropping in Virginia, has for years supplied the splendid furnaces of Eastern Pennsylvania, and extending through North-eastern Georgia into Alabama, is known as the "Red Mountain" ore of the latter State. And this grand belt lies at the very base of the coal-measures!

The East Tennessee valley extends north-east and south-west about 280 miles from Chattanooga to the Virginia line. North-west of it is the Cumberland table-land, which Andrew Jackson was wont to declare would one day be the garden of the United States; and one of the outlines of this plateau, extending from the vicinity of Chattanooga to Cumberland Gap, is known as "Walden's Ridge." This is the south-eastern limit of the great Appalachian coal-field, which covers 6,000 square miles—considerably more than the entire coal area of Great Britain. All the ridges in the "Valley" contain minerals; they are ribbed with iron ore of every variety. In some cases the veins of red fossiliferous ore extend under the coal-fields.

The numerous rivers heading in the North Carolina and Western Virginia mountains drain north-west toward the Tennessee, and form natural highways upon which to bear the ore to the beds of coal. The stores of red and brown hematites in the Alleghany chain and the Cumberland range are absolutely inexhaustible. This grand mineral-field is blessed with a delicious climate, which the high mountain walls render temperate in winter and cool and entirely free from malaria in summer.

Before 1860 numbers of furnaces were worked in the "Dyestone Belt," and excellent ore was produced; but an especial impetus has been given to the production of that section since the war. General John T. Wilder, of Ohio, while campaigning under Rosecrans against Chattanooga, in 1863, at the head of a brigade of mounted infantry, became interested in the hills, from which might be blasted thousands of tons of ore in a day, in the great veins of hematites, sometimes covering hundreds of acres, and in that mighty stretch of 200 miles along the now famous ridge, where coal and iron lie only half a mile apart, with massive limestone between them. When he laid by his sword, he continued the study of these mineral deposits, and after purchasing the site on which the village and furnaces of Rockwood now stand, associated with himself a company of capitalists, and in 1867 organized the Roane Iron

The Rockwood Iron-Furnaces — Eastern Tennessee.

Company, with a capital of $1,000,000. This company purchased the rail-mill at Chattanooga, which had been built by the Federal Government; tunneled the Cumberland mountain for coal; and in 1868 began to manufacture pig-iron cheaper than it has been made elsewhere in the country, and to supply it to the rolling-mills, sending it down the Tennessee river in steamers and barges.* Rockwood is now a brisk village of 2,000 inhabitants, of whom about one-half are workmen in the furnaces and the coal mines. It is situ-

* According to the census of 1870, there were then in Tennessee fourteen establishments manufacturing pig-iron, with twenty-three blast-furnaces and $1,103,750 capital, producing 28,688 tons, worth $1,147,707. There were eighteen rolling-mills with a capital of $253,750, producing rolled iron worth $369,222, and thirty-three manufactories of cast-iron, with a capital of $331,392, the products of which annually amounted to about $500,000. The number of establishments has much increased since that time.

ated seventy miles north-east of Chattanooga, in the heart of a rugged mountain region.*

The energetic Western men who have it in charge are confident that in a few years the city of Chattanooga will rival Pittsburg in growth, for they

The "John Ross House," near Chattanooga. Residence of one of the old Cherokee Landholders.

claim that they can manufacture iron at least ten or twelve dollars per ton cheaper than it can be made anywhere else in the United States. It would certainly be remarkable if a mineral region so vast and well stocked as that of Northern Georgia, Northern Alabama, and Eastern Tennessee,—in the midst of which Chattanooga stands,—should not produce at least one city of a hundred thousand inhabitants within a few years. The new aspirant for the honors of rapid growth has made sterling progress. Cotton-mills and car works are springing up beside the rolling-mills and foundries; many fine mansions already grace the principal residence streets, and hundreds of mechanics are building neat cottages along the slopes on both sides of the Tennessee. Swiss capital is engaged in the manufacture of cotton, and English investors are carefully studying the iron and coal fields with a view

* Twenty-five thousand tons of ore are mined at Rockwood yearly, and about 12,000 tons of pig-iron are sent thence to Chattanooga, Atlanta, St. Louis, and Louisville. The rolling-mill at Chattanooga produces about 15,000 tons of rails annually. The impetus given to the growth of Chattanooga by the establishment of this mill and the Vulcan Iron Works has been tremendous. The price paid the Government for the rolling-mill and 145 acres of land at Chattanooga by the Roane Iron Company, was $225,000. The patent puddling apparatus of an Englishman named Danks—an apparatus which is expected to revolutionize iron manufacture by an immense saving in cost—has been introduced into the works. The cost of ore at the Rockwood furnaces is about $2 per ton; that of coal, $1.40 per ton; limestone, eighty cents. It is not astonishing, in view of these prices, that the company hope eventually to manufacture rails and deliver them in Pittsburg cheaper than they can be made there.

to finally erecting large rolling-mills in the city; banks, good hotels, well-planned streets, and excellent schools and churches have arisen like magic within seven years; and the constant stream of produce transferred from the river to the railroads gives an activity and feverishness to the aspect of the streets, at certain seasons, which is quite inspiring. Even within the town limits iron ore is to be found. It lies in the north-west slopes of "Cameron Hill," a high bluff from which one can overlook the Tennessee and the busy town stretched along its banks, even to the base of "Lookout." In the Eastern, Dyestone, and Western iron belts of Tennessee there were more small furnaces before the war than at present; but it is doubtful if so much iron was manufactured then as now. Capital is fast finding out the best locations for furnaces and rolling-mills in each of the three States whose commercial centre Chattanooga properly is, and hundreds of thousands of acres have recently been purchased by companies, who will probably develop them within the next five years.

Catching a "Tarpin."

LX.

LOOKOUT MOUNTAIN—THE BATTLES AROUND CHATTANOOGA. KNOXVILLE—EASTERN TENNESSEE.

MOST persons in this country or in Europe who have heard of Lookout mountain since "the war" have also been told of the "battle above the clouds." It was my fortune to scale the remarkable palisade at a time when the broad plateau which runs along its summit was literally enshrouded in formidable mists. The rain was falling in torrents as, with two companions, I galloped through the little town at the foot of the mountain; but ere we had scaled the winding road, the shower was over, and a brisk wind began to stir the

View from Lookout Mountain, near Chattanooga.

mists. We could see little but the ledges along whose sides the route ran, but as we arrived nearly at the summit, the mist-curtain was lifted for an instant, and revealed to us a delicious expanse of valley, with sunlight's smiles here and there chasing away the rain's tears. Then we were shrouded in again; and our horses, apparently inspired by the gloomy grandeur of the occasion, rattled furiously along the hard roads, over which the boughs hung uncomfortably near our heads. The red sandy clay nourishes enormous pines, whose roots have here and there been disturbed by the sandstone bowlders, and stretched out their fibres in a desperate grasp; beside the pathways great blocks of stone, carved by the storms and polished by the winds, are scattered. We galloped nearly to the massive perpendicular wall which arises directly out of the valley, and disdainfully frowns down upon the Tennessee, spurned from its base fourteen hundred feet below; and tethering our horses, approached to the very edge. There we seemed shut off from all the world. Now and then a hum from the valley—the growl of a locomotive or the rolling of wheels—came faintly up; we heard the cow-bells and the bleating of the sheep on the hill-sides behind us; and just as we were trying to imagine how "the battle" must have been, the wind came sweeping away the mist-curtain, and—we beheld the whole!

From "Umbrella Rock" we saw "the Moccasin," that curious point of land made by the Tennessee's abrupt turn. The streets and houses of Chattanooga seemed like toys, or little blocks of wood. Mission Ridge was an insignificant blue line. The Tennessee seems to turn in deference to Chattanooga, for it might readily inundate it, and has once compelled the citizens to navigate their streets in boats. Beyond it, northward and westward, the eye encounters forests and ridges where the mountains seem to have been split asunder by some convulsion of nature—until at last, on the east, the Cumberland range springs up, and forbids you to choose any other horizon. Southward, beyond broad and quiet vales, richly cultured, are the mountains of Georgia, and westward the tree-crested ridges in Alabama.

Umbrella Rock, on Lookout Mountain.

We clambered down a flight of wooden steps to a secure point of the crags, and looked over the valley out of which Hooker hurried his troops on to the summit when he broke the left of Bragg's formidable army. It was a wild struggle, a running and leaping fight among rocks and behind trees, when men carried their lives in their hands, and their swords in their teeth, as they wormed their way through the fastnesses, and then made their charge upon the foe so strongly intrenched above the very clouds, upon "Point Lookout."

The old Government hospital still stands on its picturesque bluff, deserted now save by curious visitors; here and there along the broad plateau are scattered comfortable houses, and log-cabins; good roads lead into the northern counties of Georgia. Near "Rock City,"—a gigantic series of galleries in disrupted stone pinnacles which rise amid the ragged brush and saplings,—is another enormous uplift of limestone, from which one may see the whole of Chattanooga valley, the Raccoon and Lookout ranges, and the battle-field of Chickamauga. Descending five or six miles from the point where the turnpike from the city reaches the summit, into the valley of Walker county, in Northern Georgia, one comes to a region of precipices and waterfalls, of tarns and caves, of landslides and bluffs.

Near "Lake Seclusion," an apparently bottomless well, sunk a hundred feet below the surrounding rocks, the scenery is exquisite. In autumn the foliage on the cliffs bordering the stream which flows through this lake, and plunges farther on down a ravine in a blinding spray-cloud, which the Indians named "Lulah Falls," is so rich in color that the whole country seems aflame. From one or two of the highest points the ragged ends of the Lookout plateau, and the pleasant expanse of valley beyond, may be seen.

Riding day by day along the broad tables of the Cumberland, in the nooks on the banks of the Tennessee, and up and over the ridges near the scene of Chickamauga, it was pleasant to hear anew the story of the great fight around Chattanooga from the lips of those who had been participants. But it was all unreal, dreamlike. When we stood with our feet in half-filled rifle-pits, or among the shattered and cannon-scorched tree-trunks on the field of combat, it was still remote, indefinite. I fancy even the natives of the country round about only remember the whole struggle vaguely now and then; although a Chattanooga man once said to a newcomer from the West that when he wanted some paper which the invading army had burned up for him, or remembered the losses of property he had suffered, he "hated the whole Yankee nation for a minute or two;" but he added, "it's only for a minute or two, and those minutes don't come as often as they did."

Looking from "Lookout Cave."

Chattanooga's possession by the Union army cost many thousands of lives; but it opened the way to Atlanta and the sea. The line which stretched from Lookout's northern crag to Mission Ridge, on the night of November 24th, 1863, might have been quadrupled in strength if the dead warriors from Murfreesboro and Chickamauga could have been marshaled into it. There was an especial bitterness in the struggle for this rocky gateway. After the staggering blows which both armies had received in the terrible fight by Stone river, Bragg and Rosecrans were both willing enough to rest for a little; but when Bragg had withdrawn, and it was evident that his formidable campaign, which had carried terror even to the gates of Louisville and Cincinnati, was at an end, the Union standards led the way to Chattanooga. There, strongly intrenched, Bragg defied his old antagonist. On the morning of August 21st, 1863, General

Wilder, commanding the advance of Rosecrans' army, began shelling the city which he now makes his home, from the hills at the north side of the river.

Meantime day by day the Federal forces were investing Chattanooga, having crossed the Tennessee at Bridgeport, at Battle Creek, and at Shell Mound. On the 4th of September Burnside occupied Knoxville. Bragg moved the Confederate forces away toward Dalton, and Rosecrans entered the town, and followed the enemy, who turned fiercely, and stood at bay on Chickamauga. Longstreet's Virginians and Bragg's hardy army fought with the energy of desperation; and if, on that memorable 19th of September, when the combatants waded in blood, Longstreet had had another than Thomas to encounter, he might have carried the Federal left which he so furiously attacked. Thomas drove Longstreet back a mile or two, but, as the centre failed to keep pace with his advance, he was compelled to halt.

Then Bragg fell upon the forces under command of McCook and Crittenden, and the waves of battle flowed to and fro until night, when the Federal army still held its own ground. Early in the morning Thomas had the enemy once more hurled at him, but repulsed him as before. The Union right and centre were driven back; McCook was confused and demoralized; Thomas alone stood like a rock, and kept the enemy at arm's length until night, when he fell back to Rossville, to be attacked again, and to once more repulse his foes the next day. Fifteen thousand men had been lost to the Union army, in killed, wounded and missing, in these two days; and the Confederates had lost 18,000. The field of Chickamauga was piled with the dead, and the rivulets literally ran blood.

The flushed and defiant enemy now stood ready to again fall upon Chattanooga. They had struck some terrible blows. Rosecrans, McCook, and Crittenden, were removed from command. The Confederate forces occupied Lookout mountain and controlled the valley, cutting off rail and river communication. Provisions were hauled over the rough hill-roads and through the narrow passes on the north side

"Rock City," Lookout Mountain. [Page 537.]

of the river, for seventy miles, by animals worn to skeletons, and by men who were half starved; and so, on mountain and in forest, along the valleys and the rivers, the vigilant combatants stood, patiently awaiting the next move, when there came upon the scene a man named Grant.

As soon as General Grant had taken command of the military division of the Mississippi, communication, both by river and rail, was gradually re-established, and Chattanooga was unlocked. Sherman reinforced the army there in mid-November. Grant's next move was to allow Longstreet to do what he had several times unsuccessfully tried, pass the Federal army to the east of Chattanooga and march against Burnside and the army of the Ohio. Longstreet had 20,000 splendid soldiers, and Burnside far less; it might fare hardly with the latter, but it was one of the moves on Grant's chessboard, and there was nothing to be said. It resulted in checkmating Bragg at Mission Ridge.

Twenty thousand men having been taken from the line which the Confederates had stretched along the Lookout plateau,—eastwardly across Chattanooga valley to Mission Ridge, at or near Rossville Gap, and thence northwardly

View from Wood's Redoubt, Chattanooga.

on the Ridge toward Chickamauga creek,—by the departure of Longstreet, that line was attacked. The plan was to assault the wings, to cause Bragg to throw large forces to their protection, and then to break the centre.

Hooker and Sherman began working in earnest. The 24th of November saw the left of the enemy driven from Lookout, and the right forced out of its position. Next day the wave of war swept up Mission Ridge, over the charming slopes where now the great National cemetery is situated, up to the summit; and at sunset General Grant moved his head-quarters from Wood's Redoubt to the Ridge, which in the morning had been guarded by sentinels in gray. The enemy was next day driven from his base of supplies.

The siege was over. The pathway to the sea lay before Sherman.

Wood's Redoubt is still one of the most striking objects in the valley of Chattanooga. Standing on the grass-grown ramparts one has an exquisite view of Lookout, the Tennessee's abrupt recoil at its base, and the sharp peak of Eagle Point, and can note the two turns of the river, with the Moccasin Point between, around whose southern bend, on a November midnight in 1863, Sherman moved 3,000 soldiers in pontoons. Northward, and opposite the redoubts, overhanging the Tennessee, is Cameron Hill, from whose wind-swept height one can look down upon Chattanooga's busy streets as from a balloon. On the slopes adjacent to Cameron Hill there are many handsome residences, and Wood's

Redoubt itself will in a few years be lost sight of under the foundations of some charming villa. On many of the hills a faint outline of the old fortifications may be traced; but they will soon have vanished forever.

It would be difficult to imagine more romantic approaches than those through which the Nashville and Chattanooga railroad finds its way to the latter city. For seventy-five or eighty miles it runs through a bold, mountainous country; but about twenty-five miles before reaching Chattanooga it bends downward into the mighty passes among the Cumberlands in Northern Alabama, and crawling under rocks and on the brinks of chasms, now running on the edges of valleys clothed in perfect forests, and now shooting into long tunnels, works its way to the valley. As one approaches Lookout by this route, the effect is extremely imposing; a new and striking view is presented at each instant; the cliffs seem to present no outlet; the train is apparently about to be cast down some yawning ravine, when one sees the continuation of the route.

Sixty-two miles from Chattanooga, on a spur of the Cumberland, at Sewanee, in Tennessee, is situated the "University of the South." This remarkable institution owes its origin to the late Bishop Leonidas Polk, of Louisiana. He desired to concentrate the interests of the several Southern dioceses of the Episcopal Church upon one school where religious education might be given in a thorough manner; and in 1836 he issued an address to the bishops of the various States of the South, proposing to establish a Christian University. The result was a large assembly of bishops and lay delegates at a meeting on Lookout Mountain's summit, in 1837, at which the general principles of union were discussed; and the city of Sewanee was chosen some time thereafter. The Tennessee Legislature granted a liberal charter, and a domain of ten thousand acres of land had been secured, five hundred thousand dollars obtained toward an endowment, and the corner-stone of the central building laid, when the war began. In 1866 very little remained save the domain; but in 1868, after some aid from England, the University was definitely established, and the more important of the schools are now well organized, with able professors at their head. The institution is under the perpetual control of a board of trustees composed of the bishops of the various Southern States, the senior bishop being, *ex officio*, Chancellor of the University.

The location is charming. The University was started in the midst of an almost unbroken forest, but has now grouped around it a pleasant and refined community. It is about nine miles from the Nashville and Chattanooga railroad, and the great tunnel on that road passes under its lands. From Cowan, on the line, to Sewanee, the local coal mining company has built a good railroad. The Sewanee plateau is 2000 feet above the sea-level, in a richly-varied country, abounding in cascades, ravines, groves, and uplands.

There is an abundance of building material in the quarries of gray, blue, dove-colored and brown limestone, which lie beside the Sewanee Company's railroad, and as soon as the present insufficient endowment is enlarged, the erection of permanent buildings will be begun. There are chalybeate springs in the vicinity, and the slopes of the Cumberland here are admirably adapted for grape culture. Nearly 300 students are gathered into the various schools. Bishop Quintard, of Tennessee, has done the University great service in collecting money in England for its establishment, and he and others are now anxiously trying to secure $500,000 as an enlargement fund.

Riding through the wooded country on the Tennessee's banks, not far from Chattanooga, one autumn day, we dismounted, a large and hungry party, before the door of a log-cabin, built on a hill-side, and hailed the inmates. A fat negro woman appeared at the corner of the rude veranda, and four plump negro babies regarded us through the crevices between the logs with round-eyed fear. " Reckoned she could n't give us no dinner—no way;" finally was very positive, and said "she had nothing in the house." But persistence was rewarded by

On the Tennessee River, near Chattanooga.

permission to return in an hour, and she would see what could be improvised. At the hour's end we found in the cabin a rough table spread with bacon, and corn-bread just baked in the ashes; a few sweet potatoes were presently proffered, and some tea was made. By the fireside, rocking a black cherub, was another woman, younger and more comely than our host. These two cultivated a little field; their "husbands," or the men of the house,—for marriage is not always considered necessary among the negroes,—were away at work in another county; and the children rolled in the dirt, and had no thoughts of school. It was the very rudest and most incult life imaginable; the cabin was cleanly, but primitive in all its furnishings; the round of these people's lives seemed to be sleeping and waking, with a struggle between morning and evening to get enough to put into their mouths; they had no thought of thrift or progress. Now and then they went to a religious gathering, and, perhaps, had "experiences," and were converted; then they gradually relapsed into their dull condition.

The mountain roads in all the section bordering on the Tennessee are beautiful. There are many bold bluffs, one and two hundred feet high, which

The "Suck," on the Tennessee River.

overlook the stream; and one comes upon stretches of fertile fields. The inhabitants, white or black, are invariably civil and courteous. The farmers, clad in homespun, mounted on raw-boned horses, are willing and eager to compare notes with strangers. They have caught a touch of the inspiration Chattanooga diffuses around itself, and carefully explore their lands in the hope of finding minerals.

The Tennessee is receiving some improvement here and there. At the point called the "Suck," where the waters rush through a gorge in the mountains, over a rocky bed and in a shallow channel, we saw dredge-boats at work. The river has ordinarily more water than the Ohio, and a permanent bed, with little or no sand or gravel, so that there is no danger of the formation of those bars which obstruct the navigation of so many Western rivers.

The attention of the Government has been directed toward the needed improvements ever since 1828, and the ruins of the Muscle Shoals canal, which originally cost $700,000, testify to the thoroughness of the plans then made. If that canal were put in condition again, and the obstructions between Muscle Shoals and Knoxville were removed, America would be the richer by one grand water highway.

Knoxville, once the capital of Tennessee, and one of the most illustrious and venerable of its communities, is situated on the Holston river about 100 miles above Chattanooga. It is to-day as actively engaged in developing the mighty resources of Eastern Tennessee as is its sister of the valley, and a generous rivalry exists between the two towns, represented in the newspapers by good-humored raillery, in which the editors of both cities seem admirable proficients. Five miles east of Knoxville the lovely French Broad river empties its dancing and frothing current, released from the passes of the North Carolina mountains, into the Tennessee. Knoxville was named for that worthy Knox who was Secretary of War under the presidency of Washington. The town dates from 1794, when Colonel White, proprietor of the lands, laid it out into lots. Three years before, on the 5th of December, 1791, in the midst of Indian massacres and battles, the first Tennessee newspaper was issued by George Roulstone. Although it was printed at Rogersville, it was called *The Knoxville Gazette,* and was identified with the interests of the then territorial seat of government.

The section of which Knoxville thus became the chief town has a most romantic history. In 1760 there was not a single civilized inhabitant in Tennessee. A few daring woodsmen pushed into the wilderness a few years later, and founded settlements on the Watauga and the Holston, to which flocked settlers from North

A Negro Cabin on the bank of the Tennessee. [Page 542.]

Carolina and Virginia. North Carolina, in those days a province, was disquieted by taxation which she considered illegal; and thousands who had been compelled to fly from their homes, because they had actively resisted the oppression of Governor Tryon, took refuge with the adventurers at Watauga. In a few years the surrounding country re-echoed to the blows of the woodsmen's axes, and the Indians began to regard their encroachments with alarm and resentment. But shortly before the outbreak of the Revolution, and the downfall of royal government in North Carolina, the members of the Watauga Association had a peaceable meeting with the Cherokees and their chiefs, and purchased from them, for £2,000, all the lands on which they had settled. The Elizabethton of to-day, a little mountain hamlet, occupies the site of the old Watauga. Shortly after the purchase, the Cherokees began open hostilities, and the Tennessean had then, as for many a long year thereafter, to risk his life daily. Battles ensued; the Indians organized expeditions to cut off and annihilate the infant colonies; war raged through all the North Carolina mountains and along the Unaka range. The result was an invasion of the Cherokee towns by the militia of North Carolina and the settlements. Eighteen hundred men, armed with rifles, tomahawks, and butcher knives,—thus saith the ancient chronicle,—marched across the Holston and the French Broad, and drove the Indians everywhere before them. A pious chaplain accompanied this little army of invasion, and was the first Christian minister that ever preached in Tennessee. Immigration flowed after the army, and the Indians were dismayed. The Watauga settlement, triumphant, petitioned for annexation to North Carolina, and its prayer was granted. The Legislature of that State, in 1777, founded Washington county, which occupied the whole district now included within the present boundaries of Tennessee. Two years later explorers had planted a field with corn on the spot where the present city of Nashville stands.

The recital of the border wars, and of dashing expeditions down the Tennessee river, would require volumes. Men sprang up, rude, hardy, brave—the outgrowth of their time; their brains were filled with visions of empire; they fought by day and planned by night. After the independence of the United States had been acknowledged by Great Britain, each State endeavored to relieve the indebtedness of the country, by cessions to Congress, of their unappropriated lands; and, accordingly, North Carolina ceded her new acquisition, now known as Tennessee. This made political orphans of our brave Watauga settlers and their followers, so they forthwith created an independent State called Franklin, which was ruled over by an energetic and daring man named Sevier, and maintained a stormy existence from 1784 to 1788, during much of which time it was considered by the Government of North Carolina as practically in revolt. Sevier was engaged in many a daring battle and mountain skirmish; was once carried off by his friends at the moment a court in North Carolina was trying him for his offenses; and was, after Franklin became United States territory, sent to Congress. His associates in the Government of Franklin,—Cocke, White, the founder of Knoxville, Ramsey, Doak, Center, Reese, Houston, Newell, Weir and Conway,—were, subsequently, leading spirits in the affairs of Tennessee. Greenville, the present home of ex-President Andrew Johnson, and a pretty village set down graciously among exquisite mountains, was founded in the days of Franklin, and was the original seat of government. In 1785 the third Franklin convention was held there, in a court-house built of unhewn logs, and there the State Constitution was finally adopted.

White's Fort, the location of Knoxville, was, at the time of the fall of Franklin, a stockaded settlement, to which settlers were rapidly flocking. On the high plateau which, extending southward, terminated in a bold bluff on the Holston river, they saw excellent chances for defense; and thus the site of the city was determined. In 1794, Governor Blount, controlling the territory for the United

States, had his cabin at Knoxville, and was kept busy day and night devising measures for the defense of the young settlement against the thoroughly maddened Cherokees. At one time, when the fighting force of Knoxville was forty men, more than fifteen hundred Indians marched against the town, but were turned aside by some trivial circumstance, and the colony was saved.

As Knoxville had been the seat of the Territorial Government, so in 1796 it became the State capital, and there the convention met, and the first Constitution was adopted. There, too, the "Washington College, in honor of the illustrious

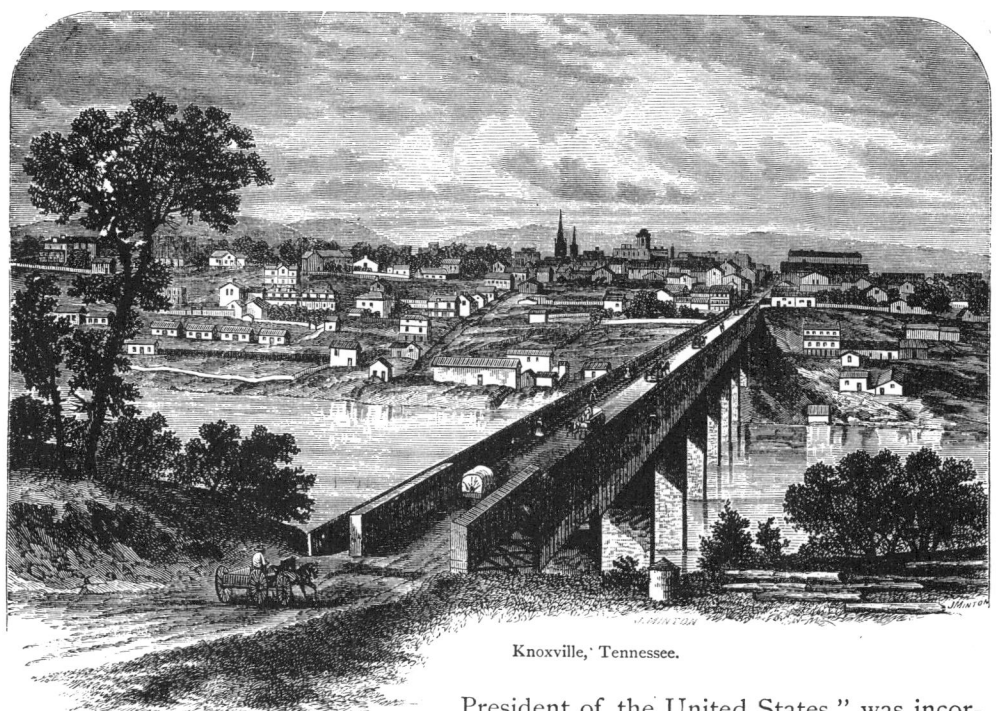

Knoxville, Tennessee.

President of the United States," was incorporated; and there General Jackson, in the convention, suggested that the new State adopt the beautiful Indian name of Tennessee. Knoxville shared the honors of the government seat with Kingston, Murfreesboro, and Nashville alternately, but in 1817 it became the capital for the last time. The centre of population moved beyond the Cumberland mountains, and the State officials went with it. To Knoxville were left the souvenirs of the bloody times in which it sprang into being, of councils with Cherokee chieftains, and struggles against their warriors, before the current of immigration came.

Knoxville is to-day a flourishing town with nearly 15,000 population. It has more capital than Chattanooga, but not the same wonderful transportation facilities. More actual business is, however, probably done there; the town has a large wholesale trade, and is a kind of supply depot for the mountains. On the line of the road from New York to New Orleans, it has hopes of other communication shortly. The subject of narrow-gauge railroads has very much interested the people of Eastern Tennessee, and they will, in a few years, traverse the valleys in all directions. A direct line from Knoxville to Macon in Georgia has been projected; and the completion of the Knoxville and Kentucky roads would be a great aid to the local commerce. The General Government is erecting a fine custom-house and post-office in the city. Thirty miles to the northward are large coal-fields, close to veins of iron; in Carter and Greene counties there are iron mines which supply the rolling-mills and car-wheel establishments at Knoxville. There is an extensive manufacture of glass in that section; the lumber interests are large, and considerable shipments are made to New England. Five miles east of Knoxville is a fine marble quarry, operated by capitalists from St. Louis. At Coal creek and Caryville, some thirty-five miles north of the town, there are extensive coal mining interests. The whole of Eastern Tennessee offers the best of inducements for the practical farmer, the wool-grower, and the investor in mines and minerals.

The social condition of the people varies with the location. In previous chapters I have described the dwellers in the mountains bordering on North Carolina; those living in other remote counties are very similar in habits and intelligence. The political sentiment is yet, as it was during the war, difficult to classify. There were then hosts of uncompromising Union men in Eastern Tennessee; but there were, also, many committed to the interests of the Confederacy, and both classes were much broken in fortune, and possibly discouraged, by the marching and counter-marching of the troops. Their farms were plundered by both armies; and they often came near starvation themselves. In Knoxville the majorities are usually Republican, although the struggle is sometimes very close. In Chattanooga Republican municipal rule is also purchased at the expense of a careful fight. In the mountain counties people are not very much engrossed with general politics; their local affairs alone occupy their attention. At the period of my visit the school law allowed each county to decide for itself as to taxation for the support of free schools, and thus far no very marked progress has been made in the State. Tennessee admits the disagreeable fact that she ranks third in illiteracy in the Union, but her population does not seem as yet to feel the situation very keenly. Knoxville has good schools, with about 1,400 scholars as an average attendance; it also supports four colored schools. Chattanooga's regular attendance is about 1,000, and it also has two large colored schools. On the whole, Eastern Tennessee seems to make as much progress in education as other sections of the State in proportion to its population. Some of its counties have totally refused to have any public schools; while others have levied small taxes for supporting winter sessions. The Peabody fund has been very active in East Tennessee, and it is largely due to its influential distribution that a feeling in favor of schools is gradually taking root among the masses. The founding of two or three Normal schools in the State is a prime necessity. In a commonwealth which has thus far succeeded in getting only one-fifth of its 400,000 pupil-children into schools, the education of capable teachers is certainly of first importance.

Knoxville is the seat of the East Tennessee University, and the State Asylum for deaf and dumb persons. The University has latterly received a large share of the $200,000 appropriated as the "Agricultural Fund" of the State, and will serve as the Agricultural College. It now has some 300 students. The Methodist Episcopal Church contemplates founding a college at Knoxville; and there, or at Chattanooga, the people of one of the grandest mineral regions on this continent should not fail to establish a school of mines.

The peaks of the Cumberland, the Clinch and the Smoky, furnish Knoxville with many beautiful mountain views; and the eye dwells with delight on the route from Chattanooga even to Greenville, upon the fields so beautifully cultivated, on the noble orchards, and the forests of mammoth corn stalks. The soil in this elevated valley is generally rich, second only to that of the Western prairies; the summers are long, but never excessively hot; there is only a light snow-fall in winter; in the valleys the water is limestone; on the hills freestone and chalybeate. On the table-lands grow rye, oats, and all vegetables; in the valleys wheat and corn attain extraordinary size. Apples, pears, peaches and wild grapes are cultivated in profusion, and the grazing-lands are no whit poorer than those of the North Carolina mountain region, which are so perfect and inexpensive. Land ranges in value from $5 to $35 per acre.

The East Tennessee University—Knoxville.

Through this fruitful country, and almost on the line of the railroad of to-day, ran the "great Indian war-path" eighty years ago. When one reflects upon the vast territory cleared, settled, and dominated within three generations, by the Tennessean, he cannot refrain from admiration, nor will he refuse to believe in the greatest possibilities in the future.

The Ducktown copper region in Eastern Tennessee, near the North Carolina line, is worth a visit from all interested in the State's development. It is the only locality in the commonwealth yielding copper ore in any considerable quantity. Although traces of the metal are to be met with in the Unaka mountains, they do not indicate veins of any importance. Ducktown is a mountain basin that belongs physically to Georgia and North Carolina. In the vicinity of the mines, 2,000 feet above sea-level, deep ravines alternate with sharp ridges, at whose base the Ocoee river worms its way toward the main Unaka range—when it becomes a torrent, roaring over huge rocks in its passage through the narrows. As early as 1836, the attention of geologists was drawn to the mineral deposits near the junction of the Ocoee and the Hiawassee rivers, and indications of copper were finally discovered by men who were searching for gold.

One of these men, while washing in the Hiawassee for gold, found great numbers of crystals of red copper ore. Soon after, the black oxide, which has thus far been the most important ore of the mines, was found; but it was not until 1850 that mining was begun in earnest. The gentlemen who opened the mines found themselves surrounded by a rough population, who took no interest whatever in any improvements; and on one occasion, when they had called a meeting of the township, and explained to the assembled citizens that civilization and wealth would follow upon the opening of the mines, one of the assembly arose and said that most of those present had come to the mountains to get away from civilization, and if it followed them too closely, they would migrate again!

This was discouraging; but the owners of the mines opened day and Sabbath schools, and built roads over the hitherto almost impassable mountains; meantime sinking shafts and employing the few whom they could prevail upon to undertake regular labor. Between 1851 and the close of 1855 a number of mines were opened and worked successfully in this region, and during that time eight of them produced and shipped 14,291 tons, worth more than a million of dollars. A few years later a consolidated company, called "The Union," was formed from a number of the most prosperous organizations, and its works now extend over 2,500 acres. Refineries were constructed, and although the company was prevented from working much of the time during the war, it has been very prosperous. The refining works have yielded nearly 1,500,000 pounds of refined copper since the war. In most of the Ducktown mines the operations have been confined to the zones of black and red copper ore, below which lie zones of iron and copper pyrites. The smelting works of the Union Consolidated Company are very extensive.

Lead and zinc are pretty liberally scattered through Eastern Tennessee, and in Bradley and Monroe counties lead mines have been opened. At Mossy Creek, in Jefferson county, and in the mountains beyond, there are numerous irregular veins of zinc ore. The gold found in the eastern portion of the State has been insignificant in quantity, although, in 1831, there was a genuine gold fever concerning the discoveries along the Hiawassee.

The most important coal mining establishments in the State are the Ætna mines, in Marion county, and the Sewanee Company's mines, which extend several miles underground, not far from the location of the "University of the South." Some of the veins at these latter mines are seven feet thick.

The coal in these mountains can be mined for three cents per bushel, and the freights for coal on all the roads south of Nashville are low. All the Tennessee coals are bituminous; but as such they present numerous varieties.

One of the sources of future wealth for Eastern Tennessee consists in its immense stores of variegated marble, the veins of which run through ten or twelve counties in that section. Besides the finer marbles, there are, in the extreme eastern counties, black or dark-blue limestones, which, when polished, would make elegant marble slabs. There is marble enough in this section to build all the public buildings of the United States for the next five centuries.

At the Ætna Coal Mines.

The siege of Knoxville, in 1863, is called to memory, but faintly, by the earthworks scattered about the town, and now nearly obliterated; but it was one of the most desperate struggles of the whole war. Longstreet and his men, fresh from their triumphs at Chickamauga, fell upon Burnside's little force in the mountain city with savage eagerness, but were hurled back into the jaws of death. They charged toward the ditches only to be pitched headlong over the wires strung to trip them, and to be massacred. But the living charged over the dead who filled the ditches, and twice had planted their flag or leaped upon the fortifications before they were finally swept away. Pools of blood six inches deep were found in the bottom of the trenches when the assault was made on the morning after the repulse of November 29th, and hundreds of corpses were hastily buried in heaps. On the 5th of December following, the little army of the Ohio, which was literally at the point of starvation, was at liberty once more. The siege was raised.

The magnitude of the mineral resources in this section perhaps affords the strongest argument in favor of the immediate removal of the obstructions in the Tennessee river; but the arguments are really legion. This noble stream, sixth in magnitude in the United States, intersecting ten rich commonwealths—in connection with the Ohio, draining the gigantic coal-areas of Tennessee and Alabama—never bearing upon its current, from its sources to its mouth, winter or summer, a particle of ice, and having half-a-dozen tributaries which could be rendered navigable by slack-water improvement, should be made one of the main commercial arteries of the South. With the necessary improvements, navigation could be rendered practicable for thirteen hundred miles above Muscle Shoals in Alabama. Only steamers of the lightest draught now succeed in running to Knoxville and beyond during six or nine months of each year.

The soil of the great Tennessee plateau, the Cumberland table-land, is no less remarkable than the climate of that favored region. For the production of fruit, and for the raising of sheep and cattle, the immigrant will find it most admirably suited. Extending across the State from north to south, the plateau is at least forty miles wide from east to west, and can furnish homes for thousands of farmers, who need but little capital.

"Down in a Coal Mine."

LXI.

A VISIT TO LYNCHBURG IN VIRGINIA.

"TIME to get up, boss!"

I hastily adjusted my garments, and hurried from the sleeping-car of the Richmond train on to the Gordonsville platform, where I was speedily

The old Market at Lynchburg. [Page 554.]

lost in a whirlpool of English and Scotch immigrants, surrounded by their numerous wives and children; of negro touters, shouting, "Dis way, boss,—

don' ye trust dat ar nigger, he don tole ye wrong 'bout de hotel,—take yer bag, *sar?*"—of stout colored damsels, hastening to and fro with platters of cold and antiquated provisions, and blue-looking eggs; of farmers coming from markets, and of through passengers shivering in the cool night air.

"Now, boss, dar 's de Orange train!"

You must know that in the South the African is wont to designate strangers to whom he is indifferent by the euphonious title of "boss." It is, perhaps, a kind of compromise with his inclination to still cling to the old word "mas'r," and, at the same time, embodies as much respect as he cares to bestow on the "casual" whom he is called to serve. When familiar with your face, he will call

The James River, at Lynchburg, Virginia.

you "captain," if you are young; "major," if you are middle-aged, and "general" or "judge," if you are advanced in years. He has even been known to heap these titles upon strangers under the genial influence of the respect-provoking twenty-five cents. But at one o'clock in the morning, in hurrying you from one sleeping-car to another, it would take the potent influence of a brand-new dollar bill to wring from him any salutation save the accustomed "boss."

The train from Washington came crawling along the Orange road, and received me, while the one I had just left rushed forward into the mountains, and by the side of the deep ravines of Western Virginia, toward the Ohio river.

Among the immigrants there were many Englishmen of education and refinement, country gentlemen's sons who had made up their minds to try farming in the new country, or to purchase coal or iron tracts for speculation. Even the least cultured and rudest of these people wore the look of health and prosperity. Their advent was an encouraging symptom.

But in the car where the colored people were seated there were a good many discouraging signs. Was it possible to mould these slouching and ragged fellows, who talked so rudely, whose gestures were so uncouth, and on whose features had been stamped the seal of ignorance, into as useful and trustworthy citizens as these newly-arrived Britons, with their hardy cleanliness and bluff ambition, were likely to become? And if not, what would be the future condition of the lately liberated slave? Was he prospering, and hastening forward to the consummation of the independent manhood promised him? These questions, idly drifting in my sleepy mind without expecting answers, served to amuse and keep awake a tired body until the train trembled to a stand-still at the foot of the steep hill along whose sides Lynchburg lies.

At midday I strolled out to survey the town. The September sun poured terrible heat upon the broad James river, which, opposite the network of tracks at the depot, flowed placidly at the base of an immense cliff, from whose stony sides quarrymen were blasting and chiseling blocks for building purposes. A few rafts and flat-boats, steered by barearmed and bareheaded negroes, drifted lazily on the stream. A long covered bridge spanned the water, and a glance through its little windows showed quaint mills and houses upon the banks; high bluffs, crowned with humble cabins, were rendered accessible by precipitous paths and flights of stone steps; and, in the distance, were blue outlines of mountains, with little cloud-wreaths around them.

Returning from the bridge toward the town I came to a wide street, stretching straight up the hill. On either side were stone pavements, crowded with negroes; colored children gamboled on the flags; colored mammas smoked pipes in the doorways of shops, where colored fathers sold apples, beer, and whiskey; colored damsels, with baskets of clean linen in their stout arms, joked with colored boatmen from the canal; colored draymen cursed and pounded their mules; and colored laborers on the streets enveloped one in a cloud of suffocating dust as he hastened by. Toward the water sloped other streets lined with roomy tobacco warehouses; half-way up the hill a broad and well-built business avenue crossed at right angles, and there, at last, one saw white people, and the ordinary sights of a city.

Finally I came into an open air market, picturesque as any in Italy or Spain. On the curbing of the sidewalk, and even on the stones in the middle of the square, dozens of negro women were seated before baskets containing vegetables, or various goods of trivial description. One venerable matron, weighing perhaps 200 pounds, had her profuse chignon overtopped by a dilapidated beaver, and was smoking a clay pipe. Many young women were cleanly and nicely dressed, and had folded back the huge flaps of their starched sun-bonnets, so that they seemed to imitate the head-dresses of the Italian maidens at Sorrento. Hosts of colored buyers, market-baskets in hand, hovered from one seller to another, talking in high-pitched voices, and in a dialect which Northern ears found difficult to understand. Leaving the market, and yet ascending, I came to another broad street lined with comfortable dwellings, and looking up saw, still far above me, the "Court-House" perched on the topmost point.

Lynchburg lies among the mountains, on the south bank of the James river, nearly in the centre of the Piedmont district of Virginia, and not far from the base of the Blue Ridge. The Virginians of all sections speak affectionately of it as "Old Lynchburg." It was once the wealthiest city in the United States, in proportion to its population, and one of the most remarkable tobacco marts in the world. Colossal fortunes were amassed and enjoyed there, in the days when internal revenue was not, and slave labor tilled the fields. Then the products of the Virginia and North Carolina plantations filled its warehouses and manufac-

A Side Street in Lynchburg, Virginia.

tories to bursting, and all Europe came to buy. An Irish emigrant gave his name, in 1786, to the town; and the famous term "Lynch law," now so universal, sprang from the summary manner in which this hot-headed Hibernian—a colonel in the Revolutionary army—treated such tories as were caught by him. During the late war the town did not fall into Federal hands. The tide of war flowed all around it, but never mounted to the reddish hills where it had safely perched.

Lynchburg's great natural advantages of situation will, in a few years, increase it from a city of 12,000 population to a huge overcrowded railway centre. It possesses superb and abundant water power. Coal is to be had in the immediate neighborhood cheaper than in most of the other cities in the Atlantic States.

Two important railway lines intersect at Lynchburg, the Atlantic, Mississippi and Ohio, now connecting Norfolk on the Atlantic with Memphis on the Mississippi, and destined also to connect Norfolk with Louisville on the Ohio; and the Washington City, Virginia Midland and Great Southern road which connects from Alexandria, in North-eastern Virginia, with Danville in the southern part of the State, and forms a link in the great Air Line between the cities on the Gulf and New York. The latter road opens to Lynchburg the whole Piedmont district, so rich in grains, grasses, fruits, tobacco, minerals and timber. The James river and Kanawha canal now extends from tide-water at Richmond, about 200 miles through the centre of the State, to a point near the base of the Alleghanies, but if carried to the Ohio, by means of liberal improvements in the Kanawha river, would revolutionize American internal commerce. This canal winds in pleasant curves between green banks through the mountains and at the base of the Lynchburg hills; and the horn of the boatmen is heard, making cheery melody at sunset. It was a grand mistake to locate the canal on the river-level. People have grown somewhat wiser since 1841, when the route was opened to navigation, and now regret that they did not place it high enough to secure the water power. The Chesapeake and Ohio rail route runs a little to the north of Lynchburg.

Finding the old town standing so "amid the fertile lands," with such excellent chances for growth, the new-comer feels, at first, like reproaching its inhabitants, despite the shock which they received in the war, for want of enterprise. But a careful examination shows that Lynchburg boasts a considerable activity. It has thirty-five tobacco factories, employing great numbers of negroes, men, women, and children. These negroes earn good wages, work faithfully, and turn out vast quantities of the black, ugly compound known as "plug," which has enslaved so many thousands, and promoted such a sublime disregard for the proprieties in the matter of expectoration. The appended note will give an idea of the trade of the tobacco district of which Lynchburg is the centre.* In the manufactories the negro is the same cheery, capricious being that one finds him in the cotton or sugar-cane fields; he sings quaintly over his toil, and seems entirely devoid of the sullen ambition which many of our Northern factory laborers exhibit. The men and women working around the tables in the basements of the Lynchburg tobacco establishments croon eccentric hymns in concert all day long; and their little children, laboring before they

*A comparative statement of the tax paid on manufactured tobacco shipped from the Fifth District of Virginia, in the fiscal years of 1871–72 and 1872–73, show that during the first period the amount manufactured was 5,351,894 pounds, on which was paid a tax of $1,501,526; and for the latter period 10,774,611 pounds, on which the taxation amounted to $2,154,922.20. The total weight of tobacco, in hogsheads, in boxes, and "loose," inspected at Lynchburg from October 1, 1870, to October 1, 1871, was 17,425,439 pounds, of which 11,629,239 pounds were brought in loose or unpacked; and for the same period in 1871–72 the total weight was 14,323,708 pounds, more than 10,000,000 pounds of which quantity was brought in unpacked. Campbell, Bedford, Pittsylvania, Halifax, Charlotte, Appomattox, Amherst, Nelson, Rockbridge, Botetourt, Roanoke, Franklin, Montgomery, Giles, Washington, Floyd, and Mercer counties furnish most of the tobacco received at Lynchburg.

are hardly large enough to go alone, join in the refrains. Tobacco is the main article of Lynchburg trade. Buyers from all parts of the Union crowd the streets; the warehouses are daily visited by throngs. Other manufactures are slowly creeping in, and the venerable town will probably yet do its share in developing the iron so profusely scattered through South-western Virginia. Lynchburg stands in the centre of a region richly supplied with educational institutions. Within a radius of sixty miles Roanoke and Hampden-Sidney Colleges, the Virginia Military Institute, the University of Virginia, and the Washington-Lee University, are all situated. Its own public and private schools are numerous and of excellent character. *The Virginian* and the other Lynchburg newspapers hold high rank among the journals of the State.

Scene in a Lynchburg Tobacco Factory.

The annual fairs of the Agricultural and Mechanical Society bring together hundreds of farmers from all parts of the commonwealth.

Down the steep hills every day come the country wagons (often with a bull, a mule, and an old mare harnessed together as the team), loaded with the dark sheaves of tobacco; and the groups of men standing about the parks and public places are almost certain to be discussing the favorite staple.

Something of the old Scotch and English manners are still perceptible among the people in this part of Virginia; and there are bits of dialect and phrase which show how little the communities have been affected during the last century by the influences which have so transformed the populations of other sections of America. While England has gone on from change to change, and has even been capable of complete revolution in certain matters, Virginia has altered but little. Until now immigration has had no inducements to come and unlock the treasure-house of the grand mountains of the South-west, and so the people have lived under pretty much the same laws and customs that prevailed in England two centuries ago. Yet the absence of the rushing, turbulent current of immigration has had its compensating advantages in allowing the growth of families in which the hereditary love of culture and refinement, and the strictest attention to those graces and courtesies which always distinguish a pure and dignified society, are preëminently conspicuous.

South-western Virginia is a region which will in time be overrun by tourists and land speculators. The massive ramparts of the Alleghanies are pierced here and there by cuts through which crawls the line of

"Down the steep hills every day come the country wagons." [Page 557.]

the Atlantic, Mississippi and Ohio railroad; and towns are springing up with almost Western rapidity. Stores of coal and iron are daily brought to light; and the farmer of the old *régime* stares with wonder, not wholly unmixed with jealousy, at the smart new-comers who are agitating the subject of branch railroads, and searching into the very entrails of the hills.

The sea-board link of the Atlantic, Mississippi and Ohio railroad was originally known as the Norfolk and Petersburg road, and was completed in 1858, under the direction of William Mahone, an engineer of decided talent. At the close of the war this line, as well as the Southside, running from Petersburg to Lynchburg, and the Virginia and Tennessee road, extending from Lynchburg to Bristol, were in a lamentable condition, having been completely worn down by the heavy traffic and constant wear and tear during the great civil struggle. A measure for the consolidation of these roads, and their rebuilding and thorough equipment as a grand inter-State highway, was brought before the Virginia Legislature, and became the subject of much discussion. The engineer, Mahone, had been for many years prominent in the railway affairs of the commonwealth, and was now the foremost advocate of the unification measure. He had also been a brilliant fighter on the Confederate side, had gone through the struggle to the bitter end, standing by Lee at Appomattox, and, as in the battle years he had been impetuous, persistent, and unsparing of self, so now, in the pursuit of this great scheme for a route from Norfolk to the Ohio and the Mississippi rivers, he was characterized by the same qualities.

Ever since George Washington plainly pointed out the advantages of a route between the Atlantic coast and the Ohio river, the attention of Virginian statesmanship has been directed to the subject; but it remained for General Mahone, with his clear logic and irresistible array of facts, to exercise the influence which finally brought about the needed legislation, and on the 12th of November, 1870, resulted in the organization of the present line, merging together the Norfolk and Petersburg, the "Southside," the Virginia and Tennessee, and the Virginia and Kentucky railroads.

By this there were placed under one management five hundred miles of railroad lying upon the best and shortest location afforded by the continent between the centres of Western trade and the finest harbors on the Atlantic sea-board. This continuous line, running east and west between the extreme western border of the State and the sea-board, will bestow its trade within, and confer its benefits upon, towns and cities in the limits of Virginia; and by building up large centres, will gradually reduce the rate of taxation levied upon the agricultural population. In its completed form it will be, in the words of a distinguished Virginian, "a line which spans one-half the continent at its narrowest breadth, which begins at that point of the very sea-board nearest the western trade centre, and reaches out not only to the proper west in its middle, but also to the north-west and the south-west"—a line, in fact, which will make the Atlantic via Norfolk 351 miles nearer Louisville, 260 miles nearer Cincinnati, and 400 miles nearer Cairo, than via New York city. Traversing the most prosperous and fertile portion of Virginia, it diverges at Bristol, to penetrate, by means of its present and future connections, the entire South and South-west, and via Cumberland Gap, the State of Kentucky and the huge North-west. The three railroads now composing this main line were placed under the management of General Mahone as early as 1869 (he having been successively chosen president of each one), but they continued for some time afterward to act under their separate charters.*

---

* In 1866–67, before the three lines above-mentioned were placed under one general management, the number of tons transported upon them was 145,000. During the year ending September 30, 1872, the amount transported by the consolidated line was 205,000 tons. In 1866–67, the average charge per ton per mile was five and a-quarter cents; in 1871–72 it was two and three-fourth cents. This great reduction of rate was followed by an increase of revenue from $1,000,000, in 1866–67, to $1,969,000 in 1871–72, and for 1872–73, to over $2,000,000. The Norfolk and Petersburg road was in active operation as an independent road in 1860. Its entire revenue for that fiscal year was $96,621.74. That same division of the consolidated road earned for the year ending September 30, 1872, $376,531. The cotton transported over this route all goes to Norfolk, except that taken by the Petersburg and Richmond mills, which yearly increases in amount. The number of bales carried in 1871–72 was 130,000; in 1872–73, 177,000, coming mainly from Memphis, Selma, Nashville, Huntsville and Dalton. Some of the other, and no less important, fruits of the consolidation measure are seen in the following statistics: In 1866–67 the quantity of minerals transported was but 13,000 tons; in 1871–72 it was 31,000 tons. In 1866–67, the weight of live stock moved was 3,000 tons; in 1871–72 it was 15,000. The contrast in the amount of wheat is still more striking: it has increased from 17,000 bushels in 1866–67, to 263,000 bushels in 1871–72. In this same latter year there were delivered to Virginia cities 88,000 tons of agricultural and mineral products, and 47,000 tons were sent North.

The traveler who hastens through Lynchburg, repelled by the uncouth and prosaic surroundings of the railway station, will lose real pleasure. A residence of a few days in the old town will show him much that is novel and interesting. He may wander along the beautiful banks of the James below Lynchburg; by the canal whereon the gayly-painted boats slip merrily to their destination; or he may climb the steep hills behind the town, and get a glimpse of the winding stream which looks like a silver thread among the blue mountains. At noontide he may hear the mellow notes of the horn by which buyers are summoned to a tobacco sale; and at sunset he may watch the curious groups of negroes returning from their labors singing and chattering, or noisily disputing some momentous political issue.

Summoning Buyers to a Tobacco Sale.

LXII.

IN SOUTH-WESTERN VIRGINIA—THE PEAKS OF OTTER. THE MINERAL SPRINGS.

IT was in the brilliant early autumn that I visited South-western Virginia. Leaving Lynchburg, just at sunset, for the mountains beyond, I was impressed with the beauty of the soft light which gently rested upon the lovely stream, and was gradually losing itself in the mysterious twilight. The foliage was at its completest still; the gay loungers at the pretty little fashion-resorts scattered through the mountains were giving their sprightliest balls before retiring to the solitude and routine of their plantations. The tobacco-fields were yet resplendent with green. The farmers were fallowing the lands on the rich hill-sides for winter wheat. Every day the sun shone with inspiring splendor on the blue lines of monarch mountains, which, clothed in their beautiful forests, reared their crests against the unclouded sky. I did not wander along the winding canal, in the recesses of the hills, as far as the famous "Natural Bridge," but he who wishes to inspect that massive arch, spanning the chasm in which flows the little stream called Cedar creek, can reach it by a night's journey along the canal, from Lynchburg to the mouth of Cedar creek, within two miles of the bridge. The route, on a moonlit evening, is delightful, as the banks of the canal afford a constant succession of beautiful mountain pictures. But we leave the description of the approach to the bridge, and the great monumental wonder's special characteristics, to the pen of a native Virginian:

"The first view of the bridge is obtained half a mile from it, at a turn on the stage-road. It is revealed with the suddenness of an apparition. Raised a hundred feet above the highest trees of the forest, and revealed against the purple side of a distant mountain, a whitish-gray arch is seen, in the effect of distance as perfect and

Evening on the James River—"The soft light which gently rested upon the lovely stream."

clean-cut an arch as its Egyptian inventor could have defined. The tops of trees are waving in the interval, the upper half of which we only see, and the stupendous arch that spans the upper air is relieved from the first impression that it is man's masonry, the work of art, by the fifteen or twenty feet of soil that it supports, in which trees and shrubbery are firmly imbedded —the verdant crown and testimony of Nature's great work. And here we are divested of an imagination which we believe is popular, that the bridge is merely a huge slab of rock thrown across a chasm, or some such hasty and violent arrangement. It is no such thing. The arch and whole interval are contained in one solid rock; the average width of that which makes the bridge is eighty feet, and beyond this the rock extends for a hundred feet or so in mural precipices, divided by only a single fissure, that makes a natural pier on the upper side of the bridge, and up which climb the hardy firs, ascending step by step on the noble rock-work till they overshadow you.

In the Gap of the Peaks of Otter, Virginia.

"This mighty rock, sunk in the earth's side, of which even what appears is stupendous, is of limestone, covered to the depth of from four to six feet with alluvial and clayey earth. The span of the arch runs from forty-five to sixty feet wide, and its height to the under line is one hundred and ninety-six feet, and to the head two hundred and fifteen feet. The form of the arch approaches the elliptical; the stage-road which passes over the bridge runs from north to south, with an acclivity of 35 degrees, and the arch is carried over on a diagonal line, the very line of all others most difficult for the architect to realize, and that best calculated for picturesque effect."

Promising myself a visit to the Natural Bridge in the future, I made all speed to the other wonder of the neighborhood—the keen, sublime and haughty "Peaks of Otter."

Tenderly outlined against the exquisite pearl gray of the morning sky was the Blue Ridge, as I looked at it from the windows of the little inn of Liberty, the shire town of Bedford county, the point of departure for the Peaks of Otter. I noticed but little life or activity in the long street on Liberty hill; some negroes were at work in one or two tobacco warehouses; farmers were bustling in on the red country roads leading toward the purplish hill-background; and miles away two sharp, yet symmetrical peaks, connected by a gap, perched high up on the Blue Ridge chain, sprang into view.

There were the mighty twins! Two splendid guardians of the sweet valley spread out at their bases, they rose in indescribable grandeur. Where they take root in the gradually ascending earth, a capricious creek, the Otter, from which they get their name, eddies and bubbles and ripples in poetic confusion through rich fields, and by humble farm-dwellings, and granaries fashioned from the mountain trees. The northern and highest peak is rarely visited; it rises 5,307 feet above the level of the sea. The other, more symmetrical in shape,—something like an enormous pyramid, and capped by a chaotic mass of rock reaching seemingly into the clouds,—we determined to scale.

The negro livery-man had promised us a "hack," and consequently arrived with a red spring-wagon, perched high upon four clumsy wheels, and drawn by two unambitious horses. The road, for a mile or two after leaving Liberty, was good; then we fell upon the ordinary back-country route in Virginia, which is simply abominable. Square brick mansions with an air of solid respectability, standing in the middle of green and well-kept lawns, occupied the environs of the town; but we gradually left them, and passing through stretches of forest, along the beds of dissolute creeks which seemed determined not to go in the narrow way accorded them by nature, and by fields rich in culture, and abounding in delicious foliage, we began to climb around the mountain base.

We followed a vagrant road skulking apparently away from the sun. Now the road huddled under oaks, and now scurried up a thinly-wooded slope; now toiled over masses of loose stones; now coursed majestically along a plateau whence one could see the valley spread out like a map; now catching a glimpse of the overhanging peak toward which we toiled, and then, as if frightened at it, entered the wood forthwith. The cabins by the way were rude; rail-fences, chin high, through which white-headed children peered suspiciously, ran by the front doors; near which the cow-yards were conspicuous. Log barns were partially filled with hay, while tobacco hung from the rafters. Glancing upward, we could frequently see the pinnacle apparently suspended in mid-air. It seemed remote from, and disconnected with, the hill up to which we toiled, frowning upon us like a giant spectre.

At last, reaching the gap, more than three thousand feet above sea-level, we saw before us a pyramid of rough soil thickly sown with trees, and dotted with cabins in a few clearings. On the right, the northern peak showed its wooded sides, where the bear still wanders undisturbed; and a little in front of us stood the primitive hotel surrounded by flourishing orchards. The vine grows with surprising luxuriance along these mountains, the dry air and genial warmth giving every encouragement for the largest experimenting in vineyards.

We now began gradually to master the ascent, and after half an hour of painful climbing over rudest roads, and a long scramble up an almost perpendicular hill-side, we came to a point in the forest where a high rock seemed to offer an impassable barrier; but around which led a path on a narrow ledge. We stumbled forward, and dizzy with the effort, stood on the summit.

Jagged and irregular masses of rock projected over a tremendous abyss, into which we hardly dared to look. A strong wind blew steadily across the height. We could not help fancying that some of the masses of stone, apparently so tightly suspended, might fall and crush us. Under the great dome of the translucent sky we stood trembling, shut off from the lower world, and poised on a narrow pinnacle, from which we might at any moment, by an unwary step, be hurled down. An old stone cabin, which had once served as the lodging for such adventurous persons as desired to see sunrise from the peak, but which had been partially destroyed during the war, was perched on one of the corners of the mighty crag; from it a slender board was laid to a sharp corner in the uppermost cliff, and up that we scrambled. Then, making our way on to the topmost stone, we gazed down on the valley

The Summit of the Peak of Otter, Virginia.

of Virginia. In front of us, looking over fertile Bedford county, it seemed a garden; from point to point gleamed the spires and roofs of villages; mountains of every imaginable shape rose on all sides; and the forests at the edges of the gaps in the Blue Ridge seemed delicatest fringes of purple. We could trace the massive and curving ranges of the Alleghanies, and the rudely-gullied sides of the nearest peaks. Their reddish soil, showing up strongly under the bright sun, produced a magical effect. Nowhere were the adjacent peaks, however, so near as to lessen the sublime illusion of seeming suspension in mid-air, produced by our climb to the highest rock of the peak. The cabins along the roads below looked like black dots; the men at work in the fields like ants. From the rocky throne one seemed to have the whole map of Virginia spread out before him; and the backbone of the Alleghanies appeared but as a toy which one might stride over, or displace at will.

Talks with the farmers and business men along the roads were full of information encouraging to would-be immigrants. Titles to land are usually good, because the estates rarely changed owners before the war, but descended from father to son, and one can more readily trace the title in Virginia on that account than in most of the other Southern States. The prices of farms in the south-western section of the State, although somewhat influenced by local causes, and, therefore, a little perplexing to the stranger, are reasonably low. Land of the best quality can be had at from $40 to $80 per acre, and the ridges of the mountains for almost nothing. The present prices there are, on the whole, an advance on the old ones.

In Rockbridge, Botetourt, and Roanoke counties, all surprisingly rich in resources, lands have declined in value so that they may be purchased at excellent bargains. In the Upper Piedmont counties prices are variable, but under the impetus given them by a steady English immigration show a tendency to rise. In Bedford, Amherst, Nelson, Campbell, and Appomattox counties, there are thousands of acres of good grazing and fruit-lands to be bought for from $2 to $5 per acre; while farms of the best quality, easily accessible to market, are sold at from $10 to $30. In the James River valley great numbers of slaves were held before the war. Emancipation ruined hundreds of planters and farmers, and caused a decline in the price of the lands. Many a fine old colonial estate is in the market at a small sum. The bottom lands in this attractive valley have been cultivated for two centuries, but are still fertile and unexhausted. The staples in the hill-country in the vicinity of Lynchburg are mainly wheat, Indian corn, oats, hay, and tobacco. The fruits are unrivaled, and along the eastern slopes of the Blue Ridge mountains the grape flourishes luxuriantly, and needs no protection from the cold. The farmers in the James River valley say that the bottom lands there will yield from sixty to one hundred bushels of corn to the acre.

The taxes are not heavy. On real estate in the counties they amount to one per cent., and the property is usually rated at only two-thirds of its cash value. Negro farm labor can be engaged for from $8 to $12 per month, with board; but "board" means only rations of bacon, molasses and corn, which the negro is supposed to cook for himself. In the forests of the hill-country black-walnut, cherry, and maple abound, and the oak, locust, chestnut, hickory, and pine are spread over one-half of the counties of the Piedmont section. Here and there one notices rank growths of pines, poplars and locusts, which have sprung up on the neglected land, whose owners have no longer capital to employ in cultivation. There is a statutory provision allowing each head of a family to hold, exempt from any process of execution or levy, real and personal property to the amount of $2,000. One-fifth of the tax money is devoted to the uses of free schools; but I am inclined to believe that in back sections of most of the counties these schools do not flourish to any extent—not so much because of any hostility toward them as because of the general apathy of the native farming population on the subject of education.

At every town throughout this region there are lovely mountain views. One has lost sight of the twin peaks of Otter ere he arrives at Blue Ridge Springs, a charming resort ensconced in a nook between two huge ridges, situated upon the railroad, and connected with the outer world by telegraph and numerous daily trains, the waters being noted for their efficacy in special cases. The route continues through a rich farming country, and passes hill-sides covered with flourishing vineyards. The farmers on the ridges are quiet and well-disposed folk. Corn-fields grow up to the very doors of their humble houses. The negroes

Blue Ridge Springs, South-western Virginia.

have little patches of land here and there, and seem industrious in their cultivation. Chalybeate and sulphur springs are the attractions around which revolves, all summer long, a pleasant *coterie* from the extreme South. The whole spring region of this section of Virginia is crowded from July until the last of October with Southern visitors.

The mountain-passes about Blue Ridge Springs, the delightful roads running out from thence to Coyner's and Bonsack's, the lovely stretches of the Roanoke valley, the mystic recesses of the hills about "Alleghany," the sweet tranquillity of the "Montgomery White Sulphur," and the half-dozen other retreats in the vicinity, are all sought by the overworked and climate-worn who have come thousands of miles for a sniff of fresh air. The railroad, seeking a way through the most practicable passes of the Alleghanies and the Blue Ridge, has established stations convenient to all these springs. For fifty miles the Atlantic, Mississippi and Ohio route runs through a wild and romantic section, abounding in richest mineral springs, as well as in minerals of value. The most noticeable of the fashionable resorts are the "Alleghany" and the "Montgomery White." Both have long been famous among Southerners; and hundreds of Northern pleasure-seekers now yearly find their way there.

Alleghany Springs, in Montgomery county, are near the Roanoke river, at the eastern foot of the Alleghany mountains. The hotel, surrounded by a chain of picturesque and comfortable cottages, is only three miles from the railroad, and in all directions there are ravines and recesses containing some of the great wonders which Nature has so lavishly scattered through the State. The saline waters which are abundant at Alleghany draw around them hosts of invalids, and the more robust visitors find health and pleasure in the exploration of such rocky cañons as Puncheon Run Falls, where, through the rent side of the hills a foamy series of cascades leap down 2,000 feet into abysses, shrouded in leaves and vines, where the black mosses cling to the blacker rocks; where the laurel sways rhythmically to the music of the spray and the sombre refrain of the fall. He who would see billowy mountains, rolling miles and miles away, should climb to "Fisher's View," at a short distance from Alleghany. Along the by-ways of this region he will meet the rustic, clad in homespun, with an ancient rifle slung at his shoulder, and will be surprised at his uncouth speech and quaint suspicions of the traveler. The mountaineer looks scornfully upon the crowds of city butterflies who flit back and forth through his country retreats in summer, and stands, dumb with amazement, before the doors of the hotel ball-room, through which he sees the gleam of rich costumes and the sparkle of jewels.

The routine at all the springs is much the same. The hotel is usually a roomy building, surrounded by porches or verandas, and stands in the middle of a green lawn, dotted with the white oak or some other of the superb trees abounding in the Virginian mountains. In the hotel are grouped the ball and dining-rooms and the general reception parlors; while in the small, neatly-painted, one-story cottages, ranged in rows, equidistant from the hotel, the visitors are lodged. There is a host of attentive and polite colored serving-men and women, ex-valets and ex-nurses of the "before-the-war" epoch, and they will tell you, with pardonable pride, "I used to belong to ole Mars' ———," mentioning some name famous in the annals of slave proprietorship. Here one can establish the charm and seclusion of a home, and combine with it the benefits accruing from a sojourn at a watering-place. Society, usually very good, crystallizes in the parlors of the hotels and in the ball-rooms, where bands of colored musicians discourse the latest themes of Strauss and Gungl. When one tires of dancing and of the promenades to the "springs," there are the mountains, and the strolls along ridges thousands of feet above the level of the sea, where the air is always pure and inspiring. There is no gam ing, save an innocent whist party by some sleepy old boys who lurk in the porches, keeping out of the strong morning sun; there is no Saratogian route of carriage and drag; no crowded street, with ultra style predominant in every costume; nothing but simplicity, sensible enjoyment, and excellent taste. In the sunny mornings the ladies and their cavaliers wander about the mountain pathways; dress does not exact homage until dinner-time, and the children join with their parents in the strolls and promenades, followed by the venerable "aunties," black and fat, who seem indispensable appendages to every Southern family having young children.

Montgomery White Sulphur Springs lie even nearer to the main route of travel than those of Alleghany. A pleasant ride of a mile and a-half from the Atlantic, Mississippi and Ohio line, on a horse-railroad brings one to a lawn, planted round about with fine trees, and watered by a rippling brook. The hotel and cottage buildings are comfortable and elegant; the sulphur and chalybeate springs are daily visited by hundreds in the season; and the ragged spur of the Alleghanies which backs the lawn is traversed by smooth, well-kept roads, over which visitors trot on the brisk mountain horses. At the season's height Southern statesmen, lawyers, planters, journalists, ex-warriors, poets and speculators make the Montgomery White their rendezvous; and illuminations, balls, tournaments and meetings follow one upon the other. Four miles south-west are the "Yellow Sulphur Springs," loftily situated near the head-waters of the Roanoke, and reached from the railway via Christiansburg. These springs, whose waters are celebrated for the cure of children's diseases, and are said to impart a rare purity to the complexion of women, are noted as a quiet resort for families.

This spring region, abounding in all the resources for the restoration of health and energy, and so rich in natural beauty, is as yet comparatively unknown to the mass of Northern and Western people. For cheapness of price and for convenience of access it has in America hardly an equal; and in Europe but few watering-places can claim any superior advantages of that nature. When the great commonwealth is thoroughly developed, these beautiful summer resorts will gradually become large towns, and the charm of the restful stillness, the possibility of intimate communion with some of nature's grandest phases which they now afford, will be gone. The mob of the summer grand tour will rob them of their chief charm.

LXIII.

AMONG THE MOUNTAINS—FROM BRISTOL TO LYNCHBURG.

A JOURNEY from the Tennessee line, northward toward Lynchburg, gave me enlarged ideas of the possibilities of South-western Virginia. Bristol bestrides the line between Virginia and Tennessee, and consequently has a double municipal existence. Two Mayors and two sets of minor municipal officers have jurisdiction within its limits. It is a pretty collection of neat houses and busy shops, ranged along lightly-sloping hills; and beyond the Tennessee boundary, the blue range of the Iron mountains stands out sharply against the clear sky.

The streets are usually crowded with wagon-trains, immense canvas-covered vehicles, drawn by sober mules, and driven by brawny, long-bearded backwoods-

Bristol, South-western. Virginia.

men, or by tattered and slouching negroes. These trains ply back and forth along the difficult routes not yet reached by any railways, and at night the men and mules camp together under the open sky. Stout farmers, splashed with the reddish mud of the highways, rattle up and down the main avenues on alert little horses. At evening the through train from New Orleans, bound for New York, shrieks the note of warning as it rolls into the overcrowded depot, and the passengers pour out to the roomy, old-fashioned brick hotel, and, seated on wooden stools around a long table, absorb the smoking fragments of hot chicken and corn-bread set before them. Here and there the noise of factory wheels is heard, and the hills are crowned with neat edifices containing flourishing schools. On the Tennessee side stands King's College, supported by the Presbyterian Church South, and there are also one or two excellent seminaries for women.

The 1,800 people settled at Bristol seem prosperous and contented, as they may well be, in view of the chances for future growth which the rapid multiplication of railway lines with important connections is to give the town. The extension of the Atlantic, Mississippi and Ohio railroad from Bristol to Cumberland Gap will develop a rich country; and when Bristol is receiving the great currents of traffic directly from Memphis and Louisville, it will fully merit the

White Top Mountain, seen from Glade Springs.

title now and then given it, of "the most active town in Virginia." The "Natural Tunnel," forty-two miles from Bristol, near the ford of the Clinch river, is a passage, about 800 feet in length, through battlements of solid stone. The vaults of the tunnel rise to the height of eighty feet; and, where the arch finally terminates in the mountain slope, there is a sheer precipice 500 feet high. In a few years, it is confidently expected, a railroad will find its way through this wonderful tunnel, and the locomotive's scream will be heard on the path over which Daniel Boone painfully toiled, more than a century ago, on his pioneering pilgrimage to the Kentucky wilds. Straight across Powell's mountain and Powell's valley to the rock-ribbed Cumberland range runs the projected route of the railway which is to forge one more link in the great chain binding the West to the East. The whole region adjacent to the main road leading to Cumberland Gap is rich in tradition and natural wonders. Not far from the Natural Tunnel is a massive cave, in whose chambers hang thousands of stalactites; and near the little town of Estillville, in Scott county, are the "Holston Springs," where chalybeate, thermal and white sulphur waters rise from sources within a few hand-breadths of each other. Around Estillville the lands are rich in minerals; iron and copper abound; and the lead deposits along the Clinch river have long been considered remarkable.

The journey backward toward Lynchburg took me through Abingdon, a flourishing trade centre in Washington county, and to Glade Springs, whence one gets a peep at White Top mountain's lofty brow. From Glade Springs I turned aside to Saltville, a busy town connected with the outer world by a branch railroad running in among the queer hill-knobs filled with plaster, and through the valleys where salt-wells are sunk. The country round about, until one reaches the Alleghany ridge, is not unlike that portion of England lying near Eastbourne, with its chalk hills sparsely covered with grass. Saltville is a neat manufacturing village, nestling in a valley near a defile in Walker's mountain. The basin of salt-water there yields nearly eighty per cent., and, ever since a Scotchman named King opened a well in 1780, the salines have been extensively worked. During the last war the Confederacy depended almost entirely upon these works for salt, and the tremendous draft of ten thousand bushels per day was promptly met by the wells. About two thousand men were constantly employed; the town was thoroughly fortified; each Southern State had its private establishment, and the various furnaces are to-day known by the names of the States which originally established them. There was some savage fighting along the mountain-sides, and in the defiles, when General Stoneman tried to force his way into Saltville and destroy the precious stores; but, after a severe repulse, he succeeded in gaining possession and burning everything. The stock company now owning and working the wells, manufacture but three thousand bushels of salt daily, sending it mainly to the Southern markets.

Making Salt, at Saltville, Virginia.

The stout negroes working over the boiling salt were both delighted and amazed when their pictures appeared in the artist's sketch-book; they had never seen "no such writin' befo'." Great stores of gypsum are annually mined and prepared for fertilizers in this valley, where also there are some superb model farms, well stocked and separated one from another by beautiful hedges. Not far from Saltville is Clinch mountain, over which the traveler to Tazewell county, a wonderfully beautiful mountain region, must climb. The fighting around Saltville was severest at the time that Burbridge came from Kentucky, intending to break up the Confederate works there. It was, I believe, the first fight in which colored troops entered as an important element, and the slaughter of them, as they came struggling up the difficult hill-sides, is said by eye-witnesses to have been dreadful. About six thousand troops were engaged on each side.

In Tazewell county, twenty-five miles from the line of the Atlantic, Mississippi and Ohio road, coal crops out literally everywhere. It furnishes a rich field for investment. The mountain population is rude, but, as a rule, law-abiding, and sensible. Along the valley of the Clinch river, in this county, are many stretches of fertile fields, contrasting strangely with the rocky cliffs rising around them. "Wolf Creek Knob," clad in laurel and ivy, and "Dial Rock," near Jeffersonville, are worthy many visits. Railroads, schools and mines will give this country great riches, and a much needed increase of education in a few years. The dialect of the people is strange and hard; their hospitality is unbounded, and their love for the peaks, among which they raise their droves of cattle, horses, and hogs, amounts to devotion. Their homes are cleanly, although simple almost beyond belief; their manners are frank, and their instincts usually noble.

At Marion Court-House—a pleasant village near the Brush mountain, and a fair type of the average Virginian county seat,—we arrived at a time when the Conservative candidate for Governor of the State, General Kemper, was addressing the citizens of the county. Marion consists mainly of one long street, on one side of which is the Court-House, with a lawn in front, and a stout jail in the rear. It was court-day as well as a political occasion; and the farmers had assembled from many miles around.

The negroes are very numerous in the vicinage; but, constituting a party by themselves, did not flock about the Court-House, although two of the better class of them lingered near, as if appointed as reporters. The court-room in which the political meeting was held, after the session of the court had been adjourned over for a day in deference to the discussion of pending issues, was small and destitute of seats. The farmers and town residents dropped in at intervals during the lucid and fluent speech made by General Kemper, and listened for some little time with respectful attention, although they did not seem to take that thrilling interest in the irrepressible conflict which I had been led to expect.

The speeches of the candidate (since elected Governor) and his friends were somewhat condemnatory of the Administration's course with regard to certain Southern States. It was evident that the hearers present, with the exception of the negroes, were all of one mind, and would vote the Conservative ticket without fail. But as soon as the farmers had seen the candidate of their party for Governor, and heard him make a few remarks, many of them strolled back upon the lawn, and began discussing crops and comparing notes on horses. They

Wayside Types — A Sketch from the Artist's Virginia Sketch-Book.

regarded the election of the Conservative ticket in the State as a foregone conclusion, and were apparently tired of all political talk, preferring to attend to their home matters, and the bettering of their agricultural prospects, rather than to a revival of past memories. By noon many of them had completed their errands, and were riding out of town on their smart horses, as grimly and silently as they had entered.

The negroes seemed to consider the Conservative triumph as certain; and those who were intelligent were basing all hope of an improvement in their condition on the influences of time rather than on anything else. They hope to make education general among their race; and, during the four years that the Conservatives will remain in power, they think that a more intelligent groundwork of politics may be formed. In the back counties it will be found difficult

Wytheville, Virginia.

to establish the free common school on a good and reliable basis; but, certainly, both whites and blacks enjoy excellent school facilities in most of the larger towns. A careful canvass of the counties in South-western Virginia, and the Piedmont district, in 1872, shows that, while there was still some marked opposition to the free public school, the sentiment of the mass was gradually becoming favorable to it.

There has never been, since the war, any inclination on the part of the whites to hinder the negro from getting as much education as he can himself pay for; and, although some resistance to the collection of taxes for school purposes was anticipated at the time the system went into operation, in 1870, there never has been any worthy of the name. The negroes in many of the counties manifest more eagerness to enter school than do the whites, but they are not always willing to pay something to support the school. On the whole, great progress has been made; the Peabody fund has done, and still does good work in Bristol, Abingdon, Marion, Salem, Wytheville and Lynchburg; the number of school edifices is increasing, and good teachers are more readily procured than at the outset. The mass of the people throughout that region, as in other parts of Virginia, would, I think, prefer that the Legislature should take the responsibility of raising the funds

Max Meadows, Virginia.

to support the schools. At present the supervisors and judges in each county have the power to regulate the local school taxes, and the result of this is that the school trustees, who are required by law to provide good school edifices for the pupils, have not the money with which to build them. But experience and improved sentiment are gradually regulating all these matters.

Near Marion, and in the mountains back of the town, the deposits of iron ores promise to be very rich, and furnaces will soon be established there. Barytes has long been mined in the vicinity. In the adjoining county, at Wytheville, a pretty town lying on the western slope of a spur of the Alleghanies, 2,000 feet above tide-water, we saw fine specimens of coal, iron, lead and zinc ore, mined in the vicinity. The Austinville lead mines, near by, have been worked for more than a century. All the zinc is at present transported to the Eastern States before being smelted.

A little more than six miles from Wytheville several extensive coal veins have been opened, and ample stores of limestone are found near these veins, so that furnaces and rolling-mills would get their material ready to hand, if erected at such an excellent point on the Atlantic, Mississippi and Ohio line as Wytheville. The water power in the vicinity is magnificent. Beyond lie Kent's Mill and Max Meadows, the latter a lovely pastoral landscape dotted with fine stock. To Max Meadows zinc and pig-iron are brought in large quantities from the country between the station and the North Carolina mountain frontier. In that section there are also extensive lead and shot works, and silver enough is scattered in the zinc-beds to pay the men mining the latter for their work. At

Dublin, a little village in the midst of fertile fields, there are large iron interests. This is a depot whence many shipments of the celebrated short-horn beef cattle are made. As soon as the railway now prompting the growth of these interests can shoot out its feeders on either side, the number of tons of minerals annually exported from Virginia will be quadrupled. Not far from this point the owners of the Radford Iron Works of Philadelphia are shipping pig-iron from a newly-erected furnace.

The banks of New river are so lovely in the autumn time, that we determined not to hasten by them in the express train; so we mounted upon a hand-car, which the strong arms of two stout negroes sent down grade at thirty, and up the toilsome ascents at five, miles an hour. The river, a few miles beyond Dublin, is broad and wonderfully clear, mirroring in its placid breast the verdure-bordered banks, and the rich foliage of the forests along the cliffs, to whose sides the railway confidingly clings.

The Roanoke Valley, Virginia. [Page 577.]

Traversing the stream, and mounting a little hill, we caught a view of "Bald Knob." The bare poll of the venerable mountain was touched by the afternoon sunlight as we looked, and the great height formed an admirable background to the richly broken landscape along the riverside. One may make a pleasant voyage on the New river from this point to Eggleston's Springs, twenty-five miles further down the current, taking one of the many bateaux which ply constantly on the stream, and simply drifting on the lazy wave until the destination is reached. Within easy distance of these springs one comes upon the greatest natural wonder of the Virginian mountains,—a pond or lake, having no visible source of supply, sunk in a kind of earth cup, on a height 4,500 feet above the level of the sea. It has been forming and enlarging for more than sixty years, and is now about three-quarters of a mile long by a third of a mile wide. Submerged trees can be seen beneath its pellucid surface; and a line hundreds of feet long, if let down its middle waters, will not touch bottom. Higher up, in the same range, is the "Bald Knob," the view from whose summit is considered quite as grand as that from the Peak of Otter.

A little beyond New river we stopped at a primitive coal station, where great heaps of the black diamonds, newly brought from "Brush" mountain, were lying. As I inquired the name of the mine from which they came, a by-stander answered, "The mountain is all coal, and every farmer is his own miner."

At Christiansburg, which is in the spring region, we were not far from the site of the new State Agricultural and Mechanical College at Blacksburg. The "farm" attached to the college comprises two hundred and fifty acres, lying in the fertile "Valley of Virginia," and with veins of coal of superior quality, and large bodies of timber within easy reach. Climbing over the huge grades which dominate the Alleghanies at this point, and passing through the deep cuts in the rock-ribbed hills near the stations giving access to Montgomery White Sulphur and Alleghany Springs, we came suddenly upon the delicious expanse of the Roanoke valley, bathed in the splendid shimmer of an afternoon autumn sun, and fading into delicatest colored shadows where the mountains rose gently, as if loth to leave the lowly retreat. The vale was filled with wheat and corn fields, and with perfect meadows, through which ran little brooks gleaming in the sun.

After crossing the Roanoke river we came into a region covered with fine fields of tobacco, which extended far up the hill-sides. Just below is the pleasant station of "Big Spring," to which we had been gradually descending for some

View near Salem, Virginia.

time on the high cliffs along the side of the Roanoke valley. At Big Spring a profusion of iron and copper ore has been found. Salem, the site of Roanoke College, is surrounded by charming hills, and stands in one of the richest agricultural regions in the United States. Near Salem are some lovely streams, bordered by rich foliage. Throughout the adjacent sections the farmers are very well-to-do, many owning from 1,200 to 1,300 acres of land, worth $80 to $90 per acre. Tobacco and the cereals are grown there in large quantities. Salem and "Big Lick," just beyond, export immense quantities of cereals. Salem stands at the head of navigation on the Roanoke, and communicates with Weldon, in North Carolina. Here, too, it is hoped that a road, opening up the Shenandoah valley, will connect with the Atlantic, Mississippi and Ohio line.

The wealth of this region is by no means developed yet. South-western Virginia proper, which remained so long unexplored after the valley and the Potomac shores had been carefully studied, has a grand future. As a field for immigrants who have capital and intelligence, for the better class of large farmers, and for workers in metal, it cannot be surpassed. An empire in itself, with every resource conceivable, it is not wonderful that that rare soldier, General Lee, boasted that he "could carry on the war for twenty years from those western mountains."

View on the James River below Lynchburg.

LXIV.

PETERSBURG—A NEGRO REVIVAL MEETING.

THE journey from Lynchburg to Petersburg calls up many memories. Eight years ago the mad rush of desperate and final battle swept across it. From the log and earth parapets of Five Forks, where Pickett's forces met their doom at the hands of Sheridan; from the Appomattox and from Hatcher's Run; from Fort Gregg, where the splendid Mississippians held on against hope and fate until nearly all of them had perished; from the intrenchments of deserted Petersburg; from Burkesville; from the road to Jetersville, over which Sheridan and the "Fifth" went clattering; from Amelia Court-House and from Sailor's Creek; from the High Bridge, and from Cumberland Church near Farmville, where Mahone made his heroic stand, and would not be driven; from all the bloody and memorable fields which stretch, sunlit and peaceful now, from the

Appomattox Court-House—"It lies silently half-hidden in its groves and gardens." [Page 580.]

hills around Petersburg to the village of Appomattox Court-House, come echoes which recall to us some faint impressions of the splendor and the grandeur of that last resistance of the broken army of Northern Virginia.

Along the line of rail where now currents of trade flow stronger and more steadily than in the most prosperous days of the old *régime*, raged a gigantic struggle, the very traces of which seem to have passed away. Now and then the eye catches the outline of a grass-grown intrenchment, in the midst of some well-cultivated field; but there are notably few marks of that wild series of battles by day and flights and pursuits by night which ended when Gordon, with the advance guard of Lee's exhausted army, had charged successfully against the cavalry ranged in front of him, only to find that behind that cavalry were the blue infantry lines which foretold the necessity of surrender.

There is nothing especially interesting in Appomattox Court-House. The little village lies at a short distance from the railway station, around which idle negroes are always lounging. It lies silently half-hidden in its groves and gardens, as if frightened at the notoriety it has achieved. The house where Lee and Grant arranged the terms of surrender is pointed out to the Northern visitor; but aside from its associations, it has nothing to recommend it to attention. The surrounding country, however, is quite beautiful. Farmville, so memorable for the battles in its vicinity, seems alert and full of energy; it has the stamp of a New England town in the vivacity of its streets, as I saw them. It has long been an important tobacco market, and the people are prosperous and progressive. Hampden-Sidney College is not many miles away; and a short distance below the town is the famous "High Bridge," simply a railway viaduct, where General Mahone had proposed, in those terrible days of April, 1865, to make one of his stubborn fights, but whence he was forced to fall back to his position at "the church." The fields on which one looks down from this great bridge—a triumph of engineering—are beautifully cultivated in tobacco and corn. The valley was delicious in color, as I passed through it in an autumn sunlight.

Below Burkesville the cotton-fields were numerous; acres were white with the pretty shrub's blossoms, and the intrenchments of eight years ago were here and there covered with them. Seen from a distance, Petersburg presents the appearance of a lovely forest, pierced by church spires and towers. On entering it, one sees many signs of commercial prosperity. Along the railroad line in the suburbs are large cotton-mills, and the much-beleaguered town now echoes to the whirr of spindles, and the ring of hammers on tobacco-hogsheads.

The negroes were slightly in the majority in Petersburg at the time of my visit. As at Lynchburg, the Northerner is at first amazed by the mass of black and yellow faces. The hackmen who shriek in your ear as you arrive at the depot, the brakeman on the train, the waiter in the hotel, all are African. In the tobacco factories hundreds of dusky forms are toiling, and an equal number are slouching in the sunshine. On the day of my visit a colored Masonic excursion had arrived from Richmond, and the streets were filled with stout negro men, decently clothed, and their wives and sweethearts, attired in even louder colors than those affected by Northern servant girls. Each was talking vociferously; officials, in flaunting regalia and sweating at every pore, rushed to and fro; bands thundered and urchins screamed. The Virginia negro has almost the French passion for *fête*-days; he is continually planning some excursion or "reunion," and will readily consent to live in a cellar and submit to poor fare for the sake of saving money to expend in frolic.

At Petersburg the negroes are from time to time largely represented in the Common Council, and sometimes have a controlling voice in municipal affairs. The white citizens have readily adapted themselves to circumstances, and the session of the Council which I attended was as orderly and, in the main, as well conducted as that of any Eastern city. There was, it is true, an informality in the speech of some of the colored members which was ludicrous, but it was evident that all were acting intelligently, and had come to some appreciation of their responsibilities. Most of the colored members were full types of the African. In some matters they readily admit the superiority of the white man in legislation, and in Petersburg willingly gave the management of the city finances into the hands of the elder Conservative members of the Council. The Commissioner of Streets and the Engineer of the Board of Waterworks were both negroes. The mayoralty and the other city offices remained, at the epoch of my visit, in the hands of white Radicals, and the negroes had made no special struggle to secure them, although they are to the whites in the city as eleven to

"The hackmen who shriek in your ear as you arrive at the depot." [Page 580.]

nine. The Conservatives allege that they are unable to compete with the negroes in tricks at election-time. They say, among other things, that they have never been able to secure burial records of the negro population, since it is their custom to make a dead voter renew his life in the person of one of his friends.

The Petersburg schools are noteworthy examples of Virginian progress since the war, and merit the warmest encomiums. No attempt has been made by black or white to insist upon the education of the races together, it being tacitly allowed on both sides that it would not be wise. Petersburg's general free system of public schools was founded in 1868, when $2,000 of the "Peabody

Fund" was contributed, on condition that the city should raise $20,000, and with it establish schools for all classes and colors. By the second year nearly 3,000 pupils were enrolled, and both whites and blacks are now given all facilities for a thorough education. The colored young men have not, as a mass,

"The 'Crater,' the chasm created by the explosion of the mine which the Pennsylvanians sprung underneath Lee's fortifications."

made any special demand for instruction in the higher branches; their main desire is for a knowledge of reading, writing, arithmetic, and such general study as will enable them to speak in public or to preach; but the girls in many of the negro schools are capable of mastering Cæsar, and can write correct French exercises.

About 5,000 negroes are at work in the tobacco warehouses; in the cotton-mills white labor exclusively is employed. Eight of these mills are established in and near the city, viz.: the Mattoaca, Ettricks, Battersea, Davis, Roper & Co's, Swift Creek, Kevan, and Lynch. Two thousand operatives are employed in manufacturing cotton. Numbers of Scotchmen have settled in the vicinity, and some of them are largely interested in the mills. Petersburg's annual receipts of cotton and tobacco are very large. During the last year 42,500 bales of cotton and 14,000 hogsheads of tobacco were received. The flouring-mills of the city have a capacity of 1,000 barrels daily. This thriving community of 18,000 persons has shrewdly thrust itself between Richmond and the northern counties of North Carolina, and has thus secured a large portion of the trade which the capital considered its own. Petersburg supplies the planters and farmers of the adjacent State with bacon and corn, and in return takes tobacco and cotton. The Atlantic, Mississippi and Ohio railroad opens up to it long stretches of fertile country.

The town contains many charming avenues, bordered with elegant mansions embowered in foliage; some of the business streets are quaint and almost foreign in aspect. The Appomattox makes here and there a picturesque waterfall; the hill on which the old cemetery and ruined, ivy-mantled Blandford Church stand commands a lovely view of the city, around which, in every direction, miles on miles, stretch the decaying intrenchments, batteries, and forts of the great siege. The lines along the eastern and southern suburbs are still pretty clearly defined; but the traces of the battles have nearly all vanished. The "Crater," the chasm created by the explosion of the mine which the Pennsylvanians sprung underneath Lee's fortifications, on that dread day of the unsuccessful assault in July, 1864, is overgrown with shrubbery; and the farmer, who points out the old lines of the two armies, says that he himself can hardly realize that his farm was once a mighty fortified camp. Along what was known as the "new intrenched line," constructed after the explosion and the consequent battle,—and around the worn earthworks of Forts "Hell" and "Damnation,"*—some marks of strife are yet noticeable. The National cemetery, with its 3,000 graves, near the "Poplar Spring Church," and the lot on Cemetery Hill, devoted to "Our Soldiers," where sleep the Confederate dead; the little church which a regiment of New York engineers erected during the weary months of the siege, and (when they left for Five Forks) presented to their enemies; the "Signal Tower," built by the same hands; and, scattered in the vales and along the slopes, some vaguely-defined ruins of rifle-pit and subterranean passage, of bomb-proof and sharpshooter's lurking-hole, are all that remain as memorials of the fierce and deadly struggle which lasted ten months, and cost many thousands of lives.

During our stay in this section a "revival meeting" was announced by the colored brethren of the surrounding country, to be held at a little station half-way between Richmond and Petersburg, and we determined to be present. On a beautiful Sunday morning we drove out through the fields, in which, the oak timber having been cut away, a rank growth of pine had sprung up; and stopping a massive coal black man, dressed in white duck, with a flaming red necktie at his throat, we inquired "the way."

"Ef yo' want to go to Zion's Hill, dat yer's de way; but ef yo' want to go whar de good preachin' is, dis yer road 'll take yo' to it."

Presently we arrived at a large frame building, much like a country school-house, save that

"The old cemetery, and ruined, ivy-mantled Blandford Church." [Page 582.]

it was neither ceiled nor plastered, and therein the revivalists were gathered. A powerful spiritual wave had swept over the colored population, and dozens of carts, loaded with dusky searchers for truth, came rolling along the rough

* Sobriquets given Forts Sedgwick and Mahone.

roads, and stopped before the primitive door. Entering, we found represented every shade of color, from the coal black full-blood to the elegantly dressed and well-mannered octoroon. The congregation was not large. Owing to the excitement which had prevailed for several previous Sabbaths, many had retired, worn out, from the spiritual feast. The women sat on the left side, the men on the right of a broad aisle, running to a plain wooden pulpit, in which were three moon-faced negroes, two of them preachers, and the third a State Senator.

In front of the pulpit, behind a little table, stood an olive-colored elderly man, neatly dressed, and with a wildness in his eyes, and an intensity written upon his lips which reminded me of what I had read of the "Convulsionists of St. Médard." The audience was breathless with attention as the preacher, a strolling missionary, supported by Quakers in Louisiana, took up the great Bible, and, poising it on his lean, nervous hand, poured forth such an impassioned appeal that I fairly trembled. I was not prepared for such vehemence. Never, in the history of New England revivalism, was there such a scene. The preacher stood with many of his hearers well around him; one of the deacons and exhorters, a black giant in spectacles, was his *point d'appui*, and to him he appealed from time to time, shaking him roughly by the shoulder, and hissing his words in his ear with fiery vehemence. The proposition with which he started was somewhat incomprehensible to us, viz.: " Christ is the creating power of God;" but the proposition was of no consequence, because every few moments he would burst into paroxysms of exhortation, before which the emotional audience rocked and trembled like reeds in a wind. He had a peculiar way of addressing himself suddenly and in a startling manner to some individual in the congregation, dancing, and pounding the table furiously with both hands, in the agony of his exhortation to that person.

From time to time he would draw in his breath with great force, as if repressing a sob, and, when speaking of love and salvation, he inevitably fell into a chant, or monotone, which was very effective. Under the hurricanes of his appeal, the fury of his shouting, the magnetic influence of his song, one of the old deacons went into a spasm of religious fervor, and now and then yelled vociferously. A milder brother ventured to remonstrate, whereupon the Quaker preacher turned upon him, saying loudly:

"Let dat brudder shout, an' 'tend to dine own business!"

Then he began preaching against hypocrisy. He seemed especially to chide the women for becoming converted with too great ease. "Woe!" he cried, "woe unto dat woman what goes down into the water befo' she ready; woe *unto* her!" with a long, singing descent on the last words; and then he added, *sotto voce*, "Dat what make so many women come up stranglin' an' vomitin' an' pukin' outen de water; de debbil dat still in 'em git hole on 'em, an' shake 'em an' choke 'em under de water! Let no woman shout for Jesus what don't know 'bout Jesus! It's one thing to git to Heaven, but it's anudder to git in! Don' ye know what Heaven is? Heaven's God! We must know what we is preachin' about, an' ef we don't we ought to SET DOWN!" (This with terrific emphasis.)

In describing the creation, he said: "Breddren, it's now 12,877 years since de good Lord made de world, an' de morning stars sung togedder. *Dat wa'n't yesterday!* Ha! read de Book o' Job, 'n see for yerself! *Dat wa'n't a month ago! I was n't dar den!*" (thus illustrating with sublime scorn the littleness of man), "but by de grace of God, I'll git dar by 'n' by!" (here his voice was faint and suggestive of tearful joy) "to join de mornin' stars, an' we'll all sing togedder!

"Oh, yes! oh, yes! Heaven's God made de world an' de fullness darof, an' hung it up on de high hooks of heaven. Dar wa'n't no nails dar; no hammer dar; no nothin' but de word of God." In hinting at the terrors of death to the unconverted, he sang wild word-pictures which had a certain rude force even for us, and then shrieked out these sentences: "Ef de brudders don't want to die in de dark, dey must git Christ to hole de candle. God's grace shall be de candle in de good brudder's heart. Devils may howl, lions may roar, but nothin' shall daunt dat brudder's heart. Angels shall come down with lighted candles in deir hands to congratulate de brudder." Then, once more screaming and dancing and weep-

"Seen from a distance, Petersburg presents the appearance of a lovely forest pierced here and there by church spires and towers." [Page 580.]

ing, he uttered these words: "Die right, brudder, 'n' yo' shall not die in de night; yo' shall die in eternal day. Ef Christ don't bring light enough, den God will come wid his candle; an' ef dat ain't enough, den de Holy Ghost 'll come wid his candle, too, an' dar can't be no more night wid dat brudder's soul."

At another period in the sermon, he said: "Ef we can't preach God, we can exhort Him; ef we can't exhort Him, we can live Him; an' ef we can't live Him, we can die Him. I've served under Him forty-two long year—longer dan Moses led Israel in de wilderness; an' ef I don' know what God is, den I'd better *shut up* an' go home!!! Jesus snatched my soul from hell forty-two year ago in Fredericksburg, in old Vaginny! Praise Him! O praise Him! Let no brudder shout for Jesus who don' know Jesus."

After the more furious passages of exhortation were over, he gave his ideas upon prayer, something in this wise: "Dar was ole Fadder Jupiter (a colored preacher). Now Jupiter he used to git a Bible in one han' an' a pra'r-book in anudder, an' a hymn-book under his arm; an' den he'd start out to see de widders 'n' de fadderless; 'n' one day I met old Fadder Jupiter, 'n' I say to him: 'Fadder Jupiter, how many pounds of meat have yo' prayed? How many pounds of sugar have yo' exhorted? How many cups of coffee have yo' sung to dem pore widders 'n' fadderless?' 'N' he says: 'Not one.' 'N' den I say: ''Pears like, Fadder Jupiter, yo 'll sing here, and pray dar, 'n' yo 'll pray every widder to death 'n' sing every fadderless child to de grave; 'n' call in help to bury 'em.' 'N' den I told him dat when he sung he must call a bar'l o' flour long metre, 'n' fur short metre he must take a keg of lard, 'n' dat 's short enough, anyhow; and fur particler metre nice ham 'n' some coffee; 'n' den he mus' take de Quaker pra'r-book, a two-wheeled cart, 'n' fill up de ole pra'r-book with coal; 'n' when de col' wedder come he must drive de ole pra'r-book down to some widder sister's, 'n' say: 'Sister, I 've come to pray six bushels of coal with yo', 'n' den open de cellar door, dump de ole pra'r-book, 'n' pray de cellar full o' coal.'"

The sermon was interspersed with impassioned recitations from Watts and Wesley. There was no logic, and no clear idea of anything except the love of God and charity. Now and then, with pompous air, the speaker would say: "An' now, breddren, we will proceed to consider de third (or fourth or fifth) point," and after a moment of solemn cogitation, would plunge into exhortation, appeal, and sarcasm, and yell until the rafters rang. His face was convulsed, and sobs shook his whole frame when he sat down. A strange wild hymn was sung, the singers waving their bodies to and fro to the measure of the music.

One of the ministers then arose, and bade those who desired the prayers of the church to come forward and lay their sins upon the altar. An indescribable rush of some twenty persons ensued. Old men and young girls hastened together to the pulpit, and knelt with their faces bowed upon their hands, and a low tremulous prayer to "O my Heavenly Fadder," was heard, as one of the old deacons poured forth his soul in supplication. During the prayer an exhorter passed around among the congregation, singling out the impenitent, and personally addressing them: "Yo' better go now!" "How 'll yo' feel when it 's too late, 'n' dar ain't no gittin dar?" In a short time the church resounded to groans and prayers, high over all of which was heard the clear voice of the colored Quaker chanting:

"For everywhar I went to pray
I met all hell right on my way,"

"but Heaven's God, 'n' we 'll get dar by 'n' by. O praise Him! O bless Him, 'n' sing 'wid de mornin' stars!"

Some of the colored preachers, although they make extravagant pretensions, are by no means so moral as our "Fadder Quaker," and, exercising absolute spiritual control over their ignorant flocks, prompt them to unworthy deeds, and fill their minds with wrong ideas. There is also a multitude of quacks and false prophets who seek to make money out of a revival of the barbaric superstitions still prevalent among certain classes of negroes.

On one occasion a huge negro created quite a clamor among the blacks in Petersburg, by announcing that he could cure any one afflicted with disease. He practically revived many of the features of Voudouism, and was rapidly fleecing his victims, when a pitying white man interposed and tried to expose the swindler.

But it was of no avail. The quack boldly challenged the would-be exposer to witness a cure of a long standing case of dropsy. At the house of the sick man the incredulous Caucasian found a large crowd of faithful believers assembled in front of a circle of bones, old rags, and other trash, over which the quack was muttering some gibberish. Finally the announcement was made that there was something in the sick man's bed which had made him ill; and, after a little search, a mysterious packet was found beneath the mattress.

While the horror-stricken crowd were bewailing this evidence of witchcraft, the white man insisted on opening the packet, found it filled with harmless herbs and minerals, and endeavored to convince the negroes that the doctor's confederate had undoubtedly concealed it there. But they would not believe him, and insisted on considering the doctor great at divination, although their confidence was a little shaken when the man stricken with dropsy died, despite the discovery and removal of the hurtful charm.

A Queer Cavalier.

LXV.

THE DISMAL SWAMP—NORFOLK—THE COAST.

CITY POINT, the historic peninsula upon the winding James river, is connected with Petersburg by a branch of the Atlantic, Mississippi and Ohio railroad, and steamers come up from the coast to carry away coal and iron. The route from Petersburg to Norfolk lies through Prince George, Sussex, Southampton, Isle of Wight, Nansemond and Norfolk counties. General Mahone's splendidly-constructed railway runs in a perfect air line for at least seventy-five of the eighty-one miles between the two cities, and is in all respects a model highway to so important a port as Norfolk. It takes the traveler

City Point, Virginia.

through fine cotton-fields; then along stretches of plain covered with thin swaying pines; now through clearings where rows of cabins are erected, and stalwart negroes are hewing wood and digging drains; now into thickets through which rough roads lead to some remote plantation; now through smart little villages, until at last he reaches Suffolk, the pretty shire town of Nansemond county. Suffolk is energetic, and well supplied with railways and river navigation; manufactories are springing up; the Sea-board and Roanoke railway touches there; the county has about 11,000 inhabitants, most of whom are prosperous. The climate in that section is usually delightful; the thermometer ranges from 22 degrees in winter to 94 degrees in summer, with seasons long enough for the maturity of all crops; and, indeed, the same land often produces two crops in one season. Cotton and all the cereals yield immensely. Many Northern people and a large number of English families have settled in the vicinity.

In Norfolk county we entered the edge of the Great Dismal Swamp, which extends far downward over some of the northern portions of North Carolina, and is intersected by canals, on which there is quite an extensive transportation business. The "swamp" is a succession of wild and, apparently, irreclaimable marshes, through which run black currents of water, and in the midst of which spring up thousands of dead tree-trunks. Many of these trunks are charred or blackened by the progress of some recent fire. Some are fantastically shaped, and have been imagined to bear resemblance to well-known statues. The passer-by has his attention invited to the "Column Vendome."

For miles the eye encounters nothing save the bewildering stretch of swamp and dead trees, or the dreary country covered with rank growth of pines and underbrush. The only signs of life are occasional groups of negroes about some saw-mill, on a "hummock," or a glimpse of dusky forms on a barge floating along one of the Stygian canals, as the train glides smoothly and swiftly by. Drummond's Lake, penetrated by a feeder from the "Dismal Swamp" canal, is about thirty miles long.

A Peep into the Great Dismal Swamp.

Norfolk has a real English aspect. It is like some of the venerable towns along the southern coast of England, and the illusion to which the traveler readily yields is heightened by the appearance of many English names on the street corners, over the doors of some business houses, and at almost every turn. The grand current of the Elizabeth (opposite Fort Norfolk) is so broad and deep that the largest ship that floats can swing around there. Midstream, there is much clatter and activity; ships and steamers arrive and depart, and the hoarse shout of the sailor is heard all day long, vying in strength with the scream of the steamboat whistle. In the streets remote from the water-side, not so much activity is apparent, but there are long rows of staid, comfortable-looking houses, embowered in trees, many fine churches, and an ambitious custom-house. The trains of the Atlantic, Mississippi and Ohio railroad discharge their freights of cotton and grain directly upon wharves at the steamers' sides, and the unusual facilities are yearly increased and improved.

The people of Norfolk are beginning to understand the consolidation policy in railroad matters now-a-days. Time was when they could hardly perceive the advantages of a road laid through the treacherous "hummocks" of the Dismal Swamp, and they called the iron bridge over the Elizabeth "Mahone's Folly" when it was first built, thinking that it would cripple the line. But now that they have grappled hold of the commerce of the West, and have begun to compare their advantages with those of New York, they cannot enough praise the sagacity of those who labored until the great through line was an accomplished fact.

The importance of Norfolk as a port of the future is certainly indisputable; and it is not at all improbable that within a few years it will have direct communication with European ports, by means of ocean steamers, owned and controlled in this country. The Norfolk people have made an effort to turn the European emigration, bound to Texas, through their town, forwarding it over the lines penetrating South-western Virginia and Tennessee. But, thus far, only a fortnightly steamer of the Allan Line has touched at Norfolk, bringing, usually, many English families for the lands around Charlottesville and Gordonsville. The Elizabeth river is not so lively now as when, at the beginning of this century, the river could not be seen, so thick was the shipping between the Norfolk and Portsmouth shores. In the financial crash which came at that time, sixty Norfolk firms interested in maritime commerce failed; the modern town does not boast as many.

Norfolk* lies within thirty-two miles of the Atlantic. Northward stretch the Chesapeake and its tributaries, navigable nearly a thousand miles; westward is the James, giving communication with Richmond, and five hundred miles of water-way; southward run the canals to Currituck, Albemarle and Pamlico, communicating with two thousand miles of river-channel. She affords

---

* The eastern and southern branches of the Elizabeth river are superior in depth to the Thames at London, or the Mersey at Liverpool. The depth of water in the harbor at Norfolk is twenty-eight feet, or nearly twice that regularly maintained at New Orleans; and the harbor is spacious enough to admit the commercial marine of the whole country. It has been estimated that thirty miles of excellent water-front for wharfage can readily be afforded.

Eastern North Carolina is the natural ally of Norfolk in commerce. Behind the barrier of sand-hills, extending along the Carolina coast, lies one of the most fertile regions on the continent, which can find no more convenient outlet than Norfolk. The Sea-board and Roanoke railroad penetrates North Carolina, a little above the point at which the trade becomes tributary to its canals, and connects with the Raleigh and Gaston, and Wilmington and Weldon railroads, at Weldon. The Norfolk and Great Western road is a projected route to run through the southern counties of Virginia, touching at Danville and terminating at Bristol. The natural seaport of the Chesapeake and Ohio railroad, which, coming from the Ohio river, penetrates the mountains of Western Virginia, is, of course, Norfolk. The Albemarle and Chesapeake canal, through which, during eleven years from the 30th of September, 1860, more than thirty-five thousand vessels of all classes passed, penetrates a country rich in cereals, woods, and naval stores, all of which it brings directly to Norfolk. The river lines of steamers, running to Yorktown, Hampton, and Old Point, Elizabeth City, and Washington, N. C., Roanoke Island, and other places, are rapidly re-establishing the local trade of the Chesapeake and its tributaries, interrupted by the war. The receipts of cotton at Norfolk in 1858 were 6,174 bales; we have seen that in 1872 they were more than 400,000.

A Glimpse of Norfolk, Virginia.

naturally the best seaport for most of North Carolina and Tennessee, besides large sections of Northern Georgia, Alabama, Mississippi, and the South-west. A thorough system of internal improvements in Virginia, giving lines leading from tide-water in that State to the North-west, would enable Norfolk almost to usurp the commercial pre-eminence of New York. Pittsburg, and Wheeling, and Toledo are geographically nearer the Capes of Virginia than to Sandy Hook; and it is almost certain that in the future many of the highways to the sea from the West will run through Virginia, and the ports furnishing outlets to the Western cities will be along the beautiful and capacious Chesapeake bay. Ingenious minds have already mapped an ocean route from Norfolk to the Holland coast—one possessing great advantages—and it is to be hoped that a company may be formed to place steamers upon it.

There are good steamship lines between Norfolk and New York, Boston, Baltimore, and Philadelphia. The Boston steamers carry a great deal of cotton to the New England factories. Norfolk received in 1873 *four hundred and six thousand* bales of cotton, an enormous increase over her receipts in 1872. The amount brought by the Atlantic, Mississippi and Ohio railroad alone in 1873 was 158,000 bales. The produce business of the port is very great; during the active season a daily steamer is sent to New York, Boston, and Baltimore, and three weekly to Philadelphia. The "truck farms"—*i. e.*, the market gardens in the vicinity,—give the shippers business at a time when "all cotton" towns are afflicted with dullness. The receipts of truck for 1872 amounted to $3,500,000; and the value of all the receipts was

$21,000,000.* The duties on imports into the district of Norfolk and Portsmouth, from 1866 to 1871 inclusive, amounted to more than $800,000.

There is a large negro population in Norfolk, and the white citizens make great struggles at each election to keep the municipal power in their own hands. They have long had excellent free schools, on which they are now expending $10,000 yearly; their city affairs are in good condition. The estimated real value of assessable property in the city is $17,000,000, and the greater part of the tax thereon is readily collected; the citizens have built fine water-works at a large expense; the shops are excellent; society is exceedingly frank, cordial and refined.

This goodly ancient town, with its 20,000 inhabitants, was laid out more than a century and a-half ago, but the British burned it in the Revolution, and it had to grow again. It has seen troublous times since then. The yellow fever has made one or two ghastly visitations, and war has disturbed the even tenor of its way. There came a day, too, when Portsmouth, the pleasant town just across the Elizabeth from Norfolk, and where one of the principal naval depots of the United States is situated, seemed enveloped in flame, and when the new-made Confederate on one side of the stream watched with mingled regret and exultation the burning of the vast ship-houses and the ships-of-war which the United States were unwilling to allow him to capture.

A promenade along the Elizabeth, in company with an ex-Confederate officer, was fruitful of souvenirs. It was toward sunset of a September day when we clambered upon the parapet of old Fort Norfolk, and gazed out over the broad expanse of sparkling water toward the horizon, delicately bordered with foliage, which masked the embouchure of the James, and the black spots further down, indicating Crany Island and the entrance to Hampton Roads, where those two sea-devils, the "Merrimac" and the "Monitor," had their fierce battle. Fort Norfolk is now, as it was when the Confederates seized it, a magazine. The powder captured there at the beginning of the war long defended many a Southern town.

From the quaint walls of the venerable fort we saw pretty villages and villas, and the noble United States Marine Hospital, on the opposite shore; could watch the schooners coming in with the tide, as the sunset deepened from blood-red until it mingled its last gleam with the strange neutral twilight; the sudden advent of a Baltimore steamer looming up like a spectre, with its dark sides and black wheels half-shrouded in smoke; could see the rows of mansions extending

* Some idea of the produce business may be had from the following enumeration of the articles which passed through Norfolk, bound mainly to Northern cities, in 1872, and the various articles received at the port. The receipts of corn were 1,628,940 bushels; of peanuts, 544,025 bushels; of dried fruit, 346,542; oats, 329,110; peas, 152,420; wheat, 75,210; flour, 100,640 barrels; rosin, 129,586 barrels; turpentine, 14,940 barrels; pitch, 3,240 barrels; tobacco, 3,525 hogsheads, 2,520 tierces, 34,270 cases, and 38,920 boxes. In the same time, 1,000,000 dozens of eggs; 14,280,170 pounds of rags; $175,000 worth of shad; 6,000,000 bushels of oysters, amounting to nearly $4,000,000; 37,775 barrels of salt fish; 8,381,860 staves, 53,392,221 shingles, and 57,496,290 feet of lumber were also received. The Sea-board and Roanoke railroad annually brings in more than 180,000 bales of cotton.

out to the very water's edge, and the piers jutting from their front doors, with rustic arbors and awnings, where one might sit and woo the fresh sea-breeze; could see the gracefully tapering masts, and the massive walls of the warehouses, and could hear the rattling of the chains, and singing of sailors.

Strolling back, we noted the barelegged negro boys sculling in the skiffs which they had half-filled with oysters, and passed through streets entirely devoted to the establishments where the bivalve, torn from his shell, was packed in cans and stored to await his journey to the far West. Driving on the hard shell road, later in the evening, we passed long trains of fish-carts, in each of which lay a

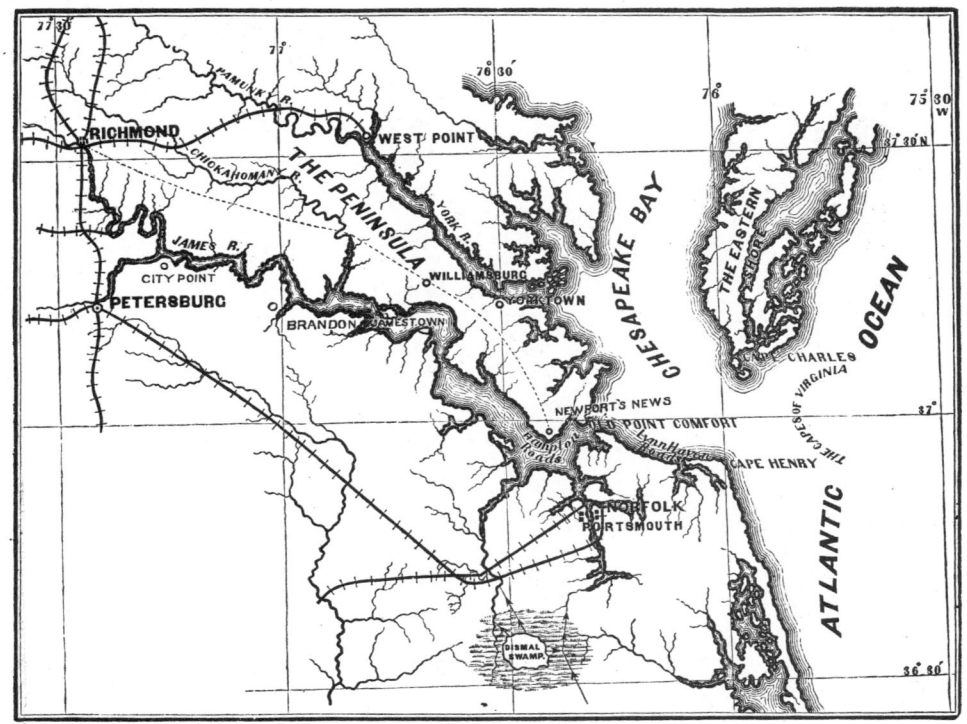

Map of the Virginia Peninsula.

sleepy negro, growling if we asked one-half of the road; saw the fields where, during the civil war, the Confederates had prepared to defend Norfolk from approach of the blue-coated soldiery by land—fields occupied by carefully-tilled farms, near which were the cabin and garden patch of the freedman; saw evidences on every hand of growth and progress, and found it hard, indeed, to convince ourselves that half a century had not passed since the "war for the Union" closed.

The map given above shows the configuration of the Virginia peninsula, and the location of Hampton Roads, one of the most superb expanses of land-locked water in the world. This grand refuge, in which all the navies of the world might at one time find shelter from storm, is but fifteen miles from Norfolk. Entering from the Atlantic, between the two capes of Virginia, Charles and

Henry, the ships of Newport, Smith, and Gosnold, the daring English explorers and colonists, penetrated more than two and a-half centuries ago to Hampton Roads and anchored opposite the point now known as Newport News. Northward from Old Point Comfort, stretches the mighty Chesapeake bay, along whose richly-indented shores are some of the finest harbors on the American coast.

Hampton Roads.

Hampton Roads and Lynnhorn bay, lying between the capes, and under their shelter, are sometimes called the "Spit Head" and the "Downs" of the United States. The York, the Potomac, the Rappahannock and the James rivers empty their ample currents into the Chesapeake bay, which the Virginians claim as "Virginia water," because it passes through her borders to the sea, and flows to it between the capes.

The "northern neck" of Virginia is that portion of her territory situated between the Rappahannock and the James rivers, and extending from the Chesapeake bay to the Blue Ridge mountains. The four counties in this section, Lancaster, Northumberland, Richmond and Westmoreland, contain four hundred and sixty-six thousand acres, on which only 26,000 people are settled. Along the rivers and the bay there are beautiful plains, which run back some two miles to a ridge two hundred feet higher than the shores. This ridge extends throughout the length of the neck, and is intersected every few miles by streams of soft, fresh water. Many of these streams are navigable, and producers settled along their banks can have easy water communication with the principal Northern ports. The prodigal abundance of food to be had with very little effort, has thus far been an effectual hindrance to the proper development of this favored region; the negroes, who constitute a good part of the population, spend a few hours of each day in securing the fish, oysters, and wild fowl with which the inlets abound, but do not possess sufficient ambition to become either fruit-raisers, market gardeners or oystermen. If they would work they might be prosperous; but they prefer a life of idleness.

The soil of the Neck along the rivers is mainly composed of alluvial deposits. It was for years cultivated recklessly, and very seriously exhausted, under the *régime* of the slave-holder; yet to-day, without thorough culture, produces paying crops. The climate is delightful; the winters are very short and by no means severe. Almost all varieties of fruit, save those peculiar to the tropics, can be cultivated to perfection there. Labor is cheap; the negro is, of course, the only workman, and does as well as his limited knowledge and indolent disposition will allow. He needs the example of ambitious immigrants to encourage him to a right development of the excellent resources so lavishly scattered around him. The white inhabitants eagerly welcome skilled workers, and offer them lands on favorable terms.

The tide-water region of Virginia extends from the coast to an imaginary line drawn across the State, and touching at Fredericksburg, Richmond, and Petersburg. It includes the northern neck just described, and consists of a series of peninsulas whose sides are washed by the Chesapeake bay, and the great tidal rivers emptying into it. Throughout this section the principal item of land culture is market gardening; good farms are to be had for small prices. The lands are well drained; reasonably free from marsh, with a soil of clay, marl and sand, and an overgrowth of pine and oak. It is estimated that 30,000,000 bushels of oysters are annually drawn from the waters in this region; a State tax is collected yearly on 20,000,000 bushels. Malarial fevers are the drawback, and historical memorials are the boast of the section. Fevers prevail only during the autumn months, and will doubtless disappear entirely as the country becomes more densely populated, and sufficient attention is given to drainage. They are at present the curse of the river-side populations, and nothing is more common than to meet a lean, discolored individual who explains his woebegone look by announcing that he has just had a "right smart shake."

LXVI.

THE EDUCATION OF NEGROES—THE AMERICAN MISSIONARY ASSOCIATION—THE PEABODY FUND—THE CIVIL RIGHTS BILL.

AT Hampton one begins to appreciate the magnitude of the revolution which has overtaken the South. There it was that, more than two hundred and fifty years ago, the first cargo of slaves was landed on American soil. There the curse began, and there its bitter leaven worked until the time of deliverance arrived, and it was ordained that, on the very ground where the negro had first been enslaved by the white man in Virginia, efforts for his elevation to a true manhood should be undertaken.

Everywhere that the Union armies went in the South, they found the negro anxious for knowledge. The wretched slave was like a blind man who heard around him tumult and struggle, and who constantly cried aloud for light, for the power of vision. He was weighted down with the crushing burden of his past life; he saw the great chance slipping away from him, and in his intense desire to become intelligent and independent, he fairly laid hold upon the soldiery for help. But the officers and men of the army knew not what to do with the negroes who took refuge in the Union camps. Sometimes they sent them back to their masters; at others they protected and fed them, while at the same time denying any intention of interfering with the institution of slavery.

But the day came when General Butler pronounced the freedmen who, by thousands, had flocked into the country around Fortress Monroe, "contraband of war." Hungry, homeless, and filled with nameless dread, these rude exiles from the plantations of their late masters turned toward the National Government, and held out their hands for protection. They knew not what to do. The future lay dark before them. The cannon still thundered throughout Virginia. The negroes stood on the threshold of liberty, still fearing that they might be dragged away to their old condition of servitude. The country came to their aid. The National Government found the key-note of the situation in Butler's sharp, coarse proclamation, and held the negro refugees under its protection. Then the American Missionary Association came to the front.

This noble Association, for so many years before the war an earnest worker in the antislavery cause, was ready and anxious to send material relief to the negroes. It was willing to aid in feeding their bodies as well as their souls. It had had its missionaries in all parts of the South, undergoing persecution and abuse for the sake of preaching the gospel and telling the truth. Its envoys had been driven out of some of the States; others, as the outbreak of the war approached, were arrested and imprisoned. But the work went on!

In August of 1861, Lewis Tappan, Esq., then Treasurer of the American Missionary Association, wrote to General Butler, at Fortress Monroe, asking what could be done to aid the negroes. The General answered, showing the unhappy condition of the freedmen and women, and welcoming any assistance. Letters came from soldiers and officers in the army to the charitable throughout New York and the East, asking help for the negroes. Rev. L. C. Lockwood was sent out to investigate the condition of the great mass of refugees in Virginia, and in September he opened a Sabbath school in the deserted mansion of ex-President Tyler. On the 17th day of the same month, he started the first day school for the freedmen. It was held in an humble house not far from Fortress Monroe, and was taught by Mary A. Peake, an excellent woman, whose father was an Englishman of rank and culture, but whose mother was a free colored woman. She, the representative of both the oppressing and oppressed races, began her work of regeneration of the blacks on the very coast where the degradation began, and near a proud seminary where the daughters of Southern aristocrats had received the education paid for by the unrequited labor of slaves.

As the war progressed, the work of teaching grew and strengthened among the freedmen. The Union forces made their way on to the sea-islands along the South Carolina coast in November of 1861, and the usual swarms of ignorant and half-starved negroes flocked around them. The envoys sent from the North to examine into the condition of these wretched people gave such thrilling accounts of their needs, that public meetings to devise measures for relief were held in Boston, New York, and Philadelphia. Societies for the establishment of schools and forwarding of supplies were speedily formed; the "Boston Education Society," the "Freedmen's Relief Association" of New York, and others, sprang into existence early in 1862. Men and women were at once sent out as teachers. They began by first relieving the physical wants of the distressed, and then tried to teach them the dignity of labor. The "Port Royal Society" of Philadelphia sent funds, provisions, and teachers. Cincinnati, Chicago, Cleveland and Pittsburg sent workers and money. Societies multiplied so rapidly that it was finally deemed advisable to consolidate them; and it was accordingly done in 1866, the combined bodies taking the title of the "American Freedmen's Union Commission." This colossal organization worked in perfect harmony with the American Missionary Association for a short time, then gradually withdrew some of its branches from the work as reconstruction progressed, and ceased to be a really national body.

From the date of the founding of the school near Fortress Monroe, the American Missionary Association pushed its work with exemplary vigor. The opening of 1863 brought with it the proclamation of emancipation, and settled forever the question of the condition of negro fugitives who escaped to the Union lines. Then the North put forth its strength. Hundreds of refined and delicate ladies voluntarily engaged in the work of teaching the blacks—living amid cheerless surroundings, on poor fare, and meeting with contempt and vulgar ostracism, which many a one who was guilty of it then would to-day be ashamed of. At Hampton, Norfolk, and Portsmouth, day and Sabbath schools for the negroes were held in the colored churches; evening schools for adults were established, and men and women flocked to them after the fatigues of the day. On the estate of ex-Governor Wise, of Virginia, near Norfolk, the Missionary Association established schools, and the Governor's mansion became a school and a home for colored teachers.

Wherever the freed negroes gathered, as at Newbern in North Carolina, at Nashville in Tennessee, on Roanoke Island, in the Port Royal Islands, at Vicksburg, at Columbus, at Memphis, at President Island, at Camps Fisk and Shiloh, teachers were furnished, charities were bestowed, and the good work went nobly on. In 1864 the Association's workers in the field of the South numbered 250, mainly employed in Virginia and along the line of the Mississippi. In Louisiana General Banks had introduced an efficient system of public instruction, supported by a military tax, and there, too, the Association sent its teachers. The colored troops enlisted in the Union armies were instructed, and while the negroes rested from drill, they pored over the Readers and text-books which had been distributed among them.

The bodily needs of the freedmen were always as great and extreme as their spiritual necessities. Thousands died of neglect and starvation. The hand of Northern charity could not reach one-third of the sufferers. Many died under the despair and unrest occasioned by their change of condition. They became wanderers, and set out upon long journeys hither and yon, blindly straying toward some dimly-defined goal. Their darkened minds were impressed with the belief that somewhere a great material heritage awaited them. They were in an attitude of intense suspense when the war ended. Virtually the wards of the National Government, which had been compelled to undertake their support wherever they claimed aid, they relied implicitly upon the promises given them. Unable to help themselves, or to understand the dignity of the future to which they had suddenly been introduced, they could but hope and wait.

Behind the army of Sherman, and the forces which entered Richmond, marched resolute teachers. Schools were established in the slave-marts of Savannah, and were in due time placed under the control of the American Missionary Association. In Augusta, in Charleston, in Wilmington, and Richmond, teachers did all they could to shape the minds of the negroes to a sense of the responsibilities of manhood and the dignity of womanhood. Early in March of 1865 the Freedmen's Bureau was formed, and placed under the direction of General O. O. Howard, who, as its chief commissioner, did much to aid the colored man in maintaining his rights. The Bureau established schools wisely and well; and under its fostering care many now prosperous institutions were started and maintained, until they showed their beneficent character, and received large support from private charities.

As the Missionary Association had been from the first frankly unsectarian, it from time to time received the cordial coöperation of the different churches. The Wesleyan Methodists went into its work with the fervor which characterizes all their movements. The Free-Will Baptists supported many of its teachers. The National Council of Congregational Churches, which assembled in Boston in June of 1865, recommended the raising of a quarter of a million of dollars, to be placed in the hands of the Missionary Association, for carrying on the work among the freedmen. This generous gift came into play in 1866, and orphan asylums and normal schools were founded. The first asylum was located at Wilmington in North Carolina; the second, founded by a donation from Hon. I. Washburn of Worcester, Massachusetts, at Atlanta, Georgia.

Aid from abroad meantime came generously in. Great Britain sent more than $1,000,000 in money and clothing to the freedmen. The envoys of the Missionary Association were gladly and hospitably received in England, Scotland and Wales.

With the advent of reconstruction came a change in the aspect of the educational situation. The Southern people were not satisfied to see the black men elevated to political power; and in many States the most barbarous and, in some cases, murderous measures of intimidation were used to prevent the negro from gaining instruction, and from demonstrating his right to be a man. Mob violence, Ku-Klux mysteries, and social ostracisms were tried as agencies to deter Northern teachers from doing their good work. But the labor was continued as zealously as before. Churches were founded, the normal schools were liberally aided and encouraged in their work of equipping colored teachers, and wherever one teacher fainted in the ranks, another was quickly found to supply his or her place.

The operation of the Peabody fund, and the constant beneficence of the wealthy in the North and West, are still doing much to second the efforts which the Southern people are now themselves making in the cause of free public education. The negroes have as yet done but little to help themselves; they are not property holders to any extent, nor do they seem likely to become such, until they have been educated for at least a generation. Instances of thrift and thorough independence among them are not wanting, it is true; but the mass of negro males in the Southern States aid comparatively little in paying for the school privileges which they receive, under the operation of school laws in most of the reconstructed commonwealths.

The North has done much; yet it is by no means a proper time for it to relax its efforts. There never was a period when the money, the intelligence and the energy of Northern people were so much needed in the cause of education in the South as now. There was never a time when so much real missionary work could be done among the negroes. Now that they are beginning to take active part as citizens in the affairs of their sections they need the best instruction and the wisest advice. Their ignorance has already been made the means of infamous tyranny; their accession to political power has been marked by much injustice and wrong, of which they have been unwittingly the instruments; and the North owes it to them and to herself to aid in rescuing them from the adventurers into whose clutches they have fallen.

The seven chartered normal schools which have grown up under the American Missionary Association in the South are annually equipping fine corps of teachers for colored schools. Hampton, in Virginia; Berea College, on the border line between the blue grass and the mountain regions of Kentucky; Fisk University, at Nashville, Tennessee; Atlanta University, in Atlanta, Georgia; Talladega College, in Alabama; Tougaloo University, in Mississippi; and Straight University, in New Orleans, are but the precursors of other similar institutions to be placed in each Southern State. The Association will not rest contented with its labors until it has established normal schools in each of the ex-slave States west of the Mississippi river. In addition to these normal institutes, the American Missionary Association now has graded and normal schools combined in Wilmington, North Carolina; in Charleston, where the Avery Institute has more than four hundred pupils, and owns twenty thousand dollars' worth of property; in Greenwood, South Carolina; in Andersonville, Atlanta, Macon, and Savannah, Georgia; in Athens, Marion, Mobile, Montgomery, and Selma, in Alabama; in Chattanooga and Memphis, Tennessee; in Lexington and Louisville, Kentucky; in Columbus, Mississippi; in Galveston, Texas; and in Jefferson City, Missouri. It has under its charge, mainly in the Southern field, although some few of the institutions are on the Pacific coast, forty-seven churches, with a membership of 2,898; the seven normal and nineteen graded and normal schools mentioned above; forty-seven common schools; three hundred and twenty-three ministers, missionaries and teachers; and more than fourteen thousand pupils. As the work of thirteen years, in the face of the most remarkable obstacles and with a degraded population born in slavery to operate upon, this merits the world's applause.

The efforts of this brave Association and kindred societies have not been in vain. The Southern States at last have school systems of their own, and seem likely to maintain them. This alone is worth all that the war cost.

When Dr. Sears, the able and generous agent of the Peabody fund, went South in July of 1867, there was, strictly speaking, no modern school system in any of the twelve States in which the fund now operates. Tennessee inaugurated one, however, in that same year, under General Eaton. To-day all of those twelve States have by law, and all but one or two have in fact, tolerable school systems. West Virginia, Virginia and Tennessee, now have the most effective plans. Tennessee, after originally taking the lead, nearly abolished its schools on changing its politics three or four years ago. It adopted the miserable county system, with no State Superintendent. But for the last year or two, it has not only recovered what it had lost, but is now surpassed in good legislation and general activity for schools by no Southern State unless it be Virginia. At this time it is, in some respects, the most zealous and active State in the South concerning educational matters, and the prospects for public schools for years to come, at least in the large towns, are most encouraging.

West Virginia, which adopted a pretty good system early after the war, did not suffer much by a change from Republican to Democratic politics. The Convention for revising the Constitution made no change in that portion relating to schools. The latest legislation, leaving it optional with the counties to supplement the inadequate State taxation, was supposed to be disastrous; but the people have fortunately shown a disposition to vote a liberal tax.

It is the testimony of Dr. Sears and other intelligent men, who have carefully studied the subject, that three of the Conservative States are now leading all the others of the South in education. The feeling in favor of schools of some kind is so strong that no ambitious man of any party, in any Southern State, dares to oppose public free education. This is certainly a radical change in seven years!

Arkansas has a good school system, inadequately supported; Mississippi has good schools in the cities, but very few in the country. Alabama's progress is marred by unwise legislation, which gives the Legislature the power to veto the laws that only a Board of Education can pass.

The American Missionary Association, and all Northern enterprises in the cause of education, cannot do better for the next decade than to put all their money and talent into the States which are now, and are likely from time to time to be, under negro rule. In South Carolina, Florida, and Louisiana, the white people either stand aloof entirely from many of the public schools, or give them but a feeble and reluctant support. Normal schools and thorough teaching are needed bitterly in those States, and will be required for ten years to come.

At the commencement of the educational work in the South, there were three grand hindrances to the establishment of public schools.

The first was prejudice against them as a Northern institution, not adapted to the condition of the Southern people. This is now so far overcome as to cause no anxiety.

The second was the burden of taxation; but men are now beginning, all through the South, to see the necessity and economy of free schools. The opposition is mainly, to-day, among the ignorant, against whom the enlightened are gradually prevailing.

The third and most potent, still existing, is the dread of mixed schools. This should not be understood, as it so often is at the North, as arising from a desire on the part of the Southerner to deprive the negro of his chances for an education. The objection to mixed schools is a graver one, and may be considered sufficient. Until the masses of the black population in the South have acquired a higher moral tone than at present characterizes them, it will not be well to admit them freely into that communion which an education in the same rooms and under the same teachers as white children would give.

It is noteworthy that where the negroes have full and unrestrained political power, as in South Carolina and Louisiana, they have not even demanded mixed schools to any extent. They know that it would be useless; and it would be quite as repulsive to most of the blacks as to the whites to have an indiscriminate mingling of the races in schools. The negro in the Conservative States gains many more educational advantages by a separate school system than he could by mixed schools. Although he rarely pays more than one-sixth as much in taxes as his white fellow-citizen, the school law guarantees him exactly equal school facilities, save in a very few instances, and supplies him with buildings and teachers. It would be as absurd on the part of Congress to pass a bill a section of which should require the co-education of the sexes in the South, as to enact the mixed school section of the proposed "civil rights" bill. The good sense of the negroes rejects the section, as it enables them to see that a law odious to the whites would have for its natural result a cessation of effort in behalf of the blacks. The mixing of the races is not a matter for national legislation. Both races now have the vote; each has an equal chance with the other to acquire property and enjoy it; each can have all the education that it is willing to buy, besides what is freely given it. The course of a Congress which seriously discusses the passage of a bill which would block the whole educational system of the South, and at the same time never thinks of voting any appropriation to aid in carrying on the work of education there, is certainly open to criticism. The practical tendency of the attempt at enforcement of the mixed school clause would be the turning out of doors of the million and a-half of white and black children now in the public schools of the fifteen ex-slave States.

Taking the statistics of the Southern public schools, as given in 1871 and 1872, it will be seen that seven years after the close of the war the impoverished Southern States had managed to bring under the operation of a school system proportionally four-sevenths as many children as are at school in the North, and to keep them at school three-fourths as long.* In view of the fact that great numbers of the Southern people (*i. e.*, the negroes) own little or no property, it may be asserted that the Southern property holder is paying a much heavier school tax than is his Northern brother.

Congress, instead of threatening the South with the destruction of her school system, should take earnest measures to foster and protect education in all the Southern States. The ignorance prevalent in that section is the cause of many phases of its unhappy condition. It is believed that the registered adult illiterates in the South constitute more than one-half the adult population. There is indisputable evidence to show that the percentage of illiteracy has increased among the whites in the South since the outbreak of the war. The reclaiming of the "poor whites" from the barbarism in which they have been plunged for so many years is certainly a proper subject for the consideration of the National Government. If that Government had carefully and wisely supplemented, by an equal sum, such a generous donation as the $2,000,000 given by George Peabody for education in the South, it would have done no more than its duty. The negroes have been called *the wards of the nation;* yet we find the Southern States and a few individuals and societies doing all that is done for them. The nation does little but look on.

* Vide Report of General Ruffner, Virginia Superintendent of Education, for 1873.

LXVII.

THE HAMPTON NORMAL INSTITUTE—GENERAL ARMSTRONG'S WORK—FISK UNIVERSITY—BEREA AND OTHER COLLEGES.

THE better class of Southerners have been for some time convinced that they must help the negroes to an education, as a protective measure. They have discovered that the free laborer must possess a certain amount of intelligence, and that he must have the incentives to work and to the acquisition of property which knowledge gives. But the great difficulty has been to procure a sufficient number of capable colored instructors for work throughout the back-country. In the cities white teachers have been readily procured; but in the interior those of their own race were needed for the negroes. To insure the elevation of the blacks, they must have before them the daily example of one of their own people who has been instructed, and who is anxious to instruct them.

The establishment of the normal schools mentioned in the previous chapter proved the solution of this difficulty. The Northern people, who had been the closest observers of the freedmen, readily recognized that the first need was the spread of rudimentary education. After the new generation had been taught to read and write, had been shown the dignity of labor, and had received the much-needed lessons in morality, it would be time enough to found a college with a classical course for the freedmen, or to insist on the privilege for them of entrance into the colleges now occupied by the whites. So the sensible Northerners went at the work of educating negro teachers.

"What the negro needs at once," wrote General Samuel C. Armstrong, in his report on the system and condition of the Hampton Normal Institute, made to the Virginia Superintendent of Education in 1872, "is elementary and industrial education. The race will succeed or fail as it shall devote itself with energy to agriculture and the mechanic arts, or avoid these pursuits, and its teachers must be inspired with the spirit of hard work, and acquainted with the ways that lead to material success. An imitation of Northern models will not do. Right methods of work at the South must be created, not copied, although the underlying principle is everywhere the same." This is the truth, and those of the negroes who have been taught under such men as General Armstrong are telling it to their fellows.

General Armstrong, who had been Colonel of the Eighth Regiment of United States colored troops during the war, was the chief official of the Freedmen's Bureau at Hampton when the thousands of blacks were helplessly gathered there. As early as 1867, he had set forth, in an able article, the need of normal schools for the colored people. The son of a missionary who was for sixteen years the Minister of Public Instruction in the Hawaiian kingdom, General Armstrong thoroughly understood the establishment of schools upon a "manual labor" basis, as they had been established in the Sandwich Islands. A man of quick sympathies, tremendous will and iron courage, he determined to see what the manual labor school would do for the freedmen and freedwomen. With the coöperation of the American Missionary Association, he began his work and, in April of 1868, inaugurated the labors of the institution which was chartered in 1867 by the Virginia Legislature as the Hampton Normal and Agricultural Institute, with a board of eminent Northern gentlemen as trustees. General Howard, as head of the Freedmen's Bureau, helped the work generously; money was given, a large farm was purchased, and in 1872 the school received its first aid from Virginia, in landscrip to the amount of $95,000, bestowed on the institution in its character of agricultural college. Thus encouraged, the school prospered, and colored pupils flocked to it from nearly all the States of the South. The division of labor and study partaken by both male and female pupils has been satisfactory to both teachers and scholars, and the pecuniary results have been better than were anticipated. Each male student has, each week, from a day and a-half to two days' labor on the farm, for which he is credited a fair sum. The young women are provided with an industrial department, where they are taught to use sewing-machines, and are familiarized with all the ordinary duties of housekeeping. There is a printing-office attached to the school, and a monthly paper is issued by the labor of the scholars. One of the fundamental principles of the school is that nothing shall be given which can be earned by the pupil, and this has the desired effect of encouraging a spirit of independence. Since the founding of the institution, it has sent out nearly one hundred well-trained teachers, earnest, honest Christian men and women, who propose to devote their lives to the elevation of their race. At the closing exercises of the term of 1874, when a large class graduated, Virginians and New Englanders united in pronouncing the school a thorough success, and one of the most effective agents for the elevation of the negro.

The normal work has had great and encouraging growth in Tennessee. The people of Nashville had the problem of the care of freedmen presented to them early in 1862, and in 1867 the Freedmen's Bureau and the American Missionary Association together had succeeded in securing the charter of Fisk University in that city. Early in 1867 the State Superintendent of Public Instruction and other Tennesseans announced that "the best way to permanently establish and perpetuate schools among the colored people is to establish good normal training schools for the education of teachers." The University was developed from the Fisk school, opened in 1866, and named for General Clinton B. Fisk, who was for a time in charge of the work of the Freedmen's Bureau at Nashville. The attendance at this school had averaged over a thousand pupils, until Nashville herself adopted a public school system. The Missionary Association then placed a suitable location for buildings at the disposition of the trustees of the new University, and a little band of the students, young men and women, went out into the North to sing the "heart-songs" in which the slaves used to find such consolation, and by means of concerts to secure the money with which to erect new University buildings. The success of that campaign, in this country and in

England, is now a matter of history. The "Jubilee Singers" have found the means to build Jubilee Hall, an edifice which would be an ornament to any university, and around which will in time be grouped many others.

This University began with the alphabet in 1867. It teaches it still, but it offers in addition a college classical course of four years, with a preparatory course of three years, and two normal courses of two years each. The following paragraph from a report of a recent commencement will show what progress the ex-slaves have already made:

"On Thursday the freshman class in college was examined in Virgil's Æneid, Geometry, and Botany, the latter with the sophomores. The sophomore class was examined in the De Amicitia and De Senectute of Cicero, and Livy, in Latin; in Homer's Iliad, in Greek, and Botany, in all of which the members of this class acquitted themselves with marked ability, showing conclusively that the people of the colored race are capable of acquiring and mastering the most difficult studies, and attaining the highest culture given by our best colleges. The promptness and beauty of their translations, together with their accuracy, showing a knowledge of the structure of the language as well as the thought of the classics they translated, was most gratifying to the friends of education, as well as to their instructors. So, too, in Botany, pursued but a single term, the examination was most satisfactory in the knowledge of the terminology of the science, the principles of classification, and the ability to analyze plants, explain their structure, and determine their order and species in the vegetable world."

The normal instruction of Fisk University is constantly supplying the colored race with efficient and pious teachers. The privations which the negro will inflict upon himself for the sake of maintaining himself in the University (for it is not, like Hampton, a manual labor school) are almost incredible. The University stands upon the site of Fort Gillam, in a beautiful section of Nashville, and the town negroes never pass it without a lingering look at the doors of the building, as if they all would enter if they could.

At Berea College, near the old estates of Cassius M. Clay, the famous abolitionist, in Madison county, Kentucky, the spectacle of both races studying in the same institution in completest harmony may be seen. A prosperous school was started at Berea several years before the war by a missionary who had been successful in founding antislavery churches in the South; but when the John Brown raid occurred, the slaveholders broke up Berea. At the close of the war the teachers returned, and found their homes and buildings uninjured. They at once opened a school into which both races were received upon equal footing. This was a source of great astonishment to the white Kentuckians for a time; but they finally began to send their children, and now the regular proportion of white students is about two-fifths, many of whom are young ladies. The annual commencement exercises bring together audiences of a thousand or fifteen hundred persons, black and white, ex-Confederate and Unionist, who look approvingly upon the progress of students of both colors. Rev. E. H. Fairchild, brother of the President of Oberlin, presides over the faculty. Donations from the North are rapidly building up this institution, one of the few in the ex-slave States where blacks and whites study harmoniously together.

The University at Atlanta met with much opposition; the Georgians seemed disinclined to believe in the sincerity of those who had come to teach the negroes.

After the institution, which was incorporated in 1867, had been in operation two years, it was visited by a committee of prominent Southern gentlemen, many of whom were severely prejudiced against negro schools, but who were forced to admit, in their report made to the Governor of the State, that "the system of intellectual and moral training adopted in the school" was eminently practical. It was evident, also, from other sentences in their report, that they began to believe in the possibility of the education of the negro masses, as they added that the satisfactory answers of the pupils "to questions tended to define the character of their moral training, their polite behavior, general modesty of demeanor, and evident economy and neatness of dress, are indicative of a conviction on the part of the pupils that they are being educated for usefulness, and not for mere ostentation or to gratify a selfish ambition." They found that the African could stand very rigid tests in algebra and geometry, and "fully comprehend the construction of difficult passages in the classics." Atlanta University has two hundred and fifty students, has received aid from the Legislature, and annually sends out well-educated colored teachers from its normal department.

The college at Talladega, Alabama, was chartered in 1869, and has already sent out many faithful workers. A paragraph from the pen of Rev. George Whipple, of New York, concerning a recent examination of the classes at Talladega, contains some important testimony:

"Those who know anything of the educational work among the colored people need not be told that they are seldom at fault in studies exercising mainly the memory; but many, if not most, have doubted their ability in studies requiring the exercise of the reasoning faculty. There was here, however, no failure. On the contrary, that which made the most marked impression on those who were familiar with schools in the North twenty and twenty-five years ago, was the well-sustained examination in English Grammar and Algebra, showing a power of analysis, under the circumstances, really surprising."

In the theological department of this University, young colored men are prepared for the ministry, and are given an impulse in the direction of real missionary work, so much needed among the reckless emotional negroes in the interior districts of the South.

The Straight University at New Orleans has nearly 250 pupils, and among the dusky attendants there are diligent students in Greek, Latin, and Algebra. The importance of this institution to the negroes of the South-west cannot be overestimated. In no other State does the negro, when left to himself, touch so closely upon barbarism as in the remote portions of Louisiana; and the training of colored teachers who can reach the untaught masses is a work of the highest beneficence. The programme of the University is certainly ample; how necessary its existence to the good of the State is may be understood from the statement of what it proposes to do:

"To train the half-heathen preachers of this State into a useful Christian ministry; to give its colored legislators so much knowledge of history and law as to make their votes intelligent, and to awaken as much self-respect as shall lift them above temptation to take a bribe; to furnish teachers to our crudely-organized public schools; to gather into 'the fold of the Church this vast Roman Catholic population; to win them to us by showing them that Straight University is, in its instructors, buildings, libraries, apparatus, discipline, Christian courtesies, scholarship, and general management, wholly superior to, and broader than, their parochial and conventual schools; to make it safe for the republic that the newly-created citizens of Louisiana should retain their franchise, and to prevent Louisiana from being Mexicanized by frequent revolutions; in brief, to infuse a wholesome Christian life into the mingled mass of negro and Latin blood,—is a work which must be done for its own sake, for the sake of the nation, and for Christ's sake."

There is but one chartered normal school for the tens of thousands of freedmen in Mississippi, the one heretofore mentioned as at Tougaloo. It has nearly 300 students; the manual labor system has been introduced to some extent; the normal school is successful; but half-a-dozen such institutions, amply endowed, are necessary to give proper facilities for education to the swarming masses of blacks.

It has been the fashion in both North and South to believe that the negro would prove susceptible of cultivation only to a certain point. But the universal testimony of the mass of careful observers is that the negro can go as far in mental processes as the white child. The blacks have wonderful memories and strong imitative propensities; eloquence, passionate and natural; a strange and subtle sense of rhythm and poetry; and it is now pretty well settled that there are no special race limitations. Why, then, should they not go forward to a good future? Is it not the duty of that section which gave them political power before they were fit to use it, to give them every opportunity to fit themselves for its exercise? It will be long before they can, of their own effort, supply the funds needed for their education; until they can, the North should not fail to foster all the schools which, like the normal institutions whose history has been reviewed in this chapter, sow the good seed.

The schools are doing much to lift up the negro's idea of the dignity of religion. Emphatically Christian institutions, they strive to inculcate that morality and self-denial which it seems so difficult for the blacks to exercise. Although there are many exemplary Christians among the freedmen and freedwomen, it may safely be said that the majority do not allow their religion to interfere with their desires. They believe in the spasmodic shouting, stamping, and groaning which characterize their meetings as essentials of true worship; they are excited to the most exalted state by the rude and picturesque harangues of their preachers, and obey them implicitly, so far as they understand them. But they often make their camp-meetings and revival assemblies the scenes of indecent orgies, and in some States where great numbers of ignorant negroes are gathered together, they turn the church into a den of roystering drunkards. The preachers are sometimes very immoral, and now and then, after exhorting for an hour or two in such a violent manner that one might imagine them possessed by the spirit, they will join in the worst carousals of their parishioners. But wherever education goes, this conduct ceases. The missionaries from the normal schools strive against the besetting sins of the African, and are gradually helping him. The school-house and the church together, with intelligent and earnest advisers in each, will transform the character of the freedman in another generation.

The negroes have a profusion of churches, organized by themselves, in all the large cities of the South and South-west; in Memphis, in New Orleans, in Richmond, and in Charleston the churches are very well sustained, and are attended by immense congregations. The preaching is sometimes absolutely fine; there are colored men of great culture and natural talent in the ministry; but, as a rule, the ministers are rude in their language, forcible in their illustrations, and possessed of an enthusiasm which, whether or not the proof of a rare spirituality, is certainly inspiring to any one who witnesses it. The emotional part of the black man's worship is, of course, that which develops the greatest number of peculiarities. It will always, even when the race is educated, remain a striking feature in his churches; but will be chastened and subdued. The rapturous shoutings, the contortions of the body, the desire to dance and to yell, the mysterious trances, now-a-days seen, as they were before the war, in assemblages of blacks overcome with religious excitement, will be greatly modified, but will never be lost sight of. Under powerful mental excitement of any kind, the American negro finds it difficult to "keep still." The exuberance of his animal spirits gets relief only in dancing, in gambols high in air, in grotesque gestures; and this is all the more noticeable from the fact that in repose his favorite attitude is slouching and inactive.

The theological department in the excellent Howard University at Washington, and the classes in theology in the other universities, are kept well recruited, and the graduates go out to teach the negroes a "different kind of religion from mere shouting and confusion." In the back-country, log churches are built; in the towns, houses are rented, or neat brick edifices are erected. The ministers who go into the interior districts make efforts to have the negroes from several contiguous plantations unite in building a church, and are generally successful. In many sections negroes have been converted from practices resembling barbarism to sincere Christian worship. But for the millions of freedmen and women in the South the work which has already been done is only as a drop in the bucket. Hundreds of thousands of dollars are needed to supply this people with the barest necessities of their intellectual improvement; a steady charity for ten years to come will be in no wise mistaken. They need, above all, to be taught how to help themselves; and by the normal schools and the complete education of the most promising individuals of their race, that will be soonest accomplished.

LXVIII.

NEGRO SONGS AND SINGERS.

THE negro would deserve well of this country if he had given it nothing but the melodies by which he will be remembered long after the carping critics who refuse to admit that he is capable of intellectual progress are forgotten. His songs of a religious nature are indisputable proofs of the latent power for an artistic development which his friends have always claimed for him. They are echoes from the house of bondage, cries in the night, indistinct murmurs from an abyss. They take directly hold upon the Infinite. They are sublimest and most touching when they partake of the nature of wails and appeals. They have strange hints and gleams of nature in them, mingled with intense spiritual fervor. In this song, which the toilers in the tobacco factories of Virginia used to sing, there is a wild faith, and a groping after the proper poetry in which to express it, which touch the heart:

> " May de Lord — He *will* be glad of me,
> In de heaven He 'll rejoice;
> In de heaven once, in de heaven twice,
> In de heaven He 'll rejoice.
>   Bright sparkles in de churchyard,
> Give light unto de tomb;
>   Bright summer, spring 's ober,
> Sweet flowers in de'r bloom."

This is the incoherence of ignorance; but when sung, no one can doubt the yearning, the intense longing which prompted it. The movement of the melodies is strong and sometimes almost resistless; the rhythm is perfect; the measure is steady and correct.

But little idea of the beauty and inspiration of the "slave music" can be conveyed by the mere words. The quaintness of the wild gestures which accompany all the songs cannot be described. At camp-meetings and revival-gatherings the slaves give themselves up to contortions, to stampings of feet, clappings of hands, and paroxysms affecting the whole body, when singing. The simplest hymns are sung with almost extravagant intensity.

The songs are mainly improvisations. But few were ever written; they sprang suddenly into use. They arose out of the ecstasy occasioned by the rude and violent dances on the plantation; they were the outgrowth of great and unavoidable sorrows, which forced the heart to voice its cry; or they bubbled up from the springs of religious excitement. Sometimes they were simply the expression of the joy found in vigorous, healthy existence; but of such there are few. The majority of the negro songs have a plaintive undertone. They are filled with such passionate outbursts as the following:

> "Nobody knows de trouble I see, Lord,
> Nobody knows de trouble I see;
> Nobody knows de trouble I see, Lord,
> Nobody knows like Jesus!
> Brudders, will you pray for me,
> And help me to drive old Satan away?"

The improvisations are in some cases remarkable. A student at the Hampton Normal School has given to the public a long rhapsody on the judgment day, improvised by an old slave who was densely ignorant, but who embodied his dreams in song, as follows:

> "I'm a gwine to tell yo' bout de comin' of de Savior,
>   Far' you well, Far' you well;
> Dar's a better day a comin',
>   Far' you well, Far' you well;
> When my Lord speaks to his Fader,
>   Far' you well, Far' you well;
> Says Fader, I'm tired of bearin',
>   Far' you well, Far' you well;
> Tired o' bearin' for pore sinners,
>   Far' you well, Far' you well;
> Oh! preachers, fold your Bibles,
>   Far' you well, Far' you well;
> Prayer makers, pray no more,
>   Far' you well, Far' you well;
> For de last soul's converted,
>   Far' you well, Far' you well;
> *In dat great gittin'-up mornin',*
>   Far' you well, Far' you well."

The terrors of the judgment day are portrayed with a vivid and startling eloquence, and these verses are usually sung with a rude dramatic force which is really fine:

> "Gabriel, blow your trumpet!
> Lord, how loud shall I blow it?
> Loud as seven peals of thunder,
> Wake de sleeping nations;
> Den yo' see pore sinners risin',
> See de dry bones a creepin',
>   Far' you well, Far' you well.

> "Den yo' see de world on fire,
> Yo' see de moon a bleedin',
> See de stars a fallin',
> See de elements meltin',
> See de forked lightnin'.
> Hear de rumblin' thunder:
> Earth shall reel and totter,
> Hell shall be uncapped,
> De dragon shall be loosened,
> Far' you well, pore sinner,
>   Far' you well, Far' you well."

Nothing can exceed in beauty and fervor this little hymn, sprung out of great sorrow and affliction. It lays hold upon Heaven, and will not be thrust aside:

> "O Lord, O my Lord,
> O my good Lord,
> Keep me from sinkin' down!
> O my Lord, O my good Lord,
> Keep me from sinkin' down!
> I tell you what I mean to do,
> Keep me from sinkin' down;
> I mean to go to Heaven too,
> Keep me from sinkin' down!"

One of the most notable of the songs refers to a "great camp-meeting in the promised land," and is said to have been first sung by a company of slaves, who were not allowed to sing or pray where the master could hear them; but when he died their mistress granted them the privilege of singing and praying in their cabins at night, and they often joyfully sang this hymn:

> Dere's a better day comin', don't you get weary,
> Better day a comin', don't you get, &c., *(bis)*
> Dere's a great camp-meetin' in de Promised Land,
> Oh slap your hands children, don't, &c.,
> Slap your hands children, don't, &c., *(bis)*
> Dere's a great camp-meetin' in de Promised Land.
> Oh pat your foot children, don't you get weary,
> Pat your foot children, don't, &c., *(bis)*
> Dere's a great camp-meetin' in de Promised Land.
> CHO.—Gwine to live wid God forever,
> Live wid God forever, *(bis)*
> Dere's a great camp-meetin' in de Promised Land.
>
> Oh, feel de Spirit a movin', don't you, &c.,
> Feel de Spirit movin', don't, &c., *(bis)*
> Dere's a great camp-meetin' in de, &c.
> Oh now I'm gettin' happy, don't you get weary,
> Now I'm gettin' happy, don't, &c., *(bis)*
> Dere's a great camp-meetin' in de, &c.
> I feel so happy, don't you get weary,
> Feel so happy, don't you get weary, *(bis)*
> Dere's a great camp-meetin' in de, &c.
> CHO.—Oh, fly an' nebber tire,
> Fly an' nebber tire, *(bis)*
> Dere's a great camp-meetin' in de Promised Land.

Throughout the South, wherever the negroes have gathered into large communities by themselves, one will generally find a very good brass band; yet probably not one of its members can read music. They play by rote with remarkable accuracy, and they learn a song by hearing it once. The rhythm mastered, they readily catch the tune, and never forget it. Every one sings; man, woman and child croon over their toil, but never with that joyous abandon so characteristic of other races. In the churches the hymns are often "lined out"—that is, each line is read by the deacon or preacher, and then sung by the congregation; but this is quite unnecessary, as all are usually familiar with the words. In hymns and songs which are purely enthusiastic, the lines are never read; the worshipers will sometimes spontaneously break into a rolling chorus, which almost shakes the rafters of the church. Then their enthusiasm will die away to a tearful calm, broken only now and again by sobs and "Amens!" The appended hymns, sung in seasons of great enthusiasm by the negroes in and around Chattanooga, Tennessee, will serve to indicate the character of all of that class:

"Oh, yonder come my Jesus,
　Hallelujah! Hallelujah!
Oh, how do you know it's Jesus?
　Hallelujah! Hallelujah!
I know Him by his garments,
I know him by his garments.
His ship is heav-i-ly loaded,
His ship is heav-i-ly loaded,
　Hallelujah! Hallelujah!
It's loaded wid bright angels,
It's loaded wid bright angels,
　Hallelujah! Hallelujah!
Oh, how do yo' know dey are angels?
　Hallelujah! Hallelujah!
I know dem by deir shining,
I know dem by deir shining,
　Hallelujah! Hallelujah!
　　*　　*　　*　　*

"O, John! my Jesus' comin',
He is comin' in de mornin';
Jesus' comin'; He's comin' by de lightning,
Jesus' comin'; He's comin' in de rainbow.
Don't you want to go to Heaven?
　Jesus' comin."
　　*　　*　　*　　*

"Oh, rock away chariot,
Rock all my crosses away;
Rock me into de Heavens.
I wish't I was in Heaven—
I wish't I was at home.
I wish't I was in Heaven—
Lord, I wish't I was at home!"

The pilgrimages of the "Jubilee" and Hampton singers through this country and England, and the brilliant success which attended their concerts, is a notable event in the history of the American negro. When the Jubilee Singers first went North to earn money for the University which was giving them their education, they met with some slights—were now and then called "niggers" and "negro minstrels," and were variously scoffed at. Here and there in the North and West they were refused admission to hotels on account of their color; their success was at first a matter of doubt; but their mission pleaded its way into the hearts of men when the sweet melodies and wild burdens of their songs were heard. In all the great cities of the North their concerts were attended by large audiences; Henry Ward Beecher welcomed them in Brooklyn, introducing them to his congregation at a Sunday evening prayer-meeting, when they sang some of their most effective songs; and straightway thereafter they were the rage in the Metropolis as well as in Brooklyn. Their tour through the Eastern States was productive of much profit, and the little band of singers carried home twenty thousand dollars to place in the treasury of Fisk University, as the result of their first campaign in the North.

Encouraged by this success, Prof. George L. White, who originally conceived the idea of teaching these emancipated slaves to sing the plantation hymns of the old times, and to give a series of concerts embodying them, took the singers to England. All the world knows how enthusiastically they were received in Great Britain. The Queen, the nobility, and the great middle class heard them sing, gave them kind words and money, and praised them highly; and in March of 1874 this little band of blacks had collected ten thousand pounds, to be used to pay for the building of Jubilee Hall, at the University at Nashville. Of the eleven singers, eight are emancipated slaves.

The Hampton Student Singers at first numbered seventeen. They made their first appearance in 1872, under the direction of Mr. Thomas P. Fenner, of Providence, Rhode Island, who was of peculiar service in aiding them to a faithful musical rendering of the original slave songs. The singers were all regular students of the Hampton Normal Institute, and, even while journeying on their concert tour, carried their school-books with them. Their songs were heard with delight throughout the Middle, Eastern, and Western States, and their concerts have been attended with financial success.

The spirituality, the pathos, the subtle plaintiveness of the fresh, pure voices of these bands of black singers, invest the commonest words with a beauty and poetry which cannot be understood until one hears the songs. Once while listening to the singing of "Dust an' Ashes," one of the sweetest and sublimest chorals ever improvised, I tried in vain to analyze its mysterious fascination. The words were few and often repeated; the melody was from time to time almost monotonous. I could not fix the charm; yet the tears stood in my eyes when the wild chant was over,—and I was not the only one of the large audience gathered to hear the singing who wept. I give some of the words; but they will hardly serve to convey to the reader's mind any idea of the beauty of the choral:

"Dust, dust an' ashes
  Fly over on my grave.
Dust, dust an' ashes
  Fly over on my grave, *(bis)*
An' de Lord shall bear my spirit home. *(bis)*
  Dey crucified my Savior
  And nailed him to de cross, *(bis)*
An' de Lord shall bear my spirit home.
  He rose, he rose,
  He rose from de dead, *(repeat)*
An' de Lord shall bear my spirit home."

One of the most effective of the spiritual songs is "Babylon's Fallin'," which is often used at Hampton Institute as a marching song. The words are as follows:

> "Pure city,
> Babylon's fallin' to rise no mo'.
> Pure city,
> Babylon's fallin' to rise no mo'.
> Oh, Babylon's fallin', fallin', fallin',
> Babylon's fallin' to rise no mo'.
> Oh, Jesus tell you once befo'
> Babylon's fallin' to rise no mo';
> To go in peace and sin no mo'—
> Babylon's fallin' to rise no mo'."

Another note of aspiration is sounded in the hymn "Swing Low, Sweet Chariot," the music of which is full of earnest prayer:

> "Oh, swing low, sweet chariot;
> Swing low, sweet chariot, *(bis)*
> I don't want to leave me behind.
> Oh de good ole chariot swing so low,
> Good old chariot swing so low,
> I don't want to leave me behind."

Even the religious hymns and songs are not devoid of that humor with which the negro is so freely endowed, and some of the words to hymns intended to be of the most serious character are highly ludicrous, as when we are informed, concerning a "pore sinner," that

> "Vindictive vengeance on him fell,
> Enough to sqush a world to hell;"

or when we hear a hundred negroes loudly singing—

> "Jesus ride a milk-white hoss,
> Ride him up and down de cross—
> Sing Hallelujah!"

It is difficult to repress a smile when listening to the story of the deluge and Noah's voyage, as detailed in the popular choral hymn entitled, "De Ole Ark a-Moverin' Along." The last verse will give the reader a taste of its quality:

> "Forty days an' forty nights, de rain it kep' a fallin',
> De ole ark a-moverin', a-moverin' along;
> De wicked clumb de trees, an' for help dey kep' a callin',
> De ole ark a-moverin', &c.,
> Dat awful rain, she stopped at last, de waters dey subsided,
> De old ark a-moverin', &c.,
> An' dat old ark wid all on board on Ararat she rided,
> De old ark a-moverin', &c.
> CHORUS—Oh, de ole ark a-moverin'," &c.

A hymn called the "Danville Chariot," which is very popular with the negroes in Virginia, has this verse:

> "Oh shout, shout, de deb'l is about;
> Oh shut yo' do' an' keep him out;
> I don' want to stay here no longer.
> For he is so much-a like-a snaky in de grass,
> Ef you don' mind he will get you at las',
> I don' want to stay here no longer.
> CHORUS—Oh, swing low, sweet chariot," &c.

The quaintness of the following often induces laughter, although it is always sung with the utmost enthusiasm:

> "Gwine to sit down in de kingdom, I raly do believe
> Whar Sabbaths have no end.
> Gwine to walk about in Zion, I raly do believe,
> Whar Sabbaths have no end.
> Whar ye ben, young convert, whar ye ben so long?
> Ben down low in de valley for to pray,
> And I ain't done prayin' yit."

"Go, Chain de Lion Down," is the somewhat obscure title of a hymn in which this verse occurs:

> "Do you see dat good ole sister,
> Come a-waggin' up de hill so slow?
> She wants to get to Heaven in due time,
> Before de heaven doors clo'.
> Go chain de lion down,
> Go chain de lion down,
> Befo' de heaven doors clo'."

Many years before the period of bondage was over, and when it seemed likely to endure so long as the masters pleased, the negroes hinted in their hymns at their coming deliverance. They often compared themselves to the Israelites, and many of their most touching songs have some allusion to King Pharaoh and the hardness of his heart. A few of the more noted of the songs, which were the outgrowth of the negro's prophetic instinct that some day he should be free, are still sung in the churches and schools. This is a favorite among the blacks:

> "Did n't my Lord deliber Daniel,
> Did n't my Lord deliber Daniel,
> And why not ebery man?
> He delibered Daniel from de lion's den,
> And Jonah from de belly of de whale,
> An' de Hebrew children from de fiery furnace,
> And why not ebery man?"

"Go Down, Moses," was another warning of the "wrath to come," which those in power did not soon enough accept. It was sung at many a midnight meeting, when the masters did not listen; and the oppressed took comfort as they joined in its chorus. The free children of parents who were born in slavery will look upon this song with a tearful interest:

> "When Israel was in Egypt's land,
>   Let my people go;
> Oppressed so hard dey could not stand,
>   Let my people go.
> Go down, Moses,
>   Way down in Egypt land,
> Tell ole Pha-roh,
>   Let my people go.
>
> "Thus saith de Lord, bold Moses said,
>   Let my people go;
> If not I'll smite your first-born dead,
>   Let my people go.
>   Go down, Moses," &c.
>
> "No more shall dey in bondage toil,
>   Let my people go;
> Let dem come out wid Egypt's spoil,
>   Let my people go.
>   Go down, Moses," &c.

The "first-born" have indeed been smitten, and Israel has come up out of Egypt.

Mr. Theodore F. Seward, of Orange, New Jersey, in his interesting preface to the collection of songs sung by the Jubilee Singers of Fisk University, makes the following remarks, which may help to a proper comprehension of the negro's heart-music:

"A technical analysis of these melodies shows some interesting facts. The first peculiarity that strikes the attention is in the rhythm. This is often complicated, and sometimes strikingly original. But although so new and strange, it is most remarkable that these effects are so extremely satisfactory. We see few cases of what theorists call *mis-form*, although the student of musical composition is likely to fall into that error long after he has mastered the leading principles of the art.

"Another noticeable feature of the songs is the entire absence of triple time, or three-part measure, among them. The reason for this is doubtless to be found in the beating of the foot and the swaying of the body which are such frequent accompaniments of the singing. These motions are in even measure, and in perfect time; and so it will be found that, however broken and seemingly irregular the movement of the music, it is always capable of the most exact measurement. In other words, its irregularities invariably conform to the 'higher law' of the perfect rhythmic flow.

"It is a coincidence worthy of note that more than half the melodies in this collection are in the same scale as that in which Scottish music is written; that is, with the fourth and seventh tones omitted. The fact that the music of the ancient Greeks is also said to have been written in this scale suggests an interesting inquiry as to whether it may not be a peculiar language of nature, or a simpler alphabet than the ordinary diatonic scale, in which the uncultivated mind finds its easiest expression."

The teachers attached to the educational mission of the Port Royal Islands carefully studied the music of the half-barbarous negroes among whom they were stationed, and the result was an excellent collection of slave songs, which, without their efforts, would have been entirely lost.

The old planters sometimes say, with a shake of the head and a frown, that the negroes no longer sing "as they used to when they were happy." It is true that the freedmen do not sing as of yore; that they sing as much, however, there is little doubt. We have seen that the better class of their songs is filled with a vein of reproachful melancholy, that it everywhere has the nature of an appeal for help, a striving for something spiritual, dimly seen, and but half understood. These were the songs which the slaves sung at their work, but since their emancipation they are no longer compelled to voice their talents in such sombre music. The Port Royal teachers took down from the lips of the colored people hundreds of songs whose crude dialect and cruder melancholy rendered the task very difficult.

According to the testimony of the teachers the negroes always keep exquisite time in singing, and readily sacrifice a word and the sense attached to it if it stands in the way of the rhythm. The voices have a delicate and mellow tone peculiar to the colored race. There is rarely part singing, as it is not generally understood, and yet the Port Royal teachers say that when a number of blacks are singing together no two appear to sing the same thing. The leaders start the words of each verse, improvising many tunes, and the others, who "base" him, as they call it, will strike in with the version, or when they know the words, will join in the solo. They always succeed in producing perfect melody, out of whose network the transcribers have found great difficulty in extracting sounds that can be properly represented by the gamut.

The teachers testify that "the chief part of the negro music is civilized in its character, partly composed under the influence of association with the whites, and partly actually imitated from other music; but," they add, "in the main it appears to be original in the best sense of the word." Passages in some of the songs are essentially barbaric in character, and the teachers believe that most of the secular songs in use among the negroes contain faint echoes from the rude music of the African savages. A gentleman visiting at Port Royal is said to have been much struck with the resemblance of some of the tunes sung by the watermen there to boatmen's songs he had heard on the Nile. Colonel Higginson, who spent some time among the negroes on the South Carolina islands, gives a curious description of the way in which negro songs were originated. One day, as he was crossing in a small boat from one island to another, one of the oarsmen, who was asked for his theory of the origin of the spirituals, as the negroes call their songs, said, "Dey start jess out o' curiosity. I ben a raise a song mysel' once," and then described to Colonel Higginson that on one occasion when a slave he began to sing, "O, de old nigger-driver."

Then another said, "Fust ting my mammy tole me was, notin' so bad as nigger-drivers." This was the refrain, and in a short time all the slaves in the field had made a song which was grafted into their unwritten literature. Another negro, in telling Mr. J. Miller McKim, one of the teachers on the island, how they made the songs, said, "Dey work it in, work it in, you know, till dey get it right, and das de way."

The "shout," one of the most peculiar and interesting of the religious customs of the slaves, still kept up to some extent among the negroes on the coast, is discountenanced by many of the colored preachers now-a-days. It is what may be called a prayer-meeting, interspersed with spasmodic enthusiasm. The population of a plantation gathers together in some cabin at evening, and, after vociferous prayer by some of the brethren, and the singing of hymns in melancholy cadence by the whole congregation, all the seats are cleared away, and the congregation begins the genuine "walk-around" to the music of the "spiritual."

The following description of the dance, which is a main feature of these shouts, appeared in the New York *Nation*, in 1867:

"The foot is hardly taken from the floor, and the progression is mainly due to a jerking, pitching motion, which agitates the entire shouters, and soon brings out streams of perspiration. Sometimes they dance slowly; sometimes, as they shuffle, they sing the chorus of the spiritual, and sometimes the song itself is also sung; but more frequently a band composed of some of the best singers and of tired shouters stands at the side of the room to "base" the others singing the body of the song, and clapping their hands together or on their knees. Singing and dance are alike extremely energetic, and often when the shout lasts into the middle of the night, the monotonous thud of the feet prevents sleep within half a mile of the 'Praise-House.'"

I append three or four of the most beautiful of the songs sung by the negroes of the lowland coast of South Carolina. That entitled "Lord Remember Me" attracted universal attention when it first appeared, shortly after the war, at the North. It was set to weird music, and had the genuine ballad flavor:

I HEAR FROM HEAVEN TO-DAY.

Hurry on, my weary soul,
And I yearde from heaven to-day,
My sin is forgiven, and my soul set free,
And I yearde, etc.
A baby born in Bethlehem,
De trumpet sound in de oder bright land;
My name is called and I must go,
De bell is a-ringin' in de oder bright world.

LORD REMEMBER ME.

Oh Deat' he is a little man,
And he goes from do' to do';
He kill some souls and he wounded some,
And he lef' some souls to pray.

Oh, Lord, remember me,
Do, Lord, remember me;
Remember me as de year roll round,
Lord, remember me.

NOT WEARY YET.

O me not weary yet, *(repeat)*
I have a witness in my heart;
O me no weary yet, Brudder Tony,
Since I ben in de field to fight.
O me, etc.
I have a heaven to maintain,
De bond of faith are on my soul;
Ole Satan toss a ball at me,
Him tink de ball would hit my soul;
De ball for hell and I for heaven.

HUNTING FOR THE LORD.

Hunt till you find him,
    Hallelujah!
And a-huntin' for de Lord,
Till you find him,
    Hallelujah!
And a-huntin' for de Lord.

I SAW THE BEAM IN MY SISTER'S EYE.

I saw de beam in my sister's eye,
Can't saw de beam in mine;
You'd better lef' your sister's door,
Go keep your own door clean.

And I had a mighty battle, like-a Jacob and de angel,
Jacob, time of old;
I did n't 'tend to lef' 'em go,
Till Jesus bless my soul.

RELIGION SO SWEET.

O walk Jordan long road,
And religion so sweet;
O religion is good for anything,
And religion so sweet.
Religion make you happy,
Religion gib me patience;
O 'member, get religion.
I long time ben a huntin',
I seekin' for my fortune;
O I gwine to meet my Savior,
Gwine to tell him bout my trials.
Dey call me boastin' member,
Dey call me turnback Christian;
Dey call me 'struction maker,

But I don't care what dey call me.
Lord, trial 'longs to a Christian,
O tell me 'bout religion;
I weep for Mary and Marta,
I seek my Lord and I find him.

MICHAEL, ROW THE BOAT ASHORE.

Michael, row de boat ashore,
   Hallelujah!
Michael boat a gospel boat,
   Hallelujah!
I wonder where my mudder deh,
See my mudder on de rock gwine home,
On de rock gwine home in Jesus' name;
Michael boat a music boat,
Gabriel blow de trumpet horn,
O you mind your boastin' talk;
Boastin' talk will sink your soul.
Brudder, lend a helpin' hand;
Sister, help for trim dat boat.
Jordan's stream is wide and deep;
Jesus stand on t' oder side.
I wonder if my massa deh;
My fader gone to unknown land,
O de Lord he plant his garden deh.

I WISH I BEN DERE.

My mudder, you follow Jesus,
My sister, you follow Jesus,
My brudder, you follow Jesus,
To fight until I die.

I wish I ben dere,
To climb Jacob's ladder;
I wish I ben dere,
To wear de starry crown.

JESUS ON THE WATER-SIDE.

Heaven bell a-ring, I know de road,
Heaven bell a-ring, I know de road;
Jesus sittin' on de water-side,
Do come along, do let us go,
Jesus sittin' on de water-side.

LXIX.

A PEEP AT THE PAST OF VIRGINIA—JAMESTOWN. WILLIAMSBURG—YORKTOWN.

AT Jamestown, on the river James, one comes suddenly upon memorials of a vanished past. The Virginia whose life once centred around the village on the placid stream has passed away. Jamestown, the first prominent Anglo-Saxon settlement on this continent, is to-day a melancholy nook where historic memories play at hide-and-seek among moss-grown ruins. The remains of the venerable church there are surrounded with a graveyard filled with mouldy tombstones, whose inscriptions are scarcely legible. Tall trees tangle their roots in the brickwork of the decaying tower. Silence and desolation brood over this ancient edifice, destroyed nearly a century and a-half ago. It is supposed to have been built a little after Bacon's rebellion in 1676, and is known to have been in use as late as 1733, for in that year a silver baptismal font was presented to it. Some of the pieces of silver plate that belonged to the church may still be seen in the library of the Theological Seminary near Alexandria.

After Captain John Smith and his brave knights, as well as all the swaggering,

The Ruins of the old Church at Jamestown, Virginia.

starveling gallants and tavern-haunting vagabonds who first colonized Jamestown, had crumbled into dust and made way for the more enterprising and industrious native Virginians, the town was deserted. The transfer of the seat of the Colonial Government to Williamsburg in the beginning of the eighteenth century ruined the prospects of Jamestown, and the swiftly-moving years have now swept everything away save this one tower of the old church, the reflection of whose image upon the river's gleaming surface seems like a ghost from the past, peering out of the depths into which the present has banished it.

Williamsburg and Yorktown, on the peninsula between the York and James rivers, contain some of the most interesting souvenirs of early civilization in America. Williamsburg, half-way between the two streams, is the oldest incorporated town in the State, was the seat of the Colonial Government before the

Revolution, and the capital of the Dominion until 1779. On the lawn in front of William and Mary College, the oldest of American educational institutions except Harvard, stands the statue of Lord Botetourt, who ruled over the Virginians some years previous to the troubles between the mother country and the colonies, and who died two years before the advent of the great Revolution.

The tide of war has from time to time swept round the College buildings, but has always respected the old statue. The Virginians of revolutionary days did not bring the good Lord down from his pedestal, for he had been a faithful Governor, zealous and never forgetful of their interests. The marble image, however, once lost its head, a college student, who afterward became Governor of Virginia, having taken a fancy to knock it off; but it was carefully replaced. William and Mary College has had the rare honor of educating several Presidents of the United States. During the late civil war it suffered much, and to-day stands in serious need of financial aid.

A century ago a noble avenue, known as Gloucester street, extended from the venerable college for a mile in a straight line to the then Capitol of Virginia. Along its sides were ranged the palace of the Governor, of

Statue of Lord Botetourt at Williamsburg, Virginia.

which only one wing remains to-day, the rest having long since been destroyed by fire; the "Court-House of James City County;" the old Raleigh Tavern; the octagonal powder magazine which served as the colonial arsenal of Virginia, and from which on the night of April 20, 1775, the royal Governor stole away all the powder; and the old church of Bruton parish. The powder magazine to-day serves as the stable for the principal inn of Williamsburg. The College chapel, designed by Sir Christopher Wren, has vanished from the western extremity of the great avenue, which it once adorned. Old Bruton Church, standing midway between the College and the site of the ancient Capitol, was erected shortly after the noted James Blair, commissary to the Bishop of London, and President of William and Mary College, became minister, when Spotswood was Governor in 1710. Whitfield often preached in the church, and the parish became noted as the ground on which, more than sixty years before the outbreak of the American Revolution, the battle of the rights of the people against privilege and irresponsible authority was fought. The Rev. Mr. Blair had a hearty quarrel with Spotswood, the Governor insisting upon the right of choosing parish clergymen, while Blair contended for the right of the vestries to make that choice. By their firm attitude the vestries at last compelled the Governor to yield his point.

Spotswood, although hard-headed and obstinate, was one of the ablest and purest of Virginia's chief magistrates in her colonial days. He it was who built the first iron-furnaces in the colonies, and who first rode across the great Blue Ridge, the barrier in his day between civilized Virginia and the wilderness beyond. When he and his goodly company returned to Williamsburg from their long and adventurous journey across the mountains, the Governor caused a golden horseshoe, set with precious stones, to be given to each of his fellow cavaliers as a badge of knighthood, bearing the motto, "*Sic juvat transcendere montes.*" This was the origin of the order of the Knights of the Golden Horseshoe.

Yorktown and Williamsburg are both destined to be important termini of the Chesapeake and Ohio railroad. Yorktown, which lies within a few miles of the colonial capital, still possesses some of the picturesque and semi-decayed mansions of the old Nelsons and Pages, and other noble families of Virginia. The traveler is yet shown the precise spot at Yorktown where, on the 19th of October, 1781, the surrender of Lord Cornwallis to the combined American and French forces took place, the remains of the intrenchments cast up by the British, on the south and east sides of the town, being still visible. An excavation in the bluff on which the village stands is called Cornwallis's Cave, and is reputed to have been made and used by Lord Cornwallis as a council-chamber during the siege. Round about both Williamsburg and Yorktown there are many newer and fresher memorials of war than those half-forgotten ones of the Revolution.

A journey up the York river from Yorktown takes one past the site of the Indian settlement which John Smith described as "Werowocomoco," and where he was rescued from death by the fair Pocahontas. Not far from the site of this romantic rescue stands "Rosewell," formerly the estate of Governor Page, a princely edifice, whose materials were all brought over from England in colonial days, and which now stands lonely on a barren hill. On the Pamunkey river is "White House," said to be the scene of Washington's marriage with Martha Custis in 1759. During the late war, White House was an important depot of supplies, and the fine mansion there and all the supplies were burned in the course of military operations.

In 1584, Queen Elizabeth licensed Sir Walter Raleigh to search for remote

The old Colonial Powder Magazine at Williamsburg, Virginia.

heathen lands "not inhabited by Christian people," and granted to him in fee simple "all the soil within two hundred leagues of the places where his people should, within six years, make their dwellings or abidings," reserving only, to herself and her successors, his allegiance and one-fifth of all the gold and silver he should obtain. Sir Walter at once sent out two ships, which visited Wococan Island, in North Carolina, and the next year he dispatched seven ships, with 107 men, who settled on Roanoke Island. The Indians there soon acknowledged themselves the homagers of the brave Sir Walter, and in 1586 and 1587 he sent a Governor, with twelve assistants and a charter of incorporation, instructing them to settle on Chesapeake Bay. They landed, however, at "Hattorask," now known as Hatteras. In 1588, when a fleet was ready to sail with a new supply of colonists and supplies, it was detained in English ports by Queen Elizabeth to assist against the Spanish Armada; and Sir Walter, who had expended £40,000 in these enterprises, was obliged to get others to adventure their money. In 1589, he therefore deeded to other colonists the liberty of trade to his new country free from all taxes for seven years, excepting the fifth part of the gold and silver ore due the Queen. At different times thereafter, however, he sent off fresh expeditions to the American coast, but the fate of the last colonists sent hither was never known, and Sir Walter died on the scaffold without seeing the realization of his bright dreams of a new empire on the American Continent.

The old Church of Bruton Parish—Williamsburg, Virginia. [Page 622.]

Those who supposed that Raleigh's grant was forfeited by his alleged treason petitioned King James, the successor of Elizabeth, for a new grant of Virginia to them. It was executed to Sir Thomas Gates and others, and in 1607 a settlement was effected at Jamestown, on the river James. This grant "was superseded by letters patent of the same King in 1609 to the Earl of Salisbury and others, incorporating them by the name of 'The Treasurer and Company of Adventurers and Planters of the City of London for the First Colony of Virginia;' granting to them and

Cornwallis's Cave, near Yorktown, Virginia. [Page 623.]

their successors all the lands in Virginia from Point Comfort along the sea-coast to the northward two hundred miles, and from the same point along the sea-coast to the southward two hundred miles, and all the space from this precinct on the sea-coast up into the land, west and north-west, from sea to sea, together with the islands within 100 miles of it." This grant was added to in 1612.

In 1621 this Company established two Supreme Councils in Virginia, one called "The Council of State," the other "The General Assembly," to be convened by the Governor once yearly or oftener, the latter body to consist of the Council of State and two burgesses out of every town, hundred, or plantation, to be chosen by the inhabitants. In due time King James and "The Company of Adventurers" quarreled, and the latter's powers were superseded by a proclamation in 1624. As Charles I. then took the government of England, the colonists of Virginia passed under his control, and in this they heartily accorded, loving and admiring the cavalier King.

But presently the northern parts of their colony were granted away to Lords Baltimore and Fairfax, the first of whom also obtained the rights of separate jurisdiction and government. After the deposition of Charles I., the English Parliament, standing in the deposed King's stead, began to tyrannize over the colony and to impose grievous restrictions upon it. But the Virginian colonists had, from the first, maintained a vigorous opposition to Cromwell and the Parliament, and did not lay down their arms until, as they fancied, they had secured their rights by a solemn covenant with the deputies from Parliament. These rights, which, with arms in their hands, they sternly insisted upon, were that Virginia's ancient limits should be restored to her; that the colony should be freed from all taxes and impositions; that the colonists should have all the rights of free-born Britons; that the Assembly should convene as formerly, and that trade should be free. Every one of these rights, so strongly insisted upon, was subsequently violated by English kings and parliaments. "The General Assembly was split into two houses; appeals from their Supreme Court, which had been fixed by law in that Assembly, were arbitrarily revoked to England, to be there heard before the King and Council."[*] The colony saw its sea-coast reduced in thirty years from 400 to 100 miles; its foreign trade was suppressed; and the gradual restriction and oppression practised by England, under the long line of royal governors, and the intolerable grants of land made to the detriment of the colonists after the Restoration, finally resulted in the Virginia phase of the revolution which became so general throughout America. England lost a proud domain when the Virginians were alienated from her. The State which produced Marshall, Madison, Monroe, Mason, Nicholas, Henry, Randolph, Lee, Pendleton, Washington, Wythe, and other members of the Convention which assembled in Richmond in June, 1788, to ratify the Federal Constitution, deserved deference and generous treatment rather than oppression and abuse. Time was when England, Scotland, Ireland, and Virginia had their arms quartered on the same shield.

[*] Jefferson's "Notes on Virginia."

RICHMOND—ITS TRADE AND CHARACTER.

THE view of the Virginian capital as one approaches it on the James river, is singularly fine. One gains the impression that Richmond is an immense metropolis, the hills seem so packed with streets lined on either side with solid blocks of stone and brick. From the ample foliage peep church-spires and towers, and the roofs of spacious mansions are seen on Cary, Main, Franklin, Grace, Marshall, Clay and Leigh streets, and in the pretty suburbs of "Chim-

View of Richmond, Virginia, from the Manchester side of the James River.

borazo" and Union, Church and Navy, Gamble's and Libby's Hills. The splendid steamers of the Old Dominion Company, which controls the line between New York and Richmond, ply slowly along the stream through the level plains bordered with forests, and give one ample time to study the city which was so lately the Confederate capital. Its grouping of houses and streets, seen at a distance, is picturesque; as one approaches it the ordinary aspects of an American city appear in their customary prosaic form.

One is not sorry to see hills again, after the lowlands of the serpentine James, and he climbs with gusto the steep streets leading to the Capitol, whence he can get a look over the broad plains beyond the stream. A few years ago the dwellers in Richmond watched those plains with keenest anxiety, when cannon thundered and battles were fought in the forests and along the roads. The traveler remembers that he saw many church-spires in the vicinity of the Capitol as he looked at the city from the river; from Capitol Square he can hardly distinguish them, they are so concealed, save their very tops, by the ample foliage. From the front porch he can look down upon the James, flowing hurriedly through the city over a rocky bed which makes Richmond the head of navigation; and can note the barges clustered about the flour-mills, and the groups of negroes at the doors of the tobacco warehouses. The State Penitentiary's whitewashed walls, on a neighboring hill, form a group as picturesque as an Italian monastery. On the Richmond bank of the river the immense array of shops, known as the Tredegar Iron Works, lies half-concealed beneath clouds of smoke, and beyond them are the "Old Dominion Nail Works," on the famous "Belle Isle," where Federal prisoners were confined during the war. Manchester, on the opposite side of the stream, is a thriving village, with two fine cotton-mills

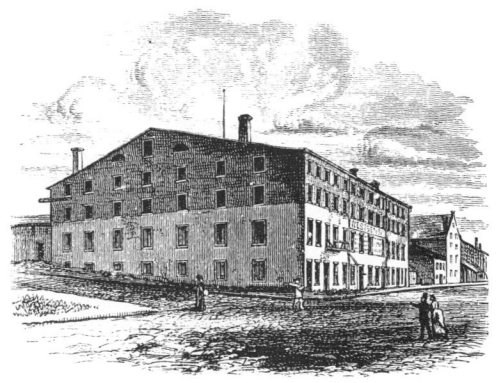

Libby Prison—Richmond, Virginia.

employing three hundred workers, and with many neat houses, which testify to the prosperity of the villagers. Farther down the James, one can see the unsightly group of buildings around the low, dirty-looking, ancient edifice, known as "Libby Prison." Not far away, on the opposite side of the street, is the famous "Castle Thunder." These once noted prisons, whose walls are covered with the names of the hapless Union officers who sweltered and starved in them during the civil war, have been relegated to their previous condition of tobacco warehouses.

At the foot of the hill occupied by Capitol Square stands the pretty Custom-House, built in the Italian style from the granite of which inexhaustible beds lie all around Richmond. From the Square, avenues running down toward the river open into Main street, a broad business thoroughfare, extending along the hills and into the valleys, and lined with the principal shops, banks and offices of the town. Below Main, on all the streets by the river-side, are located the wholesale establishments, the manufactories, and the warehouses. A vacant spot here and there, blackened by fire, is the only reminder of the great conflagration which ran riot for a mile through the business section of the city on the night when the Confederates were forced to evacuate the capital which they had defended so long and so well. Richmond lost a thousand buildings in that fire; but now builds half as many every year. In 1873, the city expended a million and a-half dollars in the erection of new edifices.

"Shockoe Hill," on which the Capitol stands, is a goodly eminence. Its picturesque height was so attractive to the eyes of old Colonel Byrd, of Westover, in 1733, that he decided to lay the "foundation of a large city there." He had found a promising site for another metropolis at the falls of the Appomattox river, where Petersburg stands, and recorded in his diary that Richmond and

Petersburg, being the uppermost landings of James and Appomattox rivers, "were naturally intended for marts where the traffic of the outer inhabitants must centre." The good Colonel's judgment has been proved accurate. "Shockoe's" height was once furrowed by deep ravines on either side, and weeds flourished where now dainty flower-beds and trim lawns delight the eye. The modest three-story wooden house in which Henry and Jefferson, when Governors of Virginia, lived, has been succeeded by a handsome "Executive Mansion." The Capitol itself, modeled, according to Thomas Jefferson's suggestion, after the celebrated Maison Carré at Nismes, in France, has an imposing front, but is insecure and insufficient for the uses of a great commonwealth. A horrible accident occurred in the building in April of 1870, by which over fifty

Capitol Square, with a view of the Washington Monument—Richmond, Virginia.

people were killed and hundreds were wounded. The flooring of the room situated directly above the Hall of the House of Delegates, and used as the Court of Appeals, gave way, and precipitated a large audience, gathered to hear the decision of an important case, into the legislative chamber.

The Capitol contains the celebrated statue of Washington, by Houdon, made in 1788, and erected in the same year by the grateful State, which would not wait until its hero was dead before it deigned to honor his deeds. In the square "hall of entrance," where this statue stands, there are also a marble bust of Lafayette, and an antique English stove, used to warm the House of Burgesses at Williamsburg in colonial days. The stove is three stories high, and when sent to the Colonies its founder, Buzaglo, wrote concerning it: "The elegance of the workmanship does honor to Great Britain. It excels in grandeur anything ever seen of the kind, and is a masterpiece not to be equaled in all Europe." It was given to the House of Burgesses by the Duke of Beaufort, and is the most interesting of colonial memorials, except the chair in which the Speaker of the House of Burgesses once sat, and which is now in the Capitol. A fine portrait of General Lee, by Elder, graces the Hall of Delegates. The only bronze statue which Richmond possesses is the most remarkable in the United States. It is the equestrian statue of Washington, upon which Crawford lavished so much labor, and in which his splendid genius shines more conspicuously than in any other of his works. The statue, completed by Randolph Rogers, stands on the esplanade leading from the Governor's house to the west gate of the Capitol Square. Around the colossal Washington, mounted on a finely modeled horse, which seems vaulting airily from a massive pedestal of granite, stand bronze figures of Patrick Henry; Thomas Jefferson; John Marshall, one of the bravest fighters in the Revolution, as well as a most illustrious Chief-Justice of the United States; Andrew Lewis, one of the giants who supported Washington in the earliest struggles against Great Britain; George Mason, author of the Virginia "Bill of Rights;" and Thomas Nelson, a Governor of the old commonwealth during the Revolution and a brilliant soldier. Around the lower pediments military and civic decorations are emblazoned in bronze. The Capitol Square also contains a marble statue of Henry Clay. Northward from the square is the City Hall, and not far from it the stately mansion which Jefferson Davis chose for his residence when Richmond was the Confederate capital. Near at hand is St. Paul's Church, in which Davis was seated at worship when the messenger brought him the fatal news of the final disaster to Lee's army, and the necessity of flight from Richmond.

St. John's Church — Richmond, Virginia.

There are three churches in the Virginian capital which possess especial interest for the traveler. One of them, St. John's, dates from before the Revolution, and is celebrated as the edifice in which Patrick Henry uttered his immortal words—"Give me liberty or give me death!" Modern improvements are crowding thickly around this venerable structure, which was also filled, long after the Revolution had been successful, by the delegates that Virginia sent up to Richmond to ratify the Federal Constitution. The second church is a long, low building on steep Broad

View on the James River, Richmond, Virginia.

street. It is known as the "Old African," and is crowded on Sundays with the dusky population of the negro quarters. During the late war, and the troublous times following it, this humble but spacious building was the scene of many tumultuous political gatherings. Now-a-days the white visitor, unobtrusively seating himself in one of the rear pews, can look over a vast congregation of blacks listening with tearful and rapt attention to the emotional discourse of their preacher, or singing wild hymns, as they are read out, line by line, by the deacon. The singing is one of the most remarkable features in all the African churches in Richmond; every one joins in it, and it is not uncommon to see the churches so crowded that the doors are blockaded, the worshipers obstructing even the sidewalks, as they unite with enthusiasm in the simple yet really beautiful service.

The third noticeable church is the Monumental, built on the spot on Broad street where, in 1811, the Richmond Theatre took fire during an evening performance, and a great number of the most beautiful women and eminent men in the State, including the Governor and other personages of distinction, were burned and crushed to death.

Richmond's principal cemetery, Hollywood, has long been noted as one of the most lovely in the South. It occupies a wide tract in the western limits of the city, picturesquely broken into hill and dale, and decorated with prettiest of shrubs and flowers. From a slope in the cemetery one gets a fine outlook over the winding James river and Kanawha Valley canal; on the fretted current of the James river itself, with its waterfalls and clusters of green islets; and on the northern and eastern hills of the city, covered with masses of well-grouped buildings and remnants of fortifications. In the southern section of the cemetery stands the tomb of President Monroe, whose remains were escorted to Richmond from New York by the Seventh Regiment several years before that noted organization had any idea that it would ever make a hostile incursion into the "Old Dominion." From the hill one can see the ruins of the old State Armory near the canal. The Confederates used it during the war, and when the evacuation of Richmond was ordered, the Armory was swept away in the conflagration kindled by the retreating army.

In the soldiers' section are the graves of hundreds of Confederate dead, and from the centre of this tract springs a rough stone pyramid, which the clinging ivy is gradually clothing in green. Soldiers from all the Southern States are buried under the shadow of this pyramid, and late in the month of May, a few days before the North observes the ceremonies of Decoration, the gray-coated veterans and the militia regiments parade in solemn procession to the cemetery, and thousands of ladies dressed in black wander silently and tearfully among the graves. There are rarely any speeches; there is no display of flags and emblems of the lost cause; the grief is too deep for words, too sacred to be associated with the vulgar details of politics.

Monument to the Confederate Dead—Richmond, Virginia.

Richmond is chief among Virginia cities, no less because of its proud position as the capital than because of its enterprise and its rapid growth. It now has nearly fifty-five thousand inhabitants, and its population is steadily increasing. The total assessed value of its real estate and personal property amounts to $37,000,000. Its exports amounted in the year 1873 to $3,026,492, an increase in one year of $1,026,123; its trade with other countries, to which it sends wheat, flour, leaf and manufactured tobacco, resin, lard, stoves, and furniture, is steadily increasing. The aggregate product of the manufactories in the city in 1872 was $16,199,870. The most important and oldest industries of the town are the manufacture of chewing tobacco and the milling of flour. The Gallego flour-mill, which produces fifteen hundred barrels daily, has a monopoly of the Rio de Janeiro and Australian trade, where the Richmond flour is preferred to all others, because it suffers no injury from transportation

The Gallego Flouring-Mill—Richmond, Virginia.

through the hot latitudes near the equator. From "Rockitt's," the "port" of Richmond, on the James, thousands of barrels of flour are weekly carried away in small sailing vessels, which ply constantly between Brazil and Virginia, bringing coffee on their trips to America. Richmond was, up to 1860, the third coffee mart in the United States, and will perhaps be the first when her Western connections have been so perfected that wheat enough to supply the hoppers of the flour-mills can be obtained, and the commerce with South America

Scene on a Tobacco Plantation— Burning a Plant Patch.

assumes the mammoth proportions it promises some day to take. The city suffered the loss of one of its largest flour-mills by fire a year since; but the citizens propose speedily to replace it by another and ampler one. The present Gallego mill has twice arisen from the ruins caused by conflagrations. This mill was owned successively by Mr. Gallego and Mr. Chevallie, both accomplished Frenchmen, the latter being especially distinguished for his literary culture and his courtly manners.

The tobacco trade of Richmond has long been of great importance to the city, and is one of the mainstays of its commerce. The trade is by no means as large as it was before the war, when slave labor made a mammoth production more certain than now, and when there was no revenue officer with vigilant eyes in every town. There are at present in Richmond about forty-five tobacco fac-

Tobacco Culture—Stringing the Primings.

tories in operation, each employing from fifty to two hundred hands, and each producing from fifteen hundred to twenty thousand pounds of manufactured tobacco daily. The revenue which this article pays to the General Government is enormous. The collections of internal revenue for the year 1872 in the Richmond district of Virginia averaged a quarter of a million dollars monthly; and during the year amounted to more than three million dollars. While the revenue collected from the tax on ardent spirits in the Richmond district in 1873 was but $34,476, that on tobacco was $3,064,293, many hundred times more than the amounts collected there by the General Government from all other sources. The collections in that district from the various taxable articles since May 1, 1869, amount to $12,251,537.

When the tobacco comes from the plantations throughout Virginia and North Carolina to the Richmond market,

A Tobacco Barn in Virginia.

it is first taken to some of the great warehouses on the border of the James, where it remains until the commission merchants to whom it is consigned desire to dispose of it. It is then "sampled" by a sworn State Inspector, who is responsible for the quality of each package from which he takes a sample. The "samples" are carried to the "Tobacco Exchange," where they are exposed for sale, either to private parties or at public auction. There are annually inspected in the Richmond warehouses from 40,000 to 45,000 hogsheads, or more than three-fourths of the entire crop of the State. The finest grades of tobacco come from Halifax and Charlotte counties in Virginia, and from Granville and Caswell counties in North Carolina. The tobacco leaf is the most troublesome as well as the most remunerative staple which the Virginian planter can raise. The old ex-slaveholders are wont to moan bitterly over the

The Old Method of Getting Tobacco to Market.

loss of the good old days when there were from six hundred to a thousand slaves upon a tobacco plantation, and when the lands were taxed almost beyond the limits of their strength that the greatest possible results might be secured. But now-a-days the work that previous to 1860 was done on one plantation is divided between a hundred "landed proprietors." *

The Richmond dealers cluster daily around the Tobacco Exchange, where they find an epitome of the whole tobacco production of the State neatly arranged in samples. Hundreds of negroes toil in the warehouses, as in Lynchburg and Petersburg, opening the hogsheads for the inspectors, and arranging the

* In 1873 there were inspected in Richmond 42,054 hogsheads, 8,201 tierces, and 1,218 boxes, besides 2,834,100 pounds of loose tobacco. The latter is mainly grown within a radius of forty miles from Richmond, and is brought to market in wagons. The Tobacco Exchange, started as a private speculation in 1857 by William Y. Sheppard, Esq., has now passed into the hands of the tobacco trade.

lots. Half a century ago the tobacco warehouses in Richmond were mere wooden sheds; the cask containing the weed was rolled to these warehouses on its own periphery. The rough farmers who had spent a whole season in cultivating a crop packed it tightly into a cask, then drove a long wooden spike into the centre of each end of the compressed mass. This served as an axletree; a split sapling was transformed into a pair of shafts, rude tires were placed around each end of the cask, and a stout horse and a steer trundled this extempore wagon to the capital, where its contents were inspected, and then sold. Near each warehouse stood a furnace, into which all tobacco unfit for exportation was thrown to be burned.

The water power of Richmond is not quite so limitless as an enthusiastic Virginian once declared it, viz.: "Sufficient to run all the machinery in the New England States;" but the best authorities have pronounced the available power very large, certainly much ampler than the entire mill privileges combined of Lowell and Lawrence in Massachusetts. There is enough for three or four times as many manufactories as are now established along the James at Richmond and Manchester, and within a short distance of this power ships drawing thirteen feet of water can come at all seasons of the year. The prominent citizens of Richmond are anxious for the establishment of more cotton-mills on the James; and it is possible that in future the Virginia capital will become the rival of Fall River and Lowell. The present ratio of increase in the value of products manufactured in the city is certainly as rapid as could be

Getting a Tobacco Hogshead Ready for Market.

expected after the trials undergone by Virginia during the last decade. The tobacco factories, the iron works, and the flour-mills showed a product amounting to twelve million dollars in 1873; and the manufacturers of agricultural implements, of fertilizers, the preparers of sumac, the makers of clothing, paper, and a hundred miscellaneous articles, are all prosperous and active. The receipts of corn, of wheat, of coal and iron are increasing immensely from year to year as the Western railroad connections are perfected and the mineral deposits in the mountains are unearthed.* The Tredegar Iron Works now employs a million dollars capital and two thousand workmen; its buildings cover fifteen acres, and it annually works up tens of thousands of tons of crude iron.

There seems but little doubt that Richmond will become one of the most important Southern centres of iron manufacture. Now that the Virginian has learned to aspire to something besides "land and negroes," and that new railroads enable him to utilize the immense coal and iron deposits of the commonwealth, it is reasonable to believe that he will improve his opportunities, and will make of the pretty capital on the James one of the most prosperous of manufacturing towns. The Richmond, Piedmont, Dan River, and New River coal-fields will add their stores to those of the mighty Kanawha valley; and the iron region

Scene on a Tobacco Plantation—Finding Tobacco-Worms.

* Leading articles brought into Richmond during three fiscal years, ending September 30th of each year:

	1871.	1872.	1873.
Coal, tons	31,220	59,188	64,916
Corn, bushels	107,456	133,696	209,225
Fish, barrels	7,824	8,153	5,819
Guano, tons	1,901	5,507	13,179
Hay, bales	1,744	3,815	12,228
Ice, tons	7,817	8,994	9,101
Iron, tons	......	36,225	21,519
Lime, barrels	28,834	18,389	17,523
Lumber, feet	5,005,000	6,771,000	6,474,419
Plaster, tons	4,916	1,903	1,208
Salt, sacks	64,798	66,773	52,230
Shingles	1,272,000	2,252,000	2,353,000
Wheat, bushels	239,213	185,383	174,355

which Richmond can draw upon is very extensive. Louisa, Spottsylvania, Albemarle, Nelson, Amherst, Fluvanna, Powhatan, Cumberland, Buckingham, Campbell and Appomattox counties possess fine deposits of iron ores; and as furnaces spring up in those sections, the capital will give added attention to the manufacture of iron. As the mineral development of South-eastern Missouri has aided in building up St. Louis, so will the unearthing of the treasures in that part of Virginia tributary to Richmond give that city added strength and size. The resources of the hematite beds of Augusta, Rockbridge, Bath and Alleghany counties, can be readily united at Richmond with those of the Kanawha coal-seams. It is safe to predict that in a generation the whole character of the city will be changed; that it will have become a sprightly centre, devoted to manufactures, and filled with huge establishments for turning raw cotton, crude tobacco, and pig-iron into serviceable articles. In twenty years manufacturers will be the aristocrats in Virginia. What planter of the Old Dominion twenty years ago would have believed such a thing possible?

The rapid growth of Richmond doubtless carries sadness to the heart of the Virginian of the old school. For in the steady progress of the capital toward prominence as a manufacturing centre he sees the symbol of the decay of the society which produced him and his. He hates large cities, with their democratic tendencies, their corruption, and their ambitious populations. He

The Tredegar Iron Works—Richmond, Virginia.

looks upon the rich manufacturer as a *parvenu;* the lordly agriculturist is still, in his mind, the only fitting type of the real aristocrat. He shudders when he sees the youth of the new school engaging in commerce, buying and selling mines, talking of opening new railroad routes, and building cotton-mills. He flies to the farthest corner of the lands that have been spared to him out of the wrecks caused by the war, and strives to forget the present, and to live as he did "before the surrender," like a country squire in England two hundred years ago.

Richmond, in the conduct of her schools, does not belie the reputation for advanced progress in education which Virginia has gained. In April of 1869 her citizens of all parties petitioned the City Council for a system of public schools, and in due time a school ordinance was adopted, and a Board of Education was appointed. To the insufficient appropriation made by the city authorities, generous donations from the Peabody fund, the Freedmen's Bureau fund, and Northern educational societies, were added, and fifty-two schools, with a pupil membership of twenty-four hundred, were opened. At the close of this first session the citizens voluntarily agreed to continue the schools, and the city took control of those for black and white alike. In the season of 1870–71, the attendance had increased to 3,300, and the schools of the city were finally made a part of the State system. The School Board turned the Davis Mansion, once the "White House" of the Confederacy, into a school building.

The Richmond schools for both white and colored pupils rank among the best in the country. The schools are grouped in houses holding six hundred pupils each, and are divided into six grades of primary and four of grammar, with an advanced high school grade. No Virginian living in Richmond is able to say that his children cannot receive as good an education in the public as they can obtain in private schools. In 1873 Richmond had fifty-five schools for white and thirty-two for colored children, and expended about seventy thousand dollars in supporting them. The instruction is the same in each, and competent white teachers are employed when good black ones are lacking for the colored schools. No one thinks of refusing to aid the negro in obtaining his education, although he contributes little or nothing toward the school tax.

The white and colored normal schools of Richmond have done noble work in sending out well-equipped teachers to encourage the growing sentiment in the State in favor of universal education and free schools. The colored normal school was incorporated by special act of the Virginia Legislature, and opened in 1867. It is supported by the Freedmen's Bureau and the Peabody fund. It receives pupils mainly from the city public schools, and gives them a careful three years' course. The Richmond Institute, for the training of colored preachers and teachers, is a protegé of the American Baptist Home Mission Society. The Baptist and the Virginia Medical Colleges, located in Richmond, are flourishing institutions; and there are more than a score of well-conducted private schools, seminaries, "institutes," and academies, in which several hundred pupils are annually received.

LXXI.

THE PARTITION OF VIRGINIA—RECONSTRUCTION AND POLITICS IN WEST AND EAST VIRGINIA.

AT the time of the secession of the Cotton States, Virginia was apparently attached to the Union. Shortly after that secession, at an extra meeting of the Legislature, a State Convention was called, the members of which were to be elected on the 4th of February, 1861. On the 23d of January of the same year, a bill was passed appropriating a million dollars for the defense of the State, and Virginia began to show signs of adhesion to the cause of the South. The Governor sent messages to the Legislature, in which hostility to the North and Northern institutions was exhibited. Ten Virginia members of Congress published an address denouncing the Republican party, and declaring that it was vain to expect reconciliation. Many of the delegates elected to the State Convention were conditional Union men; some few were unconditional in their support; but the majority avowed the doctrine of State Rights, condemned interference with slavery, asserted the right of secession, and defined the circumstances under which Virginia would be justified in exercising that right. These circumstances were the failure to procure such guarantees from the Northern States as Virginia demanded, the adoption of a war policy by the General Government, or the attempt to exact payment of duty, or to reinforce or capture forts.

On the 17th of April, 1861, after the call of the President for troops, the ordinance of secession was passed by 88 to 55 votes. War measures were begun, and on the 25th of April the Convention passed an act for the adoption of the Constitution of the Provisional Government of the Confederate States, and Virginia was fairly out of the Union.

In the western section of Virginia, a public meeting was held in Clarksburg, in Harrison county, on the 28th of April, 1861, to decide what measures should be taken in view of the recent action of the State. Delegates from twenty-five counties met at Wheeling, condemned secession, and provided for a convention to represent all the counties in the State favorable to a division thereof, in case the people of Virginia ratified the ordinance of secession, against the vote of the western section. The popular vote, ratifying the secession ordinance, is said to have given 94,000 majority for secession, Eastern Virginia voting solidly for and Western Virginia against it.

On the 11th of June, at Wheeling, the Convention of West Virginia, representing forty counties, passed a declaration of independence from the action of the State Convention, and took measures for establishing a provisional government. Later, the representatives of Western Virginia met as a State Legislature, and elected Senators to the United States Congress, passed a stay law, and appropriated $200,000 for carrying on the war, and the same amount to support the new Government. The proposition for a division of the State was voted down, but subsequently the Convention, at an adjourned session, passed an ordinance organizing the western counties into a new State to be called "Kanawha." Thirty-nine counties, with a population of nearly 300,000 people, thus gave in their adhesion to the Union.

On the 24th of October the Provisional Legislature, in session at Wheeling, sanctioned the setting off of the new State, and in October the act was approved by the people of thirty-nine counties by an almost unanimous vote. Western Virginia, as it was finally decided to call the new division, applied for admission to the Union at the first regular session of the 37th Congress, and on April 20th, 1863, after the Provisional Legislature had ratified an amendment to the Constitution, permitting free negroes to enter the State, and inserting certain provisions relative to freeing the slaves, Western Virginia was admitted to the Union, and the new State was inaugurated at Wheeling, June 20th, 1863, with imposing ceremonies.

Old Virginia thus lost one of the fairest portions of her domain, an immense amount of material resources, a mineral region almost unequaled upon the continent, and a large population.

The people of Western Virginia unanimously adopted their new Constitution in a Convention comprising 66 Democrats and 12 Republicans, on the 9th of April, 1872. The Constitution guarantees West Virginia a continued separate existence, secures free schools, and is, withal, quite liberal, although some members of the Convention tried to have the negroes deprived of their newly-acquired right to vote. It also recognizes the obligation of West Virginia for whatever she may justly owe the parent State as her share in the latter's debt of $44,000,000, and declares her willingness to pay it when it is properly ascertained. The new Constitution was ratified August 22d, 1872, by a small majority. It fixes the term of the office of Governor and other important State officers at four years, and that of the Judges of the Supreme Court of Appeals at twelve years. The Democrats, in 1872, nominated Johnson M. Camden, of Wood county, as Governor, but John J. Jacob, the then incumbent, was re-elected by a small majority.

There have been at times, serious disagreements between the Governor and the Legislature of the State; the former interpreting the Constitution as giving him appointive power with regard to almost all officers, and in 1873 these disagreements became the cause of quite serious disturbances in the new commonwealth. The estimated expenditures of the State, under the new Constitution, are somewhat more than a quarter of a million of dollars yearly, to which may be added the "State fund," distributed for free schools in 1873, amounting to about the same sum. The number of pupil-children enrolled in that year was 170,031, of which about one-half attended school. The University of Western Virginia, under the exclusive control of the State, has a permanent endowment of $100,000. The "Normal Schools" at Fairmont, West Liberty, Shepherdstown, and Marshall College are flourishing. The indebtedness of the State is very slight; taxes are not burdensome; the State institutions are well maintained, and the present population, constantly increased by immigration of excellent character, mainly from the middle classes of England, is now nearly 500,000.

After the division of territory, the progress of reconstruction in Virginia proper was marked, as in all the other States, by many political excitements and troubles. President Johnson's order, issued May 9, 1865, recognized Francis H. Pierpont, who was originally elected Governor in West Virginia, and who had subsequently moved his Government seat to Alexandria, and exercised jurisdiction over a few counties adjacent to Washington during the war. His Legislature consisted of members from ten counties, and was known to loyal men in war time as the "Legislature of Virginia." Governor Pierpont went to Richmond shortly after the surrender at Appomattox Court-House, and called a special session of the Legislature.

In October, 1865, the restriction in the Constitution prescribing the oath relative to freedom from sympathy with the late Confederacy was removed. The Legislature met at Richmond on the 4th day of December, 1865.

During this year the Conservatives attempted to inaugurate a practical serfdom of the freedmen, by means of vagrant laws; and other evidences of a determination to revert to the old system were given. But the State Government, which had been established by merely a handful of votes in the northern counties, was nevertheless honestly and creditably sustained, and Governor Pierpont suddenly found himself in full jurisdiction over Virginia.

In May of 1866, a "Republican State Convention" met at Alexandria, and a Special Committee reported a resolution declaring the so-called Legislature illegal and unconstitutional, and sent a memorial to Congress demanding the revocation of Governor Pierpont's powers, and asking for a "policy of reconstruction." How far this policy had been rendered necessary by the action of the Conservatives with regard to the negroes, it is not necessary here to inquire. As soon as the Reconstruction Act of Congress had become a law, General Schofield was placed in command of the First Military District, which comprised the territory of Virginia. The Conservatives, who had intended to hold a convention at Richmond in May of that year, and to so amend the Constitution as to make it coincide with the reconstruction policy of Congress, were too late to escape military rule. Governor Pierpont issued orders commanding all State officers to continue the exercise of their duties until a new election could be held under reconstruction. A Board of Army Officers selected the officials to superintend a new registration, which was at once begun. On the 2d of April, 1867, an order appeared, superseding all elections under the "Provisional Government," until the registration should be completed. The Commanding-General at that time made all appointments. The Conservatives were opposed to this action, and the local press was violently critical.

On the 17th of April, 1867, at the call of the "Union party of Virginia," a convention assembled in the African Church in Richmond, of which, out of two hundred and ten delegates, only fifty were white. Other political meetings were elsewhere held about the same time by freedmen and the whites allied with them. Many negroes sided with the Conservatives. General Schofield found it necessary to disband all armed organizations in the State. On the 3d of June orders for reconstruction were issued, and 116,982 white, and 104,772 colored voters were registered. In Amelia, Brunswick, Charlotte, Dinwiddie, Elizabeth, Halifax, Powhatan, and York counties the negroes were overpoweringly in the majority.

Meantime, the Conservative wing of the Union party, so called, decided to hold a convention at Charlottesville on the 4th of July, 1867, but it was finally determined to call a "convention of all the unconditional Union men of Virginia," to meet in the African Church in Richmond on the 1st of August, to secure the coalition of the two wings of the Republican party of the State. This convention was packed with ignorant negroes, and but little good was effected.

A number of ex-officers and soldiers of the Union held a convention at Richmond on the 25th of September. Vacancies in offices were filled by temporary appointees. Military commissions continued to try offenders, because the strong caste prejudice prevalent in the State endangered the lives and property of persons who sat upon mixed juries.

On the 22d of October a Constitutional Convention was decided upon by a popular vote and a majority of 45,455. Of the 105 delegates chosen to this Convention the mass were white people. The Convention, which met on the 3d day of December, proposed to provide in the organic law of the State that negroes should be allowed equal privileges with whites in horse-cars, public places, &c. Meantime the Convention of the Conservatives of the State assembled at Richmond on the 12th of December. It disclaimed all hostility to the blacks, but hotly condemned reconstruction *in toto*. The Republican Constitutional Convention finally adopted an article making every male citizen 21 years old, who had been or might be a resident of the State for twelve months, and of a county, city, or town three months, a voter, excepting only those who had been engaged in insurrection. The test oath was brought in, and the Conservatives at once rebelled against this, as did also the commander of the military district, General Schofield. The operation of the test oath, inasmuch as all the native white Virginians had been engaged in the work of secession, would not have left voters enough to carry on the Government intelligently; but the odious provision was not modified, and the new Constitution, with the test oath in it, was adopted by the Convention April 17, 1868. It had then to go before the people for ratification. Virginia remained, however, under military law.

On the 4th of April of the same year, Governor Pierpont's term of office expired. Henry H. Wells was appointed, by military authority, Governor of the State. Hon. Joseph Mayo, who had been Mayor of Richmond for fifteen years, was removed, and George Chahoon was appointed his successor. General Schofield was shortly afterward made Secretary of War, and Major-General Stoneman took his place as Military Governor of Virginia. Things went on quietly thereafter until 1869. The Constitution which the Republican Convention had adopted had not yet been presented for ratification. It was evident that under its provisions the more intelligent and capable citizens of the commonwealth were to be excluded from office. President Grant, being authorized to submit the Constitution to the voters of the State and to allow them to vote separately on the separate provisions, appointed the 6th of July as the time for ratification. Wells was meantime removed from the Governorship. General Stoneman was superseded by Major-General Canby, and the political parties continued an active canvass of the State.

Shortly afterward the Republican delegates assembled in convention at Petersburg and renominated Mr. Wells for Governor. It was my rare fortune to assist at the session of this Convention, which was held in a negro church. Never in the history of Republicanism was there a more disgraceful and lawless rabble assembled together. Gratifying as it was to see those who had lately been slaves learning something of Government affairs, it was utterly discouraging to note the violent and offensive measures which they took to obtain their ends. Brawls, shoutings, and bickerings consumed an entire day, and the police were called upon four times to clear the building before a temporary president was chosen.

Another wing of the Republican party of the State, which had always acted with the National party, but which took no part in the Petersburg Convention, nominated Gilbert C. Walker of Norfolk, an accomplished and amiable gentleman of Northern parentage, as its candidate for Governor. On the 28th of April, 1869, the Conservatives, highly pleased with this nomination, met at Richmond, and favored the election of Mr. Walker, but decided to use all their efforts to vote down the odious Constitution which the Republicans had prepared. The Constitution was accepted, however, on the 6th of July, at a general election, by a majority of 197,044 votes, but the "disfranchising clause," which had been the cause of much of the ill feeling toward the reconstruction policy in the South, was voted down squarely by a majority of 39,957 votes, and the test oath clause was also lost by a majority of 40,992 votes. Mr. Walker was elected Governor, with the coöperation of the Conservatives, by a majority of 18,317 votes. In the Legislature which then assembled there were 95 Conservatives and 42 Republicans, with 18 negroes in the House and 6 in the Senate. The Conservatives at once assumed an attitude of conciliation, and, forgetting the old issues and prejudices of the past, ratified the 14th and 15th amendments to the Constitution of the United States. The Republicans were discontented, attributing their failure to the separate votes on the clauses of the State Constitution.

Virginia was readmitted to the Union on the 26th of January, 1870. On the following day, General Canby retired from his authority; Governor Walker assumed his office, and for four years thereafter governed the State well and fairly. Had all the other Southern States been as fortunate as Virginia in escaping the major evils of reconstruction, the South would have been far more prosperous than she can now hope to be for many years.

It is noteworthy with regard to Virginia politics, that whenever the Conservative politicians make a campaign up and down the State, sometimes flying the old Confederate colors a little, they do not awaken any intense enthusiasm among the working population. The farmers of Virginia are too much occupied with their own immediate concerns to give great attention to State politics. They feel determined to keep the negro from attaining such power as he has gained in South Carolina and Louisiana; but they are apathetic, and any attempt to organize them into a party of extremists would be an inevitable failure.

The present government of the State is in good hands. The officers of the State Government are allied to the Conservative party, but seem determined to do equal and exact justice to all classes of citizens. Governor Kemper, elected over Mr. Hughes, the Republican candidate, in 1873, was a Confederate General, and is an old-school Virginian, but has a sufficient appreciation of the necessities of the time to avoid the narrow and mean-spirited policy which has latterly characterized some of the other Southern States. He has thus far done everything that he could to develop good-will and confidence between the races. When the Legislature of the State proposed, shortly after General Kemper's election, to invade the liberties of the city of Petersburg and to take from it its self-government because the majority of the voters there were negroes, the Governor stood up boldly against this movement and vetoed the bill. In his veto message, he said:

"In view of the fundamental conditions on which Virginia stands as a member of the Federal Union; in view of our own solemn and sworn recognition of the political equality before the law of all men, irrespective of race, color, or previous condition, the proposed measure, if enacted, could not fail to subject us to disastrous misconstruction at home and abroad. It would renew and intensify the race agitations of the past, which are being happily settled; it would present Virginia to the world as being torn by intestine feuds of an apparently interminable character; it would discourage and postpone, if not repel, the approach of the immigration and capital to which our most ardent hopes are directed; and, more to be deplored than all, it would sound a provocation to Federal interference in our domestic affairs."

In these words of Governor Kemper one may find expressed the attitude of the better class of Virginian Conservatives. The determination to avoid everything which might be construed as ungenerous toward the negro; to build up his character by education, and to urge him to accumulate property; the gradual change and softening of public sentiment among the elder aristocrats with regard to the introduction of manufactures and the dignity of labor,—all point to a change in the character of the Old Dominion, which will result in making her one day as rich and mighty as Pennsylvania or Missouri.

The aggregate of assessed values of taxable property of all kinds in Virginia, in 1873, was not quite $337,000,000. In 1860 the assessed value of the real and personal property actually subjected to taxation in the State was $585,099,382, and the official reports show that property of the value of $163,556,100 was then exempted from taxation, thus making the actual aggregate resources of the State in that year about $748,000,000. The aggregate value of real and personal property within the 38,348 square miles in the present limits of Virginia proper, in 1860, was $632,000,000. It will be seen from these figures that the decline in taxable values has been very great and rapid. The losses in production have in some cases been startling, as instanced in that of tobacco, the crop of which in 1860 amounted to 123,968,312 pounds, but in 1870 to only 37,086,364. The decrease in production is largely due to the fact that the slave population, which constituted the most valuable producing class before the war, numbering more than half a million persons, now produces little but a bare living for itself. Until the Virginian negroes learn to be enterprising and industrious, and to produce surplus crops, the cultivation of the great staples in the State will languish.

Of the 1,125,163 inhabitants of Virginia, more than 512,000 are blacks. It would seem that both whites and colored people spend even the small amount of ready money which they have upon things which do not profit their souls; for General Ruffner, the able State Superintendent of Public Instruction, asserts that the consumption of liquors in Virginia amounts to something like $19,000,000 annually. During the fiscal year 1872, the revenue officers of the United States collected from liquor dealers in Virginia $71,000 in licenses. General Ruffner is probably very nearly right when he puts the cost of the liquor yearly drank *as a beverage* in the State at $12,000,000, and he shows the folly and criminality of the general indulgence in whiskey, by stating that the gross annual product of seven of the best counties in the State is not sufficient to pay for the liquor consumed by the people of the commonwealth; that the gross production of nearly half the small counties would not compensate for annual loss by drink; that the Virginians drink up the value of their wheat crop every year; and that the legislative cost and the expenses of courts and civil officers and State institutions and the public free schools, and the interest on the enormous public debt, only amount to a little more than one-quarter of the sum which the people of Virginia yearly spend upon liquor. Colonel Burwell, of Richmond, estimates the annual consumption of liquor in Virginia at 2,500,000 gallons, and he latterly introduced a bill into the Legislature, imposing a tax of 30 cents per gallon upon this liquor, which would, if collected, yield the State a revenue of $750,000. But this bill has not yet become a law.

The State is now seriously considering the sources from which it may derive increased revenue, but doubts the expediency of increasing the taxation upon lands, as it would result in a virtual confiscation of private property. The State credit is severely prostrated; for, while the debt is enormous, considering the present condition of the commonwealth, the interest is largely in arrears. The act known as the Funding act pledged the State to the regular and punctual payment of interest on the debt, which it provided to be newly funded in the name of Virginia; but the State was unable to fulfill these obligations, and both debtors and creditors were but poorly satisfied with the results. The sum then funded, the interest upon which is largely overdue, was $30,478,741.48, excluding the amount assigned for settlement with West Virginia. The revenues of the State, as compared with her available resources, are quite large; yet they are usually less than enough to support the Government and to pay full interest on the debt. The Conservatives will take care to do nothing tending to impair the public credit. No partial or total repudiation will ever be considered, and the impolicy of taxing capital heavily is thoroughly understood. Virginia will not fail to treat liberally all capital invested in the establishment of new manufactures within her boundaries.

The favorable advance in public sentiment regarding general free education in Virginia grows more noticeable yearly. It is largely due to the energetic campaign upon which General Ruffner, the State Superintendent of Education, entered under the Administration of Governor Walker. By able reports, lectures, figures, and liberal as well as daring policy, he has revolutionized opinion in many parts of the State. The organization of the graded schools is rapidly becoming general in thickly-populated localities, and 160,859 pupils were in 1873 enrolled upon the books of the public schools. The total cost to the public fund for education was $707,835, and the total cost to all sources nearly $800,000, of which the Peabody fund contributed $31,450. There were 2,070 students in the various universities and colleges of the State, 1,207 of whom were native Virginians.

A Water-melon Wagon.

LXXII.

FROM RICHMOND TO CHARLOTTESVILLE.

RICHMOND is well supplied with railroads. The Richmond, Fredericksburg and Virginia road extends northward to Alexandria, the Potomac, and Washington; the Richmond and Petersburg road southward to Petersburg; south-eastward runs the rail route connecting the capital with Yorktown; southwestward the road to Danville, and thence to Greensboro' in North Carolina, and westward the Chesapeake and Ohio. By the York River railway route one may reach the battle-fields of Seven Pines and Fair Oaks, only four miles away.

A Marl-Bed on the Line of the Chesapeake and Ohio Railroad.

The Chesapeake and Ohio railroad at present extends from Richmond through the Piedmont country, the Blue Ridge, and the Alleghanies, to Huntington on the Ohio river. It was formed by a consolidation of the roads, properties and franchises of the Virginia Central and the Covington and Ohio railroad companies. Its charter privileges cover the line from tide-water on the James to the Ohio river, at or near the mouth of the Big Sandy, where the borders of the States of West Virginia, Kentucky and Ohio touch each other. This is a distance of 427 miles. Several important branches and extensions are contemplated. One is a line from Richmond down the peninsula, between the York and James rivers, to a point on the deep waters of the Chesapeake bay, near the Capes. They further propose to give Richmond its long desired direct communication with the West by the completion of the Elizabethtown, Lexington and Big Sandy railroad in Kentucky to Huntington. At Lexington this will connect with Louisville, Cincinnati and Lexington, one of the oldest roads in Kentucky, and there will then be a direct all-rail line 640 miles in length between Richmond and Louisville. The road from Richmond to the Ohio river was opened for traffic on the 1st of April, 1873. This great central highway crosses both the Blue Ridge and the Alleghany mountains by easy grades, the highest elevation attained being about two thousand feet. It offers special advantages for the transportation of the surplus productions of the

Earthworks on the Chickahominy, near Richmond, Virginia.

West directly to the largest, deepest, and most secure harbor on the eastern Atlantic coast of the United States. Along the greater portion of the route the best coals abound, in thick seams, close to and above the level of its track; and this coal can be supplied to its locomotives at the bare cost of handling. As it lies near the 38th parallel of latitude, it is never liable to obstruction from deep snows, nor interruption from severe frosts.

The journey from Richmond to the Piedmont country along this line of rail takes the traveler through little that is noteworthy. The Chickahominy river, which the railroad crosses five miles from the capital, is, at the point where the right wing of McClellan's army rested in June and July of 1862, an unimpressive stream. Various dilapidated and grass-grown earthworks are still to be seen, and are amicably pointed out and discussed by ex-Confederate and ex-Federal as the train passes. A few miles beyond are extensive marl-beds, whence Virginia draws much of her fertilizing material; although her planters also rely largely on the guano brought from the Chincha Islands for the renewal of their fields.

A little farther on is Hanover Court-House, where Henry Clay was born, and where Patrick Henry first gave evidence of his wonderful oratorical powers, by his famous plea against "the parsons," who had brought an action for the recovery of certain amounts due them by the people.

Here and there along the route are corn-sheds, unpretending buildings in which the farmers store their grain until the railway officials are ready to transport it to Richmond.

Bending northward and westward, through the rich Hanover and Louisa counties, and crossing at right angles the belt of iron and gold deposits extending through the State, Gordonsville, seventy-six miles from Richmond, is reached. This is an important junction. The line of road from Lynchburg to Washington there unites with the Chesapeake and Ohio, and the trains of the two roads run thence to Charlottesville on the same track. Gordonsville straggles along a rocky road running through a beautiful country, upon which a range of mountains looks down. There are many fine farms in the vicinity, and the English immigrants have done much to give the section the air of peace and homely thrift so marked in some British agricultural regions. The negroes, who swarm day and night like bees about the trains, look with amazement upon the brisk rosy young men and women who throng the cars, and who daily appear in increased numbers on all the fine farming tracts in·the neighborhood.

The three counties of Henrico, Hanover and Louisa, through which the Chesapeake and Ohio railroad passes between Richmond and Gordonsville, constitute a fine specimen section of the tract in Virginia known as the "Middle Country," which has an area of twelve thousand square miles, and is sixty miles

Scene at a Virginia "Corn-Shed." [Page 648.]

wide. At Gordonsville, at the South-west mountain, the surface of the country is about five hundred feet above sea-level. The light brown soil of the ridges and the rich dark brown of the bottom lands are each very productive; and even the sides and summits of the mountain are arable. Tobacco, wheat, corn, flax, oats and sweet potatoes grow in this section abundantly and well. In the three counties nearly a million and a-half pounds of tobacco were produced in 1870; and in 1860, the average production of tobacco there was 246 pounds to each inhabitant. The mud-beds, sometimes fifteen feet deep, furnish inexhaustible supplies of fertilizers; the counties contain good grazing-lands, and large herds of cattle and flocks of sheep roam in the valleys.

At Gordonsville one is at the door of the Piedmont region, which extends from the head of tide-water to the Blue Ridge mountains. The lower part of this fertile section is gently undulating; the upper is quite hilly, but nowhere so broken as not to admit of cultivation. The tier of counties included in this region comprises an area of six thousand square miles. At the outbreak of the war, nearly half the land in these counties had been put under culture, and the population of two hundred thousand persons scattered through the district raised annually about twenty-five million pounds of tobacco.* The lands are among the very finest in America; the red, crumbling loam is easily worked, and from it spring noble grass, excellent grain, and delicious orchard fruits.

The approaches to Charlottesville, the principal town of Albemarle county, afford a glimpse of the beauties of the Piedmont section. The mountains show

Gordonsville, Virginia—"The negroes, who swarm day and night like bees about the trains." [Page 649.]

their blue outlines; the slopes are dotted with rich farms; the landscape is radiant with peace and plenty. Before the war this county was a region of large plantations, principally devoted to tobacco, of which hundreds of slaves raised five millions of pounds annually. Now the production amounts to but little more than a million and a-half pounds yearly; but it will in due time regain the old number; for no section of Virginia is more rapidly recovering from the disorganization of labor, and the discouragements which followed upon the war, than Albemarle and her fertile sister counties at the foot of the Blue Ridge.

* The whole amount of tobacco raised in Virginia in 1870 was 37,086,364 pounds.

English immigrants are bringing money and accurate knowledge of scientific farming into the country, and are prompting to a new vigor the natives who had begun to yield under the pressure of the adverse fortunes of the past few years.

Charlottesville is one of the loveliest of Virginia towns. It has an air of dignified quiet which befits so ancient and distinguished a seat of learning as the University of Virginia, and the neighbor of such historic ground as Monticello, the home of Thomas Jefferson. The town stands on a moderate elevation, shut in on the south-west by hills beyond which rise the ridges known as the "Ragged" mountains. To the north-west one sees in the distance the symmetrical outlines of the Blue Ridge. On the east is the Rivanna, a pretty stream, although its waters are discolored by the reddish loam through which it flows around the base of Monticello. The railroad is an ungracious intruder, as locomotives saucily shriek at the very doors of sleepy taverns, and trains rattle through streets where everything seems to resent the outbursts of steam and the clang of wheels. The negro is omnipresent, the blacks appearing at first vastly to outnumber the white folks. Many pleasant mansions are surrounded with gardens embowered in shrubbery.

A storm was muttering overhead as I climbed, one midsummer day, the steep road which leads from Charlottesville to Monticello. Here and there a turn in the route gave me exquisite glimpses of the valley below; the old town with its many dingy brown houses, asleep on the plateau; the dome of the University peeping above the foliage, and the delicate blue of the far-away mountains. Just as I was beginning to suspect that I had lost my way, I came to an ill-kept road branching away from the main one. Ascending this, while rain-drops clattering on my face warned me to seek shelter, I came suddenly upon the tomb of the author of the "Declaration of Independence."

I rattled at the rusty iron gate set in the shabby brick wall; but, observing an enormous padlock, I turned away and continued the ascent toward the hill-top, when I noticed an ancient negro man in the pathway, vainly endeavoring to force an unruly yoke of oxen to obey him. The snows of eighty or ninety winters had frosted his wool; the labors of many years of servitude had bent him double. He did not at first hear my salutation, but continued his husky appeals to the oxen. "Debbil in dem critturs, sho;" then spying me, he took off his greasy hat with an explosive "Sah!" A sprightly negro urchin ran

The Tomb of Thomas Jefferson, at Monticello, near Charlottesville, Virginia.

out to aid the venerable blackamoor, but seeing me, grinned good-day, and led the way to the house. On the right, as we approached, stood a row of negro cabins, from one of which a black woman came out, courtesying, and as it was at last raining rapidly, I entered her door. The cabin or hovel was wretched in the extreme; a small window lighted a poor room, in which there was scarcely any furniture. On an uneven hearth a weak fire struggled with the dampness. On the lawn near the path which led, by a gentle ascent, to the mansion, was the body of an old infantry baggage-wagon, marked "U. S." Evidently the "late unpleasantness" had penetrated even to Monticello.

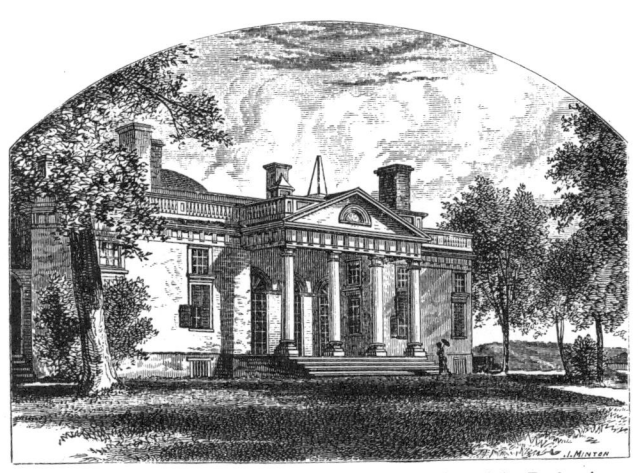

The house, surrounded by beautiful aspen trees, and with its chances for an outlook over an ocean of foliage on one side, and a lovely valley hemmed in by lofty mountain ranges on the other, must have been a pleasant retreat in the last century. I could almost fancy that the long-vanished master of the estate would throw open the great door at which I knocked, under the lofty portico, and usher me into the dining-room, where I should find the Marquis de Lafayette gayly chatting with some country squire, or mayhap reading the memoranda for the "Notes on Virginia" which Mr. Jefferson prepared mainly for the instruction of his French friends. While I stood at the door, a sharp voice inside commanded various colored servants to look "yere" and there after the key, and I was presently ushered in, not by the ghost of the great patriot, but by a sour-looking man, who collected a small fee before I could set foot upon the sacred threshold. He then proceeded to inform me that the estate was in litigation, and that it had "run down" very much, which indeed was quite easy to see. The interior of the mansion, although stripped of nearly everything placed there by Jefferson, has yet a few reminders left. A curious old clock stands in a corner of the entrance hall, and a marble bust of Jefferson himself occupies a dusty niche. The little dining-room with polished inlaid floor, and gilt Parisian mirrors, where the great man was wont to hob-nob over dinner with Lafayette, or distinguished chance visitors, is still in good order; the dumb waiter yet creaks solemnly in its grooves, and from the old-fashioned windows one can look out upon a charming lawn, and on leafy hill-sides. The house is a fair specimen of the commodious and not inelegant structures erected in Virginia in colonial times, and when filled with Jefferson's superb collections of sculpture, paintings, medallions, engravings and books, must have been an oasis of peace to gentlemen of culture who traveled slowly on horseback through the Virginia woods a hundred years ago. The library building, separated from the house, but communicating with it by means of a covered passage-way, still stands. The whole is fast decaying, however, and

Monticello—The Old Home of Thomas Jefferson, author of the Declaration of American Independence.

if the State will not, the country should, see that the home of Jefferson is, like that of Washington, preserved as an historic shrine to which the lovers of liberty may repair for many generations to come.

The little negro boy, carrying an immense key, bounded before me to the tomb, whither I went once more, despite the rain, which now came heavily. Entering, I found that the enclosure was a family burying-ground. Over the grave of the great statesman stands a simple, almost rude granite obelisk, eight feet high, on which is the epitaph which he himself desired to have inscribed on his tomb:

"Here Lies Buried
THOMAS JEFFERSON,
Author of the Declaration of Independence
Of the Statute of Virginia for Religious Freedom
And Father of the University of Virginia."

The University at Charlottesville is Jefferson's noblest monument. So long as it endures, the admirers of the great Virginian can afford to forego lamentation over the ingratitude of republics, and refrain from criticising the Government which is too niggardly to place a marble shaft over his grave. Jefferson founded the University in 1819, and watched with tender care its early growth and im-

The University of Virginia, at Charlottesville.

mediate success. Always an ardent admirer of the school system prevalent in New England in his time, he urged Virginia to adopt it, even while she was struggling in the Revolution. His zeal was so great that, after persistent labor for many years, he succeeded in influencing the State Legislature to adopt a free-school system; but its practical operation was prevented by a proviso which some

Conservative legislators managed to attach to the bill, giving the county courts, whose officials were unfriendly to Mr. Jefferson's plan, the privilege of declaring when the schools should be established in each county.

He was not discouraged, although he saw that the commonwealth gave more attention to internal improvements than to the education of her people; and he never forgot, even when seemingly absorbed in national politics, his schemes for making universal free education popular in Virginia. When, after retiring from the Presidency in 1809, he again took up his residence in the State, he returned to the work with new energy. A "literary fund" was founded by an act of the State Legislature in 1810; the proceeds of this fund were designed to be used exclusively for the purposes of common school education. The principal had at one time grown to two millions of dollars; but since the war it has yielded nothing. Its original nucleus* consisted of fines, forfeitures, and escheats. Mr. Jefferson succeeded, in 1818, in obtaining another legislative enactment, which allowed an appropriation of $15,000 yearly to endow and support a university. A report recommending the establishment of this university, various colleges, and a scheme for general public education, had been made to the Legislature in 1816, doubtless at the instance of Mr. Jefferson, and in 1821 the institution whose noble rotunda to-day rises in graceful relief against the blue mountains near Charlottesville began to receive State aid, which continued without interruption until toward the close of the late war.

Jefferson planned the University, and it still retains the characteristics which he gave it. In the departments of languages, literature, science, law, medicine, agriculture, and engineering, it has to-day eighteen distinct schools. For more than half a century it has been preëminent among the higher institutions of learning in the country, and Northern colleges and universities have borrowed from it the feature of an elective system of study. It has latterly established excellent agricultural and scientific schools, has a fine laboratory, with an extensive collection of raw and manufactured materials, and an experimental farm inferior to none in the country. Its government is vested in a rector, and two visitors from each grand division of the State, except Piedmont, which, because it is the location of the University, is entitled to three. The institution bestows no honorary degrees, and makes the attainment of its "Master of Arts" so difficult that it will serve as a certificate of scholarship anywhere. Nearly one hundred and fifty of the graduates of the several schools are now professors in other colleges. The University is by no means aristocratic in its tendencies; a large proportion of the students pay their expenses with money earned by themselves, and, since the war, there have been many "State students" who are provided with gratuitous instruction. The alumni form an army fourteen thousand strong.

The buildings of the University are not architecturally fine, although the main edifice has a rotunda modeled in part after the Pantheon at Rome. The country around the elevation a mile west of Charlottesville on which they stand, is exquisitely lovely. The great porticoes, whence one can look out upon lawns,

---

* Report of Dr. Ruffner, State Superintendent of Education in Virginia.

on the trim houses where the professors live, and on the dormitories for the students, are beautiful. In the well-arranged and amply-stocked library hangs a fine portrait of General Lee, by Elder. Among the academic groves, Long, and Key, and Silvester, whose names are eminent both in England and America, and Courtenay, Rogers, Emmett and Bonnycastle, famous instructors, once had their homes.

A Water-melon Feast.

LXXIII.

FROM CHARLOTTESVILLE TO STAUNTON, VA.—THE SHENANDOAH VALLEY—LEXINGTON—THE GRAVES OF GENERAL LEE AND "STONEWALL" JACKSON—FROM GOSHEN TO "WHITE SULPHUR SPRINGS."

THE route from Charlottesville to Staunton, through Albemarle and Augusta counties, passes some of the finest farming-land in the Piedmont section. In summer, one sees fields clad in the green of the tobacco leaf, or in the luxuriant clover, timothy, blue, orchard, and herds' grasses. The fruits flourish in perfection; the pippin, the pear and the grape attain unusual size, and yet have

Piedmont, from the Blue Ridge.

delicate flavor. Looking out from the train as it begins to scale the base of the Blue Ridge, one gazes down into fertile valleys, with little streams flowing through them; upon expanses of meadow; and on lusty vineyards clothing the hills.

The Chesapeake and Ohio railroad traverses the Blue Ridge at a point no less rich in mountain scenery than that section near the Peaks of Otter through which the Atlantic, Mississippi and Ohio road runs; but it slips under the great ridges, instead of winding among them. The Blue Ridge tunnel, seven-eighths of a mile long, was built by Virginia, under the supervision of her State Engineer, Colonel Claude Crozet, an old soldier of Napoleon the Great. This persevering engineer worked seven years at the tunnel before he saw light through it.

Coming out from the "great bore," the traveler descries the Shenandoah valley, the pride of Virginia, outspread in its loveliness before him. As far as he can see, his gaze rests upon highly-cultivated farms and noble woodlands.

"This valley," to quote the words of Major Hotchkiss, of Staunton, author of the "Resources of Virginia," "forms the north-eastern third of the great valley that extends for nearly three hundred and sixty miles diagonally across the State." This latter valley in turn "forms about one-tenth of the Appalachian valley, that, under the various local designations of Champlain, Hudson, Goshen, Kittatinny, Lebanon, Cumberland, Shenandoah, James, Roanoke, New River, Holston, East Tennessee, and Warrior, extends from the St. Lawrence to the Alabama river," a distance of fifteen hundred miles. It is walled on the east

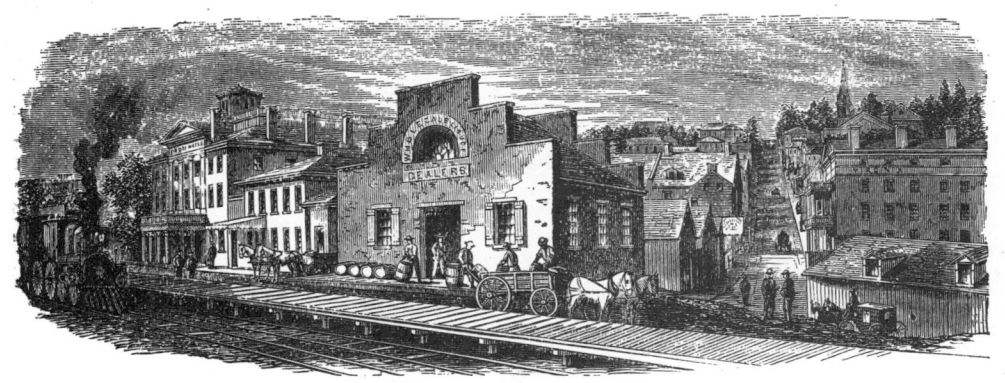

View of Staunton, Virginia.

throughout its whole extent by the Blue Ridge, on the west by the ranges locally known as the Catskill, Shawangunk, Blue, North and Cumberland, and is a limestone tract "embracing thirty thousand square miles of the best farming and grazing-land on the continent, margined on each side by inexhaustible deposits of richest hematite iron ores.

The "Shanando'," as the negroes call it, includes about five million acres of land, of which nearly two-thirds are either under cultivation or enclosed in farms; the remainder is open to immigrants. The valley is especially noted for its grain and grass-growing capacity. In 1866 its wheat product was three and a-quarter million bushels; it produced three million pounds of tobacco, and five and a-half million bushels of corn. At the outbreak of the war, it was one of the finest stocked farming countries in the world. In Augusta county, at the head of the valley, English settlers have purchased many estates. That county is well underlaid with mineral treasure. Jefferson, in his "Notes on Virginia," mentions that, in his time, iron mines were worked in Augusta county. Great impetus has been given to the mineral development there by the extension of the railroad through the Kanawha valley, which is stocked with cheap and abundant fuel, to the furnaces along the Ohio river for which the Virginia ores are always eagerly demanded. Lands which contain veins of hematite ore are easily obtainable; good agricultural tracts may be purchased from $25 to $30 per acre.

Twelve miles from the base of the mountain through which the tunnel is pierced lies the pretty hill-town of Staunton, where two of the principal State charities, the Western District Asylum for the Insane, and the Institution for the Deaf, Dumb and Blind, are located. As Staunton is also a very central point, and one of the healthiest places in Virginia, it is the seat of several seminaries for young ladies. A walk along its steep streets induces the stranger to believe that the town has more beautiful girls than are to be found anywhere else in the South; but the presence of so many lovely creatures is explained by the fact that six hundred lady pupils are gathered there from the Middle, Southern and Western States, and that they represent the best society of the whole country. The town is also the residence of Dr. Sears, the dispenser of the educational fund donated to the Southern States by George Peabody. Staunton has a large trade in tobacco and whiskey; many wealthy people have fine mansions on the hills which rise in the rear of the business section; and in summer the hotels are crowded with tourists on their way to the mineral springs of Virginia, and to the natural wonders in the vicinity of the town. One of the most remarkable of these wonders is Weyer's Cave, a "vast subterranean labyrinth of glittering grottoes and galleries," where stalactites sparkle in the light of the torches carried by the guides, and "hang from the fretted roof like the foliated pendants of a Gothic cathedral." The cave was

Winchester, Virginia. [Page 659.]

discovered in 1804, by Bernard Weyer, a hunter of the neighborhood. The direct course through it is sixteen hundred feet long; the main path usually taken by visitors to the principal apartments and galleries is six hundred and fifty feet long. Washington's Hall, the chief curiosity of the cave, takes its name from a calcareous formation six or seven feet high, which bears a close resemblance to a statue in classic drapery. "Madison's Cave," not far from Weyer's, is on the north side of the Blue Ridge, near the intersection of the line of Rockingham and Augusta counties with the south fork of the southern Shenandoah river. In Jefferson's "Notes" it is thus described: "It is in a hill of about 200 feet perpendicular height, the ascent of which on one side is so steep that you may pitch a biscuit from its summit into the river which washes its base. The entrance of the cave is in this side, about two-thirds of the way up. It extends into the earth 300 feet, branching into subordinate caverns, sometimes ascending a little, but more generally descending, and at length terminates in two different places at basins of water of unknown extent. The vault of this cave is of solid limestone, from 20 to 40 or 50 feet high, through which water is continually percolating. This, trickling down the sides of the cave, has incrusted them over in the form of elegant drapery, and, dripping from the top of the vault, generates on that, and on the base below, stalactites of a conical form, some of which have met and formed massive columns."

Northwest of Staunton, in Augusta county, are the Cyclopean Towers, formed of limestone. They rise to the height of seventy feet, and resemble the battlements of a feudal castle.

Staunton is certainly one of the pleasantest summer retreats in Virginia. The road-bed of the Chesapeake and Ohio railroad there is 1,386 feet above tide-water. The atmosphere is dry and cool. Sheltered on the east by the barrier of the Blue Ridge, and on the west by a loftier range, from which Ellsworth's Knob rises to the height of 4,448 feet above the sea-level, the piercing blasts which sweep down from the Alleghanies in winter are broken. The Valley of the Shenandoah is often free from snow when the less protected regions adjacent are covered with the white veil of winter.

The Valley railroad now runs from Staunton through Harrisonburg, Strasburg, and Winchester, to Harper's Ferry, at the confluence of the Potomac and Shenandoah rivers. I made the journey from Staunton to Harrisonburg, twenty-five miles, in a stage, before the railway was completed. The route stretches through a rich, farming country, studded with fine square, antique mansions surrounded with tall trees. The roads are excellent; the fields are divided by walls of the limestone which abounds thereabout, and are well cultivated. Harrisonburg is an old-fashioned Virginian town which has awakened into activity since the railroad reached it; the citizens are anxious to join in the efforts to make a "New Virginia" out of the "Old Dominion." The Shenandoah valley felt the shock of war as keenly as any section of the South. It was overrun by the contending armies; exhausted by the repeated foraging expeditions of Confederates and Federals; and at the close of the contest its inhabitants were pretty thoroughly discouraged.

Half-way between Staunton and the Potomac river two ranges of mountains run parallel for twenty-five miles, finally uniting in Massanutten

Buffalo Gap and the Iron-Furnace. [Page 660.]

mountain, which separates the branches of the Shenandoah river, and ends abruptly to the southward in Rockingham county. These parallel ranges hold between them "Luray," a charming valley which was the theatre of many of the exploits of Stonewall Jackson early in the war, and through which Sheridan campaigned later, leaving devastation in his train. Through the gaps the Confederates kept up communication with the forces on the lower lands of Northern Virginia, along the Rapidan and the Rappahannock.

At Strasburg, one of the prettiest towns in the valley, one gets a fine view of the Massanutten range, whose steep wooded sides seem inaccessible. The Virginians still point with pride to the pass through which Stonewall Jackson withdrew his army when closely pressed by McDowell and Fremont in 1862. The wily General saw that the Federals were determined, if possible, to capture him, so he led his hosts through the upper valley, and speedily placed the Massanutten ridge between his army and the enemy, his guides finding paths along the precipices where none but natives of the region could possibly have discovered them.

Winchester is one of the oldest towns in the valley, and has, since the earliest settlements there, been an important trade centre. It is the chief town of a region rich in historic souvenirs and beautiful scenery. Washington made it his head-quarters when commanding the army of operations against the French and Indians in 1756. Lord Fairfax and General Morgan were both buried there. Not far from Winchester, on the lower Opequan, is Traveler's Rest, whither General Horatio Gates retired after his disgrace at the battle of Camden. Leetown, still nearer Winchester, was long the home of another fallen General, Charles Lee, who conducted himself so badly at the battle of Monmouth that he received a stinging reproof from the lips of Washington. Lee and Gates were fond of each other's company, but rarely visited any of their neighbors. The former lived and died a sceptic. The skirmishes and battles around Winchester in which Jackson, Banks, Ewell and Sheridan, played important roles, are still talked of.

Returning to Staunton, and continuing along the line of the Chesapeake and Ohio railroad, the traveler will pass through a remarkable cleft in the mountains known as Buffalo Gap. It is a passage between tall cliffs which seem to have been rent asunder by earthquake or lightning stroke, and through it the buffaloes once passed in their annual migrations. Here some Baltimore capitalists have erected

Elizabeth Iron-Furnace, Virginia. [Page 661.]

an iron furnace, and six miles distant, at the ore bank of Elizabeth Furnace, rich seams of brown hematite may be seen. A little beyond this is the highest point reached by the railroad between the Chesapeake and Ohio rivers, 2,073 feet above the tide. To the west are the numerous Pasture rivers, variously known as the Cow Pasture, the Bull Pasture, the Big Calf Pasture, and the Little Calf Pasture, and Jackson's river, which are the principal sources of the James. Goshen, on the "Big Calf Pasture" river, is the point of departure for the town of Lexington, for the Natural Bridge, for the Cold Sulphur and Rockbridge Alum Springs, and for the Rockbridge Baths.

The Alum Spring—Rockbridge Alum Springs, Virginia.

Rockbridge Alum Springs, one of the most celebrated of Virginian watering-places, is in the northern portion of Rockbridge county, seventeen miles from Lexington, and is now easily reached by an eight-mile ride in a stage-coach southward from Goshen. The springs lie in a shallow basin between pretty mountain ridges. From beneath slate-stone arches issue five fountains, whose waters have proven efficacious in a variety of chronic ailments. A pretty hotel stands at the base of a high mountain; the lawns are girdled with neat cottages, secluded among the trees. The waters contain, in common with the alum which gives the Springs their name, protoxide of iron, sodium, potash, lime, magnesia and ammonia, and sulphuric, carbonic, chloric, and silicic acids. The invalid who is tired of the

The Military Institute—Lexington, Virginia. [Page 662.]

glare and bustle of the crowded Northern spring resorts can find at the "Rockbridge Alum" absolute tranquillity and the charms of a virgin forest within a mile from his hotel. The Rockbridge Baths, near the North river, are richly impregnated with iron, and are so buoyant with carbonic acid gas that the bather floats without effort in the refreshing waters.

Lexington, twenty miles from the Rockbridge Alum Springs, is filled with solemn memorials for Virginians. From the Military Institute* there, the "West Point" of the Old Dominion, went out some of the best talent engaged in the service of the Confederacy; three of its professors and one hundred and twenty-five of its alumni were killed, and three hundred and fifty of the graduates of the institution were maimed in the war. The grave of "Stonewall" Jackson, who left the peaceful retreat of his college home to fight for his State against the Union, is in the Presbyterian burying-ground. Above the simple mound a board

Washington and Lee College — Lexington, Virginia.

headstone, painted in imitation of marble, is now the only memorial of the brave General's resting-place; but latterly an effort has been made to secure funds for the erection of a memorial chapel, at the Institute where he was for fourteen years a professor, to perpetuate his memory. The Institute was destroyed in 1864 by the Federal troops, but has succeeded in securing new buildings and re-establishing itself completely without demanding the aid of a dollar from the State treasury. In a commonwealth where military discipline and training are considered as indispensable parts of a general education, the Institute is a great power, and will, doubtless, in future, be fostered and encouraged by the State. Since the war it has extended the benefits of its course to pupils from all the States of the Union.

* The Virginia Military Institute was organized in 1839 as a State military and scientific school, on the basis of the U. S. Military Academy at West Point.

"Washington," or, as it is now called, "Washington and Lee College," also located at Lexington, is one of the oldest literary institutions in the South. It was established as an academy in 1776, by the Hanover Presbytery, which then embraced the whole of the Presbyterian Church in Virginia, and was christened Liberty Hall. In 1796 it obtained its first regular endowment at the hands of Washington. The Father of his Country had received from the Legislature, as a testimony of gratitude for his services, some shares in what was then known as the "James River Improvement." He was unwilling to accept them for his private gain, and therefore presented them to "Liberty Hall." This generous act induced the trustees to change the name of the academy

Portrait of General Thomas J. Jackson, known as "Stonewall Jackson.
[From an engraving owned by M. Knoedler & Co., N.Y.]

to "Washington," and it kept it when it became a college. Rockbridge county gave birth to McCormick, the noted inventor of the reaping-machine. He has furnished the money to build an astronomical observatory at Washington and Lee College, and the Peabody Fund has also given the institution a generous sum.

After the fall of the Confederacy, General Robert E. Lee took the presidency of the college, which before the war had rarely gathered more than a hundred students at a time within its walls. The fame of the soldier-president, and the affection of the Southern people for him, brought the number up to five, and sometimes seven hundred. General Lee held the presidency of the college until his death, on the 11th of October, 1870. The name of the institution was then changed to Washington Lee, and George Washington Custis Lee, a son of the deceased General, is now president of the institution.

The University Chapel, in the basement of which are the tombs of General Lee and his wife, is a plain brick building, with an auditorium capable of holding from eight hundred to a thousand persons. The basement is built of gray Virginia limestone blocks, large and rough. The building was planned and its

General Robert Edward Lee, born January 19, 1801; died October 11, 1870.

erection superintended by General Lee himself. It is unfinished, from lack of funds. At the time of General Lee's death the basement was used as a library, and near it was the General's private office, which remains exactly as he left it when he went out of it for the last time. After his death the trustees and faculty of the University appropriated the basement as a place of sepulture for the Lee family. A vault or pit was dug, and walled and cemented in the middle of the large room formerly used as a library. The burial case containing the

The Great Natural Arch—Clifton Forge, Jackson's River. [Page 668.]

General's remains was placed in this vault, and over it were laid two strata of marble slabs, on the upper of which is the following simple inscription:

GEN. ROBERT EDWARD LEE,
Born
Jan. 19, 1801;
Died
Oct. 11, 1870.

The wife and daughter of the great Confederate chieftain, who speedily followed him to rest, repose beside him. Around the graves of General and Mrs. Lee there is a railing of black walnut, and some dark cloth hangings extend from the tops of the corner-posts to the ceilings above. The present surroundings will remain only until the monument, or sarcophagus, now in preparation by the sculptor Valentine, of Richmond, is finished. When that is completed, the whole basement will be modeled into a "Memorial Room," where as now, one of the students of the University will each day stand guard as a "watcher at the tomb." The monument will cost fifteen thousand dollars.

The railroad route from Goshen to White Sulphur Springs, the famous watering-place in the West Virginia mountains, is lined on either hand with exquisite scenery. It extends through Rockbridge, Bath, and Alle-

Beaver Dam Falls. [Page 668.]

ghany counties, entering, in the latter, the mountain or Appalachian belt of country, which has a width of from twenty to fifty miles, and is very equally divided between the States of Virginia and West Virginia. In the twenty counties—ten on each side of the State line—included in this region, there was, in 1870, a population of only 148,509 persons, or twenty to the square mile. Hundreds of thousands of acres of dense forest still clothe the mountain-sides; hickory, all varieties of the oak, wild cherry, spruce, pine, black walnut, ash, chestnut, all abound; finely-timbered land being held at from $10 to $25 per

Falling Springs Falls, Virginia. [Page 667.]

acre. All the slopes and hill-sides and the table-lands are covered with a rich and mellow soil that gives a fine yield, when properly cultivated, of wheat, corn, oats, potatoes, and all root crops. Mr. Howell Fisher, a Pennsylvania iron-master, who has carefully studied this Appalachian belt, says that cattle and sheep "fatten and flourish on the herbage and undergrowth without other food, and with literally no care." The opening of a railroad through this region has made it one of the most desirable in the two Virginias. On the extensive plateaus between the depressions formed by the washing of the streams there are fine grazing and orchard-lands, and millions of acres, now held as wild lands, are available for field culture, vineyards, or sheep pasturing, and can be purchased for trifling sums.

A little beyond Goshen the rail penetrates the rocky pass of Panther Gap, so called because the early settlers found to their sorrow that panthers loved to disport therein. From North mountain to the Alleghanies the scenery is wildly beautiful. Ravines, hill-sides, with ragged forests, log cabins beside rushing streams, vistas of perfect valleys, the high peak of Griffith's Knob, blue outlines of massive mountains, charm the eye. The "Cow Pasture" river flows beside the tracks for some distance, then disappears among the hills. From Millboro' one may take stage for the "Warm Springs," fifteen miles away, in a lovely valley in Bath county. At the lower end of this valley is the famous "Cataract of the Falling Springs," where a stream flowing down from the "Warm Spring" mountain falls over a rock two hundred feet high, jeweling with its many cascades the bright grasses and ferns below. The view from Warm Spring mountain is accounted one of the most beautiful in Virginia, and not far from it, on the banks of the Cow Pasture river, is the "Blowing Cave," from which such a current of air constantly comes that the weeds for twenty feet in front of the cavern are prostrated. The Hot and Healing Springs are but a few miles from the Warm Springs valley.

Griffith's Knob, and Cow Pasture River.

At Millboro' for many years the trains of the Virginia Central railway crossed a yawning ravine by means of a temporary track, running down one slope and up the other at a grade of hundreds of feet to the mile. But when the Consolidated railroad line was completed, this ravine was filled up, and the occupation of "Mac," the old engine driver, whose locomotive, "Mountain Climber," used to push the trains up the hill, was gone. The artist has rescued him from oblivion.

At Clifton Forge, where Jackson's river rushes through a gorge, to unite with the many bright streams flowing down to form the James, a mighty arch of a half-mile chord, and a thousand feet to the keystone, is visible on the mountain-side. In this defile the clink of hammers on the anvils of numerous forges was once heard; but only the walls of the buildings, overgrown with vines, remain. The James River and Kanawha canal is one day to have a channel here, and the wild loneliness and romance of the place will then be gone.

Covington, a sprightly town on Jackson's river, is a favorite point of departure from the railroad for the Hot and Healing Springs. On the road leading from it to the Sweet Springs, the clear waters of a little creek come rushing from a rocky cleft at Beaver Dam with a noise and patter far exceeding Lodore, which Mr. Southey made so many rhymes about; and with picturesqueness of dark green in the foliage, and brilliant refractions and reflections of broken sunlight in the descending drops.

Clay Cut, Chesapeake and Ohio Railroad.

At Covington one is confronted by the Alleghanies. Here, more than two hundred miles from Richmond, a city was once laid out, but it has never grown beyond the dimensions of a village. Covington was to have been the western terminus of the Virginia Central railroad, and the canal was to have been extended to this point. A road was to have been built from it to the Ohio by the State of Virginia, and the products of the mines and fields of the West were to be reshipped at Covington. This was a part of the internal improvement system which the Old Dominion was inaugurating when the war came. The great fight over, Virginia found that she had no funds with which to carry on the important enterprise, and offered all that had been done in improvements from Rich-

"Mac, the Pusher." [Page 667.]

mond to the Ohio river to any company that would complete the task. Both Virginia and West Virginia readily agreed upon a harmonious policy with regard to the line, and the Chesapeake and Ohio Company finished the road on the terms offered by the two commonwealths.

Jerry's Run.

At Jerry's Run a mighty ravine has been carved and cut away, to allow the road a passage among the mountains. For miles the roadway is carried over a succession of artificial embankments and through long cuttings in the crags. The train traverses the ravine so high above the stream that the water looks like a silver thread stretched through the valley. Then, at an elevation of more than two thousand feet above the level of the sea, the road passes under the mountains by the "Alleghany Tunnel," and gradually descends toward the "Greenbrier White Sulphur," the most noted of Southern watering-places.

LXXIV.

GREENBRIER WHITE SULPHUR SPRINGS—FROM THE "WHITE SULPHUR" TO KANAWHA VALLEY—THE MINERAL SPRINGS REGION.

THE White Sulphur Springs are situated on Howard's creek, in Greenbrier county, West Virginia, and on the western slope of the Appalachian mountain chain, which separates the waters that flow into Chesapeake bay from those

Scene on the Greenbrier River in Western Virginia.

that empty into the Mississippi. On the south is Kates' mountain; on the west the Greenbrier range, and northward and eastward, at a distance of five miles from the springs, the Alleghanies tower in lovely confusion. The valley in which the springs lie is one of the most beautiful in the mountain region of the South. It is planted with great numbers of noble and finely-grown trees, and in early autumn the leaves of the maple, the hickory, the oak, the chestnut, the sweet gum, and the pine, vie in color with the gay toilets in which the Southern belles clothe themselves for the final hops and "Germans" of the season. The lawn around which the cottages are grouped is rich in foliage; in the hottest days of summer, when the lifeless atmosphere of Richmond seems like a curse suspended over the heads of the citizens, the air is cool and delightful at the "White Sulphur."

The Hotel and Lawn at Greenbrier White Sulphur Springs, West Virginia.

All the region round about was once a hunting ground of the Shawnee Indians, who knew the Greenbrier valley as one of the most frequented "licks" of the deer and the elk. The valley takes its name from the river, which was christened by old Colonel John Lewis, an early explorer, who once became entangled in a brier-thicket on the banks while exploring, and vowed that he would ever after call the stream Greenbrier. Toward the close of the last century, the Indians often brought those of their number afflicted with difficult diseases to the valley, where the unfortunates were speedily cured by drinking the water and bathing in it.

But in those days there were no roads; the Indians were far from friendly, and our revolutionary fathers had neither the time nor the money to spend in improving the beautiful resort. The Virginia planters learned of its charms, and as early as 1818 the tract was somewhat improved; but it was not until 1837 that the White Sulphur Spring Company was formed by a number of Virginians, who made the place what it is to-day. They erected a mammoth hotel covering an acre of ground; surrounded it at a convenient distance with neat cottages, built upon terraces, on the hill-sides and on the borders of the lawns; laid out serpentine walks, and gave the hitherto crude valley the aspect of a fashionable watering-place. The springs had been frequented, up to the date of these changes, almost exclusively by Southern people. The planters from the lowlands came in their carriages, attended by troops of servants, scattering plenty in their path; money flowed like water during the two or three months of the season; and when the merry company departed a wail of anguish went up from the mountaineers, who saw their golden harvest checked for a twelvemonth. During the war the place was alternately a Federal and a Confederate headquarters. The cavalry of both armies clattered over the mountain roads, leaving destruction behind them. But the growth of railway enterprise in Virginia, during the last dozen years, has given the watering-place a railroad; and the lawns, the springs, and the mountain roads of the White Sulphur are rapidly gaining a national reputation.

It must have been a tedious journey to the valley in the days of stage-coaches and private carriages, for the springs lie in a difficult mountain region. The Chesapeake and Ohio Railroad Company had to build some of its highest trestles, and dig some of its longest tunnels, within a few miles of "White Sulphur." At one point between Staunton and the springs, the tunnels, within a few minutes' ride of each other, aggregate more than two miles in length. One of them, called the "Big Bend," is 6,400 feet long.

The Eastern Portal of Second Creek Tunnel, Chesapeake and Ohio Railroad.

Now-a-days, however, the traveler may ensconce himself in his berth in a luxurious sleeping-car at Richmond in the evening, and awaken at White Sulphur in the morning, just as the first breakfast bell is warning the sleepy ladies to prepare for their conquests of the forenoon. The journey from Washington to White Sulphur occupies but fifteen hours.

From July until September the season is at its height. The trains bring hundreds of passengers every evening; the cottages and hotels, as well as the few surrounding farm-houses, are crowded. The lawns are dotted with sprightly parties, representing the society of every Southern, and latterly of most of the Northern and Western States. The "hotel" is a remarkable structure, resembling the "Kursaal" at the German baths rather than the vast palaces in which the habitués of Saratoga dance, flirt, eat, and sleep in the season. It is amply provided with long and solid verandas, with a huge ball-room and a colossal reception parlor. Between ball-room and parlor is a dining-room three hundred feet long, in which twelve hundred guests may at once be seated. There are but few rooms for lodgers in the hotel. From the cottages on Alabama, Louisiana, Paradise, Baltimore, Virginia, Georgia, Wolf, and Bachelor rows, or on Broadway, or in the "Colonnade," or on "Virginia Lawn," or at the "Spring," the belles come skipping across the green sward to dinner, attired in full evening dress. There are never a dozen carriages at the White Sulphur during the season. There is no whirl and glitter of ambitious equipages, the whole life and charm of the society being concentrated in the mammoth building called the hotel. At early morning the par-

A Mountain Ride in a Stage-Coach. [Page 675.]

lor is filled with ladies who make their engagements for the day, and with the customary rows of invalids who chat cheerily, or listen to the music of the pianos or the band upon the lawn. After breakfast there are sometimes from five hundred to a thousand persons gathered in the parlor, promenading for an hour, after which the crowd separates into small parties, who linger on the verandas, or under the oaks, or along the shaded paths in that famous resort known as the "Lovers' Walk," where hundreds of hearts have been broken.

As the hour for the evening meal, dinner or tea, according to the visitors' taste, approaches, the parlor is once more crowded. At dinner an army of four hundred waiters skillfully supplies the guests with food. The scene is novel and dazzling. Hundreds of beautiful girls from every part of the South, clad in ball-room costume, are seated at the round tables in the long hall. The dark-haired, languishing Creole of Louisiana is contrasted with the robust and bewitching Kentucky belle; the delicate blonde of Richmond chats amicably with the stately Mississippian; the lovely Baltimore ladies twirl their fans and frown defiance at Northern beaux; the sparkling belles of Charleston and the pretty mountain maids from the West Virginian capital may be seen side by side. The West and the East, the South and the North seem to have forgotten their sectional bickerings, and to have come together in friendliest mood. Ex-Generals of the Confederate army—Beauregard, Johnston, the Lees—chat amicably with United States Senators from the North and West; men who would gladly have flown at each other's throats a few years ago now reviewing the war with utmost calm. The South sends its best representatives to the White Sulphur Springs every year, and the result is a delightful, unostentatious, cultured society. The "hops" and the Germans given by the fashionable Philadelphia and New York ladies are the only dissipations; neither regattas, nor horse-races, nor tumultuous tumbling in surf distract one. Every morning the groups gather in the pavilion, under which the sulphur water bubbles up from the spring; the young ladies make the wonted wry faces over the unsavory beverage; while the venerable planters from the lowlands, with many a thought upon their damaged livers and yellow faces, swallow the fluid as if it were nectar.

"Greenbrier White Sulphur," as the Southerners call it, is a pleasure resort. Not one-tenth of the throng which crowds cottages and hotel in the season comes to regain its health. It comes rather to rejoice in a superabundance of life and vigor. But the waters are singularly efficacious in many obstinate diseases.[*] As an alterative they have no superior. The effect of a free use of the

---

[*] The White Sulphur Water was analyzed in 1842, by Professor Hayes, of Boston, with the following results:

"Fifty thousand grains (about seven pints) of the water contain, in solution, 3.633 water-grain measures of gaseous matter, or about 1.14 of its volume, consisting of—

Nitrogen gas	1.013
Oxygen gas	.108
Carbonic acid	2.444
Hydro-sulphuric acid	.068
	3.633

"One gallon, or 237 cubic inches, of the water, contains 16.739-1000 cubic inches of gas, having the proportion of—

Nitrogen gas	4.680
Oxygen gas	.498
Carbonic acid	11.290
Hydro-sulphuric acid	.271
	16.739

"Fifty thousand grains of this water contain 115.735-1000 grains of saline matter consisting of—

Sulphate of lime	67.168
Sulphate of magnesia	30.364
Chloride of magnesium	.859
Carbonate of lime	6.060
Organic matter (dried at 212° F.)	3.740
Carbonic acid	4.584
Silicates (silica 1.34, potash .18, soda .66, and a trace of oxide of iron)	2.960
	115.735 "

waters much resembles that produced by mercury, without any of the disagreeable contingencies attendant on the employment of that medicine. The sulphur baths, which constitute one of the attractions of the place even for well people, are admirably kept. A visit to the spring, a bath, and a horseback ride among the mountains, or a walk along "Dry Creek" before breakfast, will certainly fit one for the fatigues of the merry "evening," even if there be a "German" which lasts until daybreak.

Within a radius of forty miles from the Greenbrier White Sulphur lies the most interesting portion of the Virginia Springs region. Northward are those already mentioned, the Hot, the Warm, the Healing, and the Alum Springs. Seventeen miles eastward from the White Sulphur are the Sweet Springs; twenty-four miles to the south the Salt Sulphur; forty-one miles to the south the Red Sulphur; and twenty-two miles to the west the Blue Sulphur. At all these springs fine hotels have been built, and as the season wanes at one it waxes at another, so that one may make a jolly round for three or four months.

Anvil Rock, Greenbrier River.

At some of these resorts the furnishings of the cottages are primitive, and one sadly misses the elegance of city life; but the natural beauties and the delicious atmosphere amply compensate for all other deficiencies. Although most of the Springs are now either directly accessible by rail, or within easy distance of the railroads, it is the fashion to make the tour in such a stage as our artist has given a picture of, although the passes in the mountains are rarely as rough as they are depicted in the engraving. Many parties adjourn to the Old Sweet Springs after the season at the Greenbrier is over, stopping on the way for picnics. The "Old Sweet" always has a company of distinguished guests. It is located in a charming valley in the eastern part of Monroe county, with the high Sweet Spring mountain on the south, and the Alleghanies only a mile away. The buildings are elegant and commodious; the lawns as beauti-

A West Virginia "Countryman."

ful and richly studded with trees as those in the Greenbrier valley. The baths are frequented from dawn until dusk by crowds who represent the best talent of the West and South. The predominance of carbonic acid in the waters of these springs induces physicians to recommend invalids who have been drinking the White Sulphur water for some time to try those of the "Old Sweet" for perfecting and fixing the cure already reasonably well established.

The Red Sweet Spring, situated but one mile from the Old Sweet, is one of the prettiest retreats in the mountains. The chalybeate and tonic waters annu-

A Freighters' Camp, West Virginia. [Page 679.]

ally draw hundreds of visitors to them. The Salt Sulphur, shut in among the mountains near the town of Union, has three springs, one of which is called the "Iodine," and is strongly recommended for chronic affections of the brain, and for nervous diseases. The Red Sulphur, in the southern portion of Monroe county, is romantically situated on Indian creek, in a deep ravine to which the traveler descends along the side of a picturesque mountain. The waters of this spring have been found a powerful adjunct in the management of difficult cases of phthisis and consumption. At the "Blue Sulphur" a spacious hotel, a beautiful lawn, and a fine establishment of medicated baths are the attractions grouped about the spring, which is covered by an imposing temple.*

The Northerner is especially welcome at all these watering-places. There is none of the bitterness and occasional small spite manifested toward him which he might perhaps encounter in some of the Southern capitals. The courtesy and hospitality of the Virginians are proverbial; their frankness and kindliness toward strangers are shown in their best light at the "Springs." The subject of politics is pretty thoroughly eschewed at White Sulphur during the season, except when the President goes there to hear what the Southern politicians have to say, or when some injudicious relict of the late war utters something fiery at a reunion or a convention. The whole company of distinguished Southerners at White

"The rude cabin built beneath the shadow of a huge rock." [Page 679.]

Sulphur, in 1873, condemned the bitter and hostile speech made by Jefferson Davis at a meeting of the Southern Historical Society at the "Montgomery White" that season. The Northern or Western man at these springs is never likely to hear disagreeable sentiments unless he provokes them by illiberality on his own part. He will find the Southern people assembled there amply able to take a fair and dispassionate view of our national politics. Gentlemen of culture and refinement will show him how possible it was for the South to believe that it was right in the war. But all will convince him that they are much more interested in the material development of the Southern States than in quarreling over

* See appendix for complete table of routes in and about the Virginia Springs region.

old issues. Leading politicians will now and then intimate that some day the Southern State Constitutions will be amended; and from this it will be easy to perceive that the South is not yet reconciled to reconstruction.

The Springs region of Virginia seems likely to become a favorite meeting-ground for Northern and Southern people. As soon as the Chesapeake and Ohio railroad was opened to the Ohio river, Cincinnati sent a large quota of visitors to the "Greenbrier White Sulphur," and the Virginians have found, much to their surprise, that there is a fair share of culture and manners at the West. The free and friendly intercourse between citizens of the different sections, which has been the result of yearly visits to the charming resorts in the mountains of Virginia and West Virginia, cannot fail to have an influence for good in their future political relations. The wild life of the mountaineers, and the strange humors and habits of the negroes scattered through the Springs region, offer an interesting study to the visitor from the North and West. The country

"The rustic mill built of logs." [Page 679.]

in the vicinity of the White Sulphur Springs has many prosperous farms; fine cattle are to be seen in the fields; the grazing is excellent the year round.

West Virginia does not bear the aspect of a slave State; its farms have the same thoroughly cultured and well-kept appearance as those at the North. But few slaves were owned in the mountain region; the wealthy families had some house-servants who, as a rule, still remain with them. The negroes who come to these mountain regions from the lowlands seem to thrive. They proved themselves one of the most useful laboring forces that could be employed in the building of the new railroad. They were endowed with vigorous health, were easily managed, sober, and quick to learn. The beautiful Greenbrier river flows downward from Greenbrier mountain

The Junction of Greenbrier and New Rivers.

through Pocahontas, Greenbrier, and Monroe counties, to unite with the New river, which rises in North Carolina, and courses through some of the most romantic mountain scenery in West Virginia, until it meets and joins with the Great Kanawha river at the entrance of the famous Kanawha valley. Along the Greenbrier and New rivers adventurous boatmen ply in "batteaux," carrying merchandise or travelers who wish to explore the wonders of the New River cañon. The lofty and thickly-wooded hills; the vales carpeted with flowers and overhung by giant trees; the camps of the "freighters" who transport goods over the rough roads along or near the banks; the rustic mill built of logs, and insecurely set beside some treacherous hill-side stream; the rude cabin beneath the shade of a huge rock; and the types of "countryman," inquisitive and suspicious—all are strangely interesting, and amply repay the traveler for the fatigues of the journey.

Our artists, who made the tour of the New river cañon in a batteau, found it an exciting experience. At the junction of the Greenbrier and New rivers they engaged one of the boats used in running the rapids. This boat was sixty feet long

Descending the New River Rapids.

by six wide, and was managed by three negroes,—the "steersman," who guided the boat with a long and powerful oar; the headsman, who stood on the bow to direct the steersman by waving his arms; and an extra hand, who assisted with an oar in the eddies and smooth parts of the river. The merry artists not only found time for exciting scrambles along the rocky banks, in search of pictures, but even when descending the New River rapids managed to obtain the necessary notes from which to give the world a faithful representation of the event.

The country near the junction of the Greenbrier with the New river literally stands on end. The people live on hill-slopes so steep that the horses can hardly keep their footing when they plough; and it is sometimes said that the farmers in the cañon stand on one bank and shoot their seed corn into the field on the other from a rifle.

The New River cañon is one of the most remarkable natural wonders of the eastern portion of the United States. It is a deep crack in the earth, a hundred miles long, a mile wide at the summit, from eight to fifteen hundred feet deep, and traversed at its bottom by a turbulent stream. The railroad builders found this cañon practicable for the passage of their route. They blasted out fragments of rock until they had made a shelf along the perpendicular rocky side of the cañon. Entering this strange gorge by train, one scarcely realizes that he is hundreds of feet below the level of the surrounding country. The scenery is grand. The journey along the rocky shelf, whence one can look upon the enormous masses of stone hurled down to make room for the track, or look up to the streams of water flowing from the sides of the cliffs, is an experience never to be forgotten.

But there is one remarkable characteristic of the cañon which the traveler through it by rail or in batteau will notice with care. He will observe that the stratification of the rocks is very singular; that they lie evidently as they were deposited; that there has been no upheaval, no disorganization. The earth has simply been cracked asunder, and the traveler is able to enter, without difficulty, a coal-shaft which is open to the sunlight, and through which a railroad runs.

A coal-shaft? Yes; out of the high bank a coal-seam crops. In some places many seams are visible. The railroad has here and there cut through veins of the best cânnel coal, and the miner has only to dig into the mountain. The mine drains itself, and the precious mineral is dumped directly into cars which carry it to Richmond. In 1871 it was impossible to ride through this cañon on horseback. Now it is as easily accessible as any manufacturing town in the North. The coal and limestone in this New River valley lie within a hundred miles of some of the richest and most important deposits of iron ore in the United States.

A hard road for artists to travel.

LXXV.

THE KANAWHA VALLEY—MINERAL WEALTH OF WESTERN VIRGINIA.

EMERGING from the New River cañon, one reaches the Great Falls of the Kanawha, a stream formed by the junction of the New and Gauley rivers. The country surrounding was the scene during the late war of much strife between the Federal Rosecrans and Wise and other Confederate officers. A few miles from Kanawha Falls, in the direction of Greenbrier White Sulphur, the "Hawk's Nest," an imposing bluff rising a thousand feet above the bed of the New river, frowns upon the railroad. From this height, to which a winding path leads, one may look down over perfect valleys, unsurpassed by those of Rhine or Moselle. The scene at Miller's Ferry, where the stream winds through deep recesses in the hills, is one of the most sublime in the South. The "Richmond" and "Big Dowdy" Falls on the New river, and "Whitcomb's Boulder," in this vicinity, are worthy of the traveler's attention.

The "Hawk's Nest," from Boulder Point.

The Kanawha and Ohio valley, or trans-Appalachian region, which lies along the western foot slopes of the Alleghany range, has an area of seventeen thousand five hundred square miles in West Virginia. Most of this area is seamed with wonderful strata of bituminous, splint, and cannel coal. Its agricultural advantages also are considerable, tobacco, corn, and root crops paying well. As a live-stock country, this valley resembles the "blue-grass" lands of Kentucky, which join it on the west. The farmers are industrious, intelligent, and reasonably prosperous.

But the mineral wealth of the Kanawha valley now usurps all the attention directed to that quarter. The coal-measures there actually cover sixteen thousand square miles. They make their appearance at the surface, in the New River and Kanawha valleys, to the number of fourteen distinct strata, "with an aggregate thickness in some places of one hundred feet, more than half of which is in workable seams from three to eight feet thick." The coal crops out on the hill-sides, high above the water and railroad levels, allowing easy and inexpensive excavation. The testimony of Mr. Howell Fisher upon this point is as follows:

Great Kanawha Falls. [Page 681.]

Miller's Ferry, seen from the Hawk's Nest.

"In respect to conditions most essential to cheap and profitable working, this region stands unrivaled. The chasm of the river renders it most peculiar service in its relation to the coal. Cutting all the coal strata for nearly its whole length entirely through, and getting down among the shales under the coal, the river has caused the numerous streams which pierce the whole coal region to cut down through most of the coal-bearing strata on their courses, leaving the coal entirely above water-level, accessible at hundreds of points by simply scraping off the surface soil, so that, as far as the mere getting of coal is concerned, two thousand dollars will open a mine ready to ship one thousand tons per week. There is no region in the world where less physical labor will prepare a mine for the delivery of coal at the drift's mouth.

"This will be made clearer by a comparison of the position of coal here and in Great Britain in this respect. In Great Britain, and in fact in almost all of the European coal-fields, the coal is deep below the water-level. To reach the seams requires the expenditure of years of labor and vast sums of money in sinking shafts or pits, and in erecting pumping and hoisting machinery, to be maintained and renewed at heavy annual expense. It is authoritatively stated that the cost of sinking shafts in the Newcastle region of England to the depth of one thousand feet, has been, in many instances, one thousand dollars per yard. In the great Northern coal-field of Great Britain, producing twenty million tons per annum, there are two hundred pits or shafts, costing, in first outlay,

Richmond Falls, New River. [Page 681.]

for sinking and machinery, fifty millions of dollars, to which must be added the necessary expense of constructing and maintaining proper air-courses, and their accessories requisite to the safety of the employés.

"Now in this great Kanawha coal-field nature has already sunk all the necessary pits and shafts, which need neither repair, renewal, nor labor to work them. The laws of gravity have provided the most perfect, permanent, and costless pumping machinery; and the ventilation of the mine and safety of the employés, instead of requiring scientific knowledge and anxious thought, is simply a matter of the most ordinary care, the freedom from noxious gases being the natural result of the position of the coal strata."

There is coal enough along the line of the railroads and rivers in this favored section to supply the American market for several centuries. Professor Ansted, of England, explored this region nearly a quarter of a century ago, and gave his testimony at a meeting of the Society of Arts in London, two or three years since, that "there was no coal-field more important than that of Virginia;

none where the coal-seams were more accessible or of a better quality. The coal-fields in the Appalachian range were nearly all horizontal, intersected by convenient valleys, could be worked from numerous points at the same time with ease, and might be looked upon as inexhaustible."

Big Dowdy Falls, near New River. [Page 681.]

Professor Hotchkiss, of Staunton, Virginia, in a paper on the Resources of the State, speaks as follows of the Kanawha coal-field:

"On the eastern border the seams of the lower coal-measures are found, having an exposed aggregate thickness of some fifty feet in the gorge of New river—the line of the Chesapeake and Ohio railway—a cañon from 1,200 to 1,500 feet below the general level of the country. One of these seams is over six feet thick, furnishing a good coking coal; another seam of block coal is four and a-half feet thick. There are several other seams three and four feet in thickness, furnishing bituminous coals of good quality. These seams have only a moderate inclination to the north-west, and are all above the river and railroad-level. These lower measures descend more rapidly than the rivers, and so pass beneath the water-level some fifty miles from their eastern outcrop. The strata of the upper coals come to the horizon as the mouth of New river is approached, and not far below the junction of that river with the Gauley to form the Great Kanawha. At Armstrong's creek, a section in the 600 feet of bluff above the level of the Kanawha shows thirteen seams of coal varying in thickness from two and a-half to nine feet, with an aggregate of sixty-one feet. Below this place, at Cannelton, on the other side of the Kanawha, there are five seams of coal open, in the 1,300 feet of the face of the bluff, aggregating twenty-nine feet. More than 100 feet of stratified coal has been proved here. The seams vary from eight to fourteen feet in thickness, and embrace gas, shop, splint, and cannel varieties. The seam producing the cannel is double, giving four feet of cannel and two and a-half of splint coal. This cannel will yield sixty gallons of oil to the ton of 2,000 lbs. A section on Cabin creek and

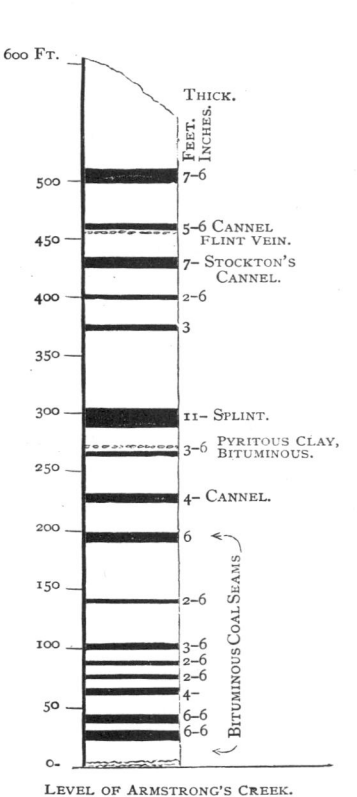

SECTION OF KANAWHA COAL-SEAMS.

Whitcomb's Boulder. [Page 681.]

vicinity, ten miles below Cannelton, by Prof. Ansted, gives sixty-eight feet of coal, in some thirteen seams, varying from two and a-half to eleven feet; twenty-two feet of these seams are cannel and from seven to eleven splint coal. At Campbell's creek, still lower down the river, in the 400 feet of bluff, are six seams, from four and a-half to six feet thick, that furnish twenty-nine feet of coal. This coal is peculiar in its formation. Near Clay Court-House, on Elk river, the coal strata are from four and a-half to eleven feet thick, making forty-one feet of coal in the 500 feet of bluff; nineteen feet of the coal being splint and six cannel. At the mouth of Coal river a stratum of coal, from four to eight feet thick, is found at a depth of 300 feet; of course the other seams are found there also, but at greater depths. These may be considered fair samples of the sections throughout this great coal-field, ample enough to satisfy the wants of untold generations, and so accessible as to require no special skill in mining; nor expenditure for drainage and ventilation. The Baltimore and Ohio railway, with its Parkersburg and Wheeling arms and numerous branches, now crosses the northern part of this field and opens it to markets. The Chesapeake and Ohio railway has just crossed it in the south, where the Great Miner has 'torn asunder the mountains,' and well and wisely cut an open gangway, more than a thousand feet deep, across the rich strata, exposed them to daylight, and at the same time made way for the railroad, at very low grades, to carry this 'bottled sunshine' to the great markets. The coals found here are used in making iron without coking, and the choice for any special purpose is very great, the quality being unexceptionally good."

Cannelton, mentioned by Professor Hotchkiss, was established by a Rhode Island company, who built works there for the milling of coal into oil. Just as the work was progressing fairly, the oil region of Pennsylvania was discovered, and the proprietors of Cannelton, unable to compete with the flowing wells of Titusville, closed their works, for without transportation facilities their coal was worthless. But with the advent of the railroad came a fortune into their hands, and to-day they let coal down an inclined plane 1,100 feet long from the almost perpendicular side of the mountain, directly into cars waiting on side tracks to receive it.

In previous chapters I have given some idea of the extent of the stores of iron in South-western Virginia and the Piedmont country. The deposits of iron ore are no less remarkable along the line of the Chesapeake and Ohio road. In that part of Piedmont penetrated by this line, there are hematite and magnetic ores of the best quality. In the spurs of the Blue Ridge, near Fisherville, a seam of hematite ores exists, and rich lodes of hematite and specular ores are found running along the foot of the Blue Ridge; at intervals, in the whole breadth of the Shenandoah valley; "and in continuous seams of great thickness along the north and parallel mountains beyond."

The Inclined Plane at Cannelton.

"The mineral wealth of the Blue Ridge," says Professor Hotchkiss, "is great, and destined to be quite important, from its nearness to the sea-board. In the ranges of foot-hills lying along the western base of these mountains, the whole three hundred or more miles of their length, are found very extensive deposits of brown hematite iron ores of the best character, giving from sixty to seventy-five per cent. of metallic iron in the yield of the furnace. It is not correct to say that these deposits are continuous, and yet they have been so regularly found, when sought after, as almost to justify the use of that term. In some places they are deeply buried in the *debris* of the mountain; at others they show themselves as interstratified masses, conforming for long distances to the formations of the district, as near where New river leaves the Ridge, at Radford Furnace, where the stratum is over thirty feet in thickness, while at other places the ore, in a soft state, forms hill-like masses, as at the Shenandoah Iron Works, in Rockingham. At one place in Rockbridge, where the stratification is nearly vertical, striking with the mountain, this one appears as a hard central stratum, forming the crest of a spur more than 600 feet above its base. The western flank of the tableland in the south-west is known as the Iron mountain, from the quantity of this ore there exposed. There are numerous furnaces now in blast, and others are being built along the line of these deposits, making charcoal iron of a high character, such as now readily commands sixty dollars a ton in the United States. One of these had a yield of sixty-five per cent. of iron from the ore put into the furnace in the run of a season. Between these hematites and the main ridge is found a deposit of specular iron-stone."

In the slopes of the North mountain there are numerous lodes or pockets of ore interstratified with limestone. The ore-beds in the western portion of Augusta county, and in one or two adjacent counties in Virginia proper, are very extensive. Their astonishing bulk and their convenient position near the surface have prompted trustworthy experts to declare them among the most remarkable on the continent. From Gordonsville in the Piedmont district, to Huntington on the Ohio river, a distance of three hundred and twenty-five miles by the railway line, there is a constant succession of minerals. All the elements of successful and profitable coal mining and manufacture are there found closely associated. The iron ores are rich and of great variety; the carboniferous limestone is excellent for fluxing purposes, and there are inexhaustible stores of coal. In Greenbrier valley the limestone is bordered by deposits of ore on one side, by coal-measures on the other.*

Fern Spring Branch, a West Virginia Mountain Stream.

* See appendix for article on the Iron of the Virginias.

Charleston, the capital of West Virginia, is pleasantly situated near the confluence of the Elk and Kanawha rivers, in a bold mountain country. A

Charleston, the West Virginia Capital.

steamboat plies between the city and the railroad depot on the steep side of a rocky ledge. The deck hands may any day be seen shoveling coal from a vein in the riverbank into the coal-bunkers of the steamer, and in the hills which overhang the stream veins crop out at points where they can be very easily mined. At the close of the war Charleston was a small village, but its selection as the State capital, and the completion of the Chesapeake and Ohio railroad, gave it a new start. It now has three or four thousand population; a cultured society; one of the best hotels in the South, the Hale House; an elegant State capitol; an opera house; fine structures for schools and churches, and many handsome private mansions. For forty years before the war the people of Charleston were wealthy and cultured. The salt-mills and furnaces along the Kanawha, and the cultivation

The Hale House—Charleston.

of the fertile bottom lands, brought plenty and prosperity. But no farmer or land-owner ever thought of opening coal mines—of developing the riches which they daily trampled under their feet. Even to-day the old-school farmers seem hardly to appreciate the value of their mineral lands, and show a decided disinclination to develop them. When they can get what they consider a good price, they will gladly sell; but they cannot be induced to risk much of their own capital in mining. Charleston is the central point and the most convenient outlet for five great sections of Western Virginia, all of which in a few years will doubtless be provided with railroads. There is no city within one hundred miles of it which can become a rival in the lumber, coal, salt, and manufacturing interests

Rafts of Saw-Logs on a West Virginia River.

of the Kanawha, Elk, and Coal River valleys. The lumber trade along the Elk river is very important; hundreds of rafts are floated down that stream to the mouth of the Kanawha, and thence into the Ohio. A single company sends twelve hundred thousand bushels of coal down the Coal river annually. The Elk River railroad will soon connect Charleston with Pittsburg and the East, and the Parkersburg, Ripley and Charleston road is an important route recently projected. Manufactures are creeping into the West Virginia capital. It begins to assume the thrifty and active appearance of a New England city. On the banks of the Kanawha there are many pleasant towns, rapidly increasing in population. Prominent among them are Point Pleasant, Buffalo, Raymond City, Winfield, St. Albans, Brownstown, Coalburg and Cannelton.

The completion of the James River and Kanawha canal would undoubtedly aid immensely in the development of the resources of the Kanawha valley. The canal is now completed from Richmond to Buchanan, 197 miles, leaving a gap of 303

The Snow Hill Salt Works, on the Kanawha River.

miles yet to be built between that point and the mouth of the Kanawha. The importance to Virginia and the Western States of a line of cheap water transportation from the Ohio river to the Chesapeake bay can hardly be overestimated.

The salt region tributary to Charleston extends from that place fifteen miles on either side up the Kanawha river. The annual product from the wells in the region is about two million bushels. It might readily be increased to twenty. The Snow Hill furnace, owned by Dr. Hale, of Charleston, is one of the largest in the world, and in 1870 produced more than four hundred thousand bushels of excellent salt.* This important interest and

Indian Mound, near St. Albans [Page 691.]

* At the Snow Hill works the brine is drawn from nine wells, each from eight hundred to one thousand feet deep. They are bored through about three hundred feet of sandstone, below which the brine is found. From forty-five to fifty gallons make a bushel of salt. Attached to the salt works is a bromine factory, where a hundred pounds of this odorous drug are daily made. The coal used for fuel for all this work is taken from a five-foot seam on the adjacent hills.

STAPLE AGRICULTURAL PRODUCTS—MOUNDS. 691

View of Huntington and the Ohio River.

the lumber trade will in a few years make Charleston a large city. The Kanawha river and its tributaries drain one of the finest bodies of timbered land in the United States. The white oak, the white and yellow poplar, the black walnut, the shell bark and "white heart hickory," grow to enormous heights; the white ash, the locust, the linden, the birch, the sycamore, and the iron-wood exhibit a development rarely seen in the Northern forests.

The agricultural advantages of the country surrounding Charleston are numerous. Not only are the river bottom lands fertile, but the mountain-sides may be profitably cultivated. Corn, wheat, rye, oats, and barley are profitable; the culture of tobacco, the grape, and orchard fruits, has proved very successful. There is nowhere a better country for sheep-raising, and the English settlers have given much attention to this specialty.

On the road from Charleston to the Ohio river, one passes through a rich and extensive timber country. Between Charleston and St. Albans there are some singular conical-shaped hills, supposed to be the work of that lost race known as the "Mound Builders." Crossing the Coal, the Scary, the Hurricane, the Mud, and the Guyandotte rivers, the Chesapeake and Ohio railroad reaches the Ohio river at Huntington, a new and pretty town, ambitiously laid out as a "future great city." It stands at the head of what is known as reliable navigation on the Ohio; steamers of light draught can reach it at all seasons, and there is never danger of any interruption of transportation. Huntington is an important supply point for the inhabitants of the lower Ohio valley, who, before the building of the route from Richmond through the mountains, often suffered a coal famine because the upper Ohio was obstructed. From Huntington the supply will be constant and regular. South of the town lie deposits of splint and cannel coal, and the neighboring counties in Kentucky are rich in both coal and iron. The State Normal School of West Virginia, formerly Marshall College, one of the elder collegiate schools of the Old Dominion, stands within the "city limits." The Chesapeake and Ohio Company have also established their construction shops, in which an army of operatives work, at Huntington.

Guyandotte is prettily situated on the river of the same name, at its confluence with the Ohio. It was once a trading place of much importance, and still has a commerce of its own with the back-country. The farmers and lumbermen from the mountain districts come down the river in barges, which they propel with long poles; and one of the most curious sights in the Southern highlands is a group of these rustic watermen storing their boats with provisions purchased from the merchants at Guyandotte.

The result of climbing a sapling—An Artist in a Fix.

LXXVI.

DOWN THE OHIO RIVER—LOUISVILLE.

THE French explorers called the Ohio *La Belle Rivière;* and certainly, when its banks are full, and a profusion of flowers dot the cliffs here and there overhanging the stream, or are reflected from the lowlands in the shining water, one readily recognizes the appropriateness of the term. But the Ohio river, on a foggy morning, late in autumn, when sycamores are stripped and flowers are gone, hardly recalls the affectionate name which the Frenchmen bestowed upon it.

The traveler, journeying from Huntington to Louisville on the Ohio, finds but little in natural scenery that is impressive; much, however, that is very beau-

The Levée at Louisville, Kentucky.

tiful. In summer, when the shores are clothed in green and the vineyards are resplendent with foliage, there are many landscapes which charm the eye. Inasmuch as the channel in midsummer contains little more than a "light dew," as the Western captains call it, navigation is attended with peculiar difficulties, and steamboats of lightest draught are often detained for days on a treacherous bank suddenly laid bare.

No river is more subject to extreme elevations and depressions. The average range between high and low water is said to be more than thirty feet. The highest stage is in March, and the lowest in August. In times of flood the variations are so rapid that the river at Cincinnati has been known to rise at the rate of one foot per hour during half a day. It requires no little skill and seamanship to navigate this peculiar stream. Obstructions were originally very numerous, and the passages between the exquisite islands and the sand-banks require the tact and courage of ocean sailors. The days of keel-boat, of Kentucky float, of pirogue, of gondola, skiff, and dug-out, are past. Lines of rail have superseded the noble packets which sailed from Louisville to New Orleans, and much of the romance of the river has departed. Yet there is a certain fascination in the journey by night along the great current which slips, although rapidly, apparently with a certain laziness, past the low shores sprinkled with log cabins.

From Huntington, the terminus of the Chesapeake and Ohio railroad, in West Virginia, to Cincinnati, the voyage is exceedingly interesting. The towns on the Kentucky shore, while few of them are large or bustling, have a solid and substantial air. Around the various taverns in each of them is grouped the regulation number of tall, gaunt men, with hands in pockets, and slouched hats drawn over their eyes. A vagrant pig roots here and there in the customary sewer. A few cavaliers lightly mount the rough roads leading into the unimposing hills; a few negroes slouch sullenly on a log at the foot of the levée, and on a wharf-boat half a hundred white and black urchins stare, open-mouthed, as if they had never seen steamboats or strangers before.

On the Ohio side of the river there are large manufacturing towns, evidences of thrift, industry and investment; iron-furnaces smoke; and the clatter of hammers and the roll of wheels are heard.

The distance from Pittsburg, in Pennsylvania, to Cairo, in Illinois, where the Ohio pours its muddy flood into the muddier waters of the Mississippi, is 967 miles. The tourist who takes a packet from Wheeling, in West Virginia, to Parkersburg, will see some noble scenery; for the upper Ohio, when navigation is practicable there, far surpasses in beauty the lower portion of the stream. Descending from Parkersburg he will pass Pomeroy, Gallipolis, Catlettsburg, Ironton, Portsmouth, Maysville, Ripley, and Cincinnati, and will note on the banks many salt, nail, and iron manufactories. From Cincinnati he can have his choice of two or three steamers daily for Louisville, and from the Kentucky metropolis can drift on to Evansville, in Indiana, and thence to Cairo. At Maysville, in Kentucky, between Huntington and Cincinnati, there are two extensive cotton factories and several iron foundries. The town contains many handsome streets, and is the entry port for the north-eastern section of the State. It is also the most extensive hemp market in the whole country.

Between Cincinnati and Louisville there are but few towns of importance on the Kentucky shore of the Ohio. At Big Bone Lick, in Boone county, great numbers of bones of the mastodon and the Arctic elephant were once found. At Warsaw, a few miles below, there are many tobacco factories. Carrollton, formerly called Fort William, stands at the junction of that beautiful stream, the Kentucky, with the Ohio.

The scenery along the Kentucky river justly ranks among the wildest and most picturesque in the United States. For more than 200 miles, as the stream flows north-west to empty into the Ohio, it passes through massive limestone ledges, arranged upon either side of its narrow channel in great cliffs, forming irregular cañons, or pours over rapids, or glides between precipices 500 feet high, whose tops almost touch, like roofs in the streets of an old Italian town.

The river flows through Middle Kentucky for the greater portion of its course. The confluence of the small streams which make it is at the spot known as the "Three Forks," in Lee county, the very heart of the coal and iron region which stretches away for miles in every direction. During the winter and spring coal and pig-iron are floated down the river in barges.

A familiar scene in a Louisville Street.

The improvement of the Ohio river and its tributaries is highly necessary. It is demanded by more than one-fifth of the States, and one-third of the whole population of the country, and inasmuch as that population has hitherto paid thirty-five per cent. of the internal taxation of the Union, and as it raises forty per cent. of the farm products of the land, owns forty per cent. of the farm-lands and of the live stock, and thirty-six per cent of the capital in farming implements and machinery, it would seem that it has a right to ask of the Government this boon. The sum demanded for the work will depend largely upon the plan adopted for its accomplishment. The estimates of engineers have varied from seventeen to sixty millions. No definite decision as to the wisest plan has yet been reached. Those most directly interested are still in doubt whether to decide upon supplying the required volume of water by aid of reservoirs, or maintaining the proper navigation by low dams with open chutes, or slack-watering the entire stream.

The commerce of the river is immense. The amount of coal transported from Pittsburg down the Ohio increased from fifty million bushels in 1869 to ninety millions in 1872, or more than twenty-six per cent. per annum. The tonnage of the port of Pittsburg in 1869 was estimated at eight hundred thousand tons; in 1872 it was one million six hundred and sixty-nine thousand tons. The commerce along the stream amounts to nearly nine hundred millions of dollars yearly. The Ohio drains an area of 214,000 square miles, and could furnish cheap transportation for the commerce of fifty millions of people.

Louisville, the chief city of the goodly commonwealth of Kentucky, lies on the southern bank of the Ohio river, at a point where the navigation of the stream was originally obstructed by rapids. For six miles above the site of the city, the stream stretches out into a smooth sheet of water, a mile wide, and embraces within its limits the mouth of Bear Grass creek, which affords a safe harbor for the myriad barges and flat-boats which drift on the bosom of the great stream. Situated centrally between the cotton-fields of the South and the grain-fields of the West, amply supplied with railways piercing both West and South in all directions, and with ten miles of river-front from twenty to twenty-five feet above highest flood mark, the city has a promising commercial future. Its levées, while they are not so picturesque, and the life along them is not so vivacious as that which one sees at New Orleans, Savannah, and Charleston, are yet quite as fine as those of any Southern or Western city. What Louisville has lost in river trade, since railroads came in, she has gained in railway commerce. The days of tedious steaming from Louisville to the Louisiana lowlands, in roundabout ways and along treacherous currents, are gone, and have pulled down with them into oblivion many noble fortunes; but the city grows and prospers despite the misfortunes that have overtaken the commerce once its mainstay. Opposite Louisville, on the Indiana shore, are the towns of Jeffersonville and New Albany; the former pretty and dull, the latter a kind of Western Brooklyn, having ready communication with Louisville by means of the great railroad bridge, a triumph of mechanical engineering, which has long spanned the stream.

A Waiter at the Galt House, Louisville, Kentucky.

West and south of the city the lots are lovely, and admit of unlimited extension; and on the broad and shapely streets which are one of its peculiar features stand many handsome mansions, each one of which is set down in a capacious yard, well kept, and now and then embellished with terraces. The streets which run parallel with the river, and not far from the levée, are long, and flanked with solid business blocks, very uniform in architecture, and as devoid of pretense and show as is the character of the men who built them. Main, Market, Jefferson and Green streets are all filled with large and handsome shops and warehouses, and many of those which cross them at right angles, extending indefinitely into the vast plains, are devoted to residences.

Scene in the Louisville Exposition.

Louisville is famous for several excellent institutions; noteworthy among which are the "Galt House," a massive stone structure in the English style, long celebrated by foreign travelers as the best hotel in the United States; the Louisville *Courier-Journal*, the successor to the old *Journal*, on which Prentice expended his wit, and upon which those who were wounded by his shafts vented their spleen; and the "Public Library," the outgrowth of an ingenious lottery scheme conducted by an ex-Governor of the State, and now a thriving institution with museums and lecture-rooms attached. The *Courier-Journal*, edited to-day by the sprightly Watterson, whose courageous attitude in reproving many of the prime faults in Kentucky politics and civilization, and whose trenchant style in his editorials, have rendered him famous, has long had a sensible influence on the political and social life of the State.

The *Commercial*, a Republican newspaper, has grown and prospered, as its party grows in Louisville, steadily and surely.

The City of Louisville was surveyed as early as 1770, when parties came from Fort Pitt, now known as Pittsburg, and examined the land adjacent to the Falls of the Ohio, with a view to parceling it as " bounty territory." In 1773, Captain Thomas Bullitt, the deputy of a special commission from William and Mary College in Virginia, moored his bark in Grass harbor, and with his little band of hunters made numerous surveys. Death, however, interrupted his labors, which were largely instrumental in the definite settlement of Kentucky. In 1778, Colonel George Rogers Clarke, who had for some time fought the British along the Ohio, took possession of and fortified Corn Island, opposite the spot now occupied by Louisville. In 1779, Louisville was permanently established; cabins, block-houses and stockades were erected. Clarke and his hunters lived in constant danger, and battled with the Indians for many a long day. In succeeding years, Louisville grew up a scraggy, rude town, whose streets were here and there intersected with ponds of stagnant water;* and so unhealthy was the location considered that it was known as the " grave-yard of the Ohio." If the denizens of the Louisville of the past could visit the thriving and healthy Louisville of to-day, with its miles of elegant streets, its smooth pavements, its fine hospitals and churches, its mammoth hotels and pretty theatres, its bustling "Exposition," and its brilliant society, they would hardly believe the evidence of their senses.

Life in this pleasant metropolis of 130,000 inhabitants is socially very attractive. Nowhere in the country is frankness and freedom of manner so thoroughly commingled with so much of high-bred courtesy. The people of Kentucky really, as Tuckerman says, illustrate one of the highest phases of Western character. They spring from a hardy race of hunters and self-reliant men, accustomed to the chase and to long and perilous exertion. The men of Kentucky, while they are not afflicted with any peculiar idiosyncrasies, are intensely individual. There is something inspiring in the figure of a grand old patriarch like Christopher Graham, now in his ninety-second year, erect, vigorous, and alert as an Englishman at sixty. Born in the wild woods of Kentucky five years before it became a State, he has lived to see a mighty change pass over the commonwealth where he cast his fortunes; and he delights to tell of the days when men went, rifle in hand, about their daily work, and when the State was constantly troubled with Indian incursions. Mr. Graham was long noted as the best marksman, with a rifle, in America, and has had, in his eventful life, a hundred adventures with Indian, guerilla, and bandit. The product of a rough, and, in some respects, barbarous time, when shooting, swimming, leaping, wrestling, and killing Indians were the only exercises considered manly, he is to-day a gentle old man, busied with works of charity, and with the upbuilding of a fine museum of mineralogy in Louisville.

* See " Casseday's History of Louisville."

LXXVII.

A VISIT TO THE MAMMOTH CAVE.

THE country along the line of rail from Nashville, in Tennessee, to Cave City, in Kentucky, whence travelers depart in rickety stages over the rough routes for the Mammoth Cave, is especially rich in fine farms. In autumn, when golden sunlight lingers lovingly over the great arched trees, and makes

Mammoth Cave, Kentucky—The Boat Ride on Echo River.

checker-work upon the reddish soil, a ride through this highly-cultivated country is thoroughly charming. The people one meets are mainly rough country farmers, plodding sturdily to court on fine horses, or journeying from farm to farm.

At Glasgow Junction and Cave City, on the Louisville and Nashville railroad, primitive hotels receive the visitor, and rival stage-drivers fill his ear with alarming rumors of each other's incapacity. At Cave City a sleepy waiter drowsily gives inexact information, and negroes, with persistent demand for *backshish*, follow the unfortunate Northerner and clutch his carpet-bag, despite his efforts to retain it.

Edmondson county, in which the Mammoth Cave is situated, is rich in natural curiosities. On Dismal creek, a perpendicular rock, 163 feet high, towers like a black spectre against the crystal vault of the sky, and the inhabitants invest it with many strange and highly apocryphal legends. Near the town of Brownsville is a large cave containing a petrified tree, and on Indian Hill are the remains of a fortification, with mounds and burial-places scattered over the acres in the vicinity.

The Entrance to Mammoth Cave (Looking Out).

The visit to the Mammoth Cave, which we made with a merry party, was in autumn, when the sunlight, tempered by fresh breezes, seemed to permeate every nook and cranny of the forests through which the road wound over hill and across plain. The vehicle in which we embarked at Glasgow was rickety and venerable, as also was the horse which drew it; and the driver beguiled the way with stories not calculated to impress us favorably with the hotel near the cave. Indeed, so great was his animosity toward the proprietors of that hotel, that he refused to set us down within the high fence which inclosed the building, and indulged in a lively passage-at-words, calculated to awaken quarrelsome feelings with the host when he came up to welcome us.

The hotel is a huge, rambling structure, built in Southern style, with long porches and surrounded by a pleasant lawn dotted with noble trees. Passing the primitive counter, on which lay the "Mammoth Cave Register," and paying the fees exacted from every visitor, we donned overalls, blouses, and flannel caps, and found ourselves face to face with an amiable darkey, who, taking up two swinging lamps, led the way down a rocky descent toward a black opening from which came a rush of cold air. Over the yawning mouth of the cave a stream of water was pouring, and around the sharp rocks on the brow of the hill were graceful fringes of mosses and leaves, and festoons of ferns. Shadows fell gloomily against the sunlight as we hastened down the declivity, and a wandering bat, giving a faint scream, flew directly in my face, and then darted back into the darkness.

A tree, apparently growing out of the solid rock, stretches its trunk over the chasm. This trunk is moss-grown, and both the moss and the leaves upon it have a pale yellowish tinge. Descending a few steps, and suddenly losing the genial warmth of the sun, we were forced to stoop, and to plunge forward, almost upon all fours, into the stony recesses.

Our dusky guide now supplied us each with a swinging lamp, by whose dim light we soon became accustomed to the narrow pathway, everywhere singularly free from obstacles. The cool air was so exhilarating, that after a march of several miles, clambering over stones, filing carefully along the edge of abysses, and escalading innumerable cliffs, we scarcely felt fatigue.

Unlocking a rude iron gate, the guide ushered us into a second narrow corridor, from the roof of which, as the light penetrated the gloom, hundreds of bats flitted down and circled about our heads, screaming, as if resentful of the intrusion. On the return journey the bats usually make the promenade through this gallery quite exciting, and many a timid lady remembers with horror the gauntlet she there ran.

We wandered on for several hours, the cheery guide singing psalms in a round musical voice, and turning from time to time to caution us against venturing into unexplored by-ways where pitfalls were numerous. Now we plodded through a mighty gallery, whose walls and ceilings seemed frescoed by the hands of man rather than incrusted with stalactite formations; now climbed miniature mountains; now looked down hundreds of feet into deep wells. Each of the galleries and recesses has been christened, but the visitor sometimes finds it difficult to detect in the fantastic forms of rock the resemblance suggested by the names. We visited the Rotunda, a vast chamber which seemed like the council-room of some ancient castle. Then, after exploring many antechambers and halls, we entered Audubon avenue. After wandering in that mighty gallery, whose roof is sixty feet above its smooth floor, we returned to the passage through which we had entered, passing into the main cave, and visiting, in rapid succession, the "Church," the ruins of some old saltpetre works, the Kentucky Cliffs, the Gothic Gallery, the Gothic Arcade and Chapel, the Register Hall, the Altar, Vulcan's Forge, and, finally, the Devil's Arm-Chair, a huge stalactite, beautiful in color, in which we enthroned one of the ladies accompanying the party. The Gothic Chapel, through which we wandered half-convinced that we were dreaming, is rich in noble ornaments, its columns rivaling in the nicety of their proportions those of the finest cathedrals. The

Gothic avenue, reached by a detour from the main cave and an ascent of some thirty feet, is two miles in length, and a promenade along it discloses an uninterrupted panorama of natural wonders which seem the work of giant architects rather than the result of one of nature's convulsions. All the stalactites and stalagmites in the cave are extremely rich in color, and look as if they had been carefully polished. The ceiling of the "Gothic Avenue" is as smooth as that of any mansion. Passing the "Devil's Arm-Chair," and stopping for a moment to inspect the "Elephant's Trunk" and the "Pillars of Hercules," we came at last to the "Lover's Leap," a large pointed rock more than ninety feet above the roadway, and projecting into an immense rotunda.

Mammoth Cave — In "the Devil's Arm-Chair."

The "Ball-Room" is a mighty chamber, admirably fitted for the dance, with a rocky gallery even, in which from time to time an orchestra has been placed when gay parties from Louisville and other neighboring cities have engaged in festivities, with music and torches. A short distance beyond looms up a huge mass of rock, known as the Giant's Coffin. Passing the deserted chamber, the "Wooden Bowl Cave," where oxide of iron and lime are sprinkled on the floor, and crossing the "Bridge of Sighs," we came to the "Star Chamber," where our guide had prepared for us a genuine surprise. Mysteriously commanding us to be seated in a dark corner, and saying that he would return to find us on the morrow, he suddenly seized the lights and withdrew. We heard his sonorous voice echoing along the galleries as he hurried back over the pathway, and while we were yet wondering what was the object of this sudden manœuvre, we saw above us twinkling stars, and seemed to catch a glimpse of the blue sky from which we had thought ourselves shut out by the solid rock. Indeed, so strange was the illusion, that we fancied we could feel the fresh air blowing upon us, and, for a few moments, imagined that the guide had conveyed us by some roundabout way to the mouth of the cave, and then had hastily left us, that he might enjoy our surprise. But presently we heard his voice, confessing the cheat. The dark ceiling of the Star Chamber is covered with a myriad incrustations, sparkling like stars; and the artful guide, by a careful arrangement of his lamps and the use of Bengal lights, had produced a magical effect. The ceiling, which was not more than forty feet from our heads, had seemed remote as the heavens. It was like the very early dawn, when the stars are gradually fading and seem no longer to belong in the sky. The guide, in the distance, imitated to perfection the crowing of the morning cock, and then burst into loud laughter as, removing the lamps, he exposed the trick, and returned to us.

From the Star Chamber we descended to "Wright's Rotunda," which has a ceiling of four hundred feet span without a single pillar to uphold it, and wandered on through the Black Chambers, where masses of shelving stone reminded us of old baronial castle walls and towers; and ascending thence into an upper room, in which we caught the whispers of a far-away waterfall, translated, upon our crossing the room, into the roar of a cataract falling sullenly down deep and hidden recesses. Next, crawling upon our hands and knees under a low arch, we entered the Fairy Grotto, whence we retraced our steps to the entrance of the cave. The bats gave us a lively reception as we passed through the gate around which they flitted as sentinels, and it was not until after we had climbed the hill, and stood in the hotel garden for some time, that we missed the sun, so accustomed had we become to the darkness during our long sojourn in the cave.

Early next morning we were once more treading the corridors, and by nightfall had made a journey of eighteen miles. The experiences of this second day were far more novel and interesting than those of the first.

The various passages of the cave have a total of more than two hundred miles in length, and many of those not often seen are said to surpass in beauty those commonly visited. To my thinking, nothing, however, in subterranean scenery can be finer than the mighty and ragged pass of El Ghor, whose jagged peaks, frightful ravines, and long recesses, filled with incrusted rocks, on which the swinging lamps threw a changeful shimmer, extend for long distances. On this day we also made the acquaintance of the "Fat Man's Misery," which the artist has faithfully depicted, and through which some of our party found no little difficulty in pressing.

Crossing the black and deep river Styx by a natural bridge, and safely ferrying over Lake Lethe, we passed

The Mammoth Cave—"The Fat Man's Misery."

through a level and lofty hall called the "Great Walk," and soon arrived at "Echo River," on whose moist and muddy shore a rude barge was drawn up. The stream seemed shut in by a huge overreaching wall of solid stone, and we turned in amazement to the ebony guide, who motioned us to take seats in the boat, jumping in when we had obeyed, and rowing boldly forward into the blackness. From time to time the wall seemed to press down upon us, and we were obliged to bend close to the seats. The guide sang loudly as we floated through the darkness, our little lights making but tiny specks in the gloom. The sense of isolation from the world was here complete. We seemed at last to have had a glimpse of the infernal regions, and imagined ourselves departed souls, doomed to a reluctant ride in Charon's bark. A deep silence fell upon all the visitors; but the guide still sang loudly his pious psalms, only ceasing them to burst into laughter when the ladies cowered as we rounded some rocky corner, and seemed about to be crushed against a lowering wall.

After half an hour of this mysterious journeying we approached another shore, and left behind us the archway. Before us lay a vast region of black and desolate pathways over high rocks and under huge boulders, along avenues brilliant with stalactites and resplendent with sparkling ceilings. Here we were recalled to a knowledge of the outer world by encountering a return party, escorted by Stephen, one of the first guides who ever penetrated the cave, and concerning whom a curious story is told.

Stephen had for many years urged a white man living near the cave to build a boat with which to explore the Echo river. When at last it was built, and a voyage under the arches was decided upon, he (Stephen) was afraid to undertake it, but was compelled at the pistol's mouth to enter the boat and proceed. Neither he nor the white man entered upon this daring feat without fear and trembling, for no one could have predicted that the stream would find its outlet beyond the cave, in Green river. Echo river is certainly one of the most remarkable streams in the world. It is here and there wide and deep enough to float a steamer of the largest class. A few fish are now and then caught in it. They have no eyes, and certainly need none.

Mammoth Cave—"The Subterranean Album."

The journey from this stream through the pass of El Ghor, Silliman's Avenue, and Wellington's Gallery, all the latter leading up to St. Mary's Vineyard and the Hill of the Holy Sepulchre, was fatiguing; and when we returned at nightfall we found that the day's journey had quite demolished our stout walking shoes.

The burning of blue lights in various places where the ceilings are covered with sulphate of iron produces marvelous effects. No palaces, no castles, ancient or modern, rival in beauty or in grandeur the corridors and passages of the Mammoth Cave. In one of the long avenues we saw the Veiled Statue, a perpendicular rock which, from a distance, as one turns around the angle of the way, looks exactly like the figure of some ancient goddess clad in draperies. Many of the incrustations or "formations," as our guide called them, are in the form of *rosaces*, some rivaling the most beautiful bits of Gothic architectural decoration. The shading is bold and beautiful, and the lines and curves delicious. The pillars seem to flit away like ghosts as one comes suddenly upon them in the dim light given by the lamps. Occasionally one reaches a place where the cave seems to afford no outlet into passages beyond; but the guide turns suddenly to right or left through narrow archways, or down little steps to new wonders. The journey is a succession of surprises. One of the most curious experiences is a look into the "Bottomless Pit," which is reached from the "Deserted Chambers;" and a glance at the Dead Sea, into which one may shudderingly peer from a precipice eighty feet high, is not without its fascination. A young telegraph operator from Michigan once descended into a hitherto unexplored pit in the cave, and found bottom 198 feet down. He narrowly escaped death, however, for the rope with which he was lowered was cut nearly in two by the sharp rocks in which it caught. The best features of the cave are the Dome, the Bottomless Pit, and the Pass of El Ghor. Their grandeur and beauty amply repay the journey of thousands of miles which European and American tourists make to see them.

Vandalism has made its way into the Mammoth Cave. The lamps given visitors are sometimes attached to a rod, by means of which industrious snobs smoke the letters of their names upon the sides and roofs of some of the corridors. Thousands of people have thus testified their thirst for notoriety, and many a shock is given the impressible traveler by finding the name and date of some obscure mortal recorded on a rock which he had fancied heretofore unseen by men.

The cave is said to have been first discovered in 1802 by a hunter, who strayed into it in pursuit of an animal that had taken refuge there. It now belongs to nine heirs, who each receive about $1,000 yearly income from it. Were the facilities for reaching it better, the heirs might readily receive $50,000 annually for an indefinite period.

The cave has repeatedly been offered for sale for half a million dollars, and Louisville capitalists have talked from time to time of forming a company for its purchase, and erecting a new and splendid hotel in its immediate vicinity.

Gathered about the great fire-place of the hotel office in the evening, the conversation drifted to Kentucky politics, and one of the Englishmen who had been exploring the cave with us inquired curiously about the Ku-Klux. The Kentuckian in charge of the hotel answered that the Ku-Klux in that section were called Regulators, and they never troubled any except bad people. "They are composed," he said, "of the gentlemen in the neighborhood, and when those gentlemen are annoyed by vicious neighbors they warn them to move away. If they will not move, they move them, and if they resist they force them." This he asserted was only done in cases when great provocation had been received, and he insisted that politics had little to do with the operations of the Klan. Carelessly dropping his reserve, the Kentuckian added: "We don't do anything wrong; we simply correct those who don't behave right," thus unconsciously intimating that he himself was one of the Knights of the "Invisible Empire."

A Country Blacksmith Shop.

LXXVIII.

THE TRADE OF LOUISVILLE.

THE trade of Louisville, long dwarfed by the oppressive slave system to which Kentucky was utterly devoted, and which prevented the growth of large manufacturing towns, is gradually springing into vigorous life. Louisville has long been one of the most important tobacco markets in the United States. Situated near the centre of the largest tobacco-growing district of the country, with an admirable system of railroad connections North and South, and a noble water outlet, she has superior facilities for this branch of trade. The bulk of the staple raised in Kentucky, the chief tobacco-growing State of the Union, is sold in the Louisville market. The Kentucky crop for 1871 amounted to 66,000 hogsheads, of which nearly 50,000 were sold in Louisville. Buyers for American and foreign markets reside permanently in the city, and those European Governments which have found it wise to enjoy a monopoly of their home tobacco trade are represented by local agents who make their purchase from the planters. Thousands of whites and blacks are employed in the huge warehouses, and nineteen factories, with a

The Court-House — Louisville.

capital of 850,000 dollars, are engaged in the manufacture of chewing tobacco. The city also produces twelve millions of cigars annually. In the whiskey trade a large capital is invested. From the distilleries in the Blue Grass region thousands of barrels, filled with the fluid which prompts so large a proportion of the homicides in the State, are brought to Louisville, and it is said that the transactions amount to five millions annually. Pork-packers also make the city their head-quarters, and in the sixty days of each year between November and January a million swine pass through their hands.

As a live-stock market, Louisville has been rapidly growing in importance for many years. The stock-yards there now cover twenty acres, and the value of the stock received annually is between twenty and thirty millions. The flour-mills yearly yield a product worth four millions. The trade in provisions aggregates from eleven to fifteen millions; the annual product of iron foots up five millions, and more than 1,500 hands are employed in the manufacture of iron work, while in the foundries 500 hands are employed. In brief, the amount of capital invested in manufacturing enterprises in the city is about twenty millions, the annual product fifty-five millions, the number of hands employed 16,000, and the amount of wages paid eight millions.

Louisville would be an admirable point for the establishment of cotton-mills, and as its capitalists have had their attention favorably directed to the large dividends which Southern mills are yearly paying, it is hoped that the city may speedily secure several mills. The building of steamboats for the Western waters has long been one of the leading industries of Louisville and the villages clustered about the Falls of the Ohio. The water power of the Ohio Falls is very remarkable, and ought to place Louisville among the first manufacturing cities of the country. It has thus far been but little utilized. The same negligent and reckless spirit which pervaded others of the slave States in regard to the improvement of natural advantages controlled the Kentuckian mind, and was even more pronounced in Louisville and its vicinity than in many places further south. The law of Kentucky, which allowed only six per cent. interest, was an effectual barrier to the investment of foreign capital in Louisville, and drove away much local capital which might have been invested. The enlargement of the present Louisville and Portland canal, which was completed in 1828 at a cost of $750,000, would render transportation to and from Louisville more feasible; and the building of a new canal through Portland town would furnish a superb location, with enormous water power for miles of factories and mills. The Louisville and Nashville railroad gives a grand trunk line from Louisville to Montgomery,

The Cathedral—Louisville.

The Post-Office—Louisville.

Alabama, a distance of 490 miles, and connection with the railroad system of the Southern States, which are Kentucky's chief market. Louisville is also connected by the Great Bridge spanning the Ohio, with all the railroads north of that river, and is directly on the through route from the north and west to the extreme south. The main trunk of the Louisville and Nashville railroad extends through Jefferson, Bullett, Nelson, Hardin, Larue, Hart, Edmondson, Barren, Warren, and Simpson counties. Branch railroads, connecting with Memphis and South-eastern Kentucky, have served largely to develop the regions through which they run. The so-called Richmond branch runs to within a short distance of the richest iron region of the State. The Elizabethtown and Paducah railroad extends from Elizabethtown, on the Louisville and Nashville railroad, forty-two miles from Louisville, to Paducah, a thriving city on the Ohio, fifty miles from its junction with the Mississippi. Paducah is the commercial market of Western Kentucky. The Owensboro, Russelville and Nashville, the Evansville, Henderson and Nashville, the Paducah and Memphis, and the Nashville and Ohio roads also traverse Western Kentucky. The last-named route gives an important connection with the city of Mobile.

Louisville has connection with the eastern section of the State and Cincinnati, by the Louisville, Frankfort and Lexington, and the Short Line, railroads. The former runs through Frankfort, the charming capital of Kentucky, to the staid and solid old city of Lexington, which is the western terminus of the Big Sandy railroad. This road passes through some of the finest agricultural districts of the State, pierces the very heart of the mineral region of

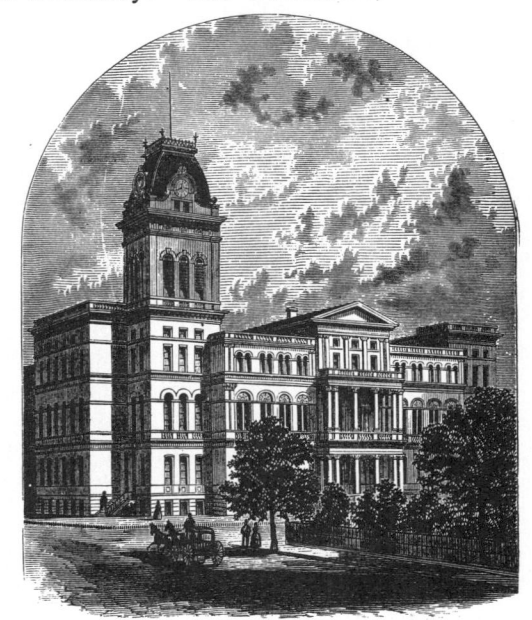

The City Hall — Louisville.

Kentucky, and is designed to furnish connection with the Atlantic ports via the Chesapeake and Ohio Railroad through Western Virginia.

At Lagrange, twenty-eight miles from Louisville, the Short Line railroad to Covington, opposite Cincinnati, on the Ohio river, crosses the Louisville, Frankfort and Lexington road. The Kentucky Central railroad runs through Middle Kentucky, and from Paris, in the Blue Grass region, the Maysville and Lexington road branches out.

Many new railroads are chartered in Kentucky, and of those most likely soon to be built, the Cincinnati Southern, intended to furnish a line from Covington, on the Ohio, to Chattanooga, Tennessee, and to pursue a central route through Middle Kentucky, is the most prominent. The Ohio and Cumberland railroad, as projected, will run from Covington to Nashville, in Tennessee, and the Louisville, Memphis, and New Orleans road is intended to pierce from Louisville through rich agricultural and mineral districts, and intersecting important lines of rail, to Union City, where it will connect with routes tributary to Memphis. The railroads that are already completed in Kentucky penetrate sixty-one counties, and the majority of them contribute directly to the prosperity of Louisville. In addition to these, as a means of distributing its manufactured wares, that city has the advantage of navigable streams, embracing an extent of 16,000 miles.

The capital stock at present invested in banks and banking houses in Louisville is about ten millions, and the deposit capital amounts to more than eight millions. In addition to these amounts, Louisville has many private capitalists. The law of Kentucky now allows ten per cent. interest upon loans, and it is probable that capital from all sections of the Union will flow to Louisville within the next few years. The bonded debt of the city was $6,153,509 in 1872, and the taxable property of the city is estimated at $80,000,000. The credit of the city is excellent; the taxation is not burdensome; the municipal government is good. There are few better lighted, better paved, or better policed towns than Louisville. For a community where three-fourths of the male citizens habitually bear arms, shooting is reasonably rare, although not properly punished when, under the influence of liquor or passion, it does occur. The city spreads over thirteen square miles, a space amply sufficient to furnish dwellings for a population of half a million. Building is cheap, tenement houses are rare, and although a motley gang of rough men from the rivers is gathered in some quarters of the city, but little lawlessness prevails.

George D. Prentice — (From a Painting in the Louisville Public Library).

The Colored Normal School — Louisville.

The public buildings of Louisville are not architecturally fine. The City Hall is the most ambitious structure, and the council-room in which the municipal fathers discuss popular measures is palatial. The Court-House on Jefferson street, the Louisville University Medical College, the Blind Asylum, the male and female High Schools, the Custom-House and Post-Office and Masonic Temple are solid and substantial edifices. In autumn and in winter, fogs hover over the city, and the coal smoke, joined to the mists, colors the walls of houses with the same brown so noticeable in London and St. Louis. The Cathedral on Walnut street, St. Paul's Episcopal Church, and the First Presbyterian, opposite it, are fine houses of worship. Louisville boasts accommodation for 50,000 worshipers, and amongst its noteworthy divines is the Rev. Dr. Stuart Robinson, whose Confederate predilections during the war were strongly marked, and whose

Louisville, Kentucky, on the Ohio River, from the New Albany Heights.

ability is unquestionable. The new Public Library at present occupies a small and commodious building, soon to be replaced, when the drawings of the Lottery are completed, by a finer structure. This library, although at present no larger than those in many New England cities one-third the size of Louisville, is admirably selected, finely officered, and contains, among other curiosities, a painting of George D. Prentice, as he appeared in middle-life. The celebrated journalist, poet and politician, lies beside his son, who was killed while in the ranks of the Confederates, in Cave Hill cemetery, near the city.

The schools of Louisville merit great praise. The public school system is taking a firm hold there, and even the "Steel Blue" tendencies of the majority of the population, and their refusal to believe in the ultimate elevation of the 222,000 blacks in the State, have not hindered them from supplying the colored population with excellent facilities for education. Louisville has two high schools, which are, in every respect, first-class seminaries, twenty-three ward schools, and a host of private institutions for English and classical training. The school buildings will seat 12,000 pupils. Nearly three-quarters of a million is invested in school buildings and lots, and $150,000 is annually paid in salaries. The German language is taught as one of the regular branches in the public schools, a measure rendered necessary, as in St. Louis, by the influx of the Teutonic population. The Colored Normal School building, dedicated in Louisville last year, is probably the finest public school edifice designed for the instruction of negroes in the country. The School Board has established training departments in connection with some of the ward schools, and these are rapidly equipping teachers.

Although there is no impressive scenery in the vicinity of Louisville, the green lowlands, the wide river, and the vast expanse of wooded plain are very imposing. From the hills back of New Albany, on the Indiana shore, one can look down on the huge extent of Louisville half-hidden beneath the foliage which surrounds so many of its houses; can note the steamers slowly winding about the bends in the Ohio, or carefully working their way up to the broad levées; can see the trains crawling like serpents over the high suspended bridge, and the church spires and towers gleaming under the mellow sunlight. In a few years, if the improvements now in progress are continued, Louisville will be one of the most delightful of American cities.

Chimney Rock, Kentucky.

LXXIX.

FRANKFORT—THE BLUE GRASS REGION—ALEXANDER'S FARM. LEXINGTON.

NOWHERE is the Kentucky river more beautiful than where it flows past the pretty and cultured town of Frankfort, the capital of Kentucky, sixty miles above its entrance into the Ohio. For many miles in every direction superb landscapes are spread out before the traveler's vision. He will have found the ride of sixty-five miles from Louisville a constant panorama of fine fields, well-

Frankfort, on the Kentucky River.

kept farms, stone-fenced and thoroughly cultivated. Their solid building and general air of thrift offers a sharp contrast to the scraggy sheds and unpainted mansions of Southern plantations. In the train the traveler will find the typical Kentuckian, tall, smooth-faced, with clear complexion, and bright eyes, his manners deferential, and his conversation enjoyable. In the manners of the better class of Kentuckians there is no familiarity, no grossness or coarseness, but a frankness only slightly tinged with formality.

We arrived at Frankfort at nightfall, and were ushered by an attentive negro into a great stone caravansary known as the Capitol Hotel, which, during the sessions of the Legislature, is crowded, but for the remainder of the year is almost empty. In the morning, while a delicious haze, through which the sun was striving to peep, overhung the hills, we walked through the still streets bordered with pretty mansions, and stole along the steep and picturesque banks of the Kentucky to the cemetery, perched on a high bluff, where stands the monument above the grave of Daniel Boone. Clambering up to this lovely spot by a flight of ancient stone steps, and passing the crags known as Umbrella and Boone rocks, we paused from time to time, fascinated with the beauty of the tranquil stream hundreds of feet below us, its banks fringed with loveliest foliage and trees. On the river lay moored great rafts of logs which had been drifted down from the mountain torrents above.

The Ascent to Frankfort Cemetery, Kentucky.

Frankfort lies in a deep valley surrounded by sharply-defined hills, the river there flowing between high limestone banks, from which is quarried the admirable building stone of which the town is partially constructed. From the cemetery bluff the town looks as picturesque as an Italian city. Clustered together on the river-bank the wide buildings form a group which has none of the unpleasant angles so common in America. The village of South Frankfort is connected with the main town by a covered bridge over the stream, and in all directions smooth, wide, macadamized roads stretch out over the hills and through the ravines. Near the city there are many fine estates, on which the noted horses and cattle of the Blue Grass regions are raised. The State Arsenal is an unimposing building on a pretty eminence. The ruins of the old State Capitol occupy a conspicuous elevation, and the new State-House, now in process of completion, stands on a handsome lawn. The Penitentiary—where, at the time of our visit, 700 convicts, equally divided among whites and blacks, were engaged in manufacturing hemp into matting—is an unpicturesque structure, whose high walls have not prevented the occasional escape of prisoners. Each convict is compelled to weave 150 yards of matting daily, and, after his task is completed, is allowed to repose until nightfall, when he is locked up in his cell. We saw several of the blacks improving their time by reading, but most of the prisoners who had finished their daily toil were sullenly chewing tobacco, and contemplating the gloomy walls of the dark rooms in which they had been working. The keepers of the Penitentiary regaled us with stories of adventurous people who in the old days had been confined for negro stealing. In the Hospital we saw a fine athletic man crouching over a table with his head held wearily behind his hands. This was the forger Atwood, whose reckless folly brought him from the centre of a brilliant society to a term of twenty years in jail.

Manufacturing is creeping into the capital, although prominent society neither seeks nor cares for it. Farming, the distilling of pure whiskeys from the golden grain which grows so abundantly in the vicinity, the breeding and care of race-horses, and visiting and junketing in all the country side, content the Kentuckians. Aside from the stir created by the assemblage of politicians there is but little thus far to trouble the dreamy repose and enviable tranquillity by which Frankfort is characterized. It is the home of many of the loveliest women in the country, and its society is largely represented in all the cities of the world. Its belles, and those of Lexington, lead the fashion at the Southern "Springs."

While we were at Frankfort the Ku-Klux were engaged in active operations in the neighboring counties, and the residents of Frankfort denounced them as a band of ruffians whose main object was revenge. One gentleman asserted that he would at any time help with his own hands to lynch a certain member of the gang, if he could be caught. In Owen and Henry counties these midnight marauders had inaugurated a veritable reign of terror. They took "niggers" from their houses and whipped them on most trivial provocation. They waylaid those who had dared to testify against them in court, and "fixed" them from behind bushes. Clad in fantastic disguises, they hovered about the confines of large towns, carrying dread into the hearts of superstitious blacks. The colored people living in the outskirts of Frankfort had deserted their homes and flocked into the town, giving as their reason that they were afraid of the Ku-Klux. It is hardly fair to presume that political bitterness has

The Monument to Daniel Boone in the Cemetery at Frankfort, Kentucky.

been so much concerned in prompting the actions of these prowlers as have ignorance and the general lawlessness—all too prevalent in the back-country of Kentucky.

Between Louisville and Frankfort, at La Grange, a branch road diverges to Shelbyville. This pretty town stands in the midst of a luxuriantly fertile country, has many manufactories, a fine court-house, numerous churches, three flourishing seminaries, and is the seat of Shelby College, founded in 1836. Thirty miles below Frankfort, on an eminence near the far-famed Salt river, so well known in political jargon, is Harrodsburg, the oldest settlement in the State, where Captain James Harrod, in 1774, erected a cabin in the wilderness. Harrodsburg has been visited by thousands from East and West, and it is to-day the most famous summer resort in the State, its mineral springs being a prime attraction. It is also the seat of old Bacon College and a good military academy. In 1819 Christopher Graham went to Harrodsburg with a few dollars in his pocket, and for thirty-two years thereafter was the patron of the springs, bringing into the State more than $4,000,000, the expenditure of visitors from all parts of the world. The Presbyterian Female College and the Christian Baptist College

View on the Kentucky River, near Frankfort.

at Harrodsburg owe their existence to Doctor Graham. He also created and paved, at his own expense, the first street in the town. In three decades, and by his own exertions, he so beautified this lovely spot that when Generals Scott and Wool were delegated by Congress to prepare an asylum in the West for invalid soldiers, they bought a site at Harrodsburg for $100,000, and built on it a fine edifice, which was long ago burned.

Nine miles from Frankfort, on the road to Lexington, stands one of the finest and richest farms in Kentucky—that owned by Mr. Alexander. On this superb stock-farm we saw 300 blooded horses, ranging in rank from old "Lexington," the monarch of the turf, to the kittenish and frisky yearling. Here also Mr. Alexander has collected $100,000 worth of cattle, comprising some of the finest stock in the world. Peeping into the inclosure where the costly cattle were kept, we saw one diminutive heifer worth $27,000, and a variety of foreign creatures whose value seemed almost fabulous. On this farm are bred the great majority of the fine trotting and running horses which appear in our parks during the racing season. Mr. Alexander's estate, which is admirably stocked with fine farm-houses, barns and stables, and is more like a ducal manor than the ordinary American farm, extends over 3,200 acres. Near by is old John Harper's modest farm of 2,000 acres. The roads, the stone walls, and the fine lawns covered with massive shade-trees, make a series of delightful pictures.

Asteroid Kicks Up.

The annual sale of horses on the Alexander farm occurs in June. Only yearling colts are sold. Hundreds of people from all the country around, and from every State in the Union, flock to this sale. An immense barbecue is held, and high wassail marks the conclusion of the occasion.

We paid a respectful visit to old "Lexington," the mighty sire of a mightier equine family. He is now quite blind, a veteran of twenty-two, afflicted with goitre, and stood gazing in the direction from which our voices came, a melancholy wreck of his former greatness. The princes of the race-course of the present galloped by, neighing and pawing the ground, as if annoyed at our presence. One of them, named "Asteroid," so far forgot his princely dignity as to charge incontinently upon the fence where we were seated, and the artist has depicted the result in a spirited sketch. The negro men who manage these erratic brutes undergo all sorts of perilous adventures, but they seem to possess as many lives as a cat, and, like that animal, always land on their feet, no matter how far the plunging and rearing horses may throw them.

Except the negligence of her people with regard to their own interests, and the prejudices which still, in many quarters, survive the death of the slavery *régime*, there is no reason why Kentucky should not already have received a mighty current of immigration. Rich in all the elements of material greatness, abounding in mineral and agricultural lands, noble rivers, and superb forests, it is astonishing that great wealth is not more general among the people of the State. Lying between 39° and 36° 30′ north latitude, her climate is delightful, and her situation, between the two greatest water-sheds of the continent, affords her easy communication with twelve of the largest and wealthiest of her sister States.

The Green, the Kentucky, and the Barren rivers are all navigable, and run through regions which can readily furnish them an immense commerce. The area of the State is 37,700 square miles, the larger part of which is more than eight hundred feet above the level of the sea. The farming region, in Middle Kentucky, which includes the territory between the mountains of the east and the lower lands lying west of the Louisville and Nashville railroad, and extending from the northern to the southern boundary, is superb. Within this tract of ten thousand square miles all the cereals, hemp, flax, and every kind of vegetable and fruit flourish magnificently. In Middle Kentucky lies the famous "Blue Grass Region," of which I have already spoken, which has long been noted for its beautiful women, its Bourbon whiskey and Bourbon Democrats, its Lexingtons and Asteroids, its Alexanders, and its "Old John Harper." Fayette, Bourbon, Scott, Woodford, Clark, Jessamine, and portions of other counties in this region, owe much to the beds of blue shell limestone and marble which underlie them, the upper soil, which is a dark loam with a red clay subsoil, being astonishingly fertile. These fair lands are carpeted throughout the year with a brilliant blue grass. Even in midwinter a deep green clothes the soil, and, when summer comes, the grass sends up slender shafts to the height of several feet, crowned with feathery tufts of a bright blue color. The effect of a landscape clad in this noble herbage, and dotted here and there with fine oaks and well-kept farm-houses, is exceedingly fine. Throughout Fayette, Woodford, Scott, and Bourbon counties, lands are worth from $80 to $140 per acre, and highly-cultivated farms of from 250 to 300 acres are abundant. There hemp yields from eight to fourteen hundred pounds per acre, and tobacco flourishes even on the second-rate lands. Montgomery county is interspersed with fields and meadows, studded with stately forests in which the blue grass grows as luxuriantly as in the cleared lands. In the forest pastures are bred the magnificent cattle and horses for which Kentucky is so famous. The chief advantage which the Blue Grass region possesses over any other in the State is in its unequaled pasturage, and in the richness of its timber-lands. From it are annually exported thousands of noble horses and cattle, and immense droves of sheep, mules and hogs are sent to the cotton-fields of the South.

Lexington, one of the most wealthy and beautiful of Kentucky cities, is charmingly situated on the lower fork of the Elkhorn river. The early pioneers and adventurers, who established the town in the midst of a wilderness, found there the remains of a great fortress and a mighty people whose history has not been written. The present city is built above the ruins of mounds and fortifications, totally different from those erected by the Indians, and evidently of great extent and magnificence. A few years before the first prominent white settlement was made there, the entrance to an ancient catacomb was discovered by some hunters, and embalmed bodies were found in it. For three-quarters of a century the entrance to this subterranean cemetery has been hidden, and the Kentuckians of to-day even doubt its existence. Lexington was the starting-point of Kentucky and the centre from which radiated all the movements that finally ended in the conquering of the savage and the domination by the whites in the West. In 1775, the hunters from Harrodsburg took possession of the north side of the Kentucky river, and the place where they first halted was near Lexington. A spring from which they drank is still pointed out. The town was named after Lexington in Massachusetts by the hunters, into whose forest retreat

A Souvenir of Kentucky.

the news had crept that King George's troops, on the 19th of April, had shot down the American rebels in Massachusetts colony at Lexington. Kentucky was then a wild territory, belonging to the royal province of Virginia, and it is not a little strange that there, in the midst of an unbroken forest, was raised the first monument to the first dead of the American Revolution.

The founder of Lexington was Colonel Robert Patterson, the compeer of Boone, Kenton, and other forest pioneers whose names are famous. For half a century after its foundation, Lexington had a brilliant history. To-day it is a quiet town, the home of many wealthy families and the Mecca of thousands of pilgrims, as it contains the old residence and the grave of Henry Clay. A monument to the illustrious statesman stands in the beautiful cemetery of Lexington, on an eminence near the centre of the grounds, and is a landmark for miles around. It was completed in 1860, at a cost of $50,000.

"Ashland," the old Clay homestead, is situated a mile and a-half from the city, in the midst of beautiful parks, closely resembling the manors of England. During Mr. Clay's lifetime the estate was ornamented with loveliest shade-trees and orchards in profusion, and the road which leads to the mansion, now the residence of Regent Bowman, of the Kentucky University, is lined with locusts, cypresses, and cedars, through which peep the rose, the jessamine, and the ivy. The old mansion, replaced in 1857 by a beautiful modern residence, was a plain, unpretending structure, in which Mr. Clay at various times had entertained a host of distinguished Americans and foreigners. Lexington is also the location of the Kentucky University and the State Lunatic Asylum; the former institution, founded on the ruins of Transylvania University, has an endowment of $500,000, a fine library, and its law and medical schools have long been renowned. The present University was incorporated in 1858, its original endowment having been obtained by the efforts of the present Regent, John B. Bowman, a native of Kentucky, who was also instrumental in the consolidation of the Universities of Harrodsburg, Transylvania, and the Agricultural College at Lexington. The first session of the Kentucky University was in 1865, and the grounds of the Agricultural and Mechanical College, which now comprise "Ashland," and the adjoining estate of "Woodlands" were purchased in 1866.

A little Adventure by the Wayside.

LXXX.

POLITICS IN KENTUCKY—MINERAL RESOURCES OF THE STATE.

POLITICAL questions in Kentucky have lately been more agitated than for many years since the war. The discussion of the Civil Rights bill has been as furious and illogical there as in any other of the ex-slave States. The freedmen do not constitute a troublesome element in the commonwealth. There are 222,000 of them, while the whole population of the State is 1,331,000 souls. Some of the oldest and stiffest Bourbon Democrats have of late shown gratifying tendencies toward liberality in educational matters, and, indeed, it may with reason be hoped that Kentucky will soon be ranked among the progressive States which desire immigration, education, and manufactures,—the three things which alone can build up States once consecrated to slavery.

A brief sketch of the progress of Kentucky politics may not be uninteresting. Kentucky was a Whig State, faithful to Henry Clay as long as he lived, and a worshiper of his theories after he died. The Whig feeling is still very strong among some of the older voters. A prominent editor in the State told me that he could remember when it was not good *ton* to be a Democrat, just as since the war it has not been fashionable to be a Republican. When the Whig party died, after Scott's defeat, the masses of the Whigs went into the Know-Nothing movement, and the Democrats opposed it, although, during the battle, a good many Whigs and Democrats changed sides. In the Fillmore and Buchanan canvass, the State sided with Buchanan, and the Know-Nothing party died.

Then the Whigs, still unwilling to coincide with the Democrats, formed what was called the Opposition Party, and, in 1859, ran Bell for Governor against McGoffin, who was a Douglas Squatter-Sovereignty Democrat; but Bell, for the purpose of making political capital, took extreme views with regard to the rights of the South in the territories, and compelled McGoffin to come on to his ground. This, it is considered, was very unfortunate in its effect on the temper of the State.

When the Secession movement came up, eighteen months afterward, it had a good deal to do with creating the neutrality position taken by the leading men of the State, in the winter of 1860, as a measure of necessity for holding the masses of the people steady for a time against the wave of Secession excitement. The division of the Democrats between Breckenridge and Douglas, in 1860, gave the State to Bell and Everett. The Douglas men were nearly all Unionists. When the Southern States began the Secession movement, after the election of Mr. Lincoln, the Kentucky Legislature, which had been elected in 1859 during the excitement raised by the Bell-McGoffin canvass for the Governorship, was found to be nearly divided between Union men and Southern sympathizers.

In the election of 1861, for "Peace Commissioners," Congressmen, and Legislators, the Union men were successful by large majorities, and they retained control of the State until 1866, although it is said that the Emancipation Proclamation, and the course of injudicious military commanders in the State, greatly weakened the Union party, which was gradually divided into unconditional Union men and "Union Democrats." The straight-out Democrats, mostly Secessionists, tried to hold a convention at Frankfort in 1862, but were prevented by the Post Commander. They sent delegates, however, to the Chicago Convention in 1864. Those delegates were received, and divided seats with the Union Democrats. The unconditional Union men, who voted for Mr. Lincoln in 1864 in Kentucky, formed the basis of the present Republican party in the State, but did not call themselves Republicans until the convention of May, 1867.

The Union Legislature, during the war, passed an act expatriating all citizens who had left the State for the purpose of aiding the Confederacy. The last Union Legislature, in 1865 and '66 repealed this act, and welcomed the return of the Confederates to their allegiance. The Democratic party was organized in 1866, and gained possession of the county offices. The unconditional Union men coöperated with the Union Democrats in this canvass. The next year the Union men took their stand with the Republican party, and nominated a candidate for Governor. The Union Democrats also nominated a candidate. They were called before the election the "third party," and after it, from their small show of strength, the "one-third party." The Democrats, embracing the Secession element, and the dissatisfied Union men, also made a nomination.

The "third party" embraced nearly all the old Union leaders, but few of the rank and file, and cast but 13,000 votes. A Democratic Governor was elected, and Secession Democrats have filled the Governor's chair ever since.

By the adoption of the fifteenth amendment about 45,000 additional voters were placed upon the lists, but not more than 35,000 of them have ever voted at an election. The Republicans have been slowly but steadily gaining ground in the Legislature for some years. They are still in a small minority. Their policy has been to win back the old Union men from the Democracy, with whom their associations have not always been pleasant. It is from that source mainly that the Republicans have gained their strength. The Democrats are divided up by lines which cross one another in a variety of ways, into the "Stay-at-home sympathizers," the Confederate soldiers, the Bourbons, and the "Progressives." The Stay-at-homes have repeatedly concluded that the Confederates were too grasping, and the Bourbons have shriekingly accused the Progressives of infidelity to party. The balance of power has swayed in every direction; but the Bourbons and Confederates now control the State. The feeling that the Democratic party of Kentucky was in many respects an "unreconciled" party, and that it sanctioned the lawlessness of the Ku-Klux, has led the Republicans to adhere to the national organization of their party, without paying much attention to the questions which have caused dissension among Northern Republicans. They still regard the predominance of the Republican party in national affairs as more important to them than the justification of party measures. If the negro question were out of the politics of the State, there would be no trouble on account of the old Union and Secession differences. The feeling in relation to it had been toned down to a manageable point, when the discussion of the Civil Rights bill revived it in all its old bitterness and intensity.

The Progressives in the Democratic party have among them individuals who take strong ground in favor of general education, but the opposition to common schools among the wealthier classes is very powerful. The first law for the establishment of a general system of common schools in Kentucky was enacted in 1838, but the continued war made upon it disgusted the friends of the movement, and they did but little for many years thereafter. In 1867 a series of liberal reforms in the then prostrate school system was planned, and a bill inaugurating the reform finally passed the Legislature in 1869–70. The result of the operation of the new law was the doubling of the number of children in the common schools, and a general advance in education throughout the State. The Board of Education is composed of the Attorney-General, the Secretary of State, and the Superintendent of Public Instruction.

While it may be said that there are free schools in most of the districts in Kentucky, it is evident that many of them are but poorly sustained for a few months in the year, and are not patronized enough by the influential classes to give them vitality and value. All the populous and flourishing towns have high schools and private academies, and the many colleges, either sectarian or established by private enterprise, receive the youth who, in other States, are educated in public schools. Outside of the cities, although some provision is made for the education of the colored children, the whites feel but little interest in it, and Berea College, in the mountain district, is probably the only mixed college in the State. An address recently made by Colonel Stodart Johnson, of Kentucky, containing a strong plea for educational progress, excited considerable unfriendly criticism.

The public debt of Kentucky is but a trifling sum, and the "powers that be" are very scrupulous with regard to incurring liabilities,—so much so that they begrudge the money which might be expended in furthering the State's interest. The total State tax, at present, is forty-five cents on one hundred dollars, and real estate is rarely assessed at more than half its value.

Eastern Kentucky may be said to be one immense bed of coal and iron. The territory of the State extends over much of the area of two of the largest and richest coal-fields on the continent. The great Appalachian coal-field extends through its eastern section, and extensive coal-measures are found, and have been worked, in a score of the eastern counties. This coal-field embraces nearly all the mountain counties drained by the Big Sandy river, the Kentucky above its forks, and the Cumberland above its shoals. The upper coal-measures of this eastern coal-field embrace very rich beds, containing from sixty to sixty-three per cent. of fixed carbon. The yield of the entire region is rich, averaging from fifty-eight to sixty-three per cent. Coal crops out along the banks of the Big Sandy river, and is easily worked and readily transportable to market. On the Kentucky and Cumberland fine workable beds of coal are also found. The iron ore is always closely associated with coal. Iron-furnaces might be established with profit throughout the entire group of mountain counties, from the Big Sandy to the level lands of Middle Kentucky, and from the Ohio river to the Tennessee line.

In many counties red and brown hematites and the Black Band ores, resembling those from which iron is chiefly made in Europe, are abundant. The minerals of Eastern Kentucky are its main resource, for the only lands of medium fertility are to be found along the streams. The hill-sides, from which the inhabitants dig with difficulty a scanty sustenance, are poor in quality. Mineral springs are scattered throughout the eastern section, and the fine climate and the lovely scenery of the Kentucky mountains will doubtless give them in due time the reputation won by those of Western and South-western Virginia.

In Estill county, on the Red river, a small tributary of the Kentucky, is an iron district which has attained a world-wide reputation. The Red River Iron Works, located near the mouth of the stream, began operations in 1808. Rude furnaces were built there in that year, and the soft ores of the district were roughly converted into pig-iron. In succeeding years better furnaces were erected, and since the war the property has passed into the hands of a wealthy stock company, which now owns 60,000 acres of mineral and timber lands, and is much in need of railroad facilities. Another corporation, known as the Cottage Iron Company, also owns 13,000 acres of fine mineral land in the vicinity. These companies together employ a thousand workmen, and annually expend half a million dollars in the manufacture of metals used exclusively for car-wheels. When these furnaces are put in connection with the markets, by an already projected railway, the number of tons of pig-iron manufactured in the State, which in 1870 was 37,548, will be vastly increased.

The coal-field of Western Kentucky is seventy-five miles in length and fifty-five miles in width at the widest part, having an average width of perhaps forty miles. The Elizabethtown and Paducah railroad runs through its entire length, and it is traversed by several other railroads. The coal and iron ores have as yet been but little developed, but will evidently repay an active mining. Through the southern portion of Western Kentucky there are large veins of lead ore said to contain considerable silver, but the operations in mining these ores have been very imperfect. Twelve of the western counties overlie coal-measures, and in Union, Henderson, and Davis counties there are many workable beds of coal with an average thickness of four feet. According to the testimony of General Basil Duke, the richest coals of the Western Kentucky fields, possessing an average of more than fifty per cent. of fixed carbon, are found in the lower coal-measures, which in a depth of 900 feet contain ten workable beds having a united thickness of more than thirty feet.

The above-mentioned counties are also exceedingly rich in agricultural resources. Alluvial deposits in the bottoms along the Ohio river, and the loam of the uplands, furnish a superb soil on which fine crops of tobacco are raised and the Indian corn is as large as that of the best blue grass land. All these counties lying along the Ohio are very fertile, and their lands command high prices. The counties near the confluence of the Ohio and Mississippi rivers, composed of the sediment of both streams, produce fine crops of tobacco, wheat, corn, and grasses. Labor and immigrants are everywhere in demand in this part of the State. Western Kentucky produces the great bulk of the tobacco crop of the State, although this staple is cultivated in many other counties. The farms in some portions of this section are now too large to be managed under the present labor system, and proprietors will occasionally sell acres which before the war brought $90, for $35 or $40. In the counties lying adjacent to Middle Kentucky small improved farms of reasonably good soil can be had at trivial prices.

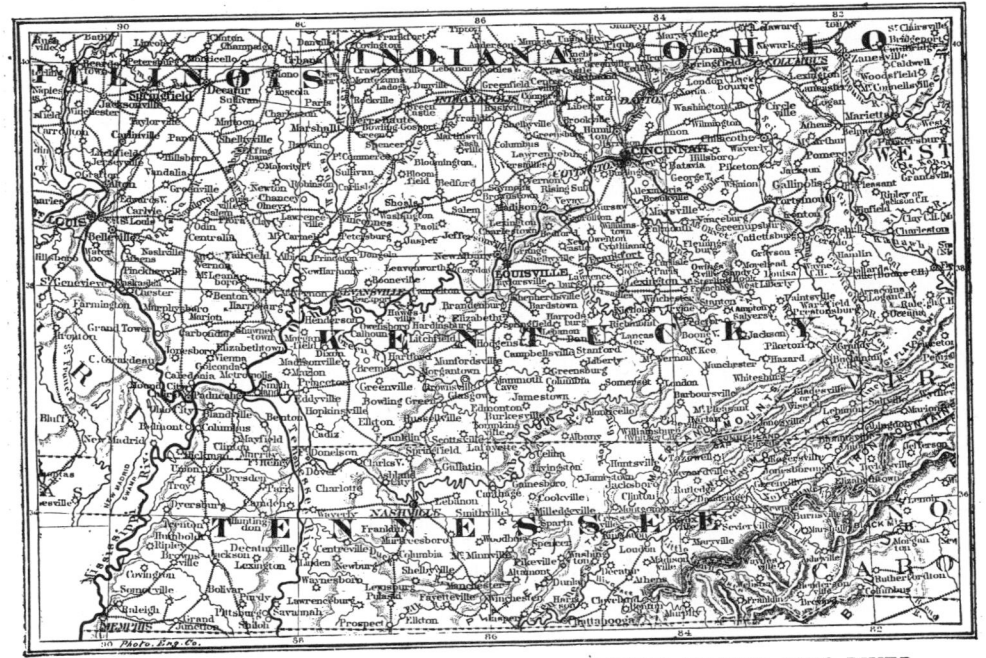

TENNESSEE, KENTUCKY, AND THE REGION DRAINED BY THE OHIO RIVER.

LXXXI.

NASHVILLE AND MIDDLE TENNESSEE.

WHEN I first saw Nashville, the capital of Tennessee, its streets were almost deserted. The only signs of activity were at the railway stations, where thousands of people were crowding the trains which were to bear them beyond the reach of cholera. The city received a dreadful visitation of this destroyer in 1873, and the dispatches which brought from Memphis the accounts of the horrors of the yellow fever were the only news which I found in the papers of Nashville. But visiting the pleasant town a few months afterward, when the cholera had passed away, and the inhabitants had regained their courage, I saw plenty of life, activity, and industry. During my stay the city was visited by a furious and protracted rain-storm which flooded the lower part of the town, and raised the Cumberland river, which at Nashville flows between high banks, so that a disastrous inundation was feared. Houses were set afloat, negroes were driven from their cabins to the streets, and poverty and distress were great.

Nashville was once one of the most famous towns in the United States. Its men and women were noted for their wit and beauty,—qualities which are conspicuous to-day, but which have not been so prominent in the society of the National Capital as previous to 1835. The town is situated on the left bank of the Cumberland river, a little north of the centre of the State. It is founded almost literally upon a rock, the river-bluffs rising nearly eighty feet above low water mark. The city stretches along irregular and gradual slopes, and is picturesquely grouped around Capitol Hill, on which stands the State-House, one of the most elegant public buildings in the country. From its beautiful porticoes one may look over the wide expanse of plain dotted with groups of houses; over the high trestle-works on which run the railways leading toward Memphis; or may gaze upon the winding Cumberland, along whose banks the high business blocks are not ungracefully packed; or out to the hill on which stand the ruins of Fort Negley, a remnant of the fierce siege during the war.

The Tennessee State Capitol, at Nashville.

The Capitol is built of laminated limestone, which softens by exposure to the air, and some of the stones are already beginning to show signs of exfoliation. On the streets near the Capitol I saw gangs of negro convicts from the State Penitentiary, which is situated in the city, working at street and wall making, while guards with cocked rifles kept constant watch over them.

Nashville now has about 40,000 population, and is rapidly growing in wealth and commercial importance. Its receipts of cotton annually amount to nearly 100,000 bales; it has a large trade in leaf tobacco, which comes from the adjacent counties; its provision trade is with the far South, and is very extensive. Its sales of dry goods annually amount to about four million dollars. It also deals very extensively in liquor. The flouring-mills in the city and vicinity manufacture 450,000 barrels of flour and 1,200,000 barrels of meal annually. The Southerner has a marked fondness for Tennessee whiskey, and Nashville sends the favorite beverage into every Southern State. During the year 1873 the sales amounted to more than one hundred thousand barrels. Nashville is also a

View from the State Capitol, Nashville, Tennessee.

central point for drovers, and thousands of cattle, sheep, and swine are yearly sent down from the great Blue Grass region to be marketed at the capital. The whole trade of the town amounts to more than fifty millions yearly, and this will probably soon be doubled by the rapid increase of the coal trade and manufacturing and mechanical interests.

Three coal-fields are easily accessible from the town. One lies along the Nashville and Chattanooga railroad, the second is drained by the upper Cumberland river, and the third, that of Western Kentucky, is penetrated by the St. Louis and South-eastern railroad. Six important railways centre in Nashville. The Louisville and Nashville, and Nashville and Decatur roads, consolidated, give a route from the Ohio river through the Tennessee capital to the junction with the road leading, by the Memphis and Charleston line, to Memphis. The Nashville and Chattanooga road runs through the loveliest mountain scenery in the South to Chattanooga. The Tennessee and Pacific road extends to Lebanon in Tennessee, and the St. Louis and South-eastern line gives a direct route via Henderson, Kentucky, and Evansville, Indiana, to St. Louis. Other roads are now under contract, and are opening up the entire country of Middle Tennessee.

The Cumberland river, upon whose banks are many flourishing towns, is navigable for nine months in the year, and large quantities of coal and lumber are floated down to Nashville during high water. The value of the exports and imports along this river exceeds ten million dollars yearly, and if the improvements could be effected which are needed to render it thoroughly navigable, even at an expense of four or five million dollars, the trade would doubtless be quadrupled. Little has been done since Andrew Jackson's time to construct the necessary dams and deepen the channel of the stream.

In North Nashville stands one of the largest cotton factories in the country. Although it has been established but a short time, the annual dividends of the company amount to twelve per cent. Factory-hands receive but little more than five dollars weekly, and the cheapness of cotton and labor enabled the proprietors last year not only to issue bonds which are at par in financial circles, but to declare a net profit of more than forty thousand dollars. Nashville is making an effort to secure the establishment of other cotton factories within her limits.

At Edgefield, across the Cumberland, there are many prosperous manufactories; and many Nashville people, finding that the neighboring town has thus far enjoyed complete immunity from cholera, have built handsome residences there. The Nashville people, during the visitation of their town by the plague, accepted the suggestion that Edgefield escaped the scourge because its inhabitants drank only cistern water; but this cannot be the case, as the water procured for Nashville by her fine system of water-works can hardly be inferior to that used in Edgefield.

Davidson county, in which the capital is situated, is highly prosperous. Manufacturing establishments are springing up in many towns; food can be produced cheaply, and great quantities of coal and iron lie within convenient distances of each other. The public schools in Nashville are exceedingly good. More than 2,500 children regularly attend them, and the course of study, which requires ten years, and embraces primary, intermediate, grammar and high school departments, is admirably comprehensive. Nashville is likely to become a prominent educational centre in the South. The Vanderbilt University, the outgrowth of the magnificent

Tomb of Ex-President Polk — Nashville, Tennessee.

donation of half a million of dollars to the Methodist Episcopal Church South, by Commodore Vanderbilt, of New York, is in process of erection. The Fisk University, for the colored people, and several excellent seminaries for young ladies, have an enviable reputation. The University of Nashville, whose buildings were used as a hospital during the civil war, has been revived, and its literary and medical departments are now successfully conducted.

From the suspension bridge spanning the Cumberland one gets a view of the pretty stream, with rafts of logs moored along its banks; of busy and prosperous Edgefield; of old Fort Negley's wind-swept height, and the many elegant streets along the hills, with cozy mansions and fine churches embowered in foliage. The market square is large, but there is not much of the picturesque activity which one finds in the markets further South; so, also, there is less of the lounging and laziness which a more genial sun prompts in the Gulf States. The town is quiet, but not sleepy. The numerous daily newspapers, and the elegant book stores, than which there are no finer south of Baltimore, as well as a good public library, and the collection of volumes at the Capitol, testify to a literary taste. The society is exceedingly cordial, and hospitality is of the genuine Southern kind, diffuse and deferential.

The Hermitage—General Andrew Jackson's old homestead, near Nashville, Tennessee.

A few miles from the town, on the line of the Louisville and Nashville railroad, is a large national cemetery, an effective testimonial to the sharpness of the fighting around Nashville in 1864, when General Thomas sallied out to meet Hood, and in a two days' battle drove the Confederates from their intrenchments, following them until they escaped across the Tennessee river.

No State is making more earnest endeavors to secure immigration than Tennessee. In the cars, on the steamboats, on the rivers, in the hotels, at the Capitol, in all public places, one hears the resources of the State earnestly discussed, and no stranger is allowed to pass without giving him thorough information as to its splendid mineral wealth and remarkable agricultural facilities.

The population of the State is at present 1,258,526, of whom 322,000 are colored. Over seventy-two per cent. of the people are engaged in agriculture. The area of improved land in the State is but small, when one considers that there are twenty-five millions of acres within the State limits.

The tendency is to small farms. The entire value of the farms is more than $218,000,000. The total valuation of the taxable property in 1873 was $308,000,000, while the true valuation was probably two-fifths more. From these few statistics it will be seen that Tennessee has an industrious and capable population, although in some parts of the State one cannot but look with displeasure upon the rough-riding, hard-drinking, quarrelsome folk who grumble at the new order of things, and spend their nights at corner-groceries, inveighing against "free niggers" and free schools.

The astonishing cheapness of land is accounted for by the want of home markets, of good roads, and cheap means of transportation in many sections in the State. The war also ruined many farmers who held slaves, and instances have been known of the sale of estates worth $100,000 for one-fifth of that sum. Among the other drawbacks to farming are the want of active capital and of good labor. Great inducements are offered immigrants who are willing to work, and who have a small capital to invest; for good lands, partially improved, may be had in the eastern, middle, or western divisions of the State for from eight to thirty dollars an acre.

Many Northern immigrants who have entered Tennessee have been disappointed because they expected to find labor less necessary than in the country whence they came. The winters are short and the products are abundant; but a farmer must labor in Tennessee as in New York or Ohio. The Secretary of the State Board of Agriculture, Mr. J. B. Killebrew, who has written an excellent book on the resources of the State, urges immigrants to go to Tennessee in colonies, as they can generally, by buying land together, secure it at much cheaper rates, and can have a society of their own, whereas a single individual settling in the back-country of Tennessee, among populations somewhat ignorant, and generally prejudiced against innovations, would find his habits constantly clashing with those of the people around him, and would end by leaving in disgust. The impression that the better class in Tennessee does not respect laboring men is incorrect. It is becoming yearly more and more disgraceful to be an idler, and the influential people heartily welcome all who go to the State for the purpose of establishing manufactures or engaging in agriculture. Outrages against persons and property are, on the whole, rare. In the rougher mountain regions, and some of the sections bordering on the Mississippi, strangers are looked upon with suspicion, and Northern men are considered as natural enemies; but this by no means represents the feeling of the mass of the people of the State.

Young Tennesseans.

Tennessee is gradually reducing her debt, which, in April of 1874, was $23,995,337. In 1875, nearly every railroad within her boundaries will be liable to taxation, and, judging from the present aspects, many millions of dollars will be invested in the manufacture of cotton and woolen goods, and the development of the coal and iron-fields so prodigally scattered over the State. The Tennessee, the Cumberland, and numerous other rivers, serve as important avenues of transportation, and the unflagging zeal manifested by the State authorities in demanding the improvement of these streams will soon result in some action by the General Government. Western Tennessee has already more than seven hundred miles of rail, and had it not been for the financial crisis of '73, the mileage would have been largely increased.

Tennessee Log Cabins.

The public school system is not yet very efficient, although much labor has been expended in its enforcement by native Tennesseans. There is a positive objection freely expressed in many parts of Tennessee to the education of the negro, but the colored element in the Republican party seems quite competent to assert its own interests and to provide for them. The blacks are clamorous for many of the privileges which would be secured to them by the Civil Rights bill, and Congressman Maynard, their present candidate for Governor (October, 1874), is helping them in their crusade. The permanent school fund for the State is more than two and one-half millions, and an additional annual income is derived from numerous sources. The school districts are authorized to levy taxes for the support of schools and the erection of buildings. As the matter of taxation is left to their option, the more illiberal of the districts are, of course, unprovided with schools. It is asserted that but thirty-five counties in the State have really levied a tax for school purposes. The fact that the whites are positively determined to provide completely separate schools for the colored people, and that the latter are not rich enough to supply themselves with schools, renders the subject a difficult and disagreeable one, especially at the present time. The scholastic population of the State was, in 1873, one hundred and seventy-three thousand. The number of teachers is insufficient, and their qualifications are not always of a high order.

The Cumberland University at Lebanon has a good legal department, and the Presbyterians propose shortly to establish a fine University, with an endowment of half a million, which shall rival the famous institution founded by Vanderbilt at Nashville.

Middle Tennessee, in which Nashville stands, is at present the most valuable division of the State. It contains more than half a million people, and several hundred prosperous towns and villages. It is one of the healthiest sections of America. The Cumberland, Duck, and Elk rivers flow down through deep gorges in the mountains, and the hundreds of small streams in the recesses among the hills furnish abundant water power. The variety of crops is almost astonishing; wheat and fruits, tobacco, corn, cotton, and everything that grows above the thirty-fifth parallel of latitude,—even the fig and the magnolia,—can be cultivated without injury from the climate. In what is called the Central Basin of Middle Tennessee, as in Kentucky, much of the fine stock used in the Cotton States is bred. The fleet horses and the slow and laborious mules, the fine short-horned and Ayrshire cattle, are sought by buyers from all the States as the most perfect types of these animals. As a wool-growing region the basin has few equals and no superiors.

Tomb of Andrew Jackson, at the "Hermitage," near Nashville.

LXXXII.

A GLANCE AT MARYLAND'S HISTORY—HER EXTENT AND RESOURCES.

WHEN the first Lord Baltimore, George Calvert, found that his efforts to establish a colony in Newfoundland were unavailing, he visited Virginia, in 1628. While there, he undertook the examination of the Chesapeake, which John Smith had explored many years before. Journeying along the mighty

View from Federal Hill, Baltimore, Maryland, looking across the Basin.

stretch of water 200 miles from the ocean, and, noting its numerous tributary rivers, he doubtless saw the wonderful advantages which these offered for colonization, and as soon as he returned to England he procured from Charles I. the promise of a grant of territory on the Chesapeake. The Virginians were not pleased with the prospects of the establishment of Lord Baltimore's colony, and took occasion to voice their discontent in the hearing of the English officials. Lord Baltimore died early in 1632, before the promised charter had been accorded; but when it was issued it passed to his son, the second Lord Baltimore, and "all that part of the peninsula lying in the parts of America between the ocean on the east and the Bay of Chesapeake on the west" was erected into a province and called Maryland. This was England's first province, and it was intended to call it Crescentia; but Charles I., when the charter was presented for his signature, struck out Crescentia and substituted Maryland, in honor of his queen, Henrietta Maria, of France. Lord Baltimore was made absolute lord and proprietary of the province, giving only two Indian arrows annually, and one-fifth of all the gold and silver ore found within the limits of Maryland, as a pledge of his allegiance to the crown. The proprietary was accorded power to enact laws, with the advice and assent of the freemen of the province and their delegates. He had arbitrary power to impose taxes, and to deprive citizens even of life and liberty.

The boundaries of Maryland were the occasion of much dispute in later days, the present limits being much less than those originally accorded the province. Delaware was formerly part of the territory of Maryland. The boundary between Maryland and Pennsylvania was disputed until Mason and Dixon drew their famous line between the two States in 1763—since recognized as the dividing line between Northern and Southern territory and sentiment. Virginia also revived her old quarrel with regard to the boundaries, and it may be said to have existed in a modified form up to the present day.

In 1633, on the 22d of November, about two hundred colonists, many of whom were Roman Catholics, set sail from the Isle of Wight, arriving off Point Comfort in Virginia early in 1634. On the 25th of March they celebrated mass on the banks of the Potomac and took formal possession of the country. They then occupied an Indian town which the natives had ceded to them, named St. Mary's, and for more than half a century this town was the capital of the province. The capital thus established was almost at the southern extremity of the province, and for many years thereafter the extension of settlements into the interior was hindered by internal commotion and wars with the Indians. The proprietary government during the first century of its existence twice met with serious interruptions: once when it was usurped by Cromwell's Commissioners during the rule of the English Commonwealth, and once when it was displaced by the rule of William and Mary. At a time when religious toleration was unknown elsewhere in America, or at all in Europe, it was inaugurated under the proprietary government. Maryland soon became a refuge for all who suffered from religious persecution. Quakers and Puritans and members of the Church of England fled thither from New England and Virginia, and Protestants from France, Portugal, and the Netherlands, took refuge in Lord Baltimore's colony from Catholic rage. The population of the province enjoyed religious equality until 1692, when the royal government which had usurped the powers of the proprietary, made, for the first time, ecclesiastical establishment in Maryland.

In 1659 Baltimore county was created. At that time the territory was almost a wilderness occupied by the Indians, but the colonists gradually extended the limits of civilization.

FOUNDATION AND EARLY GROWTH.

In 1662 the first land within the limits of the present Baltimore city was patented by Thomas Gorsuch, a member of the Society of Friends. This was a tract of fifty acres on Whetstone Point, where to-day the gigantic grain trade of the West is centring. The first actual settler on the site of the city is believed to have been a Mr. David Jones, who gave his name to the erratic little stream known as Jones's Falls, which has often overflowed its banks and caused serious damage.

In 1723 ships began to enter the Patapsco from London, and in 1729 an Act of Assembly was passed for erecting a town on the north side of the Patapsco, in Baltimore county. In 1730 the town was laid out into lots, and called Baltimore in compliment to the proprietary. It was evidently not the expectation of the early settlers that the town would grow to its present size, or they would not have established it in a location surrounded by hills, watercourses and marshes; but they found abundance of stone, lime, iron and timber, and excellent sites for water-works near the harbor. The expense to which the modern Baltimoreans have been subjected for extending and grading streets along the numerous hills, and for covering marshes and small streams, is enormous.

In 1752 Baltimore had but twenty-five houses. St. Paul's Church, which was begun by the members of the Church of England in 1731 and completed in 1744, was a quaint building occupying the site of the present church, at the corner of Charles and Saratoga streets. Although the population of the county at that time was more than seventeen thousand, that of the town was but two hundred. The sloop "Baltimore" and the brig "Philip and Charles" were the only sea-going vessels owned in the town. The warehouse near the harbor, for tobacco inspection, was one of the principal centres of trade. The growth of the city was promoted during the war between the English and the French by the necessity which the inhabitants felt of flocking together for protection, rather than penetrating into the country.

In 1755 the Indians came within eighty miles of Baltimore, and made numerous destructive raids. Palisades were constructed, and the women and children were placed by the colonists upon vessels in the harbor. In 1756 numerous Acadians, refugees from the harsh policy of the English in Nova Scotia, settled in Baltimore. The town began to grow in commerce; ship-yards were established at Fells Point, and many merchants had their residences there. In 1761 the population of the province was 164,007, of

The Oldest House in Baltimore.

which 49,675 were negroes. The good people of Maryland were greatly annoyed at this time by the number of convicts imported from England, estimated at not less than twenty thousand. These convicts were brought over under contract by private shippers, and sold into servitude for the entire term of transportation. In due time many of them were transformed into useful citizens, and some of them attained considerable distinction.

In 1761 the Maryland exports of tobacco to England amounted to 140,000 pounds. Wheat, lumber, corn, flour, iron, skins, and furs were also exported, and Maryland would have grown with astonishing rapidity from that date if England's policy of stifling manufacturing industry in the colonies, that she might send her own productions to them, had not been vigorously carried out. The iron and shipping business was greatly restricted, but, although commercially dependent upon England, the province managed to develop her natural resources to a considerable extent. Although Maryland acquiesced in the restrictions made by England upon her commerce, she heartily joined with the colonies in asserting the right to regulate her own internal government and to impose her own taxes. The freemen of the province were exceedingly jealous of the privileges accorded to them by the charter, and when England began to take the matter of taxation into her own hands by establishing the stamp tax, Maryland promptly expelled the stamp distributor from the province upon his arrival, and forbade the landing of the stamped paper which had been brought in the same ship with him. The attempted tax upon tea, which was the occasion of the sudden rebellion in Boston, was also the occasion of an outbreak at Annapolis, the then capital of Maryland. The colonists had refused from the very first to allow the tea sent from England to be unloaded, and in 1774 a vessel with eighteen packages of tea on board was burned at Annapolis.

At the time of the declaration of independence by the Continental Congress in Philadelphia, the proprietary government of Maryland was held by an illegitimate son of Lord Baltimore, who died in 1771. The people of Maryland had always entertained a strong loyalty toward the Baltimores, but this bastard ruler was promptly objected to. His government was overthrown, and a convention was called to frame a Constitution for the new State of Maryland.

The convention assembled at Annapolis on the 14th of August, 1776, and Maryland entered into the Revolutionary war with an earnestness and gallantry which made the name of the "Maryland line" conspicuous in Revolutionary annals. At the battle of Brooklyn Heights in 1776 a part of a battalion of Maryland troops repeatedly charged with bayonets a whole brigade of British regulars. They were the first American troops to use that weapon, and used it to such advantage that on many occasions thereafter they both charged and repulsed the enemy with unloaded muskets. Maryland also maintained a marine service during the Revolution, to protect her shores from the English cruisers.

After the establishment of the independence of the colonies there was for some time an almost complete paralysis of commerce in Maryland. The low price of tobacco and flour, the principal articles of export from the State, added to the distress. But a period of marked commercial activity soon followed. The tobacco trade revived, English merchants who had sought to re-establish the agencies which they had maintained before the Revolution at Annapolis, Bladensburg, Upper Marlborough and Elk Ridge Landing, being superseded by Baltimore capitalists, who began to make shipments in their own vessels and for their own account. The trade of the city was greatly improved; canal companies along the Susquehanna and the Potomac were formed; streets were extended and paved; and the population, which in 1782 was nearly 8,000, became energetic and progressive. Sugar refineries, glass-works and flour-mills were established, and the Baltimore clippers carrying their products to foreign ports became famous everywhere. As the West began to develop, Baltimore laid hold from time to time upon its trade, and became the first, as it is to-day the natural, market for the productions of that section.

Baltimore bore an important part in the war between England and America in 1814, and was one of the chief sufferers by it. The British fleet blockaded the Chesapeake bay, and commerce was seriously affected. Many privateers were fitted out at Baltimore and did good service. After the burning of Washington by the British, a force of 5,000 English was landed at the mouth of the Patapsco river, a sharp battle taking place there between this force and the Maryland and Pennsylvania militia. On the 13th of September, 1814, the British made a vigorous attack upon Fort McHenry, an important fortification which had been established on Whetstone Point in 1794. The little fort, with its finely planned batteries, completely repulsed the attacking fleet, and compelled the retreat of the invading forces. During the night of the bombardment, upon which the English admiral relied so much that he had sworn to take the fort in two hours, Francis S. Key, a noted Marylander and a prisoner in the British fleet, wrote the celebrated national song called "The Star-Spangled Banner."

This song, which has justly been accorded the honors of the "national hymn," was suggested by the hopes and fears which filled the poet's heart during the long and terrible night, and the anxiety with which he looked at the walls of the fort in the morning to see if the flag was still there:—

> "Oh, say can you see by the dawn's early light
> What so proudly we hailed at the twilight's last gleaming;
> Whose broad stripes and bright stars, through the perilous fight
> O'er the ramparts we watched, were so gallantly streaming?
> The rockets' red glare, bombs bursting in air,
> Gave proof through the night that our flag was still there.
> Oh, say does that star-spangled banner still wave
> O'er the land of the free and the home of the brave?"

While the bombs of the English ships were bursting in hundreds about the parapets of Fort McHenry, an adventurous rooster mounted the walls and crowed heartily and repeatedly. One of the defenders of the fort then declared that if he ever lived to see Baltimore the rooster should be fed with pound cake; and the day after the bombardment, although the man was so worn down with fatigue as to be unable to leave the fort, he sent to the city, procured the cake, and treated the patriotic fowl.

Maryland has an area of about 9,500 square miles of land, and the Chesapeake bay covers 4,000 more. It may be said with truth that the land beneath the waters is quite as productive as that above, for the oyster-beds, the abundance of excellent fish, the flocks of wild ducks and the multitudes of terrapins and crabs afford an immense commerce. The thousands of acres along the shores of this beautiful bay are crowded with market gardens, which supply Baltimore, Philadelphia, Washington, and New York with all the most delicate fruits and vegetables.

The estuaries and navigable arms of the Chesapeake are so numerous that there are many counties bordering on the water, no point in which is many miles from a good landing. Although the actual sea-coast of Maryland is but little more than thirty miles, the tide-water margin, including that along the islands, is over 500 miles. The largest vessels can ascend the bay, pass St. Mary's, Calvert and Anne Arundel counties to Annapolis, and, entering the Potomac river, can

Fort McHenry — Baltimore Harbor. [Page 737.]

pass up by St. Mary's, Charles, and Prince George's counties to Washington. The Chesapeake, the Nanticoke and the Patuxent, as well as nearly fifty other streams, are navigable for many miles. Maryland is divided into three sections, two of which, separated by the Chesapeake, are very similar in formation. In the tide-water district, which embraces nearly one-half of the territory of the State, and which is supposed to have formed the bed of an ancient ocean, lie rich deposits of marl and shell lime. The surface is but slightly elevated above the sea, and the forest-growths are mainly oak, hickory, chestnut, walnut, gum, cedar, pine and beech. Emery, bog iron ore, kaolin, or porcelain clay, and gray, red and blue clays are found in profusion. In this section there is an excellent opportunity for the establishment of glass manufactories, as the pure sand is admirably adapted for that purpose. Wheat, Indian corn, tobacco, and cotton in the southern sections, are the grains mainly cultivated.

On the "eastern shore," which embraces the counties of Worcester, Somerset, Dorchester, Talbot, Caroline, Queen Anne's and Cecil, the soils were originally among the most fertile in the State. Reckless management in slaveholding times injured their productive value, but careful culture is gradually restoring them. The sections remote from tide-water produce wheat and corn mainly, while in the southern portion flax and cotton are raised. In Worcester county there are immense cypress swamps, but the soil, in many portions, where it has been drained and reclaimed, is of unsurpassed fertility. Wild ducks and oysters abound along the Atlantic coast of this county.

The grape grows in great perfection along the eastern shore, and in some counties excellent wines are manufactured. Along the western shore dwell many hardy fishermen, the shad and herring fisheries of the Potomac being as extensive as those of any other portion of the United States. As many as four hundred thousand barrels of herring have been taken from the Potomac, within a hundred miles of Washington, in a single year, and sent to the Baltimore market. On this, as on the eastern shore, the lands suffered for a century from an exhaustive system of planting, and being deserted by their owners, as their fertility gradually lessened, the section had a smaller white population in 1860 than just before the Revolution; but the means of reclaiming all the lands exists in the great beds of shell marl which abound throughout many of the counties. In the southern part of the district tobacco is one of the principal crops, Prince George's county alone having produced as much as ten million pounds in a year. The clay-beds which extend through the district from the Potomac to the Susquehanna, and which here and there attain an elevation of two hundred feet above tide-water, are very valuable. The iron which the clay contains gives the pottery made from it a red shade, which renders it unfit for the choice wares; but for the manufacture of brick, these clay-beds are the best in the world. Prince George's county, whence in the latter part of the seventeenth century a hundred sail of ships annually carried tobacco to England and the West Indies, possesses the State Agricultural College, which is located near Bladensburg. On the southern border of Montgomery county are the great falls of the Potomac, one of the finest water powers in the United States. In this county many of the wealthy citizens of Washington have built handsome residences. The section suffered greatly from raids during the war, but is rapidly regaining its original prosperity. On the Patapsco river, in Howard county, there are numerous excellent granite quarries, and in Baltimore county there are fine-grained white and blue-gray marbles.

The mountain district of the State, which includes Carroll, Frederick, Washington, and Alleghany counties, is fertile and interspersed with beautiful valleys. It is admirably adapted to the raising of stock, and large crops of wheat and thousands of pounds of maple sugar are annually manufactured there.

At Wedverton, in Frederick county, a noble water power has been made available by a dam across the Potomac, and here in due time an extensive manufacturing town will doubtless spring up. In the rugged and broken Alleghany county there are extensive glades or meadows whose grasses are famed for their luxuriance, and over which, before the late war, thousands of cattle from Virginia roamed while fattening for the stall. The iron ores of Cumberland and the coal mines have already been alluded to. The capital invested in mines in Alleghany county is nearly seven million dollars.

Eighty-five thousand slaves were emancipated as the result of the war, and these persons constituted the main agricultural laboring population of the State. As elsewhere throughout the South, they have left the country in swarms and flocked to the towns, and the owners of large plantations, finding that their ex-slaves have deserted them, are anxious to divide up the broad tracts which have now become a burden to them into small vendible portions. Nowhere is there a better opportunity for the purchase of cheap and good lands, or for the practice of the highest scientific farming.

Jones's Falls — Baltimore.

LXXXIII.

THE BALTIMORE AND OHIO RAILROAD—GROWTH OF TRADE.

BALTIMORE, the Maryland metropolis, not only enjoys the honor of having received the first telegraphic message in the United States, but it was also the first to inaugurate a railroad. To that road, which has become one of the most gigantic powers in the land, it owes much of its present astonishingly rapid growth. The last surviving signer of the Declaration of Independence, the illustrious Charles Carroll, of Carrollton, laid the corner-stone of the Baltimore and Ohio railroad, on the 4th of July, 1828. Within half a century since the road was projected, Baltimore's population has increased from 62,000 to 350,000, and her trade has grown so enormously that the stranger who visited the town in 1860 would hardly recognize it now.

When the first rails were laid down, there were very few who contemplated the completion of the road even to the Alleghanies, and none believed that it would touch the Great Lakes and make Chicago and Pittsburg its tributaries. The material obstacles which beset its construction were by no means so great as the financial difficulties. From 1828 until January in 1853, when the completion of the Wheeling and Ohio railroad was celebrated, the company was engaged in perpetual struggles to maintain its existence. As soon as the first rails were laid in the city, in 1828, a car which resembled a country market wagon, and which was drawn by a single horse, was placed upon them, and the leading citizens of Baltimore made trips backward and forward in it. No one had then dreamed of employing steam to draw the cars; but as soon as steam was introduced in England, Mr. Peter Cooper, of New York, who had invented a locomotive with a boiler about the size of those used in hotel kitchens, forthwith solicited the privilege of trying his new and wondrous invention upon the Baltimore and Ohio railroad. His was the first locomotive for railroad purposes ever built

Exchange Place, Baltimore, Maryland.

in America, and Mr. Cooper successfully drove his own engine, to which was attached a car filled with the Directors and prominent citizens, a distance of thirteen miles on the new road in fifty-seven minutes. But as ill-luck would have it, on the return trip, his engine was beaten by a smart trotting-horse, whose owner, from the highway parallel with the road, saw the daring experimenters at work, and mischievously resolved to test horse-flesh against steam. The veteran philanthropist, Cooper, must look back upon those days of primitive experiments with a smile when he remembers that from New York to St. Louis is hardly a journey of forty-eight hours to-day.

From such humble beginnings the road rapidly grew, and, as it reached the Alleghanies, began to draw toward Baltimore a traffic in coal which has since been developed into colossal proportions. Millions of tons, in cars expressly constructed for the purpose, annually pass over the road; and the traveler who, seated in the hotel-station at Harper's Ferry, looks down the line of rail which runs along the ravine, sees immense trains, drawn by enormous engines of a peculiar build, whizzing over the tracks within ten minutes of each other all day long.

In 1831 the then President of the railroad, in a report made to the Governor of Maryland, boasted that the State had within her limits the longest continuous railway in the world. This was the road from Baltimore to Frederick, sixty-one miles in length. In the same report he foreshadowed the future effort to draw the trade of the West to Baltimore, when he referred to the fact that the State was so situated as to afford the surest and most convenient route of communication between the navigable Western waters and the ocean. Baltimore, with her splendid advantages of precedent, however, required many severe lessons before she could be made to improve her opportunities.

One by one her rivals laid hold of the treasures of the West, while the Directors of the Baltimore and Ohio railroad were battling with the great canal company, which had so long monopolized the trade between the Chesapeake and the Ohio; and while the legislation of Baltimore itself so restricted the road that it could not obtain proper development. In 1842 the line was opened to Cumberland, now a fine commercial town, beautifully located in the mountains; and on the completion of the road to Wheeling in 1854 the commerce of Baltimore began to increase with tremendous rapidity. The freight to the State in 1832 had amounted to scarcely 30,000 tons; in 1852 it had reached 252,000 tons; in 1854 it amounted to 661,000 tons. All the old methods of transportation were thenceforth unavailing. The products of the West were no longer floated down the Ohio and Mississippi to New Orleans, there loaded into schooners, and thence carried by sea to the Chesapeake, and so to Baltimore.

Just as the people of the State were beginning to despair, and to fancy that New York and Philadelphia had completely distanced them, their best commercial development began. Had the road been completed to the Ohio river twenty years sooner, the river system of the West would not to-day have converged toward Lake Erie. The wisdom of the commercial men of the North who had hastened to construct the Erie and New York Central road, which, with the Erie canal, seemed to secure to New York the great body of the Western trade, had been so often demonstrated to the Baltimoreans that they had quite despaired of longer endeavoring to make Baltimore a rival of New York, and were contenting themselves with the supply trade of the South. But the vigorous policy of the railroad men who pushed the Baltimore

Scene on the Chesapeake and Ohio Canal.

and Ohio road into the West, and courageously combated New York, has worked a complete revolution. Now that grain seeks quick transportation by rail, and that the Baltimore and Ohio road, whose connections extend through the length of the South and West, has reached out an arm to Chicago, Baltimore seems likely to be a most important tide-water terminus of the West.

The war interrupted the many projects which President Garret, to whose past and present vigorous management the railroad owes much of its prosperity, had been maturing, and after four years of civil strife the work was begun anew. In 1865 the company commenced to lease Western railroads, and to elaborate its terminal facilities at Baltimore. As the result, it has to-day under its management a continuous direct road of 512 miles in length, furnishing for West Virginia and much of Ohio, Indiana, Illinois, Missouri and Kansas, the surest and cheapest path to the sea. It has thoroughly attached itself to the trade of the valley of the Ohio, Pittsburg, Wheeling, Marietta, Parkersburg, Portsmouth, Cincinnati, Louisville, and other centres, which have branches extending to them from the main stem. The road to Chicago completes the system, and the Baltimoreans claim that it relegates New York to the commercial inferiority which her inactive policy of late has been bringing upon her. Within the past few years, also, the metropolitan branch of the Baltimore and Ohio railroad, shortening the line between Washington and the West nearly fifty miles, has been completed; and a new branch is in construction downward through the Valley of Virginia, and will doubtless drain that wonderful agricultural region into the Baltimore basin, opening up, by its connection with the Chesapeake and Ohio railroad at Staunton, the coal, salt and iron industries of Western Virginia. The road has also seized on the Orange, Alexandria and Manassas line from Washington to Lynchburg, and given to it and its extensions the new name of the Washington City, Virginia Midland, and Great Southern.

The House of Refuge—Baltimore.

The contest with the Chesapeake and Ohio Canal Company for the right of way along the Potomac, when the Baltimore and Ohio railroad was in its infancy, brought into play the abilities of some of the finest leaders of the bar. In the trials of the Court of Appeals, where the struggle for the choice of route was a prolonged one, and where the decision was finally given in favor of the railroads, the clear-headed Taney, the commanding Webster, the majestic and elegant Wirt, the philanthropic Mercer, the accurate Gwynn, and the then young and aspiring Reverdy Johnson, made brilliant speeches. Among the men who planned and executed the through route were some of the most noted citizens of Maryland; the names of Robert Oliver, of Alexander Brown, of William Lorman, of Isaac McKim, of William Patterson, Talbot Jones, George Hoffman, John B. Morris, William Stewart, and Philip E. Thomas, are inseparably connected with the projection of this great work. They were, in a measure, the pioneers of the railway system of this country, and to them and the thousands who have emulated their example in every State of the Union we owe our material prosperity as a nation.

The men who determined to make Baltimore the chief of American ports did not overlook the necessity for proper terminal facilities. This subject engaged the attention of the company from the moment of its organization; but during its early years, the main terminus was a small depot, which has since expanded into the great Mount Clare Station, where to-day there are acres of repair shops and locomotive houses. When the company had once resolved to provide a tide-water terminus, it lost no time in selecting and purchasing the grounds at Locust Point, a narrow strip of land at the entrance of Baltimore harbor, admirably adapted for the construction of wharves. The misguided stranger who fancies that Baltimore is a torpid town, where business enterprise is rarely hinted at, would do well to visit Locust Point, and correct his previous impressions.

The whole peninsula, of which Locust Point is the terminus, has always been considered most advantageous for shipments. Early in the Revolution an English corporation obtained possession of it; but the plans of the company were overthrown by an act of confiscation, under which the Point was taken by the State and sold. In later years, the peninsula was selected as the site for Fort McHenry, the principal defense of the harbor. The peninsula has about five miles of water-frontage, along every portion of which there is a depth of from seventeen to twenty-one feet, easily increased to twenty-five. Locust Point proper comprises a water-front of about 3,600 lineal feet, and an area of eighty acres, seamed with railway tracks, covered with gigantic sheds and warehouses, and dotted with immense wharves, on which stand two mammoth elevators, one of which has a capacity of 600,000, and the other 1,500,000 bushels. These elevators, through which the grain, poured into Baltimore by thousands of cars from the great West, passes directly into the holds of Norwegian, Danish, and English vessels, are superior to any buildings of the kind on the Atlantic coast. Their foundations rest upon thousands of piles, driven deep into the harbor-bed, and covered with oak cappings, upon which the massive granite is laid. The elevator last built stands upon no less than twelve thousand piles. Both are surrounded by water upon three sides, and the vessels flocking about them seem like swallows nestling on the sides of some huge barn. To the great steamship piers, which are covered with iron sheds and into which double track lines of railway run, come weekly steamships from Bremen, and thousands of emigrants annually pass westward through Baltimore.

The Blind Asylum — Baltimore, Maryland.

The present piers are already inadequate to the business which is poured on to them, and new ones will soon be erected. A huge ferry, upon which cars coming from the West with freight for Eastern cities are transferred to the opposite side of the harbor, where connection is made with the Philadelphia, Wilmington and Baltimore railroad, is another of the noted sights at Locust Point. When trade is busiest more than two hundred and fifty cars a day are thus transferred, and the company intends hereafter to obviate the necessity of hauling passenger trains, by horse power, through the city, by running them to Locust Point across the harbor in barges of the ferry. A huge coffee warehouse has been erected near the elevator.

The activity at this point is simply wonderful. A walk along the piers shows an immense panorama of stores of railroad iron, iron ore, bonded warehouses crammed with imported merchandise; great double piers along which hover coastwise steamers; the huge bulk of a Liverpool steam-liner discharging its freight; the graceful outlines of a "North German Lloyd," with its flat-capped and clumsy-looking sailors peering over the sides; while thousands of cars rattle forward and backward into and out of mysterious sheds, and floods of grain pour down from spouts into quaint little barks, whose captains tranquilly smoke their pipes as the process of loading goes on. When one understands that a thousand coal-cars can be daily unloaded at Locust Point, and that all the coal for the huge fleet of ocean steamers plying between New York and Europe is shipped from Baltimore, he begins to comprehend the reasons for the constant arrival of trains filled with their sooty freight.

For the month ending June 30, 1874, 13,861 coal-cars, 2,072 grain-cars, and 3,512 cars loaded with miscellaneous freight were received and emptied at Locust Point. The elevators are monuments to the astonishing increase of the grain trade of Baltimore. In 1871, the exports of bulk grain from the city were hardly 2,000,000 bushels. As soon as the first elevator was opened, they increased to 4,000,000 bushels annually, and in 1873, they amounted to 7,250,000 bushels. The citizens of Baltimore, who once fancied that the improvements in terminal facilities would only enrich the company and not aid the city, have been shown conclusively that all kinds of property in Baltimore increases in ratio with the increase of export trade. The exports for the six months ending July 1, 1874, amounted to more than $15,250,000, or $6,000,000 more than the corresponding six months of 1873, and exceeding by $3,000,000 the entire exports of 1870. Now that the elevators are in direct connection with railway tracks penetrating the West, the grain receipts for the first six months of 1874 amounted to but 600,000 bushels less than those of the entire year of 1873, and the close of 1874 will witness the completion of elevators at Locust Point and at Canton whose united capacity will increase the grain trade at Baltimore to 10,000,000

The Eastern High School—Baltimore, Maryland.

bushels for the last half of the current year. Certainly, it is not without some reason that the enthusiastic Baltimore merchants predict that they may claim $50,000,000 in exports annually in a few years.

The improvement of the harbor of Baltimore was for many years talked of as desirable, but did not become an imperative necessity until the action of the railroad company had made the town one of the most important of American ports. It was evident that if Baltimore was to have a large European trade, her ship-channel, leading from the Patapsco river into the Chesapeake, must be deepened. Large appropriations were made by Congress and the city of Baltimore, in equal portions. The new channels will permit the approach to the city at low water of vessels drawing from twenty-two and a-half to twenty-three feet; and at high water, of those drawing twenty-four to twenty-five feet. The only improvements now necessary are such as will allow vessels of the largest draft to load directly at the wharves, and this work, which is being rapidly effected by the River and Harbor Commission, comprehends the deepening of the channel to the wharves from Fort McHenry.

View of a Lake in Druid Hill Park, Baltimore.

LXXXIV.

THE TRADE OF BALTIMORE—ITS RAPID AND ASTONISHING GROWTH.

THE view of Baltimore harbor, as one enters it from the Chesapeake on one of the noble steamers of the Norfolk and Baltimore line, is highly picturesque. At the narrow mouth of the long and irregularly-shaped basin, which is thronged on either side with groups of imposing buildings, stands Fort McHenry.

On the eastward shore, and nearly opposite Locust Point, is Canton, which was laid out by a company organized in 1828, and has sprung into a wonderfully active life during the past few years. In addition to its wharf property, the Canton Company to-day owns twenty-eight hundred acres of land, and a water-front of twenty thousand feet. Many of the most important manufacturing interests of Baltimore are located in this active suburb. Oyster and fruit packing-houses, sugar refineries, brick-yards, foundries, steam saw-mills, iron and copper smelting furnaces, coal oil refineries, breweries and distilleries, ship-yards and batting factories are densely crowded together along the streets arising from the water, and five to six thousand operatives are employed in the various works.

Maryland Institute—Baltimore.

The Canton Company has shown itself capable of the largest enterprise in increasing the terminal facilities of Baltimore, and is constantly adding to its wharfage forests of piles, their scraggy heads, which appear above the dark water, testifying to the rapidity with which new wharves can be built as soon as they are needed. The railroads centring at Canton drain a vast extent of rich country, and the elevators to be erected there will make it, in time, as important a terminus as its busy neighbor, Locust Point. The Union railroad, projected mainly under the auspices of the Canton Company, was a gigantic undertaking, adding immensely to the commercial advantages of Baltimore,—its double tracks connecting the Baltimore and Potomac, the Western Maryland, the Northern Central, and the Philadelphia, Wilmington and Baltimore railroads. Much of it was constructed at great outlay through tunnels under the city and over treacherous soil; but the two million dollars which it cost are a mere bagatelle when compared with the increase of trade which it will give the city, as it affords another long-needed outlet to tide-water. It is, indeed, precisely the kind of road so much needed to-day in Boston and New York, and which neither of those great cities has yet shown sufficient sagacity to provide. All the railroads passing through Baltimore are entitled to its use at a fixed rate per mile.

When the Canton elevators are completed, Baltimore harbor will be richer in facilities for immediate and convenient shipment to Europe of Western produce than any other city on the continent. The grain trade now centring at Canton is enormous, but the elevators there are totally insufficient to meet the demand.

Woodberry, near Druid Hill Park.

The sugar refinery at Canton has large piers, and the chemical and oil works, and the distilleries, together covering many acres, require extensive wharf accommodation. Large coal oil manufactories are shortly to be established along the water-front at Baltimore, and will add much to the business of the new Union railroad.

The completion of the Baltimore and Potomac railroad, in 1873, forming a new connection between Baltimore and Washington, opened up five of the most fertile lower counties on the western shore of the State—counties which heretofore have had no ready means of communication with the metropolis except by water. The railroad included the construction of large tunnels both at Baltimore and Washington, and forms a very important link in the great Southern line of the Pennsylvania Central railroad. It has had a marked influence upon the character of the population of the western shore.

The residents of that section before the war were large slave-holders, and contented themselves with an unambitious life, devoted mainly to the raising of large crops of tobacco and cereals, and with the ordinary enjoyments of the country gentlemen of Maryland. Among them, however, there were many who, before the slavery *régime* had passed away, saw the necessity of a means of speedy transit to and from the sea-board, and at the close of the war they were prominent in aiding in the building and equipment of the road. This great work, which is one of the most solidly constructed in the United States, cost nearly six and a-half millions of dollars, one hundred thousand cubic yards of rock having been blasted through during the construction of the tunnel in Baltimore. It has already given an important impetus to forming a trade along its whole line. The Western Maryland railroad, which extends from Williamsport on the Potomac river to tide-water at Baltimore, was completed in December of 1873. It is a work which called for the best engineering talent, built as it is across the very summit of the Blue Ridge. From this summit a fine view is obtained of the vast valley of the Cumberland, which, backed with its rugged mountain slopes, and filled with flourishing farms and villages, presents a constant panorama of charming scenery. The road's main service to Baltimore will consist in the current of coal which it can pour from Williamsport on to the wharves at Canton.

The New City Hall—Baltimore, Maryland.

The Northern Central railway, formerly known as the Baltimore and Susquehanna, was one of the first routes to import locomotives from Liverpool in the early history of railroad travel; and by its connection to-day with the great Pennsylvania road, and, through that route, with the Lakes, the West, the Northwest, and the South, is a valuable feeder to Baltimore commerce. The Northern Central Railroad Company has invested very largely in lands at Canton, and proposes the erection of spacious piers, wharves, and elevators, for the reception of the grain from the West. It runs through a line of busy suburban villages, filled, like the manufacturing towns in the most prosperous sections of New England, with small manufacturing establishments; passes Timonium, where the old Maryland families were wont to attend the annual State races; passes

Lafayette Square, Baltimore, Maryland.

Cockeysville, near which marble, granite, and lime quarries, and important iron works are located; and crosses the Gunpowder river, a small tributary of the Chesapeake, which winds picturesquely among overhanging rocks. Over this route to Harrisburg, and thence by Altoona across the Alleghanies, goes a great share of the through travel from South and East to West.

The coal trade of Baltimore has been very largely increased by the rapid railroad development of the past two years. The Maryland coal regions, which stretch away through the George's Creek valley from Piedmont to Frostburg, furnish millions of tons yearly. In this Cumberland region, situated about two hundred miles from Baltimore, the stores of coal are almost inexhaustible. The city can certainly count upon supplies from them for many centuries. It is but a few years since seventeen hundred tons were considered a heavy shipment yearly from the Cumberland mines, but in 1872 1,915,000 tons were shipped thence to Baltimore, while in the same year the city received 600,000 tons of gas and anthracite coal from Western Virginia and Pennsylvania. Baltimore can to-day supply coal freights for five thousand vessels. Her coastwise trade in coal is enormous, and within the past two years her foreign trade has sprung into proportions which bid fair to rival those of any port in the world. The demand in the Baltimore market has at all times latterly been difficult to meet, and vast as are the resources of the Baltimore and Ohio railroad and the Chesapeake and Ohio canal, they are quite insufficient. It is proposed to extend the Western Maryland line until it taps the Pennsylvania railroad, thus giving a shorter route than any present one to Pittsburg, by means of which the trade will be still further increased.

In 1873 the Baltimore and Ohio railroad brought 2,752,178 tons of coal to Baltimore.

The comparative receipts of grain for four years are as follows:

	1873.	1872.	1871.	1870.
Wheat,	2,810,917	2,456,100	4,076,017	3,039,357
Corn,	8,330,449	9,045,465	5,735,921	3,831,676
Oats,	1,255,072	1,959,161	1,833,409	1,243,720
Rye,	100,519	90,938	88,956	77,778
Peas,	10,000	10,000	10,000	10,000
Beans,	30,000	30,000	30,000	30,000
Total,	12,536,967	13,571,664	11,774,303	8,232,531

The coffee and flour trades of Baltimore are very extensive. In the importation of coffee Baltimore stands second among the ports of the United States, the receipts there being more than twice the aggregate entries at the chief ports of Boston, Philadelphia and New Orleans. It has indeed become a port of entry for New York coffee merchants because of the facilities offered for economical handling. The imports for 1873 amounted to 384,808 bags. The receipts of flour for the same year from the West footed up 1,054,033 barrels, and the product of the city mills during that time was 258,579 barrels. The trade in flour has steadily increased for the past seven years, and the exports of that article from the city for 1873 amounted to 359,566 barrels, many of which went to Brazil and the West Indies.

The sugar trade of Baltimore is also very extensive, and the Baltimore, Maryland, Calvert and Chesapeake refineries work up more than 100,000,000 pounds of the crude material annually. In 1871 these refineries produced 91,000,000 pounds of refined sugar, and the total supply for 1873 was 96,387 tons. In 1873 the sugar refineries of Baltimore took 75,000 tons of sugar and 30,000 hogsheads of molasses. The six refineries which work up pure sugar and molasses produced in that same year 75,000 tons of refined sugars and syrups. Baltimore ranks now only second to New York as a sugar market. The tobacco trade has long been of great importance to the city. In colonial days it was the chief dependence of its commerce, and the old inspection laws, which were very judicious, still remain in force. The city has now six large tobacco warehouses. During 1873, 65,067 hogsheads were inspected, and more than 50,000 were exported to Bremen, Rotterdam, Amsterdam, England, France, Spain, Trieste, Italy and Antwerp. Most of the tobacco sold at Baltimore comes from the interior of Maryland, from Ohio, and from Kentucky, and is principally used in Germany and France. Baltimore has many large factories for the manufacture of tobacco, and millions of cigars are made there every year.

The City Jail—Baltimore, Maryland.

In lumber, iron, cotton, and petroleum the trade of this active commercial centre is also rapidly increasing. The export of lumber to Germany now forms a very lucrative branch of trade. The receipts of oil from Western Virginia and Pennsylvania wells in 1873 were 399,360 barrels, and there are numerous oil refineries which prepare the crude petroleum for export. The total exports of oil in 1873 were 3,470,995 gallons; and 66,415 bags of oil-cake were also sent abroad.

Not so much progress has been made latterly in the iron trade as in other branches. In 1872 there were in the State twenty blast furnaces, producing upward of 54,000 tons, but the production in 1873 did not probably reach 50,000 tons. The importations of English and Scotch iron to Baltimore are yearly decreasing. There are a number of bar and plate iron works in the city which do a very heavy business. One company alone controls four plate-mills which yield an annual product of a million dollars in value. The rolling-mills of the great railroad corporations are vast. A journey through the shops of the Baltimore and Ohio railroad at Mount Clare is the work of a day. Two regiments of laborers are employed. It is not generally known that Maryland, particularly in the vicinity of Baltimore, produces some of the best charcoal pig-iron in the country, and in such quantities that this city may be considered the principal market for that staple. Orders are constantly received, even from St. Louis, for "charcoal pig." There are eleven charcoal furnaces in the State, which produced during 1873 nearly 25,000 tons. The oldest now in operation is the Catoctin furnace, quite recently built. Pig-iron was exported from Maryland to England as early as 1717, but in 1737 the colonists were graciously permitted to make bar iron,—the act, however, providing that they should build no rolling-mills which should interfere with the manufactories of Great Britain. Along the lines of the Philadelphia, Wilmington and Baltimore railroad, and the Washington branch of the Baltimore and Ohio, for a distance of fifty miles, there is a bed of ore six to eight miles wide, and in many places fifty feet deep.

The Peabody Institute—Baltimore, Maryland.

This is a carbonate of iron peculiar to Maryland, imbedded in clay, and yielding from 32 to 40 per cent. at the furnaces. In Maryland it is known as chocolate ore.

The copper smelting works at Canton are the largest on the Atlantic coast, producing from 8,000,000 to 10,000,000 pounds of refined copper per annum.

The annual cotton receipts usually amount to from 100,000 to 120,000 bales, fully one-third of which is exported to Liverpool and German ports.

Millions of swine, slaughtered at the various packing points throughout the West, and thousands of beef cattle, are annually received in Baltimore markets, whence they are dispersed through the South and the East.

More than a thousand vessels arrive at Baltimore yearly. The total value of the imports in 1873 was $32,116,721; the exports, $23,387,812. The receipts of customs at Baltimore for the same period, notwithstanding the free entry of coffee and the reduction of duties on many other articles, amounted to nearly $7,000,000. The manufacture of boots and shoes in Baltimore gives employment to four thousand persons, and the total value of the trade in 1873 was more than $23,000,000. The jobbing and provision trade makes steady and rapid progress. More than two hundred houses are engaged in the liquor trade in Baltimore. The capital invested in whiskey is $3,000,000; the receipts from sales average $6,000,000.

The gentle oyster furnishes the means of livelihood to more than twenty thousand men, women, and children, in this liveliest of Southern cities. The resources of the Chesapeake bay and its tributaries are so vast that no competition with Baltimore in this trade is possible. More than thirty years ago, an enterprising individual established a house on Federal Hill for the canning of cooked oysters. He had discovered the secret of hermetically sealing the cans, and fancied that he was to become a millionaire, but a hundred ambitious rivals sprang up, and whole streets in Baltimore are to-day lined with the oyster packeries. Eight hundred small schooners and three thousand little boats are engaged from the middle of September until early in the spring in lifting the oysters from their tranquil beds with dredges, tongs and rakes, and in bringing them to the packing establishments, where they are ruthlessly torn from their shells, packed, raw or cooked, in cans from which air is carefully excluded, and shipped for inland consumption as a much-coveted luxury. In one single house fifty thousand cans of raw oysters are daily packed, while another establishment prepares thirty thousand cans of cooked bivalves in the same time. The manufacture of cans in which oysters and prepared fruits are transported is not a small item in the trade of Baltimore, nearly thirty million cans being annually manufactured for that market. Half-a-dozen large printing houses are occupied in preparing labels for the cans, and long lines of lime-kilns, with a capacity of one thousand to twelve hundred bushels each, dispose of the millions of oyster shells which otherwise would block the streets. One firm alone makes more than 600,000 bushels of pure white lime in a year. Farmers are paid to carry away the shells used in the construction of roads, or in the improvement of lands near the city.

When spring comes, and the great army of employés who have been occupied with the oyster during the winter would otherwise be idle, the fleet of schooners and boats penetrates all the streams flowing into the Chesapeake, and their crews purchase from the orchards and market gardens along those streams thousands of tons of fruit and vegetables. The oyster packeries are transformed into manufactories of savory conserves. Peaches, pears, apples, berries, tomatoes— pickles of every imaginable kind—are so prepared that they can be exported to any part of the world. Large kegs are annually sent to Hindostan, to China, to Japan, and throughout middle and western Europe. The oyster-beds of Maryland extend, from a point in Kent county opposite Baltimore, southward down to and up the Potomac forty miles, a total of one hundred and twenty-five miles, and east and west across the Chesapeake bay and Tangier sound, and up all their tributaries as far as salt water reaches. Maryland maintains a State oyster police force, employs a cruiser to protect her interests, has an

First Presbyterian Church—Baltimore.

elaborate oyster law, and in the shape of licenses, fines, &c., draws an annual revenue from the trade of between $50,000 and $60,000.

From this slight review of the commercial interests of Baltimore, it is easy to see that this city has become the most formidable commercial rival of New York on the Atlantic sea-board. It has the shortest inland lines to the Western granaries; its terminal facilities are superb; its rates for transportation are reasonable; imports pass with readiness and dispatch through the Custom-House, and importers are free from the many vexatious delays that have made New York a disagreeable port of entry. It requires seventy-two hours longer for a steamer of 3,000 tons to bring her cargo to Baltimore, but this extra charge is offset by the $2,000 which its owner may save by buying its coal in Baltimore instead of New York, while the difference between the terminal and berth charges of Baltimore and New York is great.

The recovery of the prestige of Baltimore has greatly encouraged her leading merchants and business men, and has done away to some extent with that provincial spirit so long characteristic of the place. In 1798, when Baltimore was a struggling village, it ranked as the third commercial port in the United States, had more than 30,000 tons of registered shipping, and exports amounting to about $12,000,000 annually. Twenty years later, the fleetest vessels that floated on the high seas under any flag were the Baltimore clippers, those renowned specimens of marine architecture whose praises were sung in every clime, and of whose captains there are yet few equals and no superiors. These clippers were schooner-rigged, and so built as to sail within four or four and a-half points of the wind. This enabled them to elude the pursuit of any vessels belonging to blockading squadrons in the stormy days between 1790 and 1807, and they did the chief part of the American and West Indian trade for this country, besides a large carrying trade for European nations. But as the clippers vanished from the seas, and Baltimore seemed overwhelmed by that disastrous lack of energy which was the natural consequence of the system of slavery, her commerce slipped away, and it was only by the projection and completion of that mighty work, the Baltimore and Ohio railroad, which spanned the Alleghanies and laid hold upon the fertile fields of the West, that she succeeded in regaining her proud position. For the first five months of 1874, the aggregate shipments of wheat and corn have been 5,277,000 bushels. The Liverpool Steamship Line has been sending extra steamers for the shipment of grain, and everything indicates a massive and tremendous increase of trade in the old city from month to month and from year to year for many decades to come.

From Federal Hill, the lofty bank south-west of the inner basin of Baltimore harbor, a fine view may be had of the city and the blue waters of the bay. Federal Hill is an historic eminence. It was christened by the Federalists of 1787, who on the adoption of the Constitution of the United States testified their joy by having a grand procession, and rigging and equipping a model ship called the "Federalist," which, after being paraded through the streets of the town, was burned on the hill. Four thousand persons there sat down to a grand dinner at which speeches were made in favor of the new Constitution. The little ship of State was afterward launched and navigated down Chesapeake bay to the mouth of the Potomac and thence to Mount Vernon, where it was presented to General Washington. It was on Federal Hill also that a disturbance occurred in the early days of Secession, when an attempt was made to display the flag of the South, and to fire one hundred guns in honor of South Carolina. There, too, General Butler posted his troops when he took possession of the city; and there are seen to-day the earthworks thrown up by the soldiers from Massachusetts and New York. Opposite Federal Hill, beyond the basin, the steep streets rise to lofty heights, along which are built the fashionable residences, many of the public buildings, the monuments, the churches, the theatres and the banks. At the foot of the hill, and grouped about the unsavory basin, which emits odors similar to those of the Amsterdam and Rotterdam canals, are long and by no means cleanly streets, lined with petty shops and crowded with piles of wood and lumber, with bustling stevedores and roustabouts, negro wood-sawyers and wholesale shipping merchants.

Looking out over this solid commercial town, and meditating on its trade's enormous growth, one is almost inclined to forget that it has any love for art. Yet it has two of the finest private picture galleries in the country. The collections of Mr. William T. Walters and Colonel J. Stricker Jenkins are world-famous. Mr. Walters' gallery is enriched with the paintings of Delaroche, Meissonier, Gérome, Edouard Frère, Corot, Plassan, Troyon, Achenbach, and dozens of other celebrated artists. The best efforts of the French pencil, and some of the finest works of American artists, grace the halls of Colonel Jenkins. Rinehart, the sculptor, who died recently in Italy, has left to Baltimore much good statuary.

The "Maryland," "Allston," and "Baltimore" Clubs are remembered with pleasure by all visitors to the metropolis. Their graceful hospitality and the memories of the luxurious terrapin which they recall can never fade away. The theatrical edifices are very good, and when the new "Academy of Music" is completed, the town will have a charming opera house.

LXXXV.

BALTIMORE AND ITS INSTITUTIONS.

BALTIMORE well deserves the name of the "Monumental City," many years ago bestowed upon it. The stately column which rises from a hill in the fashionable quarter of the city, and known as the Washington Monument, is 180 feet high. It is surmounted by a colossal statue of the Father of his Country, and on the great pedestal, from each side of which radiate pretty parks and fine avenues, are the following inscriptions:

To
GEORGE WASHINGTON,
by the
State of Maryland.

Born February 22, 1732.

Commander-in-Chief of the American Army, June 15, 1775.
Trenton, December 25, 1776.
Yorktown, October 19, 1781.
Commission Resigned at Annapolis, December 23, 1783.

President of the United States, March 4, 1782.
Retired to Mount Vernon, March 4, 1797.
Died December 14, 1799.

The square in which the monument stands is called Mount Vernon, after the home of General Washington. On the south side of the square is the Peabody Institute, founded by the famous banker, George Peabody, who never forgot, in his liberal series of donations, his adopted home and the scene of his early business success. On the 12th of February, 1857, Mr. Peabody donated $300,000 to the city for the establishment of an Institute, and appointed a number of prominent citizens as trustees of the fund. It is devoted to the selection of a fine library and the creation of an academy of music, and is intended to foster the elevation of the middle class. Every citizen of Baltimore can avail himself of the advantages of the Institute, which has already done much for the encouragement of public taste and knowledge in special branches of art.

A little to the west of the Peabody Institute stands Grace Church, and north of it the First Presbyterian Church, one of the most beautiful religious edifices in the country. A little south of the monument is the old cathedral. This noble building, which was begun in 1806, is in the form of a Roman cross, and is a massive and imposing structure. It was finally completed only in 1865. The interior is decorated with many paintings, some of which are of rare merit.

The Battle Monument, which stands in Monument Square, was erected in memory of the citizens who fell in defense of Baltimore at the battle of North Point, at the bombardment of Fort McHenry in 1814. The shaft of the monument is a fasces, symbolical of the Union, and the rods are bound together by a fillet on which are inscribed the names of those who were killed. On the north and south fronts of the base of the fasces are two excellent bas-reliefs, one representing the death of General Ross at the battle of North Point, and the other the bombardment of the fort. The column is surmounted by a statue of Baltimore, and at the feet of the statue stands an eagle. The monument is enclosed with an iron railing, outside of which are chains fastened to marble cannon. Around Monument Square are grouped the City Hall, formerly the residence of Reverdy Johnson; Barnum's Hotel, which Charles Dickens praised as one of the best hotels in the country; and the famous Guy's Restaurant, where the terrapin and soft-shelled crab are served in all the glory and perfection of Baltimore cookery.

Mount Vernon Square, with a view of the Washington Monument, Baltimore, Maryland.

Wildey Monument, on Broadway, above Baltimore street, is an imposing column designed to perpetuate the memory of Past Grand Sire Thomas Wildey, the founder of the Odd-Fellows in America. In the Green Mount cemetery stands the McDonough statue, erected to the memory of a philanthropic merchant, who was a son of Baltimore, and a prominent citizen of New Orleans; and in Ashland Square a plain but massive column commemorates the two youths who slew General Ross, the Commander of the British forces, in the battle in 1812.

Prominent among the public buildings of Baltimore is the new City Hall, which is an imposing structure of composite architecture, in which the Renaissance predominates. It fills the entire square enclosed by Holliday, Lexington, North, and Fayette streets. The dome, which adds but little in beauty to the building, is 222 feet above the level of the ground. The City Hall is situated in the business portion of the town; and, if it were not walled in by numerous inferior buildings, would be a fine ornament. The Exchange, in Gay street, is a noticeable building, with fine Ionic columns on its east and west sides, and is also surmounted by a huge dome, something like an inverted butter-bowl. The Custom-House and Post-Office are in this building, the former fronting on Lombard street, a busy and substantial avenue. On Baltimore street, the main commercial avenue of the town, is the Maryland Institute for promoting the mechanic arts. It is a handsome and commodious structure, the ground floor of which is occupied by the Centre market. The main hall of this building is one of the largest in the country, and during the annual Mechanics' Fair thousands of visitors from all parts of the State flock into it. It was in this hall that Breckenridge was nominated by the Southern politicians in 1860, and that the great Union Sanitary Fair in 1863, and the Southern Relief Fair in 1866, were held. The schools of design connected with the Institute are in admirable condition, and the library is large and constantly increasing in size. The Court-House, at the corner of Monument Square and Lexington street, is a highly ornamented marble and brick building, surrounded by streets filled with the offices of the legal fraternity. The new United States Court-House, at the corner of North and Fayette streets, is a massive building. On Madison street stand the City Prison and the State Penitentiary.

Baltimore is very rich in charitable institutions. The Maryland Hospital for the Insane, a fine building on East Monument street in the eastern part of the city; the Mount Hope Hospital, conducted by the Sisters of Charity; the Baltimore Infirmary, controlled by the regents of the University; the Washington

The Battle Monument, seen from Barnum's Hotel—Baltimore.

Medical College, the Washington Infirmary, many "Homes" for aged people, the Maryland Institution for the Instruction of the Blind; the Church Home, conducted by the Protestant Episcopal Church of the city; the orphan asylums of St. Anthony and St. Vincent de Paul (Bay View Asylum, or the Workhouse, which stands on the Philadelphia road, a short distance from the eastern limits of the city, can accommodate twelve hundred persons, and cost a million of dollars), the Maryland State Insane Asylum, on the Frederick road, six miles from the city, and the Sheppard Asylum for the Insane, are all testimonials to the liberality and beneficence of the wealthy. The will of Mr. McDonough, by which very large sums were left to Baltimore and New Orleans to be devoted to the education of poor children, gave the former $800,000, which the trustees have expended in purchasing a large farm ten miles from the city, and where they propose to erect a fine institution in which hundreds of pupils will receive constant instruction in English studies, music, and agriculture.

Beggars are rarities in Baltimore. The "Association for the Improvement of the Condition of the Poor" has the most prominent of the citizens enrolled upon its books, and all who are worthy objects of charity receive prompt assistance. A host of minor charitable institutions, under the charge of the Catholic and Protestant Churches, aid the above-mentioned useful society ; and, as the system of tenement houses is almost entirely unknown in the city, but little of the misery and wretchedness so peculiar to large towns is noticeable. The munificent donation of $600,000, left Baltimore some years ago by Moses Sheppard for the establishment of a hospital for the insane,

The Battle Monument—Baltimore, Maryland. [Page 758.]

has, by judicious investments, increased to nearly a million dollars, and a beautiful Elizabethan structure, which is to be surrounded by one of the most exquisite landscape gardens in the United States, is now arising a few miles from Baltimore. The establishment is mainly designed as a curative hospital, while Mount Hope, in the north-western centre of the city, is devoted to the treatment of the incurably insane. The Deaf and Dumb Asylum, which has been established by the State in Frederick City, has also received liberal donations from the people of Baltimore. The venerable Thomas Kelso, for eighty-two years a citizen of the Monumental City, some time since endowed a Methodist Episcopal Orphan Asylum with $100,000, and a wealthy lumber dealer has left nearly half a million for the establish-

The Cathedral—Baltimore, Maryland.

ment of an asylum for female orphans. The House of Refuge for vagrant and vicious children, opened in 1855, is a noble range of buildings situated a short distance beyond the western limits of the city, and within its walls nearly 2,000 boys and girls have been taught trades and received a plain but comprehensive education since the inauguration of the city. The Baltimore Orphan Asylum, founded in 1801, the Children's Aid Society, the Baltimore Manual Labor School, the Male Free School for Baltimore, and the Maryland Industrial School for Girls, have all been amply and generously supported since their foundation.

Mr. Johns Hopkins, one of the merchant princes of Baltimore, and identified with its history for more than half a century, left the bulk of his immense fortune to the city. The whole of his donations amount to

The Wildey Monument—Baltimore, Maryland.

nearly seven millions of dollars, two millions of which he devoted to the establishment of one of the finest hospitals in the world, for the treatment of surgical cases and general disease. The site of the old Maryland Hospital was purchased by Mr. Hopkins, and the new edifice will arise thereon. Under the supervision of the trustees of this hospital is also an asylum for the education and maintenance of several hundreds of colored orphan children. The remainder of the donation is devoted to the establishment of a university at Clifton, the beautiful country residence of Mr. Hopkins. This university will have law, medical, classical, and agricultural schools, and its endowment of $4,000,000 with 400 acres of land should make it one of the most famous sites of learning in the country. Mr. Hopkins died in December, 1873. He was connected with almost all the great

Entrance to Druid Hill Park—Baltimore, Maryland.

enterprises that have entered into the history of Baltimore; and from 1847 until the day of his death was a Director in the Baltimore and Ohio Railway

Company. When the Company was fighting through the embarrassments which constantly crippled it until 1857, he often voluntarily endorsed its notes. By the liberal manner in which he sustained the credit of the corporation the completion and success of the great road were insured. Mr. Hopkins' interest in the Company was only exceeded in value by that held by the State of Maryland and the city of Baltimore. He owned at one time shares of the stock whose actual market worth was $3,000,000. He was almost the controller of the various banks of Baltimore, and a large stockholder in them all, as well as in many of the Virginia banks. In 1873, when the news of the great panic in New York swept down through the business quarter of Baltimore, and the alarm which had been so disastrous in other cities was about to strike terror in the Maryland metropolis, Mr. Hopkins announced his determination to avert the calamity from his native town. He held at that time $2,000,000 worth of commercial paper, and had some investments which were affected by the sudden

Scene on the Canal, near Harper's Ferry.

crisis; but he put his shoulder to the wheel, loaned his money until it was exhausted, then loaned his name, which was as good as money, charging nothing for it in many cases, and, thanks to his generous efforts, Baltimore was uninjured by the financial crisis.

Prominent among the more beautiful churches of Baltimore is the superb Gothic structure near the Washington Monument, known as the Mount Vernon Place Methodist Episcopal Church, completed in 1872. The First Presbyterian Church, on Madison and Park streets, built of New Brunswick freestone in the pointed Gothic style; the Independent Methodist Church, and the Eutaw Place Baptist and St. Paul's Churches, are all imposing religious edifices. The Masonic Temple on Charles street, and the noble building which the Young Men's Christian Association of Baltimore is now erecting at the corner of Charles and Saratoga streets, the former of white marble, are substantial buildings of the modern type. It is astonishing that Baltimore is not built entirely of this marble, as there are inexhaustible supplies of the rich material within easy access of the city.

The parks and suburbs of the "Liverpool of America" are on the same magnificent scale as the charitable institutions and terminal facilities. Druid Hill park was purchased in 1860 for half a million dollars. It is within half a mile of the present city limits, and the Park Commissioners found the five hundred acres which comprise it already laid out; for the Rogers family, whose estate it once was, fashioned the superb grounds a century ago into the style of the English parks of the period. Situated on the highest point of land near the city, there are many noble views of the great town and the blue bay beyond; downward, toward Kent Island and Annapolis, and eastward and westward, fertile valleys and sweet landscapes salute the eye. The Rogers family owned the present park for one hundred and fifty years, and carefully shielded many noble sylvan monarchs from the profanation of the woodman's axe. Great bouquets and masses of superb trees dot the lawns; antique woodlands skirt the roadways; and in autumn the rich orange and crimson of the sassafras and dogwood leaves contrast charmingly with the deep browns and purples of the oaks and the gold of the hickory.*

The Bridge at Harper's Ferry.

From the terrace in front of the mansion in the centre of Druid Hill park, there are many pretty glimpses of the city, the river, the bay; and all the country may be seen through lovely frame-works of foliage. Druid Hill was once known as the largest pear orchard either in America or Europe, and on its western and south-western slopes were forty thousand pear-trees, with six hundred varieties of that fruit upon them. A tract of country has been set apart for the establishment of a botanical garden. From the noble gateway on Madison avenue lead long walks and roads, adorned with ornamental summer-houses, marble statues, vases and urns; water-ways dotted with swans and ducklings; lawns across which deer bound undisturbed, and a lake whose icy surface in winter is gay with thousands of skaters. On fine days streams of handsome equipages wend their way in procession to the centre of the park, where beauty and fashion pass in grand review. The distance to the central entrance-gate at Druid Hill from Charles and Baltimore streets, which are at present the most thickly-populated portions of the city, is two and a-half miles. Within the bounds of the park lies Druid lake, a mighty stone-wall reservoir which has a storage capacity of 493,000 gallons. This reservoir is only supplemental, however, to the ample system of city water-works which draw their supplies from Lake Roland, six miles from the city, on the Northern Central

*See Weishampel's "Stranger in Baltimore."

railway. From this lake, which is seven miles in circumference, run conduits to Hampden and Mount Royal reservoirs. The city has recently purchased, at the cost of $350,000, the water rights of the Great Gunpowder river, and has already provided a supply of pure water for a population of a million inhabitants. The drives along Charles Street avenue, which leads from the city six miles out into a lovely wooded country sprinkled with fine villas and cottages to Lake Roland, to the Sheppard Asylum for the Insane, and to numerous other institutions, are all crowded in summer with lines of carriages and pedestrians. In Green Mount cemetery, at the junction of Belvidere street and North avenue, there are many beautiful monuments, and the grounds of Loudon park, Mount Olivet, Mount Carmel, and the "Western," all within short distances of the city, are beautifully laid out and planted with fine trees.

Patterson park, in the eastern section of the city, is but small as compared with its gigantic neighbor of the west, but has been very handsomely adorned, and from it superb views of the harbor and of the mighty Chesapeake are to be had.

The proposed enlargement of the city, which now covers but 10,000 acres, will embrace within Baltimore limits Clifton park, the site of the projected Hopkins University, and many pretty suburban villages into which manufacturing enterprise has already begun to penetrate. In addition to its parks, Baltimore has many beautiful public squares scattered throughout the different sections. In the western portion are Union, Franklin, and Harlem Squares, all surrounded by choice and commodious mansions. In the north-west is Lafayette Square; in the centre stands the noble Monument Square; in the north-east and the east Madison and Jackson Squares give shady refuges to the inhabitants, and the population in the southern portion flies from the summer heats to the cool breezes in Battery Square.

The extension of the city limits is imperatively demanded by most of the citizens. The inhabitants are anxious to see the straggling villages, located within one or two miles of Baltimore's boundaries, compelled to contribute to the support of the metropolis from which they derive so many benefits. Their ambition, also, to rank Baltimore as the fourth city in the United States makes them anxious for increase of population, and many favor the annexation of the whole of Baltimore county, thus giving the city a chance for indefinite expansion. The old boundaries established by legislative enactment in 1816 are ridiculously within the proper limits of the present metropolis. Waverley, a lively village north of Baltimore, and the former

View of the Railroad and River, from the Mountains at Harper's Ferry.

seat of wealthy Maryland families; Woodberry, under the shadow of Druid Hill, an extensive cotton and machine manufacturing point; Mount Washington, perched on picturesque hills within a few minutes' ride of Baltimore by the Northern Central railway; Brooklyn, south-east of the city, possessing a land-locked harbor and a water-front nearly two miles in length; Towsontown, Govanstown, and Picksville, the last noted as the location of one of the earliest built arsenals of the General Government, are all destined to come under the control of Baltimore.

The school system of Baltimore is admirable, and will compare favorably with that of any community in the United States. The schools are under the control of a board of twenty commissioners, presided over by one chosen from their number and by the Superintendent of Schools and his assistants. The youth who passes through the primary and grammar schools and the City College of Baltimore, receives a liberal education. The total number of pupils enrolled in the public schools of the city in 1873 was 40,185; and the expenditures for white and colored schools, of which latter there are at present fifteen, amounted to nearly $500,000. The sexes are educated separately. The female high schools are the most admirable institutions of their kind in the South, and there are few in the North which equal them. The Baltimore City College, which has been granted $150,000 for the erection of a new building, has a high scholastic standard, and is eminently prosperous; and the normal school for the education of teachers yearly sends forth many competent graduates.

The press of Baltimore is enterprising in aiding to develop the commercial greatness of the city. The *American*, the *Gazette*, and the *Sun*, all have large and finely-equipped establishments. The *American* was founded in 1773 as the *Maryland Journal and Baltimore Advertiser;* the *Sun* and *Gazette* are younger. The *Bulletin* is a literary journal of much excellence. In Baltimore is also the office of the *Southern Magazine*, the only monthly periodical of any importance issued in the South.

Leaving Baltimore by the Baltimore and Ohio railroad, and crossing over Gwynn's Falls, on the superb Carrollton viaduct, the traveler will find at almost every turn a profusion of bold and romantic scenery. At Washington Junction, formerly known as the Relay House, a fine hotel has been erected by the railway company; and in summer hundreds of youths and maidens, from Washington and Baltimore, angle for trout and for each other's hearts beside the little stream which comes down from the mountains.

From the Thomas viaduct, the noble granite structure which spans the stream sixty-six feet above its bed, one can see the pretty village of Elkridge Landing. Time was when vessels of small tonnage from London used to come up the stream, which now would scarcely float a skiff, and anchor at Elkridge Landing to be loaded with tobacco.

At Ellicott's Mills, a charming old town, the Patapsco river runs through a bold and rocky passage, and from the railroad one may see the huge mass of granite known as the Tarpeian Rock. At Mount Airy and at Frederick Junction there are many fine out-looks over the fertile valleys and broken hills. At Frederick Junction, or as it is better known, Monocacy, one may visit the battle-ground where General Lew. Wallace made his gallant stand at the Monocacy bridge, on the 9th of July, 1864, and prevented the enemy from making a victorious advance upon Washington.

From Frederick Junction a branch line of rail communicates with Frederick City, a well built town with broad, straight streets, bordered with stone mansions, and possessing many handsome churches and flourishing educational institutions. From Monocacy the Baltimore and Ohio railroad traverses the beautiful valley lying between the Monocacy river and the Catoctin mountains. At Point of Rocks, a bold promontory formed by the profile of the Catoctin mountain, whose base is washed by the Potomac on the Maryland side, the railroad passes through a tunnel drilled fifteen hundred feet into the solid rock. It traverses the battle-field at South Mountain, running at the foot of a precipice for three or four miles, and, passing Hagerstown Junction, enters the great gorge at Harper's Ferry.

Thomas Jefferson immortalized Harper's Ferry by his words as John Brown did by his deeds. The rock on which Jefferson is said to have sat when he wrote his "Notes on Virginia" commands a fine view of the junction of the Potomac and the Shenandoah rivers, in the great gorge which forms one of the most picturesque bits of mountain scenery in the South. On either side of the eminence known as Cemetery Hill, on which Jefferson's Rock stands, rise up majestic mountains, rugged and difficult of access—the Maryland and Loudon Heights. The Maryland hills rise to 2,000 feet above the level of the sea, and the others are still clad in primitive forests, where the foot of man seldom treads. The Potomac, which rises in Western Virginia, and rushes

Jefferson's Rock, Harper's Ferry.

impetuously, like some mountain sprite, down through the Alleghanies, traverses the northern extremity of the valleys of West Virginia, and forms the boundary between that State and Maryland.

On the rugged cliffs are various fancied shapes and faces, and travelers are invited to discover, in a rock on the Maryland side, a fanciful and certainly feeble resemblance to George Washington.

The village of Harper's Ferry, before the war, contained 3,000 population, and was the site of a national armory, for which the immense water power rendered it valuable. When the late war broke out many of the old inhabitants cast their lot with the Confederacy, but great numbers also sided with the Government of the Union. The population has been materially changed, and to-day is composed of 1,600 whites and 700 blacks. The Baltimore and Ohio railroad has pushed its tracks across the Potomac at this point on a magnificent bridge, and the Winchester and Potomac railway has its northern terminus at Harper's

Cumberland Narrows and Mountains.

Ferry. The scenery along the Chesapeake and Ohio canal, whose banks the line of railway follows for many miles between Harper's Ferry and Washington, and by the rugged edges of the great cliffs westward from the little mountain town, is exceedingly fine. In summer a ride on the banks of this canal affords a constant succession of delicious landscapes, still-life pictures, and sweet vistas of romantic woodlands.

Harper's Ferry was named after Mr. Robert Harper, a native of Oxford in England, who established the first ferry over the Potomac in the mountains, and who was shrewd enough to join the American colonists when they made their strike for freedom. The Ferry is said to have been chosen as the site of a national armory, in 1794, by General Washington himself. The establishments there were very extensive, and their ruins—for the buildings were burned during the war—extend for a long distance beside the tracks of the Baltimore and Ohio railroad.

In the little engine-house, still pointed out from the platform of the depot of the railway station, John Brown made his defense against the excited inhabitants and the Virginian militia when he was inaugurating his raid for the purpose of liberating the slaves of Virginia. The engine-house is a small brick building near the old armory gate, and the Government would do well to see that it is preserved as an historical memorial, for around it and from it was fought the first battle of the great war which finally raged for four years throughout the South.

Not far from Harper's Ferry, on the Winchester and Potomac railroad, is the little hamlet of Charlestown, where John Brown was executed under the laws of the State of Virginia in 1859. Early in 1861 the armory buildings were burned, together with fifteen thousand stand of arms stored in them, to prevent the Confederates from profiting by their capture, and the Southern forces soon took possession of Harper's Ferry. Throughout the war it was occupied and re-occupied by the Union forces; the heights around glistened with bayonets; and the town has not yet fairly recovered from the demoralization consequent on its unfortunate condition during the civil struggle. Harper's Ferry was long the base of supplies for the armies of Banks and Fremont when they were operating against Stonewall Jackson in the Valley. In September of 1862 there was a grand artillery duel between the opposing forces stationed on the heights, when Jackson and Hill attacked Harper's Ferry with their army corps. On that occasion the Maryland heights were abandoned by a Federal officer, who was cashiered for his misconduct, but killed by a shell shortly after he had given the order for the surrender of Harper's Ferry to the Confederates.

The scene on the whole peninsula formed by the Potomac and Shenandoah, at the time that McClellan's army was concentrated about Harper's Ferry, has been described as exceedingly fine. All the heights were aglow with thousands of watch-fires, and from Camp Hill, a ridge dividing the villages of Harper's Ferry and Bolivar, one could hear the hum of voices, like the murmur of the ocean, rising up from the valleys and drifting down from the mountains.

Cumberland Viaduct, Maryland.

The village clusters picturesquely among the sides of the steep hills; no hum of spindles or plying of hammers disturbs its primitive quiet. An ancient flight of stone steps leads up to a quaint church on the hill-side, and beyond the path conducts the visitor to Jefferson's Rock. Hardly a quarter of a mile from the engine-house where John Brown struck the first blow for the freedom of the American slave, rise the walls of Storer College, an institution endowed by private munificence for the education of freedmen, and sending out every year, competent teachers of both sexes, who labor to educate the colored race.

A short distance to the west, beyond Harper's Ferry, the Baltimore and Ohio railroad passes through a projecting rock in a tunnel eighty feet long, whence a magnificent view of the pass through the mountains to the confluence of the Potomac and Shenandoah is presented. The road also passes through Kearneysville in West Virginia, the scene of many sharp cavalry fights between Generals Pleasanton, Averill, Custer, and Merritt with the Confederates under Fitz Lee and Stewart, and within seven miles of Sharpsburg, whence the tourist can reach the celebrated battle-field of Antietam.

Harper's Ferry, Maryland.

Sharpsburg bears many marks of the great fight of 1862, and near the battle-field is a monument to the slaughter of those dread September days, in the shape of a fine national cemetery.

Martinsburg, in West Virginia, on the line of the Baltimore and Ohio railroad, was the scene of many Confederate raids, but is now a prosperous town, whose chief reliance is upon the extensive iron works established there by the railroad company. At St. John's Run travelers leave the rail for Berkley Springs, a favorite summer resort at the eastern base of the Warm Spring Ridge in West Virginia. At Cumberland one enters into the mountain region of the narrow western part of Maryland, and into the magnificent valley from which Baltimore draws its enormous coal trade. Cumberland is a handsome town with many fine churches and banks. It lies in a noble amphitheatre of mountains, and all around it and beyond it the scenery is very picturesque.

At Piedmont, twenty-eight miles beyond Cumberland, the foot of the Alleghanies is reached, and the road, climbing the mountains, passes Altamont on the extreme summit of the Alleghany ridge, where the streams divide, flowing in one direction toward the Gulf of Mexico, and the other toward the Atlantic; then passes by pretty Oakland, a famous resort for summer tourists, and descends rapidly along high and precipitous embankments to the banks of the Cheat river, a turbulent mountain stream, whose waters are of sombre hue.

For many miles beyond the Cheat river the road winds down the steep sides of the mountains, and, entering the great Western coal-fields, passes through the Ringwood tunnel, 4,100 feet long, and completed at the end of five years' labor at a cost of a million dollars. From the tunnel at Newburg, in Western Virginia, the railway line descends a steep hill-side, and thence finds its way through a country rich in coal and petroleum, but only sprinkled here and there by small and uninteresting villages, to Pittsburg, on the Ohio river.

The old town of Annapolis, on the Severn, near Chesapeake, still the capital of Maryland, is the seat of the United States Naval Academy, established there in 1845. It was founded in 1649, and in 1708, in honor of Queen Anne, its name was changed from Anne Arundel Town to the present one. It was at Annapolis that General Washington resigned his commission at the close of the Revolution. The State-House, and St. John's College, founded in 1784, are the only important public buildings.

The present debt of the State, over and above its assets, is $6,219,172; but when the indebtedness of the Chesapeake and Ohio Canal Company to the commonwealth, which amounts to more than twenty million dollars, is transferred from the schedule of unproductive assets to that of interest-paying securities, a fund will be furnished by which the entire State debt can be taken up. The last Legislature appropriated $50,000 for the establishment of schools for colored children, and a colored normal school is in excellent condition.

Old John Cupid, a Negro Herb Doctor.

LXXXVI.

SOUTHERN CHARACTERISTICS—STATE PRIDE—THE INFLUENCE OF RAILROADS—POOR WHITES—THEIR HABITS.

WHILE I cannot agree with the amiable gentleman in Savannah who one day assured me that the people of the North and South were two distinct nations, and that the time would come when they would separate, I still recognize essential differences between the inhabitants of the Northern and Southern States. These differences are not merely climatic; they were inbred by the system and tendencies which have been so lately done away with. Between the citizen of Massachusetts and the dweller in South Carolina a broad and deep gulf so long existed, that it is not strange that the habits, the customs, and the language of the people should differ in many particulars.

The first thing, however, which strikes the stranger as peculiar in visiting the Southern States is that the inhabitants of each State have remarkably distinguishing characteristics. Because one knows the Virginian character he cannot safely draw inferences as to that of the South Carolinian; because he has studied the types in the bayou regions of Louisiana he cannot presume to a knowledge of the Mississippian of the Gulf coast. In short, the variety of origin and ancestry in the Southern States has left indelible marks upon the populations.

People in all the States, however, take what seems to Northern men, and also to the European, overweening pride in their State, their county, and even the immediate neighborhood in which they were born. Nothing is more common than to hear a Southerner announce himself, on being introduced, as from a certain county, and he will very likely add that it is a section famed for certain excellences and for the valor of its inhabitants. This is not said from any motives of self-conceit, because the same man who vaunts the virtues of his neighbors will willingly compare himself unfavorably with them; but it is due to a genuine love and a deep-seated affection for the soil. The Southerners have been so long emphatically an agricultural people, and have conquered at such expense and with such difficulty a great portion of the land which belongs to them, that they

Southern Types—Come to Market.

love it with an intensity and devotion equaled in the world only by the attachment of the Swiss peasant to his peaks and the Frenchman to his vineyard.

The railroads which now penetrate the South in every direction, and the prosaic yet cosmopolitan "through routes" which, to Southern eyes, dash with such irreverent lack of compunction across State boundaries, and annihilate so recklessly all local sentiment, are doubtless doing much to annul the devotion to State rights. Curious travelers in the South have remarked that, as fast as a railroad penetrates a section, sentiment with regard to matters in the outside world becomes liberalized along the line. The current of through travel pouring over the great roadways from New York to New Orleans, and from the West and St. Louis to the Atlantic coast, has done much to shake that isolated independence once so conspicuous in the Southerner of the country regions, and to render him more like his bustling and active fellow-citizen of the North and West.

However much the hundred railroads covering the South with an iron network may do to destroy the old and too earnest attachment of each individual

Southern Types—A Southern Plough Team.

to his particular State and neighborhood, that attachment will still remain for many years one of the salient points of Southern character. Two gentlemen meeting upon a railway train often introduce themselves something after this fashion:

"Are you from this State, sir?"

"No, sir, I am from Kentucky, sir," or "Tennessee, sir," as the case may be; whereupon the first interlocutor immediately defines his nativity, and the two enter into an amicable discussion of political and social issues. It is not unusual for strangers thus meeting to inquire of each other the counties and even the towns in which they were respectively born, and from the gravity and dignity of their conversation, and the evident pride which each takes in detailing the advantages and peculiar blessings of his neighborhood, one might fancy them a couple of foreigners from distant lands who had accidentally met. As a rule, two Southerners traveling in a State remote from that in which they were born find an instant bond of communion in the fact that they are from the same commonwealth.

Sometimes one sees on the cars or on the steamers a tall, lank Southerner anxiously inquiring if there be among the passengers any one from his native State; and if he finds such a one, he goes to him with effusive friendship and adopts him as his comrade. A friend has told me a curious incident of this kind which he saw in a rough part of the South-west. While traveling on an obscure railroad in some forest, the car door opened; and a lank individual thrust his countenance through the aperture, crying out in an appealing manner: "Is there any one heah from Tennessee?" No response being made, his voice was presently heard repeating the same inquiry in the neighboring car.

There are, of course, several important facts to bear in mind when one is judging of the peculiarities of the Southern people. It should be remembered

Southern Types — Negro Boys Shelling Peas.

that there were but two classes in the South under the old system, the high up and the low down, Dives in his hall and Lazarus among the dogs at the gate,— the gentleman planter and the ruffian, brawling, ill-educated, and generally miserable poor white. The negro did not count; he was a commodity, an article of barter, classed familiarly as "nigger;" had no identity; was supposed to possess little consciousness, moral or otherwise; and while practically he was every now and then treated with great kindness and forbearance by those who were his absolute masters, still he did nothing either to build up or solidify society. Now-a-days a middle class is gradually springing into existence, bridging the once impassable gulf between the "high up" and the "low down," and some of the more intelligent and respectable negroes are taking rank in this class. The low down element has perhaps received more benefit from the results of the war than has the negro or his master.

The introduction of manufactures here and there in the South has drawn into large towns some of the white population which was once utterly useless and degraded. A noteworthy instance which I have already mentioned is that of the hundreds of cleanly and handsome girls in the cotton-mills of Georgia. Many of them have been transformed from slouching, unkempt, and gawky country girls into tidy and thrifty operatives, with some little money in bank, and prospects of a social position far higher than they could ever have hoped to gain under the old system.

The poor white still clings to many of his eccentricities. One finds an excellent chance to observe the peculiar habits of this class by traveling with the great current of emigration from Alabama, Georgia, and Mississippi south-westward to Arkansas and Texas. Now and then, in our long journeys from one end of the South to the other, we fell in with, and traveled for days in the company of, representatives of what was formerly the low down class. We chatted in the friendliest and freest manner with the pretty, soft-voiced girls from Alabama, as we rode across the great plains of Texas, and were no whit deterred from conversation by the fact that they dipped long pine sticks in yellow snuff, and chewed the sticks while they talked with us. Sometimes, however, we felt like remonstrating with the mothers who gave their children sticks from the family snuff-bottle, and taught them the disgusting habit.

The men were almost without exception clad in homespun garments of a blue or butternut color, always neatly made. A slouch hat was their invariable head-gear—a hat, too, which seemed to have undergone more than the ordinary vicissitudes, which one could never imagine to have had band or buckle or definite color—a hat much battered by the elements, and occasionally perforated with buckshot. Out of ten thousand people of this class, not one had in his face a particle of color; all had the same dead, pallid complexion. The women whom we saw, and who were doubtless fair specimens of their class, were, when young, quite pretty; gracious, but exceedingly timid. On the whole, when the snuff-stick was laid by, and their lustrous brown eyes were playing at hide-and-seek with thought, they seemed charming as Italian peasant girls, or maids of Marseilles; but when from their sweet lips came the flat and harsh accents of their native mountains and plains, the illusion was dispelled.

My observation justifies me in the conclusion that the poor white always has a numerous family. It was not at all uncommon to see lean fathers and lank and scrawny mothers entering the cars, followed by a brood of ten or more children of all sizes. There was something touching, too, in the rough sympathy and helpfulness of the members of these families one for another, during their long and weary journeys. The little girls, whose thin but pretty faces were hidden beneath sun-bonnets, and the rough boys, with fists like sledge-hammers, and faces drawn down with wrinkles of fever and ague, each carried some bundle of household gear; the mother usually bore a basket containing a ham, some coarse corn-bread, and, mayhap, a package of fruit, as well as the snuff-bottle; and the father bore the family rifle, its long barrels weather-stained and rusty.

The ignorance and timidity of these poor people, during their journeys to new homes, was painful as well as ludicrous to witness. Sometimes a family on entering a car would stand utterly bewildered, not seeming to know whether to sit or slink into a corner, until the conductor, or the "captain," as he is called in the South, marshaled them to seats. On one occasion, being startled by the pressure of a brawny hand on my shoulder, I turned to confront the father of an interesting family of eleven, who, pointing to his wife, said in a hoarse whisper:

"Stranger, the captain did n't give her no yaller ticket; I reckon he done forgot."

Then showing me the yellow check which the conductor had given him in return for his ticket, he earnestly inquired the meaning of the lettering upon it. Surprised that a man whose appearance indicated intelligence of no mean order could not read, I ventured to ask him if such was the case, and if his family was unable to read or write. I found that no member of the party had the slightest acquaintance with anything educational, and that in the whole course of half a century of toil, the old man had rarely been more than ten miles from home. Now he was about to try the far-away plains of Texas, and he looked forward to it as a mighty change. The future seemed a great gulf before him, and he informed me, with the ghost of a sigh, as he shifted his tobacco from one cheek to the other, that he never would have believed "befo' the surrendah" that he could have undertaken a wholesale emigration.

Few people who have not wandered up and down the highways and byways of the South can appreciate the immensity of the emigration from the old cotton States to the extreme South-west. That Texas will speedily have

Southern Types—A "Likely Girl" with her Baby.

a vast population, drawn from these cotton States, and bitterly necessitous in matters of education and elevation, there is no doubt. The destiny of these poor whites, who have fled before the changed order of things in their homes, is somewhat uncertain. If they could but acquire habits of solid industry, and learn to accumulate in their rough way some little surplus means, they might easily be redeemed from their present degraded condition; but Texas is vast, the means of living easily to be had there, and so it is to be feared that the mass of the poor white race will be improved in little except its material condition. Those who remain at home are certainly, as I have said, improving as a whole; yet the Sand-hillers of South Carolina, the Crackers of Georgia and Florida, the wretched masses along the lowlands of the Atlantic coast, and the mountaineers in some portions of Virginia, Eastern Tennessee, and

Western North Carolina, present many discouraging signs. In some cases, they do not advance as rapidly as does the negro; but the latter, immediately after the war, had a great incentive to a rapid growth, and it was to be expected that he would improve his newly-acquired opportunity. I do not think the mass of poor whites really appreciated the immense difference which the war effected in their social position, nor will they thoroughly understand it for many years to come—not until the progress of events under the new *régime* has wiped out the old aristocracy, and brought its genuine leveling influence wholly to bear. Should immigration make as great progress in the other States of the South as it is now making in Virginia, there will, of course, be a radical change in the character of the poor white population. We may expect in a few years, as the country fills up, and the persistent idlers are crowded to the wall, to see the Southern poor white transformed into an industrious and valuable member of society. The pride of State, heretofore alluded to, has doubtless made it much harder for the native Southerner to emigrate than it would have been for citizens of other sections. I shall not readily forget the intense delight with which a Mississippian, returning from a disastrous colonization experiment in Brazil, hailed the bluffs and the rose-embowered gardens of beautiful Natchez as we drew near to them one spring evening.

Southern Types—Catching his Breakfast.

"Thar," he said, "is ez good a country ez the sun shines on, and if all them cussed fools as went to the Brazils was hyar now, they would say so too. Give me old Mississippi in mine."

The affection for the State as distinguished from the section was shown all through the late war. When we were called upon to listen to the recital of battles, in which, by the way, it was noteworthy that the Confederates always won, we remarked the pride and dignity with which the superior excellences of any special State in question were asserted. In fact, we learned to believe that the Southerner often thinks, as the Englishman said of all Americans, that "he is as good as any one else, and better too."

LXXXVII.

THE CARRYING OF WEAPONS—MORAL CHARACTER OF THE NEGROES.

SOME people are inclined to place a good deal of stress upon the supposed fact that the mass of Southern males carry weapons, and that their sense of honor is so highly wrought that their conversation is guarded. While it must be admitted that great numbers of Southerners habitually go armed, and that in some States they are prone to fight on small provocation, my experience has been that the most cultured and refined gentlemen rarely bear a weapon, and scoff at the idea of the necessity of carrying one. In our journeys, we traveled not unfrequently in regions remote from the railroads, or along rivers, where the people were somewhat rough, but never on any occasion did we see pistol or knife drawn or displayed during our fourteen months' stay in the South. While, however, we never saw weapons displayed, we heard plenty of stories to confirm the impression, that large classes carried them and used them freely.

There is no doubt that a great proportion of the Southern people believe that they must avenge any fancied slight upon their honor by personal punishment of the individual who has offered it, and so they have recourse to the revolver and the knife, where the Northern man would carry the case into the courts. The worst phase of the Southern character is illustrated in the unwillingness to adopt legal methods in the settlement of disputes.

Southern Types—Negro Shoeblacks.

Under the *régime* of reconstruction the juries of the Federal Courts are detested, appeals to them being considered a greater ignominy than those to the State Courts. The higher class of gentlemen rarely settle disputes by shooting or stabbing, but it is probable that the only thing which will restrain the rougher whites from a practice unworthy of our civilization, and from ideas of personal satisfaction which are alike murderous and contemptible, will be the progress of education.

It is, perhaps, too true that the recent accession of the Democrats to power in Texas and Arkansas has increased the number of misdeeds there. That the Democratic party in the South is the party of law and order is by no means strictly true; the leaders of the Democratic party are unfortunately people of inflammable methods of speech, and often, in the excitement of political harangues, give advice which their rude followers interpret to suit themselves, and which sometimes results in bloodshed. The public, however, should be extremely careful not to judge of the Southern character by the greatly exaggerated accounts of outrages with which many political newspapers are filled during the progress of a campaign. The fact that in a journey of 25,000 miles, nearly a thousand of which I traveled on horseback, through mountain regions, I saw no weapons drawn, and not a single instance of assault, lynching, or even drunken brawls, ought to be considered as good testimony in favor of the Southerners. The Northern people in their judgment are too apt to confuse the classes, and it is undoubtedly true that in some parts of the North prejudiced persons still fancy the South a barbarous region infested with ruffians of the old border type.

The negroes certainly rejoice in the possession of weapons to a large extent. Since the war every black man has felt himself called upon to own a shot-gun, but to his credit be it said that very rarely in his history as a freedman has he been guilty of the murder of white people for purposes of vengeance. He is deterred in a large measure from the greater crimes to which his ignorant condition and lack of moral training may impel him by the certainty of punishment, just as he is deterred in some of the States, where he has not political power, from petty and grand larceny. When traveling through sparsely settled regions in many of the Southern States one may generally leave his personal property unprotected by lock or key. The negro will not steal it. In some of the States petty larceny by negroes is punished with undue severity, in imitation of the barbarous English sentences which send a man to jail for eighteen months for taking a loaf of bread. Rape and similar crimes, of which in all the States negroes are occasionally guilty, are invariably punished with death; and the rape, justly considered a capital offence by all nations, is almost always avenged at the hands of Judge Lynch.

The negro is far from being a savage, even in his most degraded condition. Whiskey, however, operates as badly upon him as upon the whites; it prompts him to an indiscriminate use of the revolver and the knife, when, if he were in his sober senses, he would be contented with a solid bout at fisticuffs. The negro, however, rarely cherishes a feud for many years, as the low whites do. His vengeance is prompt, or his careless nature leads him, if he delays, to forget it. No Southern man, even when surrounded by a hundred negroes politically hostile to him on any remote plantation, fears for his life. A kind of tacit confession of his superiority pervades his dusky dependents, and he might kill half-a-dozen of them without incurring any danger of Lynch law. In the cities where the negroes flock together idly and become more vicious than in the country, occasional cutting and shooting among themselves are not uncommon; and now and then when a white man kills one of their number, they resent the slaughter by riot, but they rarely bring the offender to justice. It would, I think, be perfectly fair to say that not half-a-dozen white men have been hung in the South since the war, for the murder of negroes. I believe conviction for such a crime would be quite impossible in the present state of opinion in some Southern States.

That there is a large class of negroes who are intrinsically mean and gravitating steadily downward toward the worst phases of rascality, there is no

Southern Types—A Little Unpleasantness.

doubt. About one-third of the negroes in the South is in a very hopeful condition; another third seems to be in a comparatively stationary attitude; another third is absolutely good for nothing, prefers theft to honest labor, and makes no steady progress in morality, refinement, or education of any kind. The religion of the negroes in many parts of the South appears pretty completely divorced from morality.

It is difficult to persuade one's self that the blacks as yet deserve recognition as a moral race. Their best friends will admit that, though very religious, they are also very immoral. Adultery, which is a mortal sin among the Northern and Southern white religionists, is simply venial to the black man. His conversion to the religion of the Lord does not seem to build up the negro's conscience. The tough moral fibre of the Anglo-Saxon, which came only by slow growth, is not perceptible in the negro; neither could it be expected, considering that he was brought from the jungles of Africa into a comparatively wild region in America, and that, under the dominion of slavery, his moral growth was but lazily helped. That the negro has made progress no one will be inclined to dispute, but he started from such a low and bestial condition that he has as yet reached only the confines of real Christianity. He tries to be a good Christian, and yet is not always satisfied with one wife. He is not restrained by the fear of what people will say of him, as the whites universally are. The moral

Southern Types — "Going to Church."

tone of all his fellows is so low, the temptations to occasional lapses from virtue on the part of his spiritual advisers of his own color are often so great, that it is not astonishing that his backslidings are frequent. His idea is that salvation is attained by shouting. The Anglo-Saxon believes that salvation can only be attained by self-denial, faith, and hard work. In some parts of the South the negro, while under conviction, goes into spasms, and is unfit for his daily duties If he is a cook he spoils the dinner, and if he is a field-hand his master finds occasion to complain of him. In Virginia, and doubtless in many other States, the negro alludes to this spiritual condition as being "in the wilderness."

He has found no peace, he cannot profess to be converted until he sees a great light, hears a voice from Heaven, and has a visitation from an angel of God. Then his spirit is filled at once with brightness and light, and in the public revival-meetings he often jumps six feet into the air, embraces with effusion all the deacons and ministers, and in some of the States he is not considered as converted unless he can say this formula:

"The Lord has taken my feet out of the miry clay and set them on the rock of ages, where the very gates of hell shall not prevail against them."

If the brother or sister under conviction cannot say this phrase exactly, the preachers and deacons will tell them that they are not yet out of the wilderness, and will refuse to admit them to religious communion.

All the negro meetings which I attended were marked by intense convulsions of the muscles on the part of all the people present. Even the best educated colored ministers seemed to rely upon theatrical contortions of face, and mighty stampings of feet and waving of arms, for effect on the congregations. Listening outside the open windows of a negro church in Florida one evening, I heard the preacher furiously pounding the Bible which lay on the sacred desk. His words were incoherent, his logic was sadly at fault; some of his appeals seemed ludicrous, but every thump on the holy volume brought a tempest of shoutings, sighs, and moans from the dusky hearers. On the plantations the camp-meetings and revivals sometimes totally unfit the negroes for labor during the whole week. Men and women foam at the mouth, wander about the fields and forests half distracted, a spasm of spiritual insanity having taken possession of them. In such moments of rare enthusiasm they sometimes descend to orgies; whiskey and licentiousness do their work, and the whole meeting will be transformed into an assembly of blackamoor maenads and satyrs. A clever Northerner, who has for many years dwelt in the South, once told me that he considered the Christianity of the negro as Fetichism with a Christian cloak on.

Southern Types— A Negro Constable.

This may seem a hard and unfriendly judgment of negro character, but the careful observer who studies the characteristics of the whole black population will yet not fail to see signs of encouragement. He will discover that a mighty uplifting has really been going on since 1865, and that an influx of good teachers, who shall teach industry, thrift, continence, and self-respect, will in another decade raise the four and a-half million negroes in the South to pretty near the level of Christian manhood and womanhood. Such discouraging views of the negroes in the Gulf States as are taken by many of the native whites, are the result of a mistaken judgment. Even Caucasian ministers of the gospel, whose hearts are supposed to be filled with charity for and faith in all men, refuse to see any tendency on the part of poor Sambo to improve his advantages. They do not seem to understand that moral growth is slow, and that so long as the negro remains in ignorance, and, in a measure, uncertain as to his future condition, he will not develop very rapidly.

Traveling one day from Jackson to Grenada in Mississippi, I observed a bright, intelligent-looking negro woman seated near me in the smoking-car which I had entered for a moment. By her side was her little girl, three or four years of age. At one of the wayside stations a smart mulatto man entered the car, and, being acquainted with the young woman, speedily addressed her thus:

"Why, Sister Smith, how is you?"

"Why, Brudder Brown, tol'able, thank you; how is yourself?"

"I's tol'able; always tol'able, thank you."

"Is you quite sho' you is tol'able?"

"Oh, yas; I's tol'able, very tol'able, thank you."

"Whar is you gwine, Brudder Brown?"

"Oh, I's gwine up hyar to 'tend a meeting; is dat your little gal, Sister Smith?"

"Yas, dat's my little gal."

"How is your little gal, Sister Smith?"

"Oh, she is tol'able, thank you, very tol'able; is your children tol'able?"

"Yas, yas thank you."

"Is you married, Sister Smith?"

"No, Lor! I is n't married; what would I be married for?"

"Whar did you get dat little gal, Sister Smith?"

"Dat's one I done foun', Brudder Brown;" whereupon the two indulged in a sympathetic giggle.

But the teachers of the various Freedmen's Aid and Missionary Associations, as well as Southern people of high character, such as the daughters of Christian ex-Confederate soldiers, who do not count it a shame to teach the ignorant negro, are gradually shaping opinion favorable to marriage among the blacks; and while great numbers of ex-slaves still prefer the old fashion of living together so long as they can agree, without having any sacred compact between them, they feel that they still have a duty toward their offspring, and illegitimate birth is slowly becoming among the blacks, as among the whites, a cause for reproach.

In many of the States until very recently, the railroad stations had rooms over the doors of which were signs marked, "For colored people only." But this odious distinction against race is, I believe, gradually dying out. I do not remember to have noticed it often. In some sections of Georgia it may perhaps still be seen, but I would not affirm that it is general even in that State. Negroes and whites, however, do not ride together in the same railway cars, in those States where the blacks are absolutely masters of the political situation, nor do I believe that the whites would tolerate the admission of the black race to an equal share in the first-class accommodations of travel. The blacks usually buy second-class tickets, and as the Southern railroads are very poor in rolling stock, black men and black women are crowded together into smoking-cars of trains where the white men who enter to smoke, pay as little attention to the etiquette of travel as if no members of the female sex were present. There is an occasional outburst on the part of the whites when an aggressive negro attempts to assert his right to a berth in a sleeping-car or to enter a first-class carriage.

In South-western Virginia I once entered the smoking-car of a through train, and was suddenly accosted in a fierce manner by an intelligent looking mulatto who inquired if I was born in the South, and if I ever owned slaves. Responding in the negative, he began a violent harangue against the railroad authorities, saying that it made his blood boil to be refused a first-class ticket; that he was from Tennessee, and as good as any white man, and added very bitterly that he was "damned if he appreciated it." He was well dressed, cleanly, and appeared decently educated. In a New York horse-car, room would have been made for him even on a crowded seat, but the Southern people dislike to establish a precedent for the admission of the colored race to the same facilities of travel enjoyed by the whites.

In Louisiana and South Carolina the negroes do from time to time monopolize the trains, and create disturbance when their presence is objected to; but if they insisted upon it as a general thing the whites would arm themselves and speedily check any such aggression. The negroes as a mass have not, however, even where their civil rights are practically gained, been difficult to manage in this delicate matter. They avoid a collision with white prejudices as much as possible; as great numbers of them are ragged and engaged in menial occupations, their presence in a car where elegantly-dressed ladies and gentlemen are seated would certainly be far from agreeable, and they recognize this fact quite as readily as they could be expected to do. Until they have gained much more property than they at present possess as a class, they will not be likely to secure the recognition of their equality, which they certainly desire, however little they may assert it.

LXXXVIII.

DIALECT—FORMS OF EXPRESSION—DIET.

THE noticeable differences in dialect and mode of expression between the North and South have been noted, caricatured, and exemplified hundreds of times. The lower class of Southern whites have undoubtedly caught some methods of speech, and certain fatal defects of pronunciation, from the negro.

Southern Types—The Wolf and the Lamb in Politics.

Sometimes, as we have seen in South Carolina, the rude and coarse dialect of the plantation hand, who never in his long life had an instant's education, is reflected in the speech of the haughty and high-bred gentleman's son. But this will no longer be so. The intimate communion which was possible in the days of slavery between the white and the black is now, for a dozen obvious reasons, impossible. The intermixture of dialects is as sure to be stopped as the commingling of bloods. Competent observers say that miscegenation was nearly ended by the war and the emancipation of the slave; that the social equality which certain of the whites in the South now seem to fear has been rendered impossible by the very event which established the independence of the negro. The two races are steadily drifting apart, so far as all intimate association is concerned.

No one can doubt that the negro who was born a slave still retains the profoundest respect for, and in general also a kind of admiration with regard to, his late master; but, except on remote plantations where, thus far, but small change in the habits and customs of the natives has resulted from the war, the white and black children do not associate in the friendly comity of old; a kind of barrier seems to have been erected between them, and it is but right it should be so. There seems no reason for believing that the negro cherishes any insane desire to promote miscegenation. There is a tendency in some sections of the South among the full-blacks to marry, as the whites phrase it, "above their color," or, as the negro himself would express it, "into America, and not back into Africa." A jet black man often shows a marked preference for a mulatto woman, and a full-black girl will not hesitate long in expressing her preference for a smart yellow boy of the modified and subdued African type over the thick-lipped, long-heeled negro who may also be enamored of her charms. A pupil in one of the Virginia schools for the colored people told a teacher that of her two suitors she liked the character of the one who was jet black the best, but that, altogether, she preferred the mulatto who also wooed her, because of his color and his refinement. But the full-blacks are gradually beginning to assert themselves, and certainly in South Carolina, and in many other sections, they have as much pride of race as has the haughty Caucasian.

Just how much influence the incapacity of the negro to pronounce many of our English words has had upon the speech of the Southern people it would be difficult to say. It is not probable that the masses in the lower class at the South would feel flattered if told that their speech much resembles that of the Africans. It may be said without exaggeration that all classes of Southerners find it impossible to pronounce the letter "r." They seem to have the same difficulty that the Parisian has in giving it its full roundness and completeness. Such words as "door" and "floor," and "before," are transformed into " do' " "flo' " and " befo' " by the lower class, while some educated and refined people pronounce them " doah," " floah," and almost invariably allude to our late unpleasantness as the "waw." The use of " I reckon," for " I guess," or " I think," is, of course, universal. Now and then the Southerner says " I calculate," or " I allow," but rarely " I guess," or " I think," unless in delicate deference to his Northern visitor.

The highly educated people of the South speak an elegant and chaste English, in which, by the way, they take an especial pride. The planter, the city merchant, the factor, the professional man of eminence, the lawyers and physicians, the doctors, and even the country squires, judges, and militia colonels, all are distinguished for an exactness and nicety in the use of language which is very agreeable. There is a refinement and courtesy in the manners of the country gentlemen, and an absence of anything like a relapse into the slang of the day, or familiar forms of expression, which are perhaps more noticeable in the North and West than in the South.

The joking and chaffing so common among acquaintances, and even strangers, in many parts of the North, is not understood at the South, and a Southerner will often fancy his dignity seriously offended by some sally which would pass unnoticed among other people. There is also an occasional undue assumption of dignity on the part of employés in public offices.

On one occasion, remonstrating with a clerk in the office of a Texas stage company because he demanded the moderate sum of four dollars and a-half in gold for transporting my trunk eighty miles, he flew into a towering passion and inquired if "I meant to tell him that he lied." Nothing would have been easier than to quarrel with him, yet a moment afterward he was convinced that my inquiry was justifiable.

A Northern gentleman, venturing to question the price of a telegram in the office of the telegraph company in a Mississippi town, was haughtily reminded by the chief clerk that he did n't allow his statements to be questioned. This excess of individualism, however, is perhaps a mark of provincial manners quite as much as of Southern breeding, and does not in any sense apply to the educated and refined Southerner.

To note the characteristics of the South properly, one would be compelled to classify them by States, as the citizen of Maryland would be loth to admit the justness of a judgment which would be reasonable with regard to Texas, and the Virginian would repel with indignation the assumption that he has a few traits which might very properly be ascribed to the people of Louisiana.

Recurring to the matter of speech and its peculiarities in the Southern States, it may be said that it is among the poor whites that eccentricities are mainly found.

The Union soldiers brought home with them an inexhaustible fund of stories illustrating the dialect of these people, and relate with gusto the anecdote of the venerable Georgia cracker dame, who, when a company of Kentucky Confederate cavalry passed her house, inquired:

"Be you-uns kim all the way from Kintuck, critter back, to fight for we-uns?"

The use of "we-uns" and "you-uns" is very noticeable in North Carolina and Eastern Tennessee, both in the mountains and valleys. The same thickness of pronunciation in certain words which is remarkable in the West, but never in the East, as in the words "there" and "where," and "here," which become, "thar," "whar" and "hyar," are observable among the lower classes in the South.

There are also certain shibboleths by which the traveler from south of Mason and Dixon's line is always marked in the North and in Europe. These are the before-mentioned inability to give the letter "r" its due, and the transformation of such words as "car" into "cyah."

Some waggish Northern critic has asserted that the mass of ex-slave-holders find great difficulty in pronouncing the word "negro," from their long habit of alluding to the black man only as a "nigger," and that they now-a-days call him a "niggro." But I suspect that there is a spice of malice in this hypercritical statement.

The use of "I don't reckon" sometimes strikes one unpleasantly, coming, as it often does, at the end of a sentence. "Right smart" is used in a variety of ways never employed at the North. The Southerner says, "We shall have a right smart crop this season," or, "There was a right smart of people at the last meeting," or, "I shall have a right smart chance of business." "Right" is used pretty generally throughout the South in the sense in which Northerners use "very." Of a lady they say that she is right pretty, of a fruit that it is right good, of scenery that it is right magnificent.

Southern Types — Two Veterans Discussing the Political Situation.

With regard to distance, there seems in the back-country a charming disregard of actual measurement. The negro is especially vague in his statements as to the number of miles between any two towns. He will either tell you that it is a "right smart distance," or may state that it is "two good looks and a dog bark," or that it is "a hop, skip, and a go-so." This would hardly be credited unless one heard it. The negro was, up to the date of the war, intensely local in feeling. The boundary of his little neighborhood was to him the horizon where the world stopped, and, traveling but little, he got but slight idea of distances. In some portions of the Southern mountains we found the whites were very familiar with distances in their own State and counties, but not outside of those limits. The chief difficulty in obtaining accurate information from the negroes seemed to be their disinclination to assertion. A visitor to the Virginia springs noted as curious that the negroes there would not, as a rule, dissent from remarks by white people. If asked, "Does this stream run up hill?" the negro would be apt to say: "Yas, sah, reckon it do, sah;" but if the question were put in a leading form, as: "This stream runs down hill, of course, does it not?" he would say: "Sartinly, sah."

The use of the word "stranger," as applied to an individual whose name one is not familiar with, so common in the extreme West, we found to prevail among the mountain populations of the South, but so far as my observation went, nowhere else. Sometimes the natives whom we encountered would say, "Mistah," and pause, as if expecting you to supply your name. If you did not do so they would inquire, "What did you say your name was," or more frequently, "What mout your name be?" A curious form of assent, which must be heard to be appreciated, and which Dickens caricatured mercilessly when he first visited this country, prevails in the mountains of Eastern Tennessee and Western North Carolina. The following will serve as an example:

While discussing the outer world with old Parson Caton, in a remote mountain district of Tennessee, he inquired if New York was not a right smart place, and being assured that it was, he said with a rising inflection, "Yes, sir?" Whereupon I responded, "Yes, sir." "As likely a place as Louisville, I reckon," he added; to which I answered, "Yes, sir," he chiming in interrogatively, "Yes, sir?"

These mountain peculiarities of speech demand more study than we were able to give them. They strike the visitor at first very strangely, but he gradually becomes accustomed to them. They differ considerably from the barbarous nasal Yankee slang spoken in certain sections of New England, but they have, nevertheless, many points of resemblance to it. There is nowhere in the South any such conspicuous difference from Northern habits of speech as is found between the dialects of the French peasants living in two towns near each other. Some of the mountaineers speak of "hit," instead of "it," and emphasize the word as in this case: "I meant to have brought my gun, but I forgot *hit*."

Words of endearment between husband and wife in the South often show an unconscious borrowing from the negroes. Where the Northern husband habitually calls his wife "dear" or "darling," the Southern man says "honey," alike to his spouse and to his offspring.

The negro in South Carolina, and in other adjacent States, shows a tendency to render the English language more musical than it is when spoken by Anglo-Saxons. He gives an extra syllable to words which end abruptly, and puts a kind of rhythm into all that he says. The Virginia negro, especially when he shows the influence of mixed blood, copies the speech of the whites as nearly as possible, making some ludicrous errors when he attempts to catch the sonorous refrain of long words. He still speaks of people who impress him favorably as "quality folk," and now and then, when disdainfully describing some unimpressive people, will denominate them "white trash," or even admit that they are "worse than niggers." Entering Barnum's Hotel, in Baltimore, one evening, I found the colored bell-boys gathered round an old negro servant, who was reading from the evening paper some instance of unparalleled meanness which a white man had been guilty of. After he had finished the anecdote he said: "Boys, dat 's— dat 's real niggerism," thus expressing his contempt for the conduct of the white man in question.

In Natchez, on the Mississippi, I noticed that some of the white children, even those who attended private schools and were evidently kept from street communion with the negroes as much as possible, copied the defects of the colored man's speech. Our landlord's son, for instance, pointing to our carriage which had arrived at the door, said: "Da he," which was plantation slang for "There it is." Since the negroes gained their freedom, those among them who had been servants of wealthy gentlemen, and who had consequently been thrown into the company of white people, speak very good English, except when they endeavor to use long words, when they sometimes mix their meanings.

In San Antonio I saw an officer of the garrison handing some invitations for a reception to the old darkey who was to distribute them through the town.

"Now, Uncle," he said, "mind you do this promptly." "Yes, sah," said the old man, "I will regenerate dem," meaning that he would distribute them.

Here and there the polite black servants in the first class hotels hinted that "renumeration," instead of "remuneration," would be agreeable. The negro is almost as quick of wit of a certain kind as the Irish peasant. He is disposed, as European servants are, to presume upon the good-natured familiarity of his superiors in position, and serves one best when a dignified and distant demeanor is maintained toward him.

At Lynchburg we noticed that "Charles," one of the colored waiters, black as the traditional ace of spades, and very clumsy withal, made extravagant professions of his willingness to serve us, but managed to make his fellow-servant, "Harry," do all the work. I therefore ventured a remark something in this wise:

"It appears to me, Charles, that Harry does all the waiting and you do all the talking."

"Yas, sah," he answered, civilly but quickly, "I does de talkin', and de smokin' too, when de gemmen gives me cigars."

After that we considered Charles incorrigible.

The negro valet, taught by years of experience under the slave system, is probably the best in the world. He is always civil, attentive, deferential, and adheres to his master's fortunes, good or ill, with remarkable tenacity. It is not from him that you will hear complaints of his old position. Indeed he looks backward half regretfully to the days of the slave-holders' domination, and often gazes with proud scorn upon the struggling blacks who are playing fantastic tricks in the political world.

The teachers on the Port Royal islands, in South Carolina, in the book called "Slave Songs of the United States," give many interesting instances of what is probably the most remarkable negro dialect in the South. They say that, "With these people the process of 'phonetic decay' appears to have gone as far, perhaps, as is possible, and with it an extreme simplification of etymology and syntax. There is, of course, the usual softening of *th* and *v*, or *f*, into *d* and *b*; likewise a frequent interchange of *v* and *w*, as *veeds* and *vell*, for *weeds* and *well*; *woices* and *pumkin wine*, for *voices* and *pumpkin vine*. 'De wile' *(vilest)* sinner may return.' This last example illustrates also their constant habit of clipping words and syllables, as *lee' bro'*, for *little brother; plant'shun*, for plantation. The lengthening of short vowels is illustrated in both these (*a*, for instance, rarely has its short English sound) 'Een (in) dat mornin' all day.'

"Strange words are less numerous in their *patois* than one would suppose, and, few as they are, many of them may be readily derived from English words. Besides the familiar *buckra*, and a few proper names, as Cuffy, Quash, and perhaps Cudjo, I only know of *churray* (spill) which may be 'throw' way;' *ouna* or *ona*, 'you' (both singular and plural, and used only for friends), as 'Ona build a house in Paradise;' and *aw*, a kind of expletive, equivalent to 'to be sure,' as, 'Dat clot' cheap.' 'Cheap aw.' 'Dat Monday one lazy boy.' 'Lazy aw—I 'bleege to lick 'em.'"

These interesting quotations illustrate the linguistic peculiarities of the South Carolina negro. It is supposed that the fashion which the negroes in all parts of the South have of speaking of their elders as uncles and aunts, or as daddy and mammy, arose originally from a feeling of respect, and as they were not allowed to call each other Mr. or Mrs. they adopted this.

Almost universally on the sea-islands they call their equals also cousin. Their speech has but little inflection or power of expressing grammatical relation in any way. Even to-day they make little distinction of tense, gender, case, number, or person. "He" is most common as a possessive pronoun. Thus the teachers say that "him" might mean a girl as well as a boy. I quote the following specimens of negro talk from the volume published by the teachers mentioned above, as it gives, better than any one else has been able to show, the peculiarities of this remarkable dialect.

"A scene at the opening of a school:

"'Charles, why did n't you come to school earlier?' 'A-could n't come *soon* to-day, sir; de boss he sheer out clo' dis mornin'.' 'What did he say to you?' 'Me, sir? I ain't *git;* de boss he de baddest buckra ebber a-see. De morest part ob de mens dey git heaps o' clo'—more 'n nuff; 'n I ain't git nuffin.' 'Were any other children there?' 'Plenty chil'n, sir. All de chil'n dah fo' sun-up.' 'January, you have n't brought your book.' 'It *is*, sir; sh'um here, sir?' 'Where is Jim?' 'I ain't know where he gone, sir.' 'Where is Sam?' 'He did n't been here.' 'Where is the little boy, John?' 'He pick up he foot and run.' A new scholar is brought: 'Good mornin', maussa; I bring dis same chile to school, sir; *do* don't let 'em stay arter school done. Here you, gal, stan' up an' say howdy to de genlm'n. De maussa lash 'em well ef he don't larn de lesson.' 'Where's your book, Tom?' 'Dunno, sir. Somebody mus' a tief 'em.' 'Where's your brother?' 'Sh'im dar? wid bof he han' in he pocket?' 'Billy, have you done your sum?' 'Yes, sir, I out 'em.' 'Where's Polly?' 'Polly de-de.' Taffy comes up. 'Please, sir, make me sensible of dat word—I want to ketch 'em werry bad, sir, werry bad.'"

Probably, no Northern traveler ever went South without returning to complain with great bitterness of the poor food which he finds even in prosperous regions. Horace Greeley told the people of Texas that their prime need was a thousand good cooks; and, doubtless, a few regiments of Frenchmen, well dispersed throughout the South, would succeed in giving the Southern people some much needed instruction in this respect. Yet criticism of the Southern cuisine cannot be general. Nowhere in the world is there better cookery or a richer bill of fare than that offered in Baltimore, in Charleston, in Savannah, and in New Orleans; yet within a few miles of any of those cities one comes into a region where coarse bread, coarser pork, and a few stunted vegetables are the only articles of diet upon the farmers' tables. In regions where the best of mutton and beef can be raised at trivial expense, where with slight cultivation the land will produce a profusion of vegetables, and where good wines can be raised from vines of two or three years' growth, the farmers are a lean, ill-fed race. Nowhere was this more apparent to us than in the mountains, where, save at the hotels and in the comfortable mansions of well-to-do agriculturists, we were usually invited to partake of hot and indigestible corn bread, fried and greasy ham, or bacon, as it is universally called in the South; and whenever by rare chance a beefsteak found its way to the table, it had been remorselessly fried until not a particle of juice remained in its substance.

People who subsist upon such food as this must of necessity use some stimulant, and they make up in corn whiskey and leaf tobacco what they lack in nourishing meats, good soups, and a general variety of vegetables. Wherever culture and refinement prevail, however, there one finds the best of cookery, an educated taste in wines, and a thorough appreciation of good things.

LXXXIX.

IMMIGRATION—THE NEED OF CAPITAL—DIVISION OF THE NEGRO VOTE—THE SOUTHERN LADIES.

THERE is much that is discouraging in the present condition of the South, but no one is more loth than the Southerner to admit the impossibility of its thorough redemption. The growth of manufactures in the Southern States, while insignificant as compared with the gigantic development in the North and West, is still highly encouraging; and it is actually true that manufactured articles formerly sent South from the North are now made in the South to be shipped to Northern buyers.

There is at least good reason to hope that in a few years immigration will pour into the fertile fields and noble valleys and along the grand streams of the South, assuring a mighty growth. The Southern people, however, will have to make more vigorous efforts in soliciting immigration than they have thus far shown themselves capable of, if they intend to compete with the robust assurance of Western agents in Europe. Texas and Virginia do not need to exert themselves, for currents of immigrants are now flowing steadily to them; and, as has been seen in the North-west, one immigrant always brings, sooner or later, ten in his wake. But the cotton States need able and efficient agents in Europe to explain thoroughly the nature and extent of their resources, and to counteract the effect of the political misrepresentation which is so conspicuous during every heated campaign, and which never fails to do those States incalculable harm. The mischief which the grinding of the outrage mill by cheap politicians, in the vain hope that it might serve their petty ends, at the elections of 1874, did such noble commonwealths as Alabama, Georgia, and Mississippi, can hardly be estimated.

The Italians have been favorably looked upon by the Southerners as possible immigrants, and many planters in some of the States have offered them liberal inducements to settle on the lands which now lie wholly uncultivated; but it will probably be some years before any considerable body of Italian settlers take up those lands. Many foreign immigrants show an indisposition to settle among the negroes, and an especial unwillingness to accept the wages offered them by the old school of planters—namely, a trivial sum yearly, and the rations of meal, pork, and molasses, with which the negro is easily contented. The immigration question can only be settled by time; but an exposé of the material resources of the South is an important aid to such settlement, and I have endeavored, in the foregoing pages, to give some adequate idea of those resources, and the possibility of their development. The attentive reader of this book will not fail to discover that the mineral wealth ascertained since the war to exist in some of the States of the South is likely to be of far more importance to their future than all the broad cotton-fields, once their sole dependence.

Until her people have recovered from the exhaustion consequent on the war, capital is and will be the crying want of the South. The North will continue to furnish some portion of that capital, but will be largely checked in its investments in that direction, as it has been heretofore, by its lack of confidence in the possibility of a solution of the political difficulties.

If we may rely upon the figures given in the last census, the black race is increasing in numbers. Many travelers through the South, however, have expressed a contrary opinion, some enthusiastic correspondents asserting that the negroes, by flocking into the large cities, and there living in idleness and vice, are contracting the seeds of disease, which will eventually sweep the race away. But in spite of the fact that on many of the plantations fœticide, which in the days of slavery was of course almost unknown among the negroes, has become quite common, there seems no good reason to doubt that their numbers have increased nearly half a million within ten years. The black population will long be migratory, and will show the same tendency which has been so noticeable since the war to seek the attractive life of the town.

Still, as white families are, as a rule, much larger in the South than in the North, and as the increase of the native Caucasian population there is, on the whole, greater than in any other section of the country, there is not much danger of the Africanization of any of the States of the South. The whites and blacks will have to learn to live and vote amicably together, and in time they will do so.

As soon as the negro vote in the South is divided, and the black man learns to respect the merits of a candidate in spite of his political complexion, there will be but little of the trouble now-a-days so conspicuous in Louisiana, Alabama, and some of the other States. Within the last few months the South Carolina Conservatives have frankly allied themselves with those of the negroes who have shown a disposition to encourage honest government in the State, and this is a movement which will be general throughout the South as the abuses of reconstruction are corrected, and some of the more odious carpet-baggers, who have arrayed the negro wrongfully against the principal property-holders, are summarily dismissed from the arena of politics.

The South can never be cast in the same mould as the North. Its origin was too different; it will not be thoroughly emancipated from the influence of the old system for several generations. It will still cherish some prejudices against that utter freedom of speech, that devotion to "isms," and possibly that intense desire for immediate material development that distinguish the North; but it will be progressive, more progressive and liberal every year. Its provincialisms will fade gradually away; its educational facilities, despite the occasional hindrances imposed by such unwise manœuvres as the projected passage of the Civil Rights bill, will increase and flourish. The negro will get justice from the lower classes of whites as soon as those classes are touched by the liberalizing influences of the times. There is, of course, still much objection to sitting with him on juries, or otherwise acknowledging his equality.

It is not the province of this volume to indulge in theories as to the grave dangers which many politicians fancy still environ the Southern question, nor is it important to speculate upon the possible determination on the part of the planters to demand compensation some day for their emancipated slaves, or to hint that they may try to establish a labor system which shall relegate the negro to serfdom. Time alone can disclose the rôle which the Southern Conservative will play when he returns to power.

The Southern ladies during the trying years since the war have developed many noble qualities. It is hardly necessary to eulogize their beauty, their wit, their vivacity, or even to hint that they still cherish a few of the animosities which their husbands, brothers, and lovers have long ago laid aside. It is but natural that they should yet feel some of the bitterness of the war, for latterly its burdens have fallen quite as heavily upon them as upon the survivors of the Confederate ranks. They have toiled unceasingly and uncomplainingly.

The frankness and earnestness with which these ladies accepted a changed order of things, the smile with which they have cheered the humble homes for which many of them have been compelled to leave noble mansions, and the charity and kindliness that they have shown toward their ex-slaves, entitle them to the highest honor. They have not been ashamed to teach negro schools now and then; they have contentedly worn calico instead of satin when rude poverty made it necessary, and they have graced with the nameless charm of their manner circumstances which have made many men harsh and sour for life. It is but natural that, as they stray among the graves of the loved and lost, or amid the ruins of their homes and hopes, they should sometimes recall with strange affection the memory of a lost and mistaken cause, to which they gave themselves with a passionate devotion which has few parallels in the history of the world.

XC.

RAMBLES IN VIRGINIA—FREDERICKSBURG—ALEXANDRIA. MOUNT VERNON—ARLINGTON.

THE journey from Richmond to Washington, via the battle-scarred town of Fredericksburg, takes one through Henry, Hanover, Caroline, Spottsylvania, Stafford, Prince William and Fairfax counties. This route is now a favorite one from Wilmington in North Carolina, and other large cities in the Southern Atlantic States, to the North, and sleeping-cars daily cross the Rappahannock, which a few years ago was red with the blood of Northern soldiers. In the vicinity of Ashland, the site of a flourishing Methodist college, fifteen miles from Richmond, there are thousands of uncultivated acres which might readily be turned into profitable farms. The birthplace of Henry Clay is not far from Ashland. Fredericksburg is a venerable town, pleasantly situated on the south shore of the Rappahannock, seventy miles from Washington. The "Falls," a mile above the place, afford an extensive water power. Falmouth, on the north side of the river a little above Fredericksburg, is a small village of the ordinary Virginian type.

Fredericksburg is, historically, one of the most interesting places in Virginia. The birthplace of George Washington is near the town, half a mile from the junction of Pope's creek with the Potomac, in Westmoreland county, on the "Wakefield" estate. The old farm-house, a rude building with enormous stone chimneys at each end, in which Washington was born, was destroyed some time before the Revolution. The only memorial on the spot to-day is a freestone slab, erected by George Washington Park Custis in 1815, and bearing these words:

"Here, the 11th of February (O. S.),
1732, George Washington
was born."

Near Fredericksburg, too, repose the remains of the mother of Washington, who lived for many years in the town. Some time before her death, she selected the spot, and often retired to it for meditation and prayer. In 1833 the corner-stone of a fine monument was laid above the grave by Andrew Jackson, then President of the United States; but the monument is still unfinished. The house in which the last memorable interview between the mother and her distinguished son occurred still stands in Fredericksburg. The old Masonic Hall, in which Washington was initiated into the Masonic Order, is also yet standing.

But the reverence which the mass of Americans a generation since felt for these important memorials has been dulled by the newer and sadder souvenirs which fill the minds of all visitors to the Fredericksburg of to-day. The heights on either side of the little river have been the scene of one of the greatest battles in our history; the old town has echoed to the noise of fratricidal strife, has been riddled by shot and shell, and some portions of it have been burned. It is wonderful that it was not entirely torn to pieces by Burnside's guns in 1862. Many a European village, far more solidly built, was crushed into ruins under the shock of battle between the contending hosts in the last struggle in France, while Fredericksburg yet shows a smiling front. The old steeples, around which raged tempests of bombs and bullets, still point serenely heavenward; and the rows of houses by the river, past which went the torrent which poured up Marye's Hill to attack the Confederate position, seem but little damaged. The stranger can readily convince himself, however, that the tide of battle has swept over Fredericksburg, if he will but climb the hills which lie beyond the plain at the rear of the town—those eminences along which Lee posted his army of defense, from Hamilton's Crossing to Marye's Hill. There he will find, charmingly laid out in terraces like some vast garden, a huge national cemetery, where many thousand soldiers sleep the sleep that knows no waking upon earth.

At the foot of Marye's Hill may still be seen the stone wall behind which the Confederate infantry were posted on that dread day in 1862 when the Northern troops, time and time again repulsed, were finally compelled, by the artillery fire from the hill, to retire across the Rappahannock. That stone wall is a monument to the bravery of the Irish troops who there fought for the Union. If mortal men could have taken it, it would have been theirs; but it was an impregnable position. Blackened with smoke, and scarred with bullets, it is a ghastly reminder of the days when Northern Virginia was a battle-ground where two giant antagonists had declared war against each other to the death. Lee's Hill, where General Lee stood during the fight in December of 1862, and Chatham, on the north side of the river, where General Burnside had his head-quarters, are interesting points, both offering a good view of the surrounding country.

A journey into the battle-grounds of the "Wilderness"—that vast tract stretching southward from the Rapidan, and westward from Mine Run, may be readily made on horseback or in private conveyance from Fredericksburg. The Wilderness, which has been described as a "darkling wood" covered with "a dense undergrowth of low-limbed and scraggy pines, stiff and bristling chincapins, scrub oaks, and hazel," is not looked upon with much affection by Virginians, as the lands in that section are not valuable. On the road to Chancellorsville one passes Salem Church; and not far from that point is the "Mountain Way" estate, where General Sedgwick had his head-quarters when he was fighting his way to Chancellorsville in 1863. The view of Fredericksburg, the Rappahannock, and the distant summits of the Blue Ridge from this place, is delightful. In the vicinity of Chancellorsville one may still see the outlines of the Federal works, the tree under which Stonewall Jackson lay for a time after he received his fatal wound, the old Wilderness Tavern, and the Wilderness Church.

Hanover, Caroline, and Spottsylvania counties produce excellent crops of tobacco, winter wheat, rye and Indian corn; the farmers are intelligent and capable, and saw enough of Northern men during the war to wear away a good deal of their old-time prejudice against the "Yankees." There are still large tracts of unimproved land in these counties; industrious and frugal immigrants can readily turn them into paying farms.

The old town of Alexandria, seated on the Potomac shore, seven miles from Washington, is now accessible by rail from Richmond. Before the completion of the Richmond, Fredericksburg and Potomac railroad, trains from the Virginian capital stopped at Acquia creek, on the river, whence passengers were conveyed in boats to Alexandria and Washington. The Orange, Alexandria, and Manassas railroad procures for Alexandria trade with many of the counties along the line, and, by the "Washington and Ohio," lays hold upon fertile Halifax and Loudon counties. The town has a cotton-mill, a brewery, some private iron workers and machinists, a few repair shops for railroad works, and it makes extensive transfers of coal. It occupies a position admirably fitted for large industrial activity. Its frontage on the Potomac is better than that of any other town on the river, and yet it languishes. Its inhabitants seem to lack the vigor and the enterprise needed to seize upon and improve their fine advantages. They are in the attitude of waiting for something to turn up, yet do not even display the impracticable enthusiasm of Micawber when an opportunity presents itself. The streets were not paved until a Northern officer, during the occupation in war times, insisted upon having a pavement of cobble stones laid down, and met the expense by fines levied upon whiskey-selling. Few repairs have been made, and the avenues are filled with ruts and hollows. The inhabitants seem to feel, with regard to the changed order of things upon which they have fallen, very much as did the old negro whom I met there in 1869.

"'Pears like, boss," said the venerable darkey, as he looked up the river toward the dome of the National Capitol, the Mecca of his dreams, and then glanced over his broken down chest and withered limbs, "'pears like I's come too late for de good times."

One sees nerveless unthrift in many small Virginian towns. It seems graven in the nature of whites and blacks. An occasional conversation with the negroes led me to believe that they offer as many hindrances to the advent of capital as their ex-masters do. Both seem suspicious that some improper and undue advantage is to be taken of them. The negro appears oftentimes suspicious of those who are making strenuous endeavors to elevate him out of his shiftless and helpless condition into something like manly independence.

Alexandria was once a part of the District of Columbia, but was retroceded to Virginia in 1846, when the Old Dominion regained all the territory which had before been national ground. The town was founded in 1748; Washington was a frequent visitor there, and the pew in which he used to sit, in Christ Church, is still pointed out. The hourly steamboat line which plies between Washington and Alexandria affords communication with the Washington City and Potomac line of steamers, with Norfolk, Philadelphia, New York and Boston.

A new commercial exchange, and a fine Government custom-house and post-office have recently been erected in the town.

In summer and autumn the journey down the Potomac from Washington is usually interesting. There is a certain picturesqueness in the great stream and the quaint towns and fortifications along its banks; Forts Foote and Washington, on the Maryland side, being especially noticeable. On the little steamer which plies regularly to and from Mount Vernon, the old home of the Father of his Country, may sometimes be found a few Virginians clad in rusty black, who confidentially discuss with the stranger the painful issues of the present.

Mount Vernon is fifteen miles from the Capitol, and the traveler will not fail to observe, while sailing down the river, that the fields on the Virginia side have not yet recovered from the devastation of war. The whole country has the trampled aspect which the passage of the myriads of men and horses, and the location of the thousand camps, naturally gave it. Fort Washington, on the Maryland side, was blown up in 1814 when the British occupied Washington, but is now thoroughly restored. On a fertile slope on the Virginia shore, in the midst of noble groves and on a pretty lawn, overlooking the wide and winding river, one may see here and there a few substantial mansions, once the homes of prosperous planters. The woods near Mount Vernon, like many bits of forest along the Potomac, are untamed, but a pretty road leads up the hill-side to the tomb, and thence wanders to the lawn, where stands the Washington mansion with its little cupola, its quaint roof and its veranda with eight stately pillars.

Nothing can be simpler than the tomb in which the first President of the United States reposes. It is of quadrangular form, built on a sloping hill-side, painted red and white, a high iron gate guarding the entrance. Above the gate is the inscription, "Within this enclosure rest the remains of General George Washington." There is no attempt at decoration. One sees nothing but two marble coffins lying on the brick floor; the one on the right has upon its lid a spread eagle, a flag and a shield, and beneath these emblems the single word, "Washington." The coffin on the left is plain, and contains the remains of Mrs. Washington. Above the door which opens into another vault are the following words:

"I am the resurrection and the life; he that believeth in me, though he were dead, yet shall he live."

Near the tomb are several other family monuments, much more showy and pretentious than that which covers the mortal remains of our chief patriot. The old tomb, in which the body of Washington remained for thirty years, was situated between the present vault and the house.

The mansion commands a fine view of the river, and, were it not for its low ceilings and its lack of all the comforts of modern residences, would be a desirable country residence for a century to come; for, although it is now more than one hundred and twenty-five years old, it is still solid and enduring. The wood of which the house is built is cut in blocks in imitation of stone; on the sloping sides of the roof there are dormer windows, and the portico, which covers the whole front of the building, is quite imposing.

The gardens and the lawn in the rear of the house, with the walks extending to what were formerly the negro quarters, are extensive and pleasant, and one or two colored families supply the visitor with luncheon, and nosegays from the garden. Mrs. Cunningham, the present guardian of that portion of the estate purchased by the patriotic ladies of the country some years ago and preserved as a National treasure, lives at Mount Vernon some portion of the year. The farms round about are owned by Northern men, and the old lordly life of the planter and country gentleman, which prevailed so extensively in all that region when Washington inhabited Mount Vernon, has passed utterly away. The whole surroundings of the estate are calculated to remind one of the English country seats which still remain, in some parts of England, much as they were two centuries ago. The quaint staircases, and odd little angular passages in the mansion, are thronged by fashionable tourists from the cities, who never fail to express their wonder that the Father of his Country lived in such a simple, unostentatious style.

Below Mount Vernon on the Virginia side one comes upon naked sand-bluffs standing out into the stream here and there; on shad and herring fishing stations, where in spring time, when the herring shoals come in, hundreds of fishermen are busy; and upon forests, where in autumn the hickories and cedars, the oaks and the ashes, the chestnuts and the beeches clothe the hill-sides in brilliant colors. At Acquia Creek, a dreary and forlorn little place to-day, but an important military depot during the war, one may take the railroad for Fredericksburg. In the vicinity of Acquia Creek there were many Confederate batteries, which of course did their best to injure the Federal shipping on the Potomac in the early years of the war.

A journey by land from Mount Vernon to either Alexandria or Fredericksburg may be made along the main road, which extends through a wild country, and which those who have traversed it declare to be not only the worst road in any country, but probably much worse now than it was when Washington was wont to ride over it.

On the road from Mount Vernon to Fredericksburg one passes Pohick, where stands a ruined church, which the family of Washington attended until the close of the Revolution; and crosses a pretty river, called Occoquan, which empties into the Potomac near the headland known as High Point, upon which, during the fall after the battle of Bull Run, the Confederates established their nearest river battery to Washington.

Southward, on the Washington City, Virginia Midland and Great Southern railroad, is Clifton Station, twelve miles from the old Bull Run battle-field. This was a famous depot during the war for army supplies, and is now a prosperous summer resort, frequented by visitors from Northern cities. In Prince William county, on the same line of rail, is the flourishing village of Manassas. It is situated on the summit of a high table-land, twenty-seven miles from Alexandria, and commands a beautiful view of the surrounding country. Six miles to the right of it, in the direction of Fairfax, the first battle of Manassas was fought, and here and there a ruined earthwork marks the site of the old struggle. In 1868 there was not a fence or a building on the spot where the town now stands, but since that time many Northern and Western people have flocked into it. The centre of a prosperous county with ample facilities for transportation, with a fine free school system, and with the best of hematite iron ore in its vicinity, it can but have a prosperous future. Throughout this entire section the tide of battle raged during 1862 and 1863. Hooker and Ewell, Warren and Hill, marched and countermarched over the devastated country, which to-day is rapidly recovering from the shock of war.

In Fauquier county are situated the Warrenton White Sulphur Springs, where formerly a brilliant society annually gathered. Warrenton, fifty miles from Alexandria, now receives many fashionable visitors yearly. Nine miles from the town is the birthplace of Chief-Justice Marshall. In Culpepper county stands the town of Culpepper, founded in 1759, and first named after Lord

The Potomac and Washington — Seen from Arlington, Virginia.

Fairfax, the original proprietor of the section. The little town looks down upon the beautiful and vast extent of the Blue Ridge, has a handsome and costly court-house, and many prosperous manufactories, and is also the site of the annual fair of the Piedmont Agricultural Society, of which General Kemper, the present Governor of Virginia, was, for two years, the chief executive officer. Near Mitchell's Station the battle known as that of Cedar Mountain was fought in August, 1862. Magnetic iron ores and fine grasslands are gradually attracting Northern immigration to the surroundings of the old battle-field. From Culpepper the Washington City, Virginia Midland and Great Southern railroad runs through Gordonsville, Charlottesville and Lynchburg to Danville, four miles from the North Carolina line in Pittsylvania county, whence it connects with the Piedmont air line via Charlotte in North Carolina, to Atlanta in Georgia.

The railroad known as the Manassas Division, and running through the town of Manassas, through Warren, Shenandoah, and other counties in Northern Virginia, passes Front Royal, near which is the finest and most profitable vineyard in the whole South. The Northern visitor, while at Front Royal, has his attention directed to the exploits of General Stonewall Jackson, who, in 1862, in a severe battle near this town, drove General Banks out of the Shenandoah valley. At Rivington Station, the junction of the North and South forks of the Shenandoah river, much of the brown hematite and magnetic iron ore which comes down the river in flat-boats from the counties of Rockingham, Page and Warren, is received and exported. A joint-stock company of Northern capitalists, with a million dollars of capital stock, is now operating in this region.

The traveler along the romantic gaps of the Shenandoah passes the sites of the battles of Chester Gap, Cedar Creek and Front Royal, and, straying by the ruins of burned bridges and devastated farms, cannot but wonder that the Virginians of the section have so soon recovered their courage and shown a disposition to rebuild after the prostrating struggle. Five miles from Strasburg, the present western terminus of the "Manassas Division," Ashby's Confederate cavalry and Banks's infantry fought a sharp battle in May of 1862, and a little north of this, at Cedarville, that dashing and gallant West Virginian, McCausland, met, in a severe fight, part of General Phil Sheridan's forces. Shenandoah county, originally called Dunmore, after the Tory Lord of that name, but later more properly named after the beautiful and picturesque Shenandoah river, which wanders by cliff and through meadow within its limits, is extremely fertile. Strasburg was so named because its original settlers came from Germany. It will in due time be a place of great importance, and the Capon and Orkney Springs near it will give it a good tide of summer travel. One mile south of the town is Officers' Hill, where Early and Sheridan met in a tremendous fight in September of 1864, and in October of the same year severe battles were fought in the immediate vicinity. This region is one of the most beautiful in Virginia. The rugged and mighty slopes of the Massanuttan contain much delightful and wild scenery, and near Newmarket Station there is a beautiful cataract.

Along these lines of rail many fine bodies of land are offered to capitalists and actual settlers. Many of the lands are admirably adapted to the production of the grape; and the fine air, the beautiful springs of fresh water, the short and mild winters, the long and equable summers, offer superior attractions to the emigrant from England or from middle Europe.

The traveler along the Potomac will do well to scale the hill opposite Georgetown, in the District of Columbia, on which stands Arlington House. The famous mansion, once the residence of George Washington Parke Custis, one of the last survivors of the Washington family, stands more than two hundred feet above the Potomac; and from its massive portico one can look out over Washington, and can see the white dome of the National Capitol gleaming through dark green foliage. Arlington was, for many years before the late war, a part of the estate of General Robert E. Lee, but when that valiant soldier unsheathed his sword in the Confederate cause, the grand old mansion and the beautiful grounds about it were confiscated to Government use, and are now held on an arrear of taxes title. The ravages of war have destroyed many of the beauties of the parks and gardens. To-day, the fields of Arlington, which the proud leader of the Confederate hosts cherished as one of his favorite resorts, are covered with national cemeteries. Fifteen thousand graves, on the head-boards over many of which is written the word "Unknown," dot the slopes and lawns. Near the mansion is a short but heavy granite monument, on which is the following inscription:

"Beneath this stone
repose the bones of two thousand one hundred and eleven
unknown soldiers, gathered after the war, from
the fields of Bull Run and the route to the Rappahannock.
Their remains could not be identified, but their names and deaths
are recorded in the archives of the
country, and its grateful citizens honor them
as of their noble army of martyrs.
May they rest in peace.
Sept. A. D. 1866."

Thousands of negro soldiers and "contrabands" who died during the war, are also buried at Arlington. In the eastern division of the largest of the three cemeteries are monuments to the memory of George Washington Parke Custis and Mary his wife. Thousands of visitors yearly come and go, over the hills, under the oaks, and among the graves at Arlington; and now and then old soldiers, who for long years fought fiercely against each other in opposing ranks, pause in friendly converse by some grassy mound, beneath which sleeps an unknown and forgotten member of the great army that has passed into the silence and shadows beyond.

APPENDIX.

FACTS AND FIGURES CONCERNING THE EX-SLAVE STATES, AND DELAWARE AND THE DISTRICT OF COLUMBIA.

POPULATION.

Compiled from the United States Census of 1870.

STATES.	WHITES.	BLACKS.
Alabama	521,384	475,501
Arkansas	362,115	122,169
Delaware	102,221	22,794
Florida	96,057	91,689
Georgia	638,926	545,142
Kentucky	1,098,692	222,210
Louisiana	362,065	364,210
Maryland	605,497	175,391
Mississippi	382,896	444,201
Missouri	1,603,146	118,071
North Carolina	678,470	391,650
South Carolina	289,667	415,814
Tennessee	936,119	322,331
Texas	564,700	253,475
Virginia	712,089	512,841
West Virginia	424,033	17,980
District of Columbia	88,288	43,404
Totals	9,466,355	4,538,782

APPENDIX.

MANUFACTURES OF COTTON IN THE UNITED STATES.

NEW ENGLAND STATES.

STATES.	1860. RAW MATERIAL USED. POUNDS.	VALUE.	1870. RAW MATERIAL USED. POUNDS.	VALUE.
Maine	23,733,165	$3,319,335	25,887,771	$6,746,780
New Hampshire	51,002,324	7,128,196	41,469,719	12,318,867
Vermont	1,447,250	181,030	1,235,652	292,269
Massachusetts	134,012,759	17,214,592	130,654,040	37,371,599
Rhode Island	41,614,797	5,799,223	44,630,787	13,268,315
Connecticut	31,891,011	4,028,406	31,747,309	8,818,651
Total	283,701,306	$37,670,782	275,625,278	$78,816,482

MIDDLE STATES.

New York	23,945,627	$3,061,105	24,783,351	$6,990,626
Pennsylvania	37,496,203	7,386,213	32,953,318	10,724,052
New Jersey	9,094,649	1,165,435	7,920,035	1,964,758
Delaware	3,403,000	570,102	2,587,615	704,733
Maryland	12,880,119	1,698,413	12,693,647	3,409,426
District of Columbia	294,117	47,403	. . . .	. . . .
Total	87,113,715	$13,928,671	80,937,966	$23,793,595

WESTERN STATES.

Ohio	3,192,500	$374,100	2,226,400	$493,740
Indiana	1,813,944	229,925	2,070,318	542,875
Illinois	95,000	11,930	857,000	177,525
Iowa	. . . .	. . . .	20,000	4,950
Utah	12,000	6,600	23,500	7,051
Missouri	990,000	110,000	2,196,600	481,745
Kentucky	1,826,000	214,755	1,584,625	375,048
Total	7,929,444	$946,710	8,908,443	$2,082,934

SOUTHERN STATES.

Virginia	7,544,297	$811,187	4,255,383	$937,820
North Carolina	5,540,738	622,363	4,238,276	963,809
South Carolina	3,978,061	431,525	4,756,823	761,469
Georgia	13,907,904	1,466,375	10,921,176	2,504,758
Florida	200,000	23,000	. . . .	. . . .
Alabama	5,246,800	617,633	3,249,523	764,965
Louisiana	1,995,700	226,000	748,525	161,485
Texas	588,000	64,140	1,079,118	216,519
Mississippi	638,800	79,800	580,764	123,568
Arkansas	187,500	11,600	66,400	13,780
Tennessee	4,072,710	384,548	2,872,582	595,789
Total	43,960,510	$4,739,371	32,768,570	$7,042,962
Total United States	422,704,975	$57,285,534	398,248,257	$111,735,973

APPENDIX.

STATISTICS OF THE MANUFACTURES OF COTTON IN THE UNITED STATES.

NEW ENGLAND STATES.

STATES.	1850. Value of Product.	1860. Value of Product.	1870. Value of Product.
Maine	$2,630,616	$6,235,623	$11,844,181
New Hampshire	8,861,749	13,699,994	16,999,672
Vermont	280,300	357,450	546,510
Massachusetts	21,394,401	38,004,255	59,493,153
Rhode Island	6,495,972	12,151,191	22,049,203
Connecticut	4,122,952	8,911,387	14,026,334
Total	$43,785,990	$79,359,900	$124,759,053

MIDDLE STATES.

New York	$5,019,323	$6,676,878	$11,178,211
Pennsylvania	5,812,126	13,650,114	17,490,080
New Jersey	1,289,648	2,217,728	4,015,768
Delaware	538,439	941,703	1,060,898
Maryland	2,021,396	2,973,877	4,832,808
District of Columbia	100,000	74,400	....
Total	$14,780,932	$26,534,700	$38,587,765

WESTERN STATES.

Ohio	$594,204	$723,500	$681,335
Indiana	86,660	344,350	778,047
Illinois	....	18,987	279,000
Iowa	....	....	7,000
Utah	....	10,000	16,803
Missouri	142,900	230,000	798,850
Kentucky	445,639	315,270	251,550
Total	$1,269,403	$1,642,107	$2,792,585

SOUTHERN STATES.

Virginia	$1,446,109	$1,489,971	$1,435,800
North Carolina	985,411	1,046,047	1,345,052
South Carolina	842,440	713,050	1,529,930
Georgia	1,395,056	2,371,207	3,648,973
Florida	49,920	40,000	....
Alabama	398,585	1,040,147	1,088,767
Louisiana	....	466,500	251,550
Texas	....	80,695	374,598
Mississippi	22,000	176,328	234,445
Arkansas	17,360	23,000	22,362
Tennessee	508,481	698,122	941,542
Total	$5,665,362	$8,145,067	$10,873,019
Total United States	$65,501,687	$115,681,774	$177,022,422

COTTON TRADE OF THE UNITED STATES FOR FORTY-EIGHT YEARS.

YEARS ENDING AUGUST 31.	PRODUCTION. BALES.	CONSUMPTION. BALES.	EXPORTS. BALES.	AVERAGE NET WEIGHT PER BALE. LBS.	AVERAGE PRICE PER LB. IN NEW YORK. CENTS.	AVERAGE PRICE PER LB. IN LIVERPOOL. PENCE.
1825–26	720,027	....	....	...	12.19	5.85
1826–27	975,231	149,516	854,000	331	9.29	5.79
1827–28	720,593	120,593	600,000	335	10.32	5.84
1828–29	870,415	118,853	740,000	341	9.88	5.32
1829–30	976,845	125,512	839,000	339	10.04	6.44
1830–31	1,038,847	182,142	773,000	341	9.71	5.72
1831–32	987,477	173,800	892,000	360	9.38	6.22
1832–33	1,070,438	194,412	867,000	350	12.32	7.87
1833–34	1,205,394	196,413	1,028,000	363	12.90	8.10
1834–35	1,254,328	216,888	1,023,500	367	17.45	9.13
1835–36	1,360,725	236,733	1,116,000	373	16.50	8.97
1836–37	1,423,930	222,540	1,169,000	379	13.25	6.09
1837–38	1,801,497	246,063	1,575,000	379	10.14	6.28
1838–39	1,360,532	276,018	1,074,000	384	13.36	7.19
1839–40	2,177,835	295,193	1,876,000	383	8.92	5.42
1840–41	1,634,954	267,850	1,313,500	394	9.50	5.73
1841–42	1,683,574	267,850	1,465,500	397	7.85	4.86
1842–43	2,378,875	325,129	2,010,000	409	7.25	4.37
1843–44	2,030,409	346,750	1,629,500	412	7.73	4.71
1844–45	2,394,503	389,000	2,083,700	415	5.63	3.92
1845–46	3,100,537	422,600	1,666,700	411	7.87	4.80
1846–47	1,778,651	428,000	1,241,200	431	11.21	6.03
1847–48	2,439,786	616,044	1,858,000	417	8.03	3.93
1848–49	2,866,938	642,485	2,228,000	436	7.55	4.09
1849–50	2,233,718	613,498	1,590,200	429	12.34	7.10
1850–51	2,454,442	485,614	1,988,710	416	12.14	5.51
1851–52	3,126,310	689,603	2,443,646	428	31.9–50	5.05
1852–53	3,416,214	803,725	2,528,400	428	11.02	5.54
1853–54	3,074,979	737,236	2,319,148	430	10.97	5.31
1854–55	2,982,634	706,417	2,244,209	434	10.39	5.60
1855–56	3,665,557	770,739	2,954,606	420	10.30	6.22
1856–57	3,093,737	819,936	2,252,657	444	13.51	7.73
1857–58	3,257,339	595,562	2,590,455	442	12.23	6.91
1858–59	4,018,914	927,651	3,021,403	447	12.08	6.68
1859–60	4,861,292	978,043	3,774,173	461	11.00	5.97
1860–61	3,849,469	843,740	3,127,568	477	13.01	8.50
1861–62	....	....	....	...	31.29	18.37
1862–63	....	....	....	...	67.21	22.46
1863–64	....	....	....	...	101.50	27.17
1864–65	....	....	....	...	83.38	19.11
1865–66	2,269,316	666,100	1,554,664	441	43.20	15.30
1866–67	2,097,254	770,030	1,557,054	444	31.59	10.98
1867–68	2,519,554	906,636	1,655,816	445	24.85	10.52
1868–69	2,366,467	926,374	1,465,880	444	29.01	12.12
1869–70	3,122,551	865,160	2,206,480	440	23.98	9.89
1870–71	4,362,317	1,110,196	3,166,742	442	16.95	8.55
1871–72	3,014,351	1,237,330	1,957,314	443	20.48	10.78
1872–73	3,930,508	1,201,127	2,679,986	464	18.15	9.65